The Roman Republic

Cognella Antiquities Series

The Roman Republic

A HISTORY FOR STUDENTS

Joseph McAlhany

University of Connecticut

Bassim Hamadeh, CEO and Publisher
David Miano, Senior Specialist Acquisitions Editor
Michelle Piehl, Senior Project Editor
Abbey Hastings, Production Editor
Emely Villavicencio, Senior Graphic Designer
Trey Soto, Licensing Coordinator
Natalie Piccotti, Director of Marketing
Kassie Graves, Vice President of Editorial
Jamie Giganti, Director of Academic Publishing

Cover image: Jean-Paul Laurens, "La Mort de Caton d'Utique," 1863.

All Livy excerpts were translated from *Livy, Ab Urbe Condita.*

Printed in the United States of America.

Brief Contents

Detailed Contents

Chapter 12: The Republic Is Dead. Long Live the Republic! 275

ACTIVE LEARNING

This book has interactive activities available to complement your reading.

Your instructor may have customized the selection of activities available for your unique course. Please check with your professor to verify whether your class will access this content through the Cognella Active Learning portal (http://active.cognella.com) or through your home learning management system.

Foreword

As its subtitle declares, this book is written for students. In structure, selection of material, approach, and even in the way sentences were written and vocabulary chosen, every choice was dictated by students. Of course, every author has their own idea of a student. In my case, students are intelligent and curious, but come to the study of Roman history (and much else) unequipped with some of the background information that many authors and their textbooks take for granted. Moreover, many Roman history textbooks are written with future Roman historians in mind, or at least future history graduate students. This book is aimed specifically at students whose only exposure to Roman history, or any history, may be in a single class, perhaps taken as a requirement. The concern is less with what that history is than what that history—and any history—means, less about small answers than big questions.

I would like to thank Arieta Jakaj, Renee Semple, and Jake Webber for their comments, criticisms, and suggestions. These three students made the book immeasurably better. I would also like to thank the staff at Cognella, especially Michelle Piehl, for shepherding this project to its completion. And, finally, I thank Clare for many things, not least putting up with me.

CHAPTER 1

Last Things First

Of Kings and Consuls

FIG. 1.1 A coin with a portrait of Julius Caesar wearing a laurel wreath issued shortly before his assassination. The text reads *Caesar Dict Perpetuo*—Caesar, dictator for life.

OVER THE COURSE of the year, the inhabitants of ancient Rome celebrated over forty religious festivals, known as *feriae* in Latin. Priests performed the appropriate sacrifices, officials made the necessary arrangements, and all legal and political business came to a halt. Some festivals included games and entertainments (*ludi*) such as chariot races, musical and theatrical performances, or gladiator fights and staged animal hunts (gladiator combats were at first only performed in connection with a funeral). One of the major annual festivals, celebrated every February 15, was the Lupercalia. Its origin and meaning were already obscure to Romans at the end of the republic in the first century BC, and they were not even sure to which god it was dedicated. Some believed the Lupercalia was rooted in a fertility ritual, perhaps going back to an ancient Greek religious festival; others thought it was an ancient rite of purification. Whatever its true origin, a connection to Rome's founding seemed likely. The name of the festival appears related to the word for she-wolf (*lupa*) and, according to the legend of Rome's founding, a *lupa* nursed the twins Romulus and Remus. In the best-known version of the story, these twins, grandsons of a king who had been driven from the throne by his brother, had been left in a spot outdoors to die. A she-wolf nursed them until a shepherd found them and raised them together with his wife. Eventually, they discovered their true identity, restored their grandfather to the throne, then set off to found their own city. An argument arose, and Romulus killed his twin brother, becoming the first king of the new city he named Rome after himself. To most Romans, when or why the

Lupercalia first began was of no importance. As far as they were concerned, this festival had always been celebrated, ever since the beginning of Rome itself, and they continued to celebrate it every February for centuries. In fact, it lasted until 494 AD when a pope converted the holiday into a Feast of the Purification of the Virgin Mary.

We know the basics of what happened at the Lupercalia, even if many details remain unclear. First, a group of young men, known as *luperci*, slaughtered a dog and a goat at the base of the Palatine hill in Rome, where Romulus and Remus were believed to have been nursed by the she-wolf. With the knife used to sacrifice the animals, they smeared the foreheads of two young *luperci* (perhaps new initiates) with the animal blood, and then wiped the blood away with pure wool dipped in milk. Next, the *luperci* cut the hide of the goat into strips and, wearing nothing but goatskin thongs, ran around the Palatine hill and into the Forum at the center of Rome. During their run through the city, they playfully struck spectators with the strips of goat hide, especially young women. According to the traditions of the ritual, women who were hit would become pregnant. An ancient writer even describes young women holding out their hands to be struck just like naughty schoolchildren about to receive a whack on the hands from their teacher.

We might wonder how seriously the Romans took this strange ceremony, though the answer would vary depending on an individual's social status and level of education. The ruling elite who were in charge of Rome's religion, including the *luperci* themselves, likely found the whole ritual somewhat ridiculous, if entertaining. A prominent Roman of the first century BC once wrote that two Roman priests passing each other in the street would have to stop themselves from laughing, since they both knew much of what they did was silly. But even if some Romans thought the religious traditions were sometimes laughable, all Romans considered the observance of the Lupercalia and other religious festivals extremely important to the continuation of the community of Rome. They believed Rome had become great because of its traditions, and this was good enough reason to continue observing festivals like the Lupercalia in the same way their ancestors were believed to have done. Thus, in the very center of Rome, the seat of power of an empire that controlled much of the Mediterranean by the second century BC, men who were current or future leaders of this imperial power considered it a serious honor to run through the streets nearly naked while the inhabitants of Rome looked on.

We know some of these details about the Lupercalia because of a notable incident that took place in 44 BC, when Marcus Antonius (often known as Mark Antony or simply Antony) was the leader of a group of *luperci*. At the time, he held the highest political office in Rome, the consulship, together with Julius Caesar, and was arguably the second-most powerful person in the ancient Mediterranean world, second only to Caesar himself. In fact, after Caesar's death, Antony would join together with Cleopatra, the ruler of Egypt, in a war against Caesar's young great-nephew and adopted son Octavian. These two infamous lovers would lose this war for supremacy at Rome and over the entire Mediterranean, and Octavian would later be known as Augustus, regarded as the first emperor of Rome. But before his exploits with Cleopatra in the war that gave rise to the Roman Empire, Antony ran around Rome in a goatskin thong as a *lupercus*. The *luperci* would finish their ceremonial run in the Forum, at the heart of Rome, and on this occasion, when

ROME & ITS HILLS

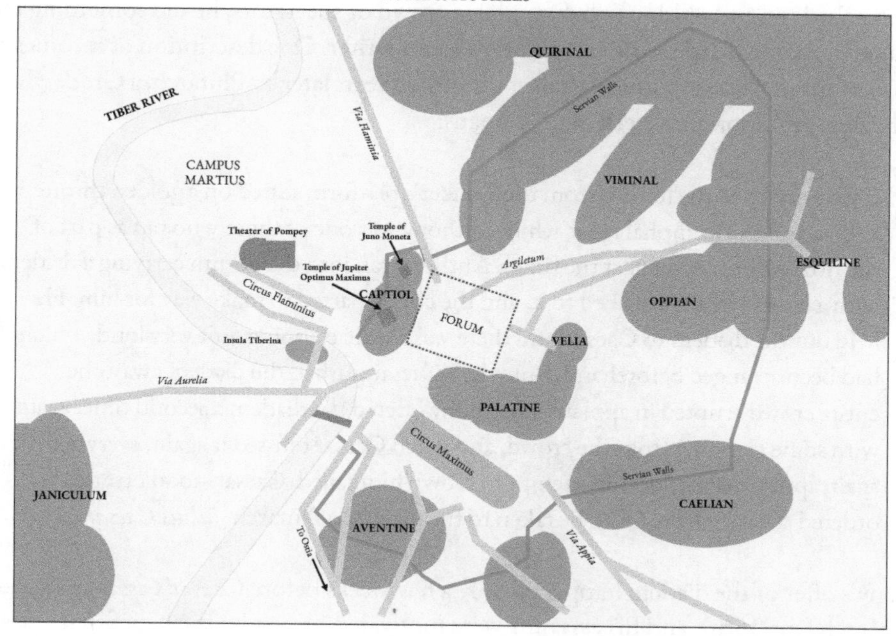

THE ROMAN FORUM IN THE 2nd SECOND CENTURY BC

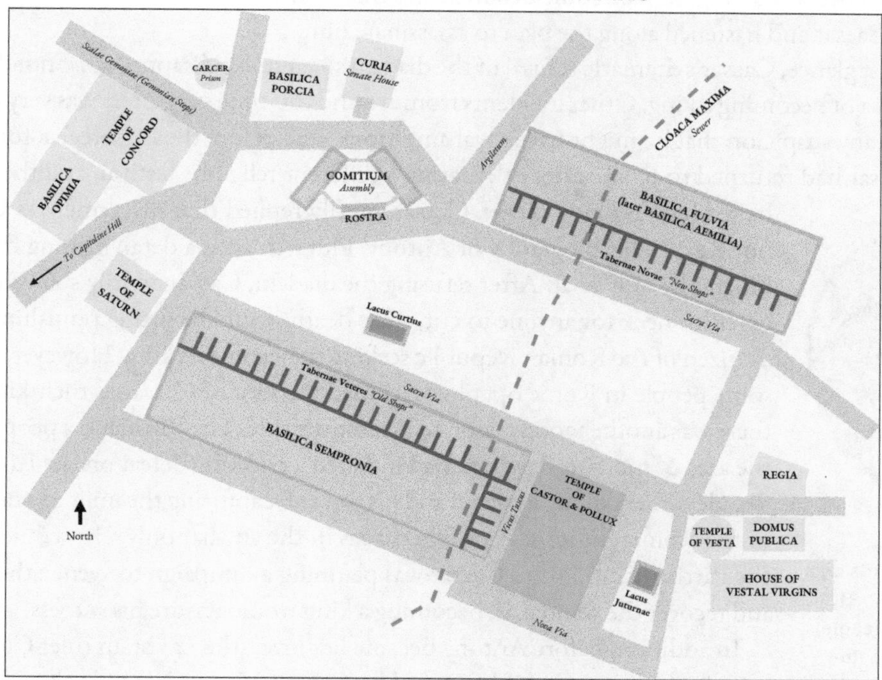

FIG. 1.2 Rome and the Roman Forum.

Antony reached the end of his run before a large crowd of spectators, he did something remarkable enough to be recorded by more than one ancient writer. One description of it comes from a biography of Julius Caesar written well over a hundred years later by Plutarch, a Greek who wrote about the lives of important Greeks and Romans:

> Caesar watched the festival from the speaker's platform seated on a golden throne and wearing a triumphal robe, while Anthony was one of those who ran as part of the ritual (he was consul at the time). Anthony ran into the Forum carrying a diadem with a laurel wreath attached to it, and the crowd parted to make way for him. He held out the diadem to Caesar, and there was a little clapping, not very loud, which had been arranged beforehand. But when Caesar pushed the diadem away, the entire crowd erupted in applause. Anthony offered the diadem a second time, again with some clapping from the crowd, and when Caesar refused it again, everybody again applauded. After this attempt to crown him failed, Caesar stood up and ordered the laurel wreath to be taken to the Capitol. (Plutarch, *Julius Caesar* 61)

Antony's offer of the diadem happened only a few weeks before Caesar's assassination on the Ides of March (the 15th), and his assassins were motivated in part by the belief that Caesar was seeking to become a king. In fact, some believe it was this incident that solidified the conspiracy against Caesar and hastened along the plan to assassinate him.

At first glance, Caesar's dramatic refusal of the diadem suggests his disapproval, if not disgust, at the idea of becoming a king. Other incidents from around this time suggest he was very careful to avoid any suspicion that he might have royal ambitions. Just before the Lupercalia, for example, Caesar had returned to Rome after celebrating a different religious festival, and the crowd

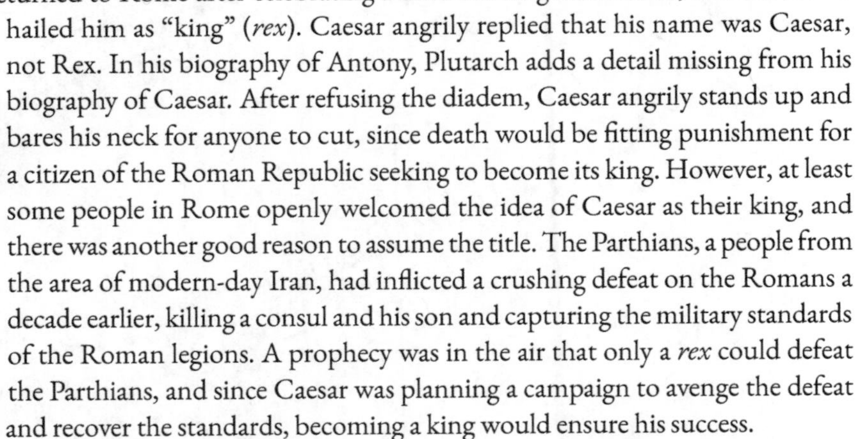

hailed him as "king" (*rex*). Caesar angrily replied that his name was Caesar, not Rex. In his biography of Antony, Plutarch adds a detail missing from his biography of Caesar. After refusing the diadem, Caesar angrily stands up and bares his neck for anyone to cut, since death would be fitting punishment for a citizen of the Roman Republic seeking to become its king. However, at least some people in Rome openly welcomed the idea of Caesar as their king, and there was another good reason to assume the title. The Parthians, a people from the area of modern-day Iran, had inflicted a crushing defeat on the Romans a decade earlier, killing a consul and his son and capturing the military standards of the Roman legions. A prophecy was in the air that only a *rex* could defeat the Parthians, and since Caesar was planning a campaign to avenge the defeat and recover the standards, becoming a king would ensure his success.

FIG. 1.3 Legionary standards on a coin issued by Antony in 32/31 BC. In the center is the *aquila* (eagle) carried by each legion. The Romans would go to great lengths to recover standards captured by the enemy.

In addition, before Antony became her lover, the Egyptian ruler Cleopatra had given birth to a child fathered by Caesar. Might Caesar, looking beyond the horizons of Rome, seek to become a Mediterranean monarch, founder of a new royal dynasty with its capital in Egypt, rather than an officeholder of the

Roman Republic? There were rumors to this effect, no doubt spread by Caesar's enemies. The Lupercalia, with its clear associations with Romulus, founder of Rome and its first king, would be a fitting occasion for a flirtation with kingship and the establishment of a new government for Rome.

While the Romans maintained one of their oldest traditions with the celebration of the Lupercalia in 44 BC, Antony's offer of the diadem to Caesar made it seem that another tradition was in danger of ending. The Roman Republic had begun over 450 years earlier with the expulsion of the last king from Rome, and now, to many Romans, the monarchy was on the verge of returning in the person of Julius Caesar, effectively bringing the republic to a close.

The Man Who Would Be King?

Although Caesar seemed to be very careful about associating himself with monarchy, or at least with the title of king (*rex*), he was at the same time accumulating special privileges and extraordinary powers, to the extent that his opponents could easily accuse him of being a king in everything but name. Seated on a golden throne and dressed in a purple robe in the middle of the Forum during the Lupercalia, Caesar might look to many people very much like a king or an emperor. Yet as long as he did not accept the title or the diadem, he could still claim to be upholding the traditions of the republic.

In Plutarch's account, Caesar is wearing what is described as a "triumphal robe," which is a purple-dyed toga embroidered with gold thread. Purple dye was obtained from shellfish on the eastern coast of the Mediterranean and was very expensive. A purple cloak on its own could be associated with royalty, but Roman generals wore this particular toga (the *toga picta*) during a triumph, the spectacular ceremony in which the victorious commander paraded through Rome with his soldiers and members of the senate (see the end of chapter 5 for more on the triumph). The triumphal robe was a marker of extraordinary status, and by tradition it was worn only during the ceremonies associated with a triumph. An earlier commander and relative of Julius Caesar, Gaius Marius, deeply offended the senators when he wore his triumphal dress at a senate meeting—he quickly went home and changed. While Caesar's wearing of the triumphal toga on this occasion was at first glance extraordinary, he had in fact been granted this as a special privilege by his fellow Romans.

Plutarch also notes that Caesar is sitting on a golden throne. Traditionally, high-ranking Roman officials sat on an ivory stool known as a curule chair (*sella curulis*), and thus a golden throne seems to break with tradition and move a step closer to monarchy. Moreover, the placement of the throne on the speaker's platform, known as the rostra, would carry symbolic weight. This platform, named from a Latin word for the prows of captured ships used to decorate it, was in front of the senate building. Speakers mounted this platform when they wanted to deliver a speech to the public. By occupying an elevated position atop the speaker's platform, Caesar demonstrated his political dominance. But again, the golden throne was a special privilege that had been granted to Caesar by the Roman Senate, and the Lupercalia of 44 BC was the first time he had made use of it. In addition, as pontifex maximus, the chief priest of Rome, Caesar was entitled to a privileged position at a religious celebration.

This brings us to the laurel wreath, which in some accounts Caesar is already wearing when Antony offers the diadem. Whether the diadem was a replacement for or an addition to the laurel wreath, this small change in headwear carried important meaning for the Romans. The wreath, traditionally made from the glossy green leaves and branches of a laurel tree but sometimes fashioned in gold, was worn by victorious Roman generals. It would be an appropriate accessory to the purple-dyed triumphal robe Caesar was wearing. This laurel "crown," like the purple robe and golden throne, was an honor conferred by the Roman Senate, and thus still in accordance with the normal practices of the republic. A diadem, on the other hand, is a kind of crown that has its own history, which is important for the context of the incident at the Lupercalia. A cloth band wrapped around the head and tied in back, but like the laurel wreath sometimes fashioned out of precious metals, the diadem was a symbol of royal rule, worn by kings and queens around the Mediterranean. Alexander the Great, for example, appeared on coins wearing one, as did the kings who ruled in the eastern part of the Mediterranean after Alexander's death.

The offer of the diadem to Caesar was thus a critical moment when the existence of the republic was in danger, at least symbolically. Monarchy was a boundary that Romans who professed to defend the republic would not allow anyone to cross, since the republic began when the rule of the kings ended. Referring to someone as a "king" (Latin *rex*) or accusing him of seeking to establish a monarchy (*regnum*) was tantamount to charging him with treason against the republic. Indeed, the history of the Roman Republic provides several examples of the murder of a politician suspected of harboring regal ambitions. One example from the early history of the republic, shrouded in legend, is Spurius Maelius. In the fifth century BC he decided on his own initiative to purchase grain and sell it at a low price to the people of Rome, who were suffering from a shortage of food. What to some seemed a noble and generous deed was to others an attempt to win popular support for his own regal ambitions, and for this reason he was killed by a fellow Roman. His killer would later be hailed as a hero who saved Rome from possible tyranny. Centuries later, a few generations before Caesar's assassination, a young Roman from one of the most important families in Rome attempted to push through major reforms to benefit the poorer members of Roman society. During the riot that resulted from both his

FIG. 1.4 Left: Julius Caesar wearing a laurel wreath, from a coin minted in 44 BC. Right: Ptolemy I, former general under Alexander the Great and then king of Egypt, wearing a diadem.

zealous efforts and the stubborn resistance to them, he was seen to point to his head. It was, some sources say, an innocent signal to his followers that his life was in danger, since he could not be heard in the confusion. His opponents, however, claimed it was proof he was seeking a royal crown for himself. This was used to justify killing him, at the instigation of the pontifex maximus, the chief priest at Rome.

Caesar's assassins would also claim they were following in this tradition of eliminating a potential king and restoring liberty to the Roman people. At the Lupercalia, however, Caesar's denial of the crown would send the message that he should not be considered in the same light as those earlier examples. Numerous honors had elevated him, literally and figuratively, above everyone else, but up to this point he had only accepted honors that had been officially granted to him by the "Senate and People of Rome," the SPQR that defines the republic. Caesar and his supporters could thus claim he was operating within established republican tradition and was using his special powers and privileges to fix a corrupt and broken government. But whether Caesar refused or accepted the diadem, the way in which it was offered may have been more alarming than the offer itself, and a clearer sign that the republic was finished.

In 44 BC it would be abundantly clear that Caesar was the most powerful man in Rome and throughout the Mediterranean, yet he and Antony were still fellow consuls, colleagues in the highest elected office who were legally equals. In their own understanding of their history, the Romans established the new political structure of the republic after overthrowing the monarchy in 509 BC, expelling the seventh and last king from their city. In this new form of government, there were two individuals chosen every year for the highest political office, the consulship. For the Romans of the republic, the rule of a single individual meant the subjection of citizens to a kind of slavery (and as slave owners themselves, many Roman citizens had at least a vague idea of what slavery meant). By having two people occupy the highest office, the republican form of government avoided placing political authority in the hands of a single man. Roman citizens believed this political structure meant freedom instead of servitude.

To the Romans who feared Caesar's power and were suspicious of his ambitions, Antony's offer of a diadem to Caesar at the Lupercalia was bad enough, but the fact that Antony made the offer while he was a consul made it even worse. A contemporary witness to this event was the great orator and former consul Cicero, who made the remark about two Roman priests containing their laughter. In a series of speeches attacking Antony for his behavior after Caesar's assassination, he gives his own brief version of the incident at the Lupercalia:

> Your colleague [Julius Caesar] was up on the rostra sitting on a golden throne, clad in a purple toga and wearing a laurel wreath. You climb the steps, approach the throne, and hold up a diadem. You were acting as a *lupercus*, but you should've remembered you were a consul! The entire Forum groans. Where did the diadem come from? You didn't just pick it up off the ground—you brought it with you, a crime carefully planned in advance! You start to place the diadem on Caesar, the people cry out; he rejects the diadem, and there is applause. So

> you were the only one there, you crook, who tried to find out what the Roman people would put up with, since you wanted to establish a kingship and make the man who was your colleague in office your master. (Cicero, *Philippics* 2.85)

Cicero's description closely corresponds to the account in Plutarch, in part because Plutarch used Cicero as a source for his biography of Caesar. However, unlike Plutarch, Cicero specifically criticizes Antony for forgetting that he was a consul. In offering the diadem to Caesar, Antony was turning his colleague in the consulship into his *dominus*, a word that specifically means the master of a slave. Thus, as Cicero portrays him, Antony was willingly enslaving himself. It does not get much more disgraceful than that for a Roman citizen, especially a consul of the Roman Republic.

A King by Any Other Name

Among the honors and powers Caesar had received by 44 BC, however, there was one not mentioned in Plutarch or Cicero, and it was this one more than any other that blurred the line between king and consul, and between republic and monarchy. At the beginning of the second century AD, during the reign of the emperor Trajan, the Roman historian Tacitus wrote the *Annales*, a history of the first emperors of Rome, beginning with Caesar's adopted son Augustus and ending with the infamous emperor Nero. It opens with a brisk overview of Roman history, surveying over 700 years in the span of a short paragraph. Tacitus begins with the monarchy, quickly moves on to the civil wars that tore apart the republic, and ends with Augustus, who after his victory over Antony and Cleopatra took on a title that made him an emperor in all but name:

> Kings controlled Rome at the beginning. Lucius Brutus established liberty and the consulship. Dictatorships would be used temporarily, the rule of the decemvirs lasted only two years, and the consular authority of the military tribunes did not endure for long. The tyranny of Cinna and Sulla was brief, then the political power of Pompey and of Crassus soon yielded to Caesar, and the military forces of Lepidus and Antony to Augustus. When everyone was worn down by civil wars, Augustus received power over Rome under the title of *princeps*. (*Annals* 1.1)

For Tacitus, liberty (*libertas*) and the consulship together mark the change from monarchy to republic (Lucius Brutus is the hero who led the overthrow of the last king in 509 BC, and another Brutus, a descendant of Lucius, would be one of the leading assassins of Caesar.) "Liberty" (*libertas*) is a troublesome word and came to mean different things to different people, according to their political views and their personal ambitions. It makes for a convenient political slogan. Yet in this particular context, Tacitus equates liberty with the distinctive political office of the republic. "Liberty" could only arise when the rule of a single king was replaced by the two consuls, elected for a term of one year. If monarchy returned and the consulship disappeared, liberty would disappear as well.

Tacitus mentions other political offices, all set in contrast to the consulship. Two of these—decemvir and consular tribune—existed for only a brief period at the beginning of the republic, but the dictatorship remained in place throughout its history. To modern ears, dictator is an ugly term with an ugly history, yet the dictatorship was an established office among the Romans. However, as Tacitus highlights, it was used only occasionally, and was not a regular elected office. In an extreme crisis, the senate would appoint one individual as dictator, with supreme authority for a period of six months. A dictator was very much like a temporary king.

The last dictator of the Roman Republic was none other than Julius Caesar. Shortly before the Lupercalia, he had been appointed "perpetual dictator," or in other words, dictator for life. The senate had already appointed Caesar dictator four times, so, in some sense, naming him "perpetual dictator" simply dispensed with the pretense of reappointing him. But from another perspective, "dictator for life" and "king" are only different names for the same thing. The difference still mattered, however, just as the difference between a laurel wreath and a diadem mattered. To some in the crowd at the Lupercalia, even if in reality nothing in their daily lives would change if Caesar took the diadem, and even if for all practical purposes Caesar already had the power of a king, his acceptance of the diadem would signal a symbolic rebirth of monarchy and the death of the republic. As silly as it might seem to give a Roman all the powers of a king but refuse to call him one, it was no more silly than continuing the tradition of running around Rome in a goatskin thong every February.

Caesar had reached the extraordinary position he held at the Lupercalia because of his victory in a civil war that pitted him and his supporters against fellow Romans under the command of Gnaeus Pompeius Magnus, usually known as Pompey the Great (*magnus* is Latin for "great"). Before he entered into armed conflict against Caesar, Pompey had been one of the most successful Roman commanders ever and was one of the most politically powerful men of his generation. For a while, he worked closely with Caesar, and was even married to Caesar's daughter. Though it was never wise to bet against Caesar, Pompey would have been a safe choice as the individual who would emerge as the undisputed leader of the Roman Republic, and many who feared Caesar thought Pompey would be its savior. Yet during his time of political and military supremacy in the Roman state until his defeat by Caesar's forces in the last civil war of the republic, Pompey had himself broken norms at almost every step of his exceptional career.

Pompey had been elected to the consulship three times, first in the year 70 BC at the age of 36, before he had held any of the lower offices normally considered as stepping-stones to the highest office. He celebrated a triumph before becoming a senator, something that had never happened before. In the 60s BC, he had been granted two extraordinary military commands, one of which gave him supreme authority over the entire Mediterranean to deal with the problem of pirates. Less than a decade before Caesar's assassination, during a period of civil disturbance when it had become impossible to conduct elections at Rome, Pompey was even made "sole consul," an unusual step taken in recognition that there was the need for an individual with extraordinary authority to deal with the crisis. There were prominent Romans who opposed placing so much power in the hands of a single individual, but Pompey, like Caesar after him, had been granted these extraordinary honors in recognition of him exceptional abilities that made him so well suited to tackle the crisis of the moment. Also like Caesar, Pompey could be suspected of harboring his own regal ambitions. Once, when Pompey held a linen band to wrap around a wound on his thigh, a political enemy claimed the strip of cloth was a diadem and accused Pompey of planning to become king.

Caesar's extraordinary powers and privileges were thus not as unprecedented as they might first appear, even if he accumulated more than anyone before him. The Romans of the republic had always been willing to make exceptions to the rules or invent new ones when they felt it necessary. From one point of view, Caesar's honors and offices were only modifications to republican traditions, different in degree but not in kind to what other outstanding Romans had received in the past. Extraordinary times call for extraordinary measures, some might argue, and exceptional individuals deserve exceptional treatment. The cases of Caesar and Pompey reveal that while Rome has a reputation for conservatism and a respect for tradition (a reputation fostered by the Romans themselves), they were more than willing to break with the traditions they upheld as the foundations of who they were. In truth, the Romans were innovators as well as traditionalists, but their innovations were usually cloaked in the mantle of tradition. Whatever norms Pompey and Caesar may have broken in reality, they had kept up the appearances that they were adhering to the long-held customs of the Roman Republic, not upending them. Caesar's position as "dictator for life" was just such an innovation made within a traditional form.

Even when the rule of one man became the norm for Rome shortly after Caesar's assassination, the idea of the republic and its political traditions remained strong, and emperors continued to use the vocabulary and imagery of the republic. Yet, in a grand historical irony, the door opened by the assassination of Caesar, the man who would *not* be king, led not to a restoration of the republic, but to the establishment of undisputed rule by a single individual. Augustus, too, would not be king. Instead, as Tacitus noted in the passage quoted above, he assumed the title of *princeps*. The word had already been in use during the republic: *princeps senatus* ("leader of the senate") was the title given to the individual recognized as the most respected member of Rome's ruling body. It was an honorific title, which meant the person who held it got to speak first when the senate deliberated an issue, but it had no other legal authority. *Princeps* gives us the English "prince," but Augustus would argue that his assumption of the title simply meant he was the "leading citizen" of the Roman Republic. But in history books he is more often called by a name that suggests a power beyond even that of a king—emperor.

Reading History: The What and the Why

In Plutarch's account of the incident at the Lupercalia, the mention of prearranged clapping might suggest Caesar and Antony had staged the offer of the diadem to test the Roman people's acceptance of him as a king. Perhaps if more people had joined in with the applause, Caesar would have accepted the diadem and assumed the title of king, the first at Rome since the beginning of the republic over 450 years earlier. In this interpretation, Caesar turned the failure to his advantage by having the diadem taken as an offering to the Temple of Jupiter Optimus Maximus, overlooking the Roman Forum from the top of the Capitoline hill. On another interpretation, the entire drama was staged in order to give Caesar the opportunity to prove before the eyes of all that he would never assume the title of king and instead would continue in the traditional office of dictator in the nontraditional form he held it.

Although Plutarch might have assumed Caesar and Antony were working together, Cicero places all the blame for the incident at the Lupercalia on Antony, implying that Caesar was completely innocent. He was the only one there, Cicero claims, who wanted to test the Romans' willingness to accept a king. This seems unlikely, but is not impossible, and it is one of the historian's primary tasks to imagine the possibilities provided by the evidence, which is never as straightforward as it might appear. Cicero was more interested in attacking Antony than criticizing Caesar, and in another passage he even accuses Antony of staging the offer of the crown as a prelude to Caesar's murder. Antony had, in fact, been suspected of planning a coup, and according to Plutarch, he was approached by those conspiring to kill Caesar. He refused to join in the plot, but he did not tell Caesar about the threat to his life. We might be tempted to trust Cicero more than Plutarch or other authors because he was closest to the event. But if Cicero's account might be more trustworthy about *what* happened, that does not mean it is more trustworthy about *why* it happened. (And even in terms of what happened, the source that is closest to the event is not necessarily the closest to the truth.) For his own purposes, Cicero wants to portray Antony in the worst possible way, and does not want to implicate Caesar, who at the time of the speech was dead and soon to be made a god (or "deified").

The lack of clarity about the motives behind Antony's offer of the diadem at the Lupercalia is not only a modern problem. Another version of this incident is found in a biography of Augustus by Nicolaus of Damascus (a city in Syria), who was a young man at the time it happened. He sums up the different reactions to Antony's offer of the diadem as follows:

> People had different opinions about what happened. Some were annoyed because it was a clear demonstration of political power that was contrary to a democratic form of government, while others went along with it, thinking they would find favor with Caesar. Others spread the rumor that Antony had done it with Caesar's approval. And there were many who wanted Caesar to become king without any doubt about his status. Among the crowd there were rumors of every sort. (*Life of Augustus* 21.8)

Nicolaus adds complexity to the interpretation, and adds confusion as well. Cutting through all the possible political intrigue and complex web of motivations, what is at stake in all the accounts of consul Antony's offer of a diadem to Caesar the dictator? The meaning of the republic itself. Caesar's angry refusal, whether play-acting or not, shows how the republic's history and its traditions, already ancient to the Romans of 44 BC, could shape both events and their meaning. The crowd's different reactions, as described in Cicero, Plutarch, and Nicolaus, show that the idea of the republic still had some hold on their beliefs, even if it no longer corresponded to the current political reality. There were those who genuinely wanted Caesar to be king, while there were others who wanted Caesar to look like one only so they could undermine support for him and justify his assassination. On the other hand, for Romans to whom the republic still meant "liberty and the consulship," the offer of the diadem may have meant very little. All of Caesar's special privileges and honors, especially the title "dictator for life," already told them more than enough: The word "republic" no longer meant anything and was in real danger of being lost forever under the powerful sway of an extraordinary individual, no matter what he wore on his head.

In fact, Caesar's rejection of the diadem may have been less about the traditions of the republic and more about securing his power and preserving his life. Would accepting the diadem have given him anything he did not already possess? And as for his opponents, when they appealed to republican liberty as opposed to slavery under King Caesar, did the republic and its anti-monarchial traditions truly mean something to them, or were they merely using "liberty" as a way to attack a political opponent? In other words, did they oppose the idea of a king, or only Caesar as king? Were they in truth more anti-Caesar than pro-republic? If we have a relatively clear picture of *what* happened when Antony offered Caesar the equivalent of a royal crown, much less clear is *why* it happened. And it is the *why* that is the true arena where history is practiced, because ultimately history is about meaning. What did it mean to the people who lived it, to the people who wrote about it, and to the people who now read about it?

Writing shortly after Caesar's assassination about an earlier conspiracy against Rome in 63 BC, the historian Sallust provided an account of a debate between Julius Caesar, who at this point was starting to make a name for himself, and Cato, a staunch and unyielding supporter of the republic and its traditions. Sallust puts a speech in the mouth of Cato, that echoes the words of the ancient Greek historian Thucydides, who wrote about the war between Athens and Sparta in the fifth century BC. At this point, Cato laments the current state of the Roman Republic:

> We have already lost the true names for things: Generosity now means giving away someone else's wealth, courage is now daring in doing wrong, and because of this the Republic is at the point of collapse. (Sallust, *Catiline's Conspiracy* 52)

In this passage, Sallust has a true believer in the republic and its history say something important about lost meanings, at a date twenty years before the incident at the Lupercalia. According to this view, the traditional values and ideals of the republic have been so badly corrupted, wicked behavior parades under the name of virtue. Cato, the speaker of these words, fought together with Pompey against Caesar in the civil war that led to Caesar's position of supreme authority, and eventually to Antony's offer of the diadem. When it was clear Caesar would emerge victorious in this war, Cato committed suicide, preferring to die along with his republic.

But Caesar may well have agreed with Cato that many high-sounding words had become empty labels, and perhaps this was true not only of terms such as "courage" and "generosity," but also of "liberty" and "republic." Caesar, however, chose to recognize this reality rather than fight against it. In fact, at some point (we do not know when) Caesar reportedly said that the republic was nothing but a name without substance, without form (Suetonius, *The Deified Julius Caesar* 77).

The incident at the Lupercalia allows us to see the different meanings the republic had to the Romans during its final years, and these different meanings were shaped by the history of its earliest years: Both what the republic was and what it meant connect the end of its history with its beginning. And if the republic came to an end after nearly five centuries, it continues to exist today in our historical imaginations. If we examine how the republic came to acquire meaning, and also how it came to lose it, we can better understand how our own institutions and values came to have meaning, and how these, too, might lose their meaning for us, because of exceptional individuals, corrupted institutions, and an exhausted populace. In the next chapter, then, we will begin with the legend of the republic's birth, and over the course of the book continue to ask ourselves if Caesar was right to believe that the republic had lost all meaning, and, if so, he was right to take the actions he did.

The Nuts and Bolts of the Roman Republic

The Romans of the republic did not have a written constitution that set out the structure of their government, but instead developed their political system over time. As should be expected, the political institutions of the Roman Republic underwent substantial changes over the nearly five hundred years of its existence, and the Romans themselves often wrote their own history with the assumption that later developments had an earlier origin. Without worrying about the details of these changes, the following overview of the basic political and social structures of the Roman Republic will provide a framework for the chapters to follow and will also introduce most of the terms essential to understanding the history of the Roman Republic.

SPQR: The Senate and People of Rome

These four letters, found today on the manhole covers of Rome, are for many people synonymous with ancient Rome. This abbreviation, written in full as *Senatus Populusque Romanus*, means the Senate and the Roman People, a useful starting point for a history of the Roman Republic and for an understanding how the Romans thought of themselves. SPQR represented an ideal, when the two essential elements of the Roman Republic, the ruling elite of the senate and the general citizen body, worked together for a common good. But while the two were joined together in the abbreviation, they were in reality often at odds. In fact, conflicts between members of the senatorial elite and politicians who represented (or claimed to represent) the interests of the Roman people are one of the major themes of the republic's history.

The Senate (senatus)

The Roman Senate, as the forerunner of many modern senates, might appear somewhat familiar, but there are important features unique to it. The Romans traced the origin of their senate to the first king and founder of Rome, Romulus. After establishing his new city, the story goes, he selected one hundred older men to serve as an advisory body, on the assumption that older men were wiser and possessed greater self-control. The Latin terms *senatus* and *senator* are related to the Latin for old man, *senex* (root of the English word "senile"). Roman senators were usually referred to as *patres* (singular *pater*), a word that means "fathers," and is one hint to how patriarchal Roman society was.

In contrast to the modern US Senate, the Senate of the Roman Republic did not have a fixed number of senators. Though the first senate supposedly had 100 members, the number varied over the course of the republic. Records of attendance at senate meetings near the end of the republic show around 400 members, and there was a quorum (the minimum number of participants required to conduct business) of 200. Under Caesar, the total reached 900, but for much of the republic there were around 300 senators. Also, individuals were not directly elected as senators. Although the early history of the senate is obscure, it seems at the beginning of the republic senators were first chosen by the consuls, and then by the censors. Later, election to one of the more important political offices qualified the officeholder for membership in the senate. It is not clear if senators were legally required to meet a minimum standard of wealth, but there is no question that senators were always expected to be among the wealthiest citizens of Rome. Membership in the senate was for life, though a senator could be expelled for misconduct. Ultimately, the censors were in charge of senate membership. Senators were distinguished in public by a special toga with a broad purple stripe (known as the *latus clavus*) and also special red shoes; they also had special seats reserved for them in the theater. They were forbidden from engaging in business, but found ways around this restriction.

A meeting of the senate could be called only by high-ranking officeholders, and though there was a senate house (known as the *curia*), the senate could meet anywhere in Rome or up to a mile outside the city limit, as long as the space had been consecrated by a religious ritual. Thus, the Senate could meet in a temple, and often did. Even though the senate was the most influential and important body for the governance of the republic, it could not pass laws. Instead, the senate would issue a "decree" (*senatus consultum*), usually a recommendation for action or specific instructions to an officeholder to carry out some action. When a proposal was made before the senate, each senator would be called on to give his opinion, in order of rank, beginning with the individual designated as the *princeps senatus*. To express support for a speaker, a senator would often go stand next to him, and voting would often be done by walking to one side or another. The Senate controlled the state's finances, managed foreign relations, directed the disposition of military forces, and supervised all religious matters. For all practical purposes, the senate was the governing body of Rome, and senators were a small elite ruling class that dominated Roman history, both in making it and writing it.

The Roman People (populus Romanus)

As in English, "people" can be understood simply as everyone, but in political contexts the word can carry the sense of "regular people" as opposed to an elite group who are marked out by having more wealth, more power, and more education (such as senators). In Latin, *populus* can carry the same range of meanings, and as the republic developed, the word often carried more of the sense of the "have-nots" as opposed to the "haves," or, as some might characterize it, the 99 percent as opposed to the 1 percent (in Rome, actually closer to the 99.9 percent and the 0.1 percent). But *populus Romanus* also had a more restrictive sense, which it carries in the abbreviation SPQR. In this case, the phrase referred specifically to the citizen body of Rome, who were entitled to vote in the assemblies. The division between citizens and noncitizens is one of the most crucial elements of the organization of the Roman Republic. In simple terms, a citizen was free, as opposed to a slave, and able to participate fully in political life at Rome.

There were different types of citizenship with different rights. Full Roman citizenship included the right to vote, while more limited forms granted particular rights, such as the right to settle in Rome (*ius migrationis*), to trade with Romans (*commercium*), and to marry a Roman citizen (*conubium*), but did not allow access to political office or participation in politics. There was also a limited form of citizenship known as "Latin rights" (*ius Latii*), granted to the communities around Rome at the end of the fourth century BC, and later extended to other peoples in Italy as well as Spain, Gaul, and North Africa. One particular right fundamental to Roman citizenship was *provocatio*, the right of a citizen to appeal to the judgment of the people, the *populus Romanus*, against a Roman official. This right made the *populus Romanus*, as represented by a voting assembly, the ultimate judge in the case of a citizen against a political official and ensured that, ultimately, no Roman citizen would be subject to the arbitrary or corrupt exercise of power by an individual with political authority. In this regard, *provocatio* is a form of protection against an individual who wishes to act like an absolute monarch.

In contrast to most other ancient civilizations, Rome was rather generous with its citizenship, and was willing to grant it, usually in one of the limited forms, to other peoples, especially those who willingly became subjects to Rome's authority. While being born to parents who were citizens automatically granted citizenship, there were other ways to become a Roman citizen, and birth to noncitizens did not prevent someone from becoming a citizen. For example, a freed slave would become a Roman citizen, and military service could result in citizenship for soldiers and their families.

The grant of citizenship was not motivated by pure good will. Individuals who possessed some form of Roman citizenship had rights, but also obligations, such as paying taxes and, more importantly, military service. The limited rights possessed by communities in Italy that provided much of Rome's military manpower would prove to be a major source of conflict during the last century of the republic, especially when military service meant spending several years far away from home.

Slaves and Freedmen/Freedwomen

In the narrow sense, *populus Romanus* did not include inhabitants of Rome and its territories who did not possess citizenship and were not considered "free." The largest category of such people were slaves, and Rome was a society that depended on a steady supply of slaves for economic production. Slave trading and selling captured individuals as slaves was a prime source of income for pirates as well as dealers around the Mediterranean. The Greek island of Delos, for example, was a major market for slaves, and thousands would be bought and sold in a single day. Inhabitants of cities conquered by Rome (as well as by others) would often be sold into slavery, if they were not ransomed or killed. The slavery practiced at Rome and in the ancient Mediterranean was not based on race, as it was in the US. In general, the Romans did not regard skin color as a marker of any particular character traits, which would have been difficult given the multiethnic Mediterranean. There were stereotypes about different peoples, but these were based on the part of the world from which someone came, not skin color. (To the Romans, the peoples who inhabited the colder regions of present-day Germany and Great Britain were the prime examples of uncivilized barbarians.) There was a wide variety of types and conditions of slavery, ranging from those who worked in mines (essentially a death sentence) to the highly educated tutors of the Roman elite, who were usually Greek intellectuals. While slaves did sometimes run away from their owners, slave revolts were not as common as might be expected. These were not uprisings against the institution of slavery, however, and there was no abolitionist movement in ancient Rome. In fact, freed slaves would often own slaves.

Slaves could obtain their freedom in a few different ways. An owner could simply free the slave through a legal process known as manumission, and it was not uncommon for slaves to be freed at the death of their master, as long as the master stated so in the will. Slaves could also purchase their freedom; they were often allowed to have savings, though everything they possessed was still technically the property of their master. A freed slave was known as a *libertus* (male; plural *liberti*) or *liberta* (female; plural *libertae*), and upon being freed they acquired the citizenship rights of the community to which they belonged. Children born to freed slaves would be treated the same as freeborn citizens, though a child born to a slave mother, regardless of the father's status, would be a slave. There was a social stigma attached to having slaves in one's family past, and freedmen and their sons were not normally permitted to be senators.

Like most people who were not part of the Roman elite, slaves are mostly absent from the historical record seen only through their eyes of their owners. We thus we have little information about their lives—those we do hear about were usually from the educated rank of slaves who were part of wealthy households, not from the vast majority who toiled in fields, in mines, or in workshops. Slaves do feature in Roman literature, especially as caricatures in comic plays. A stock character of Roman comedy was the "clever slave," who outwitted his master and made jokes about being whipped and punished. Obviously, this portrayal was for the amusement of free, slave-owning Romans, and has as much correspondence to reality as racist stereotypes in contemporary media.

Women

The status of freeborn women as members of the *populus Romanus* was limited and might be compared more to the status of slaves than full citizens. While women could be full citizens, with few exceptions they could not vote or attend political meetings, and thus in the political world of the Roman Republic they could play only an indirect and largely invisible role though their influence on men. The ideal woman, as constructed by elite Roman males, was a producer of legitimate children who managed the household. The ideal activity of a dutiful wife and mother was spinning wool at home. For women, marriage often occurred at a very young age, in general between the ages of 15–18, though marriages as young as 12 are recorded. (Men were in general slightly older, around 20–23, at the time of their first marriage.) The young woman's preferences were not usually taken into consideration, and marriage was often used for political purposes. Caesar, for example, married his daughter Julia to the much older Pompey to cement their political alliance.

Since women are presented to us almost exclusively through the eyes of men, they are frequently portrayed as one of two extremes: either idealized and virtuous wives, mothers, and daughters, or conniving and dangerous sexual monsters. Roman women, as women in many societies ancient and modern, were considered inferior to males, and thus were often very restricted in the roles they could play in society. In reality, women's lives were richer and more complex than our sources usually represent them. As we will see in the next chapter, women often play a prominent role at important moments in the historical narratives of the Roman Republic, but we must be careful when interpreting these narratives and their relation to reality.

Roman Social Organization

Ancient Rome was a hierarchical society, and in addition to their legal status, free citizens belonged to groups that determined their place in society and politics. These groups were based on birth, wealth, and social relationships. Family history was always extremely important in Rome, and birth to a family of wealth and prestige, with a long record of military and political accomplishments, would make access to wealth and power much easier for a young male. In fact, a son born into such a family would be expected to achieve the same success as his ancestors. Those who did not belong to such families faced a far more difficult path to a political office, and in the first centuries of the republic, holding political office or a priesthood would have been impossible.

Patricians, Plebeians, and Nobles

One of the fundamental divisions in Roman society was between patricians and plebeians, groups sometimes referred to as "orders" (from the Latin *ordo*). All Roman citizens would belong to one of these two groups, and the political battles between them during the early republic are often called the "Conflict of the Orders" or the "Struggle of the Orders." However, these two groups were never clearly defined. By tradition, a "patrician" was someone who could trace his family lineage back to the first senators (*patres* in Latin) established by Romulus, the legendary first king of Rome, or to some prominent family associated with the legends surrounding the founding of Rome. This ancestry gave the individual an elevated status in Roman society, and it was very much an aristocracy by birth. Though this seems like a clear enough definition, the Romans themselves did not have precise family histories. Nonetheless, certain family names, such as Claudius or Fabius, would identify someone as a patrician. Scholars have attempted to identify the number of patrician families, with the totals ranging from 14 to well over 100. "Plebeian" is even less well defined, but one shorthand definition of a plebeian is anyone who is not a patrician. "Plebeian" comes from *plebs*, which is often is used in the same sense as the "people," but many plebeians, especially those that make it into history books, were wealthy and powerful, distinguished from patricians only by their name.

Patricians and plebeians are sometimes treated as economic classes—the very rich and everyone else—but this is inaccurate. While a patrician would almost always be one of the wealthiest members of Roman society, plebeians could also be extremely wealthy. However, the vast majority of plebeians would be of much lower social and economic standing than the patricians. As well, patrician families could fall onto hard times. At the beginning of the republic, there was some fluidity between patrician and plebeian families, but the division between the two groups soon hardened. While patrician and plebeian are primarily social categories, the distinction had important consequences for access to positions of power, namely political offices and priesthoods. During the first two centuries of the republic, plebeians were barred from most political offices, and patricians retained exclusive control of priesthoods even longer. Even when plebeians were allowed to hold political office and priesthoods, the patricians continued to dominate them. In short, patricians were far fewer in number, but far more powerful and influential in Roman society and politics.

A third category that overlaps with both patrician and plebeian is "noble." "Nobles" (*nobiles;* singular *nobilis*) were individuals with an ancestor who had held high political office, and in a strict sense, the highest office, the consulship (the Latin term *nobilis* originally meant "well-known.") Both patricians and plebeians could belong to the nobility, though patricians would have a distinct advantage, since plebeians were at first barred from holding the higher offices. Most patricians would have a family tradition of achieving positions of prominence, and a patrician who failed to be elected to high office could be considered something of a disappointment. Plebeians would not necessarily have the same expectation, though if an ancestor had reached a high office, thereby elevating the family into the nobility, there would then be an expectation for his descendants to measure up to his example. The plebeian nobility would thus consist of individuals who possessed the same wealth and family traditions as the patricians, with the only difference being the supposed connection to the earliest "senate" under Romulus. The combined patrician and plebeian nobility would often share the same interests, and starting in the third century BC, formed the ruling class of the republic. To sum up briefly:

- **Patricians:** Members of an exclusive set of wealthy elite families who traced their origins to the early years of Rome.
- **Plebeians:** In the simplest definition, everyone who was not a patrician.
- **Nobles:** Anyone, either patrician or plebeian, whose family included an ancestor who had obtained high office, and strictly speaking only those whose ancestor had reached the consulship.

Patrons and Clients

Connected to the distinction between patricians and plebeians is the Roman institution known as *clientela*, which is a formal relationship between an individual known as a *patronus* and anyone who was his *cliens* (plural *clientes*). While related to the modern English words "patron" and "client," their meanings are very different. In the Roman Republic, a patron is a wealthy and powerful citizen, a patrician or a noble, who has established a formal relationship with individuals and entire families known as his clients. The patron looks after the well-being of his clients, providing legal and financial assistance and other kinds of protection. In turn, the clients provide services for the patron when called on, particularly in helping to pay for his expenses, such as a fine or a daughter's dowry. A client would also be expected to support the patron and the patron's preferred candidates in elections. The patron–client relationship was not simply a social arrangement, but carried serious obligations. In fact, if a patron failed a client, there were potential legal consequences. The relationship was also hereditary and would be passed down through generations, so a patron's son might inherit his father's clients. (Some see the patron–client relationship as an early forerunner of the relationship between a mafia godfather and individuals who seek his "protection.") Clients were not necessarily of low standing, and there were different types of *clientela*. Freed slaves automatically became the clients of their former masters, while entire communities might become the clients of Roman politicians who helped them. Kings in the eastern Mediterranean might become clients of a powerful Roman politician, and Roman military commanders often became patrons of peoples they had conquered.

Equites *("Knights"): The Equestrian Order*

In addition to patricians and plebeians, the term "order" was also applied to a class of individuals known as *equites* (singular *eques*), who make up the "equestrian order." *Equites* were of high social standing, second only to senators. *Eques* (sometimes translated as "knight") and equestrian are terms connected to the Latin word for "horse" (*equus*), and the origin of this group, like the others, goes back to the stories surrounding Romulus's founding of Rome, when he is said to have established a special cavalry. Over time, the military significance of the *eques* as a member of the cavalry faded, and the primary qualification for the equestrian order was a minimum amount of wealth, which was extremely high. There was also a standard for physical and moral fitness, but this was largely ignored. *Equites* are often contrasted to senators because of a preference to engage in business rather than politics, and they are closely associated with the infamous tax-collectors (*publicani*) of the late republic. (Senators were legally barred from engaging in certain lucrative forms of business, such as lending money and large-scale trading, but most found ways around it.) However, this contrast is often overstated because of the political conflicts between the two orders during the last century of the republic. Much of the time, the equestrian and senatorial orders shared the same interests, given that they both were extremely wealthy. As well, many ambitious individuals left the equestrian order to pursue a political career and enter the senate. Somewhat strangely, some members of the equestrian order were provided with a horse at public expense, which they had to turn in after they had completed their military service and wished to enter the senate. In short, when you see someone referred to as an equestrian or a knight, in most cases it means they were from a wealthy but not politically prominent family.

Assemblies and Elections

To hold elections for political offices and to pass laws, the Romans would assemble into a body, known as a *comitia*, that was divided into subgroups. Instead of counting each individual vote and deciding a winner based on a majority of the votes, Roman voting took place according to these subgroups. In principle, it is similar to the way US presidential elections work, in which the winner of the popular vote in each state determines which candidate receives the state's electoral votes, and the electoral vote determines the winner of the presidency rather than the popular vote. (It is thus possible for a candidate to win the popular vote but lose the election, which has happened five times in US history.) There were three different *comitia* and all three voted in subgroups formed according to different criteria. Of the two important assemblies, one had subgroups determined by wealth, and the other according to place of residence. While these assemblies could be called democratic, since they are the bodies representing the "Roman people," they are democratic in a very limited sense. In particular, the assemblies were structured so that wealthier and older citizens had a distinct advantage in voting.

Comitia Centuriata

This assembly, known as the Centuriate Assembly or sometimes the Military Assembly, was summoned to elect the higher political offices and to pass legislation, as well as to issue formal declarations of war and to ratify treaties. As with many institutions of the Roman Republic, the Centuriate Assembly changed over the course of the centuries, but the basic structure remained. For the purposes of voting, Roman citizens were divided into five (or six) property classes. Property class was determined by a census, carried out in theory every five years by officials known as censors. Each of the property classes was then divided into "centuries." These groups were originally connected to the organization of the Roman military into centuries, groups nominally consisting of a hundred soldiers, though in practice the number varied. In the Centuriate Assembly there were 193 centuries in total, and each century cast a single vote, determined by the majority vote of its members. However, the 193 centuries were not equally distributed among the property classes, and the centuries did not have the same number of citizens. The wealthiest class had the fewest citizens, but these wealthy citizens were distributed into more centuries than any other property class. Far more citizens were in the lower property classes, but they were placed into a smaller number of centuries. In fact, the lowest property class consisted of only a single century of individuals, so for all practical purposes, a vote by a member of this century,

FIG. 1.5 Roman voting portrayed on a coin of the first c. AD. To vote, Romans walked across a narrow "bridge" (*pons*). The figure on the left receives a ballot, and the figure on the right drops his ballot into a voting urn.

which had the most citizens, counted for almost nothing. In short, the wealthier you were, the more your vote counted. The members of the two wealthiest property classes controlled 98 of the 193 centuries, and since it took 97 centuries to win a majority, the wealthiest classes could on their own win an election if they voted the same way. Moreover, the centuries in each property class were at times divided between young men (*juniores*, between 17 and 45 years old) and older men (*seniores*, over the age of 45). There were fewer older men, so there was also a bias toward older men in the voting, though not as pronounced as the bias toward the wealthy. The centuries would vote in order from wealthiest to poorest, and votes would be counted as the voting went on, so if a majority of 97 was reached before the centuries in the lower property classes had voted, they would not get to vote. Because voting in the Centuriate Assembly was designed to favor the upper classes, the wealthiest members of Rome were essentially guaranteed to control access to those offices and determine the most important policy decisions of the Roman Republic.

Comitia Tributa *and* Concilium Plebis

The *comitia tributa*, also known as the Tribal Assembly, elected lower offices and could pass laws. Voting was by tribe, rather than property class, and thus this assembly was less heavily weighted in favor of the wealthy citizens than the Centuriate Assembly, but still tilted in their favor. Every Roman citizen was assigned to a tribe, determined by the region where he lived or owned property. The number of tribes in the early republic was 17, but eventually reached 35. Similar to the Centuriate Assembly, each tribe cast one vote determined by the majority vote of the tribe's members. Unlike the Centuriate Assembly, in which the centuries voted in order until a majority was reached, the tribes voted simultaneously. The number of citizens in each tribe was unequal, so the larger a tribe, the less an individual vote counted. Most of the poorer citizens who lived in the city of Rome belonged to one of the four tribes known as the "urban tribes." These four urban tribes contained far more citizens than the 31 rural tribes, which not only had fewer citizens, but also had a higher concentration of wealthy land-owning citizens. New Roman citizens, such as freed slaves, would be assigned to a tribe, but even as the number of citizens increased, the number of tribes did not. Assignment of new citizens to tribes became a contentious political issue at the end of the republic.

The *concilium plebis* functioned in the same way as the *comitia tributa,* and thus could also be called a Tribal Assembly. However, only a tribune of the plebs could summon a *concilium plebis* and, as the name implies, patricians were excluded. The *comitia tributa* included the entire *populus*, not just the *plebs*. As a result, the *concilium plebis* is sometimes called the Plebeian Assembly, to distinguish it from the Tribal Assembly. The *concilium plebis* elected tribunes of the plebs and plebeian aediles. Decisions voted on by the Plebeian Assembly, known as *plebiscita* ("plebiscites" in English), eventually acquired the same validity as laws passed by the Centuriate Assembly. Since laws that were favored by the plebs and opposed by the senatorial elite would normally have a difficult time passing in the Centuriate Assembly, given its extreme bias toward the wealthy citizens, politicians who wanted to pass "popular" laws would make use of the Tribal or Plebeian Assembly, since they had a far better chance of success.

There is still debate about the difference between the *comitia tributa* and the *concilium plebis*, and the English terms Popular Assembly and Tribal Assembly are sometimes used for both. For most purposes, they can be treated as the same.

Comitia Curiata

This assembly, also known as the Curiate Assembly, was likely the oldest of all the assemblies, but for much of the republic had a limited role, mostly approving adoptions and overseeing some religious matters. It consisted of thirty *curiae*, which were subgroups of the original three "tribes" of Rome, by tradition established by the first king, Romulus. Each of the three tribes was divided into ten *curiae*, resulting in a total of thirty. In voting, each *curia* was represented by a single individual.

Political Offices

The political offices at Rome are often called "magistracies" and officeholders are called "magistrates." A basic principle of Roman politics is "collegiality," which means every officeholder had at least one colleague who possessed equal authority and could prevent him from taking any action. No one individual would ever possess unchecked power, with the exception of dictator, a temporary office used only in emergencies. The relationship between colleagues in an office was usually not adversarial, since the officeholders would come from the same elite class. However, there were exceptions, and both personal ambitions and political issues could create serious conflicts. Hostile relations between colleagues in the same office was usually a sign of a major crisis.

With the exception of censor, all elected offices had a term of one year, and normally at least one year had to pass before holding another office. A political career would begin after at least ten years of military service. Over time, the custom developed of holding a series of offices in order, and a Roman politician was expected to hold the lower offices before running for the higher offices. This sequence eventually became codified in law and was known as the *cursus honorum* ("the course of offices," sometimes called "the ladder of offices"). Moreover, by the second century BC, there were minimum ages for higher office (36 for aedile, 39 for praetor, 42 for consul). However, exceptions were made, particularly for an individual who had acquired prestige and popularity through military service. The political offices that follow are presented in the order of the *cursus honorum*, from lowest (quaestor) to highest (consul). Two other offices, tribune of the plebs and censor, were not part of the regular *cursus*, but were extremely important. Aside from the offices listed, there were several other minor offices, some of which were elected while others were appointed by the senate.

Quaestor

Elected by the Tribal Assembly, this office was the lowest of the offices in the *cursus honorum* and was usually held by young men in their late twenties, after their initial military service. The number of quaestors increased over the course of the republic until there were twenty, and it eventually became the first step in a political career that would lead to higher offices. By the late republic, election to this office automatically qualified the officeholder for the senate. There were specific types of quaestors: The "city quaestor" (*quaestor urbanus*) was in charge of the treasury of Rome, while "consular quaestors" served as staff assistants to consuls and other higher officials, especially as part of a mission overseas. Quaestors often kept financial records for the commanders of military campaigns, and in general were the accountants and administrative assistants of the Roman government.

Aedile

Aediles come in two flavors, plebeian and curule, and there were two of each. The plebeian aediles, elected by the *concilium plebis*, had to be plebeian, and were elected by the Plebeian Assembly. Curule aediles, elected by the Tribal Assembly, were originally patrician, but later plebeians could hold this office as well. "Curule" refers to a political office for which the holder had the right to use a special ivory chair (*sella curulis*), which carried with it special prestige. Plebeian aediles did not have this privilege. While the plebeian and patrician aediles had different names, for much of the republic their functions were similar. Always concerned with the city of Rome itself, they maintained temples, supervised markets and the supply of grain, organized the entertainment for religious festivals, took care of roads and the water supply, and regulated the sale of slaves. Because of these highly visible responsibilities, especially supervising the games (*ludi*), a successful aedileship was crucial to winning popular support and was a key step to higher political office.

Offices with Imperium*: Praetor and Consul*

The next two offices, praetor and consul, were elected by the Centuriate Assembly, and are distinguished from the lower offices because holders of these offices possessed *imperium*. The holder of an office with *imperium* had practically supreme authority in military command and in legal matters, including the ability to execute citizens. Without *imperium*, an official could not command an army, and any command issued by an official with *imperium* could be disobeyed only in extraordinary circumstances. An official with *imperium* would be accompanied by lictors, who were essentially bodyguards. Lictors walked before the magistrate carrying a bundle of rods known as *fasces*, and when outside the city of Rome, the bundle included an axe. The rods symbolized the power to administer beatings, the axe the power to execute (these *fasces* give us the English word "fascism"). A praetor had six lictors, while a consul had twelve.

Praetor

The original two heads of state in the republic may have been called praetors instead of consuls. Eventually the praetors became the office second only to the consuls in authority, though they retained many of the same functions as the consul. They would command the army in place of the consul, and when neither of the consuls were in Rome, the praetors served as the chief executives in the city. One of the most important duties of a praetor was to serve as judge in legal disputes, both civil and criminal. The law courts of Rome were highly politicized, and political disputes often played out in criminal trials. Over the course of the republic, the number of praetors grew from two to eight, and there was a specific praetor to oversee the courts in Rome (*praetor urbanus*) and another to oversee legal disputes involving foreigners (*praetor peregrinus*).

Consul

The consulship is the highest elected office of the republic, and the summit of the *cursus honorum*. Two individuals are elected each year for a term of one year. By tradition, it was the first office established under the republic. Consuls could call a meeting the senate or one of the assemblies, but one of the most important functions of a consul was command of a Roman army. Usually, one consul would take command of the legions while the other remained in Rome, though if both consuls were on campaign at the same time with the same army, they would alternate days in command. One of the honors of reaching the consulship is that the names of the consuls were used to date the years of the republic (for example, 44 BC would be known as "in the consulship of Caesar and Antony").

Beyond the Cursus: *Censor, Tribune of the Plebs, and Dictator*

The remaining offices were not part of the *cursus honorum*, but were no less prestigious. In fact, because of their particular powers, each of these offices was as important the consulship in the political history of the republic. In particular, the growth in the power and independence of the office of tribune of the plebs became one of the main factors in the constitutional crises during the last generation of the republic.

Censor

Two censors were elected every five years by the Centuriate Assembly for a term of eighteen months. As the name suggests, the censors were in charge of the census that determined the property classes for the Centuriate Assembly, and also oversaw most aspects of citizenship, including maintaining the official list of citizens. The censors were also responsible for senate membership and could have senators removed for various offenses. In a broader sense, they also had authority over public morality, which included upholding standards of decency. Lastly, censors were in charge of state contracts for collection of taxes and public works, such as building roads and aqueducts. Because of its oversight of official lists of citizens and senators, it was usually held by prominent men who had already served as consul. The censorship was considered the culmination of a political career, and, since there were fewer censors in comparison to other offices, competition was intense.

Tribune of the Plebs (tribunus plebis)

The tribune of the plebs is often called by different names, such as tribune of the people, popular tribune, or plebeian tribune. As its name suggests, the primary purpose of this office is to represent the plebeians, and only plebeians could hold it. It was often considered the people's defense against the ruling elite of the patrician class. By tradition, the plebeians had won the right to establish this office as part of the settlement after their conflicts with the patricians. Although at first there may have been only two tribunes of the plebs, for most of the Roman Republic there were ten. The tribunes presided over the Plebeian Assembly, where the resolutions known as *plebiscita* were passed, and in the early third century BC these resolutions acquired the force of law. However, the most important power held by a tribune of the plebs was the "veto" (Latin for "I forbid"), which meant they could halt any legislation or official act, prevent the senate from meeting, and even stop someone from speaking publicly. Moreover, they could intercede on behalf of a citizen to prevent an official, including another tribune, from carrying out any act against that citizen. Tribunes themselves were also considered "sacrosanct," which meant it was a serious offense, a religious violation, to lay a hand on them. No one could touch them, and no one could interrupt them while they were speaking—at least in theory.

The power of the tribunes was only effective within the city limits of Rome, and only in special cases could a tribune spend a night away from Rome. Yet it was an extremely powerful office, one that would eventually become a major source of discord at the end of the republic. Given that every year there were ten individuals who could block any legislation or action, even by another tribune, it is remarkable that anything got done. This fact highlights how much traditional norms directed Roman behavior, and how ambitious and wealthy plebeians might wish to play nice with the upper class.

Dictator

As briefly discussed, the dictatorship was a special office, appointed by the senate for a period of six months in times of crisis. The dictator possessed *imperium* and had supreme authority for the duration of the office. While dictators were appointed with some frequency in the first two centuries of the republic, it fell out of use until the first century BC, when it was revived during the civil wars of the 80s BC and then held by Caesar. This was the only office without a colleague, though the dictator did have an assistant, known as the *magister equitum* (usually translated as "master of the horse," in the sense of a cavalry commander).

Roman Names

The basic form of a name for a Roman male has three parts: the *praenomen*, the *nomen*, and the *cognomen* (*nomen* is the Latin word for "name"). For example, in Gaius Julius Caesar, Gaius is the *praenomen*, Julius the *nomen*, and Caesar the *cognomen*. The *praenomen* is simply a given name, much like the first name in English. The *nomen* indicates the *gens*, often translated as "clan"; this is the family name, though holders of the same *nomen* were not necessarily closely related. The *cognomen* indicates a specific branch of the *gens*, and thus holders of the same *nomen* and *cognomen* would belong to the same family. For example, Marcus Tullius Cicero had a brother Quintus Tullius Cicero. Some Romans had only a *praenomen* and *nomen* (for example, Gaius Marius), which may have been the original form of Roman names.

Another kind of *cognomen* is an honorific title, usually indicating the name of a territory or people that an individual conquered as a commander of an army. For example, in the name Publius Cornelius Scipio Africanus, the "Africanus" was added because Publius Cornelius

Scipio had defeated the Carthaginian general Hannibal, from North Africa. Other examples of *cognomina* are *Macedonicus* (Macedonia), *Creticus* (Crete), and *Numidicus* (Numidia in North Africa). Examples from later in Roman history include *Germanicus* and *Britannicus*. Honorific names could also be added for other reasons. Quintus Caecilius Metellus Pius, for example, acquired the honorific Pius because he tried to restore his father from exile (*pius* means dutiful, similar to "pious" in English). An honorific *cognomen* could also be passed on to descendants and become a regular part of the family name.

One source of confusion in the study of Roman history is that males often had the same name as their father, grandfather, or other ancestor. Gaius Julius Caesar's father, for example, was also named Gaius Julius Caesar, and there are several well-known individuals with the name Appius Claudius Pulcher. In some cases, modern historians are not sure to which generation a name applies.

Women, on the other hand, are usually given the feminine form of their father's *nomen*, which almost always ends in *-a*. For example, Gaius Julius Caesar's daughter is Julia, and Marcus Tullius Cicero's daughter is Tullia. Even when there is more than one daughter, each daughter would carry the same name. Marcus Antonius had two daughters, and both were named Antonia. To distinguish these in history books, they are often designated as Antonia Maior (Antonia the Elder) and Antonia Minor (Antonia the Younger). Additional daughters would sometimes be known by a name indicating which number they were among the daughters, such as Tertia, which means third.

There were a limited number of *praenomina*, and these are often abbreviated. The most common are as follows:

A.	= Aulus	Post.	= Postumus
Ap.	= Appius	Q.	= Quintus
C.	= Gaius (C is an older form of G)	S.	= Sextus
D.	= Decimus	Ser.	= Servius
L.	= Lucius	Sp.	= Spurius
M.	= Marcus	T.	= Titus
M.'	= Manlius	Ti.	= Tiberius
P.	= Publius		

Some of these names originally had some particular significance, but it is not always clear what these were and in most cases the meanings of the name have been forgotten. For example, *Quintus* ("Fifth"), *Sextus* ("Sixth"), and *Decimus* ("Tenth") may have originally referred to the birth month, but someone with one of these names was not necessarily born in that month. *Postumus* was a name given to a child born after the death of the father; *Marcus* was likely associated with the god of war Mars, while *Tiberius* was taken from the name of the god of the Tiber river.

Dating Roman History

For dating events we now commonly use a numerical year that by tradition is based on the supposed birth year of Jesus as calculated by a monk over 1500 years ago. Since the birth of Jesus was taken as the starting point, dates before his birth count the years backward and are designated with BC, short for "before Christ," or BCE ("before the Common Era" or "before the Christian Era"). For years BC, the lower the number, the later the year. Thus, the date for the beginning of the Roman Republic is 509 BC, while the assassination of Julius Caesar 465 years later would be 44 BC. For events after the birth of Christ, the number of the year increases and is designated with AD (from the Latin *anno domini*, "in the year of our Lord") or CE (for "Common Era" or "Christian Era"). AD and CE are sometimes placed before the year, so you may see a date range expressed as 63 BC–AD 14. Note one possible confusion when speaking in terms of centuries (often abbreviated "c."): The 1st century AD (or CE) means the years 1–100 (there is no year 0), the 2nd century AD means the years 101–200 AD, and so on. Thus, "mid-3rd century AD" would be around 250 AD. The situation is the opposite for years BC: The 1st century BC (or BCE) would be the years 100–1 BC. Thus, a reference to the early 3rd century BC would mean roughly the years 300–270 BC. Lastly, some Roman historians as well as some older history books use the abbreviation AUC to designate a year. AUC is from the Latin *ab urbe condita*, which means "from the foundation of the city," the city being Rome and the year of its foundation 753 BC. Thus, the number of the year AUC has to be subtracted from 753 to arrive at a year BC. For example, the year 353 AUC would be the same as 400 BC. One final note: "c." or "ca." before a date means "around" (from the Latin *circa*), and so c. 125 BC would mean approximately 125 BC. It might seem easy to confuse the abbreviations c. for *circa* and c. for century, but context will make it clear.

CHAPTER 2

Origin Stories

The Birth of the Roman Republic

FIG. 2.1 *The Oath of Brutus* by François-Joseph Navez (1787–1869). Brutus holds the dagger out toward Lucretia's father and his companion, Publius Valerius Publicola. Lucretia dies in the background with her husband Collatinus kneeling at her side.

Overview

The legends of Rome's founding, going back to the arrival in Italy of Aeneas, refugee from the mythical Trojan War, provide the backdrop for Rome's encounters with the other peoples inhabiting the Italian peninsula. Aeneas' line of descendants, who are little more than names, leads to the founding of the city of Rome by Romulus, the first of seven kings. The last of these kings, Tarquinius Superbus, sets the stage for the dramatic story of the republic's founding, which according to the traditional history was motivated by an act of sexual violence. The establishment of the republic, however, does not lead to stability and security, but produces a series of internal crises and external threats that threaten the existence of this new state.

Timeline

1184	Traditional date for the end of the Trojan War
753	Traditional date for the founding of Rome
753–509	The Regal Period
509	Overthrow of the monarchy, beginning of the Roman Republic
508	Lars Porsenna's siege of Rome
499 or 496	Defeat of the Latins at the Battle of Lake Regillus

Rome Before Rome

The Romans traced their origins back to Aeneas, a Trojan warrior who plays a minor role in an ancient Greek epic poem, the *Iliad*. Believed to have been the work of a poet named Homer, the *Iliad* tells the story of the greatest of the Greek warriors, Achilles, and is set during the last year of the Trojan War. For ten years, a large army composed of various Greek forces set siege to the city of Troy, on the coast of modern-day Turkey. The Greeks, under the command of their king Agamemnon, had sailed across the Aegean Sea in an attempt to recover Helen, the wife of Agamemnon's brother. According to legend the most beautiful woman in the world, Helen had been either kidnapped or seduced by a Trojan prince named Paris. (In an old saying, Helen's was "the face that launched a thousand ships.") Although there is no certainty that this war really happened, 1184 BC is the traditional date for the fall of Troy and the end of the war, thanks to the famous trick of the Trojan horse. According to Roman tradition, Aeneas rescued his aged father and young son from the flames engulfing his city and set sail with other Trojan survivors to find the new home appointed to him by the gods. The story of Aeneas's wanderings is best known from a Latin epic poem, the *Aeneid*, which was modeled on Homer's Greek epics, the *Iliad* and *Odyssey*. Composed by Vergil near the end of the first century BC, after the end of the republic, the *Aeneid* became the national epic of Rome and one of the most influential works of literature in the Western tradition.

In the story of the *Aeneid*, Aeneas eventually lands on the coast of Italy, encounters both allies and enemies among the people living there, and marries the daughter of a local king named Latinus. However, this marriage does not come about easily. The ruler of another local people had expected to marry the king's daughter, and since he was also suspicious of these foreign immigrants, he started a war against Aeneas and his Trojan followers, who had become allies of a Greek people living on the future site of Rome. This conflict ends when Aeneas kills his rival in single combat, and after he marries the daughter of King Latinus, the Trojans and Latinus' followers unite into a single people, the Latins. We now recognize "Latin" as the name of the language spoken by the people of Rome, which became the dominant (but not only) language spoken throughout Italy and the ancient Mediterranean world.

Aeneas was considered the "father" of the Roman people, but not the founder of Rome. In the Romans' own historical tradition, there is a gap of just over 400 years between Aeneas's arrival in Italy after the Trojan War and the founding of Rome, traditionally dated to 753 BC. Later Roman scholars and historians filled this gap with a list of Aeneas' descendants, all of whom were kings of Alba Longa, a city founded by Aeneas's son just 15 miles south of the future site of Rome. However, these individuals are nothing more than names to us, and even to the Romans were not much more than that. In the twelfth generation of this line of Alban kings were two brothers, and the younger of the two, named Numitor, seized the throne, driving out his older brother and his brother's only child, a daughter. Because Numitor feared his niece might give birth to a son who would claim the throne, he made her a Vestal Virgin, a special priesthood that committed a woman to chastity. However, despite Numitor's efforts to isolate her, she became pregnant. According to legend, the father was none other than Mars, the god of war, though others said this was only an attempt to hide the fact that a Vestal Virgin was having sex. She gave birth to twins, Romulus and Remus, whose story is one of the most famous and important from ancient Rome.

Numitor, still the king of Alba Longa, did not want these two boys to reach adulthood, so he ordered them to be taken to the Tiber River and left there, presumably to die. ("Child exposure," as the abandonment of infants is known, was a widespread practice in the ancient world, often, but not always, leading to their death.) Because the river had flooded and spilled over its banks, the twins could not be placed directly in the river, and instead were left nearby in a marshy area. By chance, a shepherd came upon them and saw a she-wolf (*lupa*) nursing them, a scene that supplies the famous symbol of the city Rome, still in use today.

The twins were raised by the shepherd and his wife, enjoying a simple and rustic upbringing. Eventually, their true identity and royal lineage were revealed when both the shepherd and king Numitor put two and two together. Realizing that their life was in danger, Romulus and Remus took swift action against the king and restored their grandfather to his rightful place on the throne of Alba Longa. They then set off to found their own city at the place they had been found as infants along the banks of the Tiber. Their grandfather and great-uncle were brothers who could not share power, and likewise these brothers could not agree which one of them would be the new city's founder and ruler. There are different versions of how the argument began and how it ended, but the result is the same: Romulus kills his twin brother Remus, founds a city that he names Rome after himself, and becomes Rome's first king. There will be six more kings after him, and the period from the traditional date of Rome's founding in 753 BC until the overthrow of the monarchy and the foundation of the republic in 509 BC is known as the "Regal Period."

FIG. 2.2 The Capitoline Lupa (she-wolf). The statue may be a forgery from the Middle Ages; the infant twins were added in the Renaissance.

The stories of early Rome are more myth than history, but while Aeneas and Romulus are not considered historical figures today, for the Romans they were an important part of their history and of their identity as Romans. This history was never settled or agreed on by all, and there were no facts fixed beyond any shadow of a doubt. Even ancient Roman (and Greek) scholars and historians debated the story of Rome's founding, and while they made an effort to determine correct dates, true names, and real events, they often had different aims and perspectives than historians today. Of course, they recognized many elements of their history as the stuff of legend and sought to give rational explanations for them, though they might accept more as factual than we would. For example, few believed that the god Mars was the real father of Romulus and Remus, and one ancient explanation was that king Numitor dressed in armor to disguise himself and, looking much like the god of war, raped his niece. In a similar way, the miracle of the she-wolf nursing the abandoned infants was explained as an attempt to mask the fact that the wife of the shepherd who found the twins had a reputation as a prostitute. In Latin, the word for she-wolf, *lupa*, also means prostitute, so it was an easy substitution. Such interpretations as these show a healthy skepticism about a divinity impregnating a captive princess, or about a wild animal feeding human infants rather than eating them, but they still accept the fundamental story that Romulus and Remus were twins, and that one of them founded Rome.

There are other ways to interpret these early legends as representations of a historical truth even if they are not historically true. Mars as the father of Romulus and Remus can be interpreted not as an accurate account of a real event, but as a way to symbolize the war-like character of the Romans. The same kind of interpretation can be applied to Romulus's killing of Remus. There are different reasons for the killing given in the sources, but one of the best known is that Romulus killed his brother for jumping the half-built walls of his new city. After striking him down, he exclaimed, "That'll happen to anyone who jumps over my walls!" Whether anyone believed this actually happened is less important than what it meant to them. On one reading, the story offers the lesson that Rome will defend its walls to the death against any attack, now or in the future, but it also hints at a tension between family and state. A real Roman, it suggests, should be loyal to his political community above all else, and should be willing even to kill even his own brother in its name. That fact that a twin brother is killed emphasizes this message, since no one can be more closely related than a twin, who is almost another version of oneself. In this "history," bonds of citizenship are more important than friendships or blood ties, and this is an important notion in Rome's transition from monarchy to republic. On the other hand, when the republic devolves into civil war in which Roman kills Roman, it is hard not to think of Romulus and Remus, brother killing brother in a bid for political supremacy.

These stories, in all their different versions, were the Roman history of Rome. The way Romans of the republic thought and wrote about the regal period tells us as much about the Roman Republic as it does the regal period, and maybe more. Just as some in the modern world look back on the history of the Roman Republic as a "distant mirror," which the modern world can use to reflect upon itself, so too the Romans of the republic would see themselves reflected in the early history of their city. These reflections, however, are sometimes distorted in complicated ways, so that Aeneas, a "foreign" refugee from the losing side in a war, can still be an ideal Roman hero, and Julius Caesar could boast that Aeneas was his ancestor. Different and competing versions of history often arise less from different sets of facts than from different ideas about what the facts mean.

The Romans had a rich historical tradition about the regal period, filled with dramatic stories about the individual kings and other notable figures, both heroes and villains. They knew of wars won and lost against neighboring peoples of Italy, and of the building of temples and other structures, such as the Circus Maximus and Cloaca Maxima (the "Great Sewer"), that gave shape to the city they recognized. But much of this early history would look familiar to later Romans because their historians tended to project back onto the beginning of their history features that they recognized from their own time. It would be the same if a historian of the US described the Constitution ratified in 1789 as if it already had all the amendments that were in reality added much later, such as women's right to vote (19th amendment, 1920), the two-term limit for presidents (22nd amendment, 1951), or the elimination of the poll tax (25th amendment, 1964). Such a history would radically distort the long and often difficult struggle toward a "more perfect union" and make the country appear as if it was already far "more perfect" at its foundation than it really was.

For the Romans, placing the origins of republican institutions and customs at the very beginning of their history also served to justify preserving them. If this was the way their ancestors, who made Rome great, had done things, then it would be foolish and dangerous to change them. The Romans were suspicious of change and innovation, even though they were, in fact, remarkably innovative. If change was necessary, it would be justified by finding—or inventing—a precedent in their early history. Their own history served as one of their most powerful arguments, especially in politics, and they often appealed to what they called the *mos maiorum*, "the ways of our ancestors." Likewise, a political revolution was simply called *res novae*, "new things."

Because their own history was often fabricated, if not completely false, it is usually presented in very dramatic scenes featuring characters more suited to the stage than real life. The story of Romulus and Remus is a terrific tale, which is one reason it remained one of the best-known "historical events" of Rome for centuries. It is not history in the strict sense, since it describes neither real people nor actual events, but it is not entirely false nor utterly useless as history—it is a matter of what kind of history it is, and for the Romans, it was a meaningful one, and remained so throughout the republic and even later under the emperors. One of the primary reasons a modern historian should try to determine what *really* happened in Roman history is to better understand how the Romans themselves viewed it and crafted it. Of course, trying to determine historical truth in early Rome is extraordinarily difficult, given the lack of trustworthy literary sources and the problems of interpreting the archaeological remains. But this difficulty is also a reason why there is always more to be done, and new eyes can often see new things in old evidence.

For modern historians, the early history of Rome as written by the Romans does not tell us very much about the actual events of Rome's first centuries, and for a different perspective, a historian can turn to archaeology. Unfortunately, archaeological remains are extremely difficult to interpret, especially on the site of Rome, which has been continuously inhabited for millennia. Moreover, archaeology never presents a neat story like one would find in a Roman history book, and it sometimes creates more confusion than the literary record. Yet archaeology does confirm the very basics of the traditional history of early Rome. There does seem to be a permanent settlement on the site of Rome around the middle of the eighth century BC, which fits with the traditional date of Romulus's founding. There is also evidence that many urban developments, such as the drainage and paving of the Forum, the first foundations of larger temples, and the beginnings of the Circus Maximus, took place during the sixth century BC. This development fits the chronology of the last kings of Rome and to the building programs attributed to them in the literary sources, even if the exact details are not accurate.

The Kings of Rome

For the entire regal period from 753 to 509 BC, Rome had only seven kings, which is an average reign of almost 35 years. This fact alone renders the traditional history of this period very suspicious, and the kings themselves often seem more symbolic than real. Romans had a special reverence for the first two kings, Romulus and Numa Pompilius, both considered brave and wise leaders who laid the foundations of Rome's future greatness. Romulus, in his guise as a son of Mars, embodied military prowess. He was the original model of a military commander who could lead Rome to victory over its enemies, and by the seizure of enemy territory, start Rome on its way to empire. Romulus's successor Numa was a different type of king, credited with establishing Rome's religious practices. In contrast to Romulus, he is portrayed as a king who cultivated the arts of peace and helped the Romans show proper devotion to the gods. The next two kings, Tullus Hostilius and Ancus Marcius, are lesser figures than Romulus and Numa, without the fuller personalities given to their predecessors in written sources. After the peaceful Numa, Tullus Hostilius is said to have returned Rome to the war-like footing of Romulus. His *nomen* Hostilius is related to the Latin word for "enemy," *hostis* (root of the word "hostile"), and his grandfather is said to have fought in battle alongside Romulus. Tullus is also said to have neglected the religious observances established by Numa, dying from a lightning strike sent by Zeus as punishment. The fourth king, Ancus Marcius, was Numa's grandson, and though he had some military success, one signature achievement was publicizing the religious writings of Numa to prevent the neglect of religion that marked the reign of Tullus Hostilius. These latter two kings thus serve as a kind of doublet to Romulus and Numa, representing the same balance of the arts of war and the arts of peace. Their role in Rome's history is to emphasize the necessity of maintaining both, and to demonstrate the dire consequences of neglecting either.

According to tradition, the fifth king, Tarquinius Priscus, was the first king to come to the throne without being chosen by the senate. (In truth, it is not known how kings came to the throne.) Priscus's father had fled from Greece to escape a civil war and arrived in the Etruscan city of Tarquinia, on the coast of Italy north of Rome. There, he married an aristocratic Etruscan woman and they had a son. This son, Tarquinius Priscus, was ambitious and wealthy, but in the

Etruscan city where he was born he was still considered an outsider because of his Greek father. He decided to migrate to Rome with his Etruscan wife Tanaquil, because at Rome, his status as a foreign immigrant would not hold him back as it would in his home city of Tarquinia. At Rome, he worked to make friends and cultivate connections until he became a trusted adviser to the current king Ancus Marcius, who made Priscus tutor to his children. Unlike his predecessors on the throne, Priscus openly campaigned to be made king and gave speeches to the Roman people explaining why he would be the best choice to rule Rome. He was elected easily by the people—it didn't hurt that he sent the king's sons out of the city on a hunting trip when they were making their choice.

The sixth king, Servius Tullius, has a mysterious background. His parents were unknown even to the Romans, and his name hints at a servile background (*servus* is Latin for "slave"). His rise to power was orchestrated by Tarquinius Priscus's wife Tanaquil. One day, she saw flames shoot from the head of Servius, a lowly servant in the royal household, and encouraged her husband to pay special attention to him. After a botched assassination of Priscus by the sons of Ancus Marcius, who felt they had a right to the throne, Tanaquil disguised the king's death, telling everyone that he was recovering from the wounds he suffered during the assassination attempt. The delay in announcing the death of Priscus gave Servius time to acquire enough power and prestige that his placement on the throne was accepted by all. He even married a daughter of Priscus and Tanaquil, ensuring that the family of the Tarquins maintained a hold on the throne.

With Tarquinius Superbus, the seventh and final king, the monarchy declined further into corruption and tyrannical behavior, reaching a historical breaking point. His rise to the throne began with a marriage to his sister-in-law, who in our sources is as ambitious and wicked as he was. In order to secure their marriage, they both killed their spouses, who also happened to be their siblings (that is, two daughters of Servus Tullius had married two Tarquin brothers). While Superbus's father-in-law Servus Tullius, still alive and ruling as king, was away from Rome, Superbus simply took his place on the throne. When Servius returned to find his throne occupied, Superbus took the old king outside and hurled him down the palace steps, killing him. Adding to the outrage, his new wife Tullia, riding by in a carriage, ran over her father's corpse, which in the story serves to demonstrate how wicked her ambitions made her. Because his tyrannical nature made him unpopular, and the way he came to the throne made his rule illegitimate, Superbus unleashed a reign of terror. He exhausted the people of Rome by keeping them occupied with construction projects and fighting in wars. Under Superbus, wars were undertaken not to increase Rome's territory or its glory, but to provide money for his building projects out of the wealth seized from conquered peoples.

In contrast to the first four kings, the last three start to look more like a family dynasty, whose claim to rule is not based on any recognition of their merits by the people or the senate, but on blood ties—in other words, a hereditary monarchy. These last kings also begin to exhibit more of the negative characteristics associated with evil tyrants rather than with good kings. Still, they are credited with many achievements, both military victories against neighboring peoples and new buildings that magnified the city of Rome. Tarquinius Priscus started construction of the

Cloaca Maxima, the "Great Sewer" that drained the Forum and made it suitable as the civic center of Rome. His successor and the sixth king, Servius Tullius, receives credit for developing the census system used for voting assemblies, and also for completing the massive stone walls around Rome, known as the "Servian walls." (Both of these, in fact, were accomplishments of the republic.) Even the wicked Superbus gets credit for beginning construction of the Temple of Jupiter Optimus Maximus, which by tradition was dedicated the same year as the republic's founding, 509 BC. (Archaeology confirms that it was built at this date, or very close to it.) These achievements, however, often came on the backs of the people. According to sources, the construction of the Cloaca Maxima was so difficult and exhausting that many laborers chose to commit suicide rather than continue working. Priscus is said to have crucified the suicides and put their corpses on display as a warning to others who might think of "quitting."

As a family dynasty, these last three kings present a picture of increasing corruption and wickedness. Each of them acquired the throne in a somewhat irregular manner, at least from the perspective of our sources. The involvement of the senate and the people in the selection of a new king diminishes, until Superbus simply seizes the throne by murdering the current king, his father-in-law. As a result, both the elite class of Romans represented by the senators and the common people of Rome had good reason to be hostile to monarchy, even if the early kings had ruled admirably. The overall arc of the regal period demonstrates why Romans in the republic had such a negative reaction to anyone or anything associated with kingship, and it also justified their aversion to the idea of monarchy. Tarquinius Superbus in particular embodies many of the political anxieties that plagued the republic, especially concerns about an ambitious individual aiming for a kingship. For example, once he took the throne, he is said to have won over the people of Rome by distributing land to them. In the later years of the republic, land reform was a contentious political issue. Politicians who made proposals that called for the government to grant plots of land to poorer Romans would be accused by their political opponents of trying to win over the people by using free handouts. Even if their proposals were motivated by a sincere desire to address a serious issue for the greater good of Rome, opponents would claim the politicians making such proposals had monarchical ambitions. (Of course, both might be true.) Superbus also governed without the consent of the senate or the people, the SPQR that represented the republic. In fact, it is said that when he sought advice, he ignored the senate entirely, consulting only his close friends. Moreover, he used trumped-up charges to jail or execute political enemies. In short, he was a stereotypical tyrant, with none of the positive qualities of a good king.

The traditional history of the regal period is a combination of "origin stories" and tales of kings gone bad, always told with an eye toward the later years of the Roman Republic, when many of these histories were written. If this traditional history does not always help us to understand the regal period itself, it tells us a great deal about how the Romans of the republic thought about their history, and about themselves. An essential element of their view of the republic was that it was *not* a monarchy, and the traditional history of the kings offered the Romans ample justification for their hatred and fear of monarchs. At the same time, the Romans did not think of all their early kings as bad, or consider the regal period a dark time in their history. On the contrary, they traced many of the developments that shaped their city, their customs, and their culture to the time of the kings. The stories of Rome's founding have been shaped to glorify the later institutions and ideologies of the Roman Republic, and also reflect a belief in a larger historical pattern of governments, one which the constitution of the republic might bring to an end.

The Cycle of Constitutions

Romans under the republic found the idea of a king problematic, and their concerns about monarchy were based on a belief that humans were prone to corruption, especially when they were wealthy and powerful. (Many know the quotation by the nineteenth-century historian Lord Acton "Power tends to corrupt and absolute power corrupts absolutely.") In this view, when people in power became corrupt, as they inevitably would, they would govern badly, committing acts of injustice and placing their own interests over the welfare of the community they ruled. This would in turn create the conditions for a change in government, often via the violent overthrow of the existing constitution. Many political thinkers of ancient Greece and Rome believed that forms of government went through a cycle, and that no one political constitution could endure for long, because human nature would necessarily lead to its corruption. They developed a theory about the cycle of governments, which could be reduced to three basic types: The rule of one, the rule of a few, and the rule of many. Each of these had a good form and a bad form.

The changes from one form of government to another followed a natural sequence: A line of good kings will eventually produce a bad one, an oppressive tyrant, just as the line of kings beginning with Romulus and Numa led to Tarquinius Superbus. Once the tyrant becomes overly oppressive, a small group of good men will rise to overthrow him and form an aristocracy (from the ancient Greek for "rule of the best"), until this small group of rulers in turn grows corrupt and becomes an oligarchy ("rule of the few"). At this point, the people will seize control and form a democracy ("rule of the people"), which will eventually degenerate into mob rule. Out of this disorder a single man will emerge and rule as a good king, and the cycle begins again. When the Romans wrote about their own history, they often used this cycle to shape their view of the political changes it underwent, particularly in the transition from monarchy to republic. There is already a hint of this cycle in one version of Romulus's death, in which the senators murder him because he had become overbearing. After they hack Romulus into pieces, each senator hides a little part of his body in his toga so the corpse could be disposed of without the people realizing what they had done. In this one episode, the three basic forms of government are represented: the rule of one by Romulus, the few by the Senators, and the many by the people. Of course, whether Romulus was a king or tyrant, the senators an aristocracy or an oligarchy, or the people a democracy or a mob, is a matter for debate. The story reveals a fundamental tension between these political elements, since the aristocratic or oligarchic senate takes action against a ruler whom they find increasingly tyrannical, but whom the people revere as a good king. In addition, the senators fear how

	Good		Bad
Rule of one	King	⟶	Tyrant
Rule of a few	Aristocracy	⟶	Oligarchy
Rule of many	Democracy	⟶	Mob rule

FIG. 2.3 Cycle of constitutions.

the people will react to what they have done, while the people are suspicious of the senate. The senators, in fact, seem to distrust the people as a whole, since they do not believe the people have a proper understanding of Romulus's reign. Throughout the republic, as we shall see, political and social conflicts can be viewed as arising from the tensions among the people (the many), smaller groups of the elite such as the senators (the few), and an ambitious individual (the one) who is often popular with the people.

Some Romans saw the political structure of the republic as a solution to this endless cycle, since the republican form of government incorporated elements from each of the three types of rule. The Senate and People of Rome (SPQR) represented two of the categories. The people of Rome were given a role in government through the voting assemblies, allowing for a limited version of the "rule of many." During the first centuries of the republic, the power of the assemblies increased, which tilted the constitution toward the democratic side of the spectrum, without ever becoming truly democratic. The Senate of Rome was a version of "rule of the few." Though there could be several hundred senators, there were still a small number in comparison to the number of citizens, and they were not directly representative of or answerable to the citizen body. Rather, they saw themselves as the rightful superiors to an unruly and ill-disciplined citizen body. For the "rule of one," the Romans cheated and had two consuls as their executive power, which shows how deeply suspicious they were of monarchs. In theory, each part of this three-fold "mixed constitution" counterbalanced the other two parts, serving as a check and balance to the inevitable corruption of any one part. Since all three types of rule were incorporated into one system, the cycle would be frozen, and the republic could endure forever—in theory. The idea of a "mixed constitution," as it was called, proved enormously influential and shaped the thinking behind the Constitution of the United States. When in 1788 Alexander Hamilton, James Madison, and John Jay wrote *The Federalist Papers* in support of the US Constitution, they made frequent references to the Roman Republic's "mixed constitution" and even used the pen-name "Publius," after Publius Valerius Publicola, one of the founders of the Roman Republic involved in the overthrow of the monarchy.

Setting the Stage for the Republic

In reality, the mixed structure of the Roman Republic did not arise fully formed immediately after the overthrow of the last king of Rome, but developed over the course of various political struggles, in particular between the people—the *plebs*—and the senatorial elite. These struggles, lasting over a century and leading to fundamental changes in the way the republic was governed, will be the focus of the next chapter. But the first step on the journey to a full-fledged republic was the end of the monarchy.

As with many events from the early history of Rome, the origin story of the republic is dramatic and sensational. Also like many of these stories of early Rome, the momentous event that brought about a decisive change centers on a woman. Women in Roman history, at least as they appear in histories written by Roman men, are often portrayed in extremes, representing both male fantasies and male fears. The incident that in the Roman historical tradition sparked the overthrow of the monarchy demonstrates both. The spark that set off the overthrow of the last king was an act of sexual violence against an ideal Roman wife. The story, once one of the most famous stories of Rome and a popular subject for artists and writers through the Renaissance and beyond, is traditionally known as "The Rape of Lucretia." (William Shakespeare even wrote a poem with that title.) Though Lucretia is the subject of the story, she is better thought of as its object, since the founding of the republic took place over her dead body.

The wicked deed that brought about the end of the monarchy occurred during the reign of Tarquinius Superbus. It was not something the king himself did, but one of his sons, which highlights the dangers created not only by a king, but by a royal family. The Roman army, under the command of the king, was on a military campaign, besieging the nearby town of Ardea. Siege warfare was long and arduous, sometimes lasting many years (think of the famous ten-year siege of Troy). The attacking army set up camp around the walls of the city they wished to capture, blocking anything or anyone from going in or coming out. The inhabitants of the city would hunker down to wait out the siege. Though the army besieging the city might try at times to scale the walls, knock them down, or even tunnel under them, the city's defenders would take countermeasures, and also try to sneak supplies into the city or sneak people out. Sometimes the besieged city might try to launch an attack against the forces surrounding them, but more than anything, a siege required patience and endurance.

During a lull in the siege of Ardea, one of the king's sons, named Sextus Tarquinius, was relaxing and having some drinks with other young men who were members of the king's family. A friendly argument arose, as often happens at such gatherings, about whose wife was the best. Sextus's cousin, Lucius Tarquinius Collatinus, boasted that no one's wife could compare to his Lucretia back in Collatia, about ten miles east of Rome. To settle this debate, the band of drunk young men first rode their horses back to Rome to see what the other wives were doing. To their dismay, they discovered that all their wives, instead of behaving with the decorum expected of a noble lady, were having a party (much like their husbands). They next rode to Collatia to see Collatinus's wife Lucretia. When they arrived, they found her hard at work, spinning wool into thread that could be used to make clothing. (She's often pictured using a spinning wheel, but these were not put into use until much later; she would have used a spindle and a weight).

FIG. 2.4 A Roman woman spinning wool. The weight at the bottom spins to turn the clump held on the stick (known as a distaff) into thread.

In contrast to the other hard-partying aristocratic wives, Lucretia presented to the gaze of the young men a vision of the ideal wife, at least from a Roman man's point of view: chaste, dutiful, and industrious. There was no question who won the bet, but the sight of the virtuous Lucretia filled Sextus Tarquinius with lust. A few days later, he rode back alone to see Lucretia, and she treated this son of the king and relative of her husband with courtesy, welcoming him into her home and offering him a room for the night. When everyone in the household was asleep, Sextus entered Lucretia's room and confessed that he was inflamed with passion for her. When Lucretia rejected his advances, Sextus resorted to a vile threat: If Lucretia did not submit to his desires and have sex with him, he would force her to and then kill her. He would also kill one of her slaves and place his naked body next to hers, to make it look like she was having sex with a slave while her husband was away. Sextus made it clear to Lucretia that he would get what he wanted—the only choice left Lucretia was whether to bring lasting dishonor to her husband and family. As to what she must suffer, she had no choice. Lucretia unwillingly submitted to Sextus, but as soon as he left, she sent messengers to tell her husband and father to come to her as soon as possible. They soon arrived, her father accompanied by Publius Valerius Publicola, and her husband Collatinus by his friend Lucius Junius Brutus, who was also a relative of the king. The *cognomen* Brutus means "stupid" (the origin of the word "brute"), though this Brutus was no fool. He had only pretended to be in order to escape the notice of the tyrannical king, who had killed Brutus's brother and might worry that Brutus would seek revenge.

When these four men were all gathered before her, Lucretia told them exactly what had happened. They consoled her and assured her that she had done nothing wrong, reminding her that "the mind commits a wrong, not the body" (*mens peccare, non corpus*). Lucretia, however, had another plan in mind, and after a stirring speech fashioned to address future generations of Roman women, plunges a knife into her chest. Her final exclamation, as composed by a Roman historian of the first century BC:

> No unchaste woman should continue to live because of Lucretia's example! (Livy 1.58)

After Lucretia commits suicide, her husband and father are overwhelmed with grief, but the supposedly slow-witted Brutus pulls the bloodied knife from her chest and swears to drive from Rome the king along with his wife and all his descendants. His speech, like Lucretia's, has a dramatic conclusion, written to echo in the ears of Romans in the republic:

> I will not allow the Tarquins, or anyone else, to be a king at Rome! (Livy 1.59)

The others also swear the oath, and a plan to overthrow the monarchy is set in motion. Lucretia's body becomes a political prop, put on display at Collatia and then the Forum at Rome. Brutus, the former dimwit, gives another rousing speech to urge the Romans to banish the ruling family and revoke the king's authority.

The king hurries back to Rome only to discover he is no longer allowed in the city. Brutus and the others return to the army at Ardea in order to convince the soldiers to join their cause. Sextus and the king's other sons are sent into exile, and the Tarquin family is expelled from Rome.

Brutus and Collatinus are made consuls, the new office for this new republic—everything comes together suspiciously fast and easy.

The episode of Lucretia and Brutus reads very much like a script for a play, complete with dramatic speeches and a rousing climax. It is worth asking how much of this story, including the sudden change from a monarchy to a republic, is true, though a better question might be what kinds of truth it reveals. In fact, the sexual violation of women was a traditional sign of the excessive and tyrannical behavior of kings and tyrants. When the Greek historian Herodotus, writing in the fifth century BC, portrays three Persians debating which form of government is best—democracy (the rule of the many), aristocracy (the rule of the few), or monarchy (the rule of one)—the Persian who argues for democracy criticizes monarchy because of the outrageous behavior of kings. The three worst things kings do, he says, are ignore traditional customs, execute men without trial, and violate women. The first two items can be charged against Superbus himself, while his son commits the last crime.

FIG. 2.5 Two portraits of Lucretia (dated 1664 and 1666) by the Dutch painter Rembrandt.

The excessive and uncontrolled lust of tyrants, though it may have been real enough, is a way to characterize their unrestrained abuse of power. Sexual violence against women, who would be viewed as powerless and innocent victims, represented the extremes to which a tyrant (or anyone close to him) would go if there was no check on his power. Moreover, Roman men believed a primary function of wives was to produce children in order to extend their family line. When a king's tyranny reached into the private homes of citizens, it became truly intolerable—a violation of something sacred to every Roman male, and a threat not just to society, but to the family. It was one thing to attack a man in public, quite another to attack a woman in private. Lucretia's sacrificial suicide is thus politically symbolic, and as her speech makes clear in its appeal to future generations of Roman women, she sacrifices her own personal interests in the name of a larger civic cause. The city and its future become more important than her own family and its future; the bond between fellow citizens supersedes family ties. Even when women in Roman history are given a voice, the male writers who give them voice make them say what Roman men would want them to say.

That Brutus's first reaction to Sextus's act of sexual violence would be the overthrow of the monarchy is not obvious. Revenge against Sextus, the villainous perpetrator, might be the first item on the agenda, and Lucretia herself asks for this. Moreover, in his speech over Lucretia's body, Brutus does not focus on Tarquinius Superbus, but on the institution of kingship for all future Roman history. This alone might suggest the story is not meant to be taken as literal truth (or only as a literal truth), but as symbolic of political concerns of later Romans. The story also has a framework that matches the ideal Roman republican government. A member of the ruling elite, in the person of Brutus, joins together with Publius Valerius Publicola, whose *cognomen* means "helper of the people," to avenge injustice and remove a king and his family from the borders of Rome. In other words, the senate and the people of Rome join forces to defeat the tyrannical rule of a single individual.

Yet if the characters of Lucretia and Brutus seem to come from the stage rather than real life, they were real enough for the Romans throughout their history. The Romans continued to hold up Lucretia as an ideal for women, and Lucius Brutus was an example for men who claimed to defend the freedom of the republic, which meant above all eliminating those who had regal ambitions, or at least appeared to. In fact, when Caesar was suspected of seeking to become a king, one of the leaders of the conspiracy was another Brutus (his full name is Marcus Junius Brutus). Supporters encouraged him to carry out the plot against Caesar's life because he was believed to be a descendant of this first Brutus and should thus live up to his ancestor's example.

Threats Inside and Out: The First Years of the Republic

The expulsion of the Tarquins and the establishment of a republican form of government did not bring stability to Rome. During the first year of the republic, there was turmoil with the consuls. Along with Brutus, Lucretia's husband Collatinus was one of the first two consuls, but a decree was passed expelling all members of the king's family from Rome. Because of his family ties to the Tarquins, Collatinus was forced to leave the city, even though he of all people might be expected to be hostile to the return of Tarquinius Superbus. Brutus himself, it should be noted, was also related to the king, on his mother's side, and seems to have been spared from the decree. Collatinus was replaced in the consulship by Publius Valerius Publicola, who had accompanied Lucretia's father when she had sent for him. When Brutus later died in battle against Tarquinius Superbus, he was replaced in the consulship by Lucretia's father, who died only a few days later. Yet another consul was elected in his place, the fifth consul of this first year of the republic. It might strike some as a suspiciously remarkable coincidence that the first four consuls were the men who witnessed Lucretia's suicide.

Although the Tarquins had been exiled, they had not been defeated. They still had resources at their disposal, as well as potential allies who would see Rome as an emerging threat and thus gladly assist Tarquinius Superbus in a bid to regain power. The first serious danger to the new republic, however, came not from an invasion by outside forces gathered by an exiled king, but from the family of the founder and first consul himself.

Family Troubles: Brutus and His Sons

Thanks to a dutiful slave, a conspiracy to return the Tarquins to the throne was discovered during Brutus's time as consul. Two of the conspirators were his own sons, and others involved were

Brutus's brothers-in-law and nephews of Collatinus. As a consul, Brutus had an obligation to punish these traitors with death, but as a father, we might assume he would wish to spare the lives of his sons.

A father in Rome had extraordinary legal authority over his children, and this authority did not come to an end when the children reached adulthood or, in the case of sons, when they married. The term used for a father as a holder of this authority was *paterfamilias*, "father of the household." The Latin word *familia*, root of English "family," means not just the immediate family, but covers the entire household, including slaves and other dependents. A *paterfamilias* had almost total control of those under his authority. He legally owned any wealth or property acquired by his children and could sell his children into slavery if he so chose. A *paterfamilias* could even kill a member of his household for any reason. In practice, a *paterfamilias* would not exercise these powers to their full extent, and examples of a father killing one of his children are rare. Brutus kills his sons as consul, not *paterfamilias*, and the few other recorded examples in Roman sources take place in a military context, where the son is serving as a soldier under his father's command. Moreover, an early law forbids a father from selling a child into slavery more than three times, and his penalty for doing so was the legal emancipation of the child from the authority of the *paterfamilias*. (In fact, some fathers took advantage of this law to legally free their sons from their authority by arranging three sham sales to a friend.) Nonetheless, the authority of a *paterfamilias* was extensive and real, part of the deeply rooted patriarchal nature of Roman society. *Pater*, the Latin word for "father," is also found in the use of *patres* as a term for senators, the name of the patrician order, the term *patronus* (who had authority over his clients), and even the Latin term for one's home country, *patria*, literally "fatherland."

Though Brutus had the right as *paterfamilias* to execute his sons, in our sources he feels compelled to do so out of a civic duty that conflicts with his feelings as a father. According to the story, though he would not be expected to witness the execution of his sons, he did so with a blank look on his face that never changed. This incident, like the story of Lucretia, is more symbolic than real. It speaks to internal tensions in the new republic and symbolizes the conflict between loyalty to the new state and devotion to family. Note that this would not be an issue under a monarchy, when the ruling family *is* the state. The expulsion of Collatinus after he was made consul suggests the Romans were not confident that the bonds of citizenship in this new republic could overpower family ties. But with the execution of his sons, the other consul at the republic's origin supplies a brutal ideal of the republic's triumph over family.

Virtue Conquers All: Lars Porsenna's Siege of Rome

Rome's transition from a monarchy to a republic was likely not occasioned by a single horrific act carried out by a member of the king's family. Nor did the republican form of government, with two annually elected consuls and other magistrates, emerge spontaneously after the suicide of Lucretia. In reality, the republic continued to develop over the centuries, with constitutional fits and starts and occasional reversals, including changes in the nature and number of political offices, some of which disappeared, and some of which grew in number along with Rome's increasing population and power. That the monarchy did end in some fashion and the republic did begin in some form at the end of the sixth century seems beyond dispute—almost. Some scholars deny there was any real overthrow of the monarchy and believe there was instead a gradual transition lasting until the 450s BC. The basic story of Lucretia and Brutus, stripped of all its dramatic elements, sounds plausible enough: An overbearing king with corrupt relatives is overthrown in a revolt led by a band of young aristocrats, defenders of justice and liberty, who rise up after a violent assault on a virtuous young woman. In fact, archaeological evidence, always difficult to interpret for Rome, hints at the possibility of a violent overthrow, but this is little more than a possibility. However, there are other hints in later Roman historians that the overthrow of the monarchy may not have been a Roman achievement at all, but rather the result of the capture of Rome and expulsion of the king's family by a different Etruscan ruler, Lars Porsenna.

According to the traditional narrative, shortly after his banishment from Rome, Tarquinius Superbus joined forces with Lars Porsenna, ruler of the Etruscan city of Clusium, in order to invade Rome and reinstall Superbus as king. The story of Porsenna's siege of Rome, after he set up camp across the Tiber river, is highlighted by three dramatic episodes, each portraying the courageous and virtuous actions of an individual Roman. The first is the story of Horatius Cocles, who stood firm as sole defender of a narrow bridge across the Tiber. Covered in arrows, he withstands blow after blow from the enemy, even losing an eye, all to prevent the Etruscans from reaching Rome while his comrades escaped the onslaught. In another episode, a brave young female slave, Cloelia, offers herself and other female slaves as hostages to Lars Porsenna so that the daughters of the nobles do not have to undergo such an indignity. Taken to the enemy camp, she manages to climb a tree and send a signal back to the Romans, informing them of an opportunity to attack. Third, there is the daring Mucius Scaevola, who undertakes a secret mission to the enemy camp to assassinate Lars Porsenna. He infiltrates the king's inner circle but fails when he stabs the wrong person. When he is captured and threatened with torture, he places his right hand into a fire and keeps it there as it burns (earning the *cognomen* Scaevola, which means "lefty"). He tells Porsenna that there are many more Romans like him ready to succeed where he has failed. Porsenna, in awe of Scaevola's endurance of pain, decides he would rather not tangle with such a people, and so packs up camp, abandoning the siege of Rome.

By this account, Porsenna is defeated not by Roman military might but the virtuous behavior of two Roman soldiers and a female slave, who all act in just the way the way Romans would like such individuals to behave. The reality was certainly far different, and many historians today believe these stories mask a bitter truth. Lars Porsenna may, in fact, have conquered and occupied Rome, and it was he, not a few brave Romans, who ultimately defeated the Etruscan dynasty of the Tarquins. Later Roman sources seems to suggest as much, and one even mentions that Porsenna passed a law forbidding the Romans to have any iron implements, a condition one would impose on a subjugated people. Whatever the truth of the matter, the last years of the monarchy and first years of the republic appear to be an attempt to liberate Rome from Etruscan rule. However, we must be careful to distinguish between Etruscan domination and occupation of Rome versus domination by a powerful family who happened to be Etruscan. Brutus's oath over Lucretia's corpse called for the expulsion of the Tarquin family and the abolition of the monarchy, not a purge of Etruscans. Only later, when the Romans had developed a sense of national identity, would the story of the last kings of Rome acquire an additional layer of Romans versus Etruscans.

However it may have happened, the republic's first real military encounter with a foreign enemy is only the beginning of a long series of wars between Rome and neighboring peoples. While there are many setbacks and defeats, numerous truces and alliances, the military victories that begin with the very founding of the republic will come to define Rome. The Romans will bring all of Italy much of the Mediterranean world, under their control. But even as the republic began to exert itself and slowly rise to dominance, more threats from within will push the new state to the point of dissolution, this time coming not from any monarchial sympathizers, but, as we will see in the next chapter, from the conflicts arising between plebeians and patricians.

Becoming Roman

Rome was situated on the banks of the Tiber river, about 15 miles from the west coast of Italy, in a region known as Latium (modern-day Lazio). This geographical location made it an important crossroads for those traveling north and south in Italy. Traders from around the Mediterranean frequented the port of Ostia at the mouth of the Tiber, using the river to bring their ships and goods inland to Rome itself. As a result, numerous peoples, languages, religions, and cultures mixed together in and around Rome from its earliest history. Because the Romans were the ultimate victors in the military conflicts that consumed the Italian peninsula, our sources focus almost exclusively on Rome, and all events are viewed from the Roman perspective. This can make it appear as if Rome was already a dominant power at the beginning of the republic, and thus being "Roman" seems something easy to define, though this is far from the case. When we speak of someone or something as "Roman," we should be aware of the different meanings the word can have, especially among the Romans themselves. Much of the legendary history of early Rome is written as if "Romans" were already a clearly defined group, yet these stories also show traces of the various peoples who over time come together to form Rome.

In Vergil's epic poem the *Aeneid*, composed near the end of the first century BC, the followers of the Trojan hero and exile Aeneas encounter the indigenous peoples of Italy as well as Greek settlers, eventually merging together with the Latins. The story of the *Aeneid* projects into the mythical past a slow process that in reality took place over the centuries and extended into the republic. In fact, some of the republic's first wars were fought with the Latins (whose legendary ancestor was King Latinus).

When Romulus founded Rome, there was still no "Roman" people to speak of, so he declared his new city an "asylum," a special word that means a place of refuge for anyone who has committed a crime or a religious offense. Romulus offered membership in his new community to murderers, runaway slaves, and other criminals and outcasts, who were given a fresh start in exchange for providing manpower. This initial openness to all newcomers is reflected in the stories of the regal period. The second king, Numa, was an immigrant to Rome from the neighboring Sabines, a people whose king had briefly ruled together with Romulus. Tarquinius Priscus, who had a Greek father and an Etruscan mother, rose to the position of supreme power at Rome, while Servius Tullius was reputed to be a former slave or a descendant of one. The early history of Rome is filled with interactions, in both war and in peace, with the other peoples who inhabited the Italian peninsula. Many individuals among these peoples would eventually identify as Roman in some way or another, but their own cultural, linguistic, and religious identities did not completely disappear.

Greeks, Etruscans, Latins, and Sabines all played an important role in the formation of Rome, and these are only the most prominent of the peoples who shaped its history. There were many others living on the Italian peninsula before the coming of Rome—Samnites, Oscans, Volscians, Umbrians, Iapygians, and Ligurians, to name a few. All of these peoples would have to confront the growing power of Rome, and would over time fall under its control.

Latins

The Latins traced their origin back to King Latinus, whose daughter married Aeneas, according to the early legends. They had a culture and language distinct from the other peoples of Italy, long before Rome or the identifier "Roman" existed. At some point after Rome's founding, a number of Latin communities (thirty is the traditional count) joined together in a loose federation known as the Latin League, though they never referred to themselves in this way. Members of this league shared certain rights, such as the right to marry a citizen from another Latin community (*conubium*) and the right to trade with other Latins (*commercium*). The league also allowed a Latin to become a citizen of a different Latin community by taking up residence there (*ius migrationis*). But what tied these communities together more than anything else was worship of their shared ancestor Latinus, who in a process known as "deification," came to be identified as a god, Jupiter Latiaris. Once a year, the Latin peoples would gather for a ritual celebration, the *feriae Latinae*, at a sanctuary on the Alban Mount, a hill near Alba Longa, the city founded by Aeneas's son and later ruled by the grandfather of Romulus and Remus. The highlight of this festival was a feast, at which representatives of the thirty different Latin communities would receive a portion of the meat from a sacrificed bull. (Sharing a meal was an important way of forming a social bond, much as it is today.) Despite their common bonds, however, and their unified resistance to Rome, these communities often waged war against one another, so political unity was not a hallmark of the Latin League. Nonetheless, the Latin League would remain in effect until it was dissolved after a final defeat at the hands of Rome in 338 BC. The Latins, of course, provided the name for the language that would be Rome's, and over time gave birth to the Romance languages of western Europe.

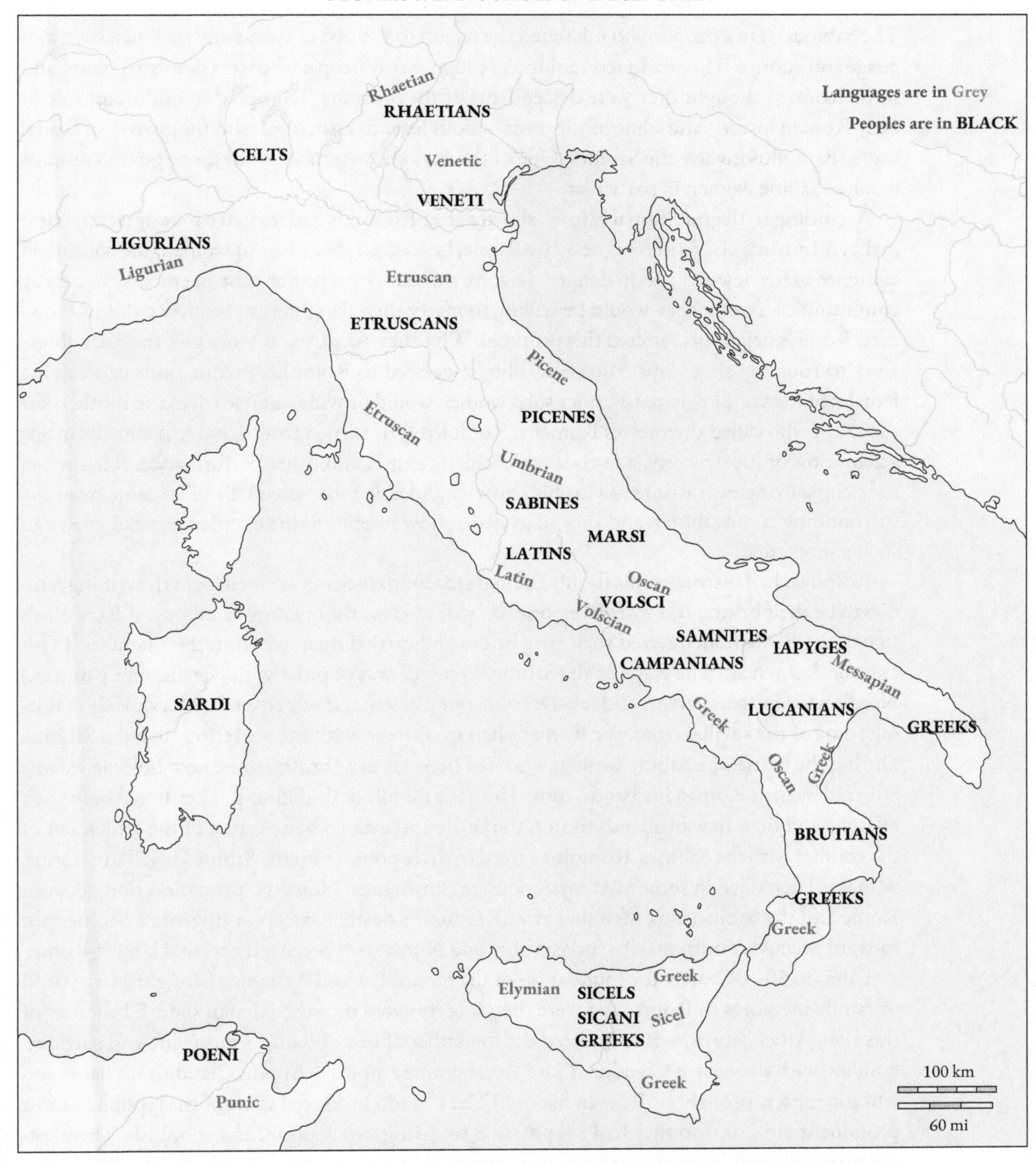

FIG. 2.6 Peoples of Italy.

Sabines

The Sabines were a people who inhabited the region to the east of Rome and had their own language and culture. They had a reputation as a tough, hardy people who were deeply religious, and some Romans thought they were descendants of the Spartans. They play an important role in early Roman history, and some of the most famous legends associated with the growth of Rome under Romulus involve the Sabines. One of the best-known stories from the reign of Romulus involves Sabine women in particular.

According to the traditional history, shortly after Romulus had invited runaway slaves, criminals, and anyone else to join his new city Rome, he realized that without women, the continued existence of his new city was in danger. To solve this difficulty, he first sent an embassy to nearby communities to see if they would be willing to marry their daughters to his new citizens. However, Rome's neighbors rejected this proposal. Why, they asked, would they give their daughters away to runaway slaves and criminals? They suggested to Romulus that he put out a call for females of the same lowly status, since such women would provide suitable wives and mothers for the scum who called themselves Romans. Romulus thus turned to a trick. He planned a major celebration of his new city, a festival with athletic games and other performances. He invited the people living near Rome to visit his new city and enjoy the festival. Families came from the surrounding communities, and they marveled at how much this little settlement had grown in such a short time.

Romulus had instructed his freshly minted citizens to pick out women from the visiting families to be their brides, and when everyone had gathered for the opening ceremony, at Romulus's signal, the Roman men seized their new brides and carried them off from their families. (This episode, known as "The Rape of the Sabine Women," was popular with Renaissance painters.) Needless to say, their parents and relatives were not pleased, and war ensued. After quickly defeating some of the smaller cities, the Romans had to contend with a more serious foe, the Sabines. During the battle, the Sabine women who had been taken as brides, some now holding infants fathered by their Roman husbands, rushed into the middle of the fighting. They urged both their relatives and their new husbands to stop the battle and make peace. As part of the settlement of the conflict with the Sabines, Romulus agreed to share power with the Sabine king, Titus Tatius, who was later killed in somewhat mysterious circumstances. However, the connection between Rome and the Sabines was such that after Romulus's death, a vocal contingent of Sabines put forward a fellow countryman to succeed him, and Numa then became the second king of Rome.

Later, in 504 BC, after the foundation of the republic, a leading Sabine brought a large band of family members to Rome who were then incorporated into the Roman state. The leader of this clan, Atta Clausus, was considered the forefather of one of Rome's most elite and patrician families, with the *nomen* Claudius. (And Atta became Appius—Appius Claudius is a name you will encounter throughout Roman history.) The Claudii produced some of the republic's most prominent citizens, and they had a reputation for being overly proud and snobbish. Their lasting prominence in Roman history is demonstrated by the designation used for the first line of Roman emperors, the Julio-Claudians.

Despite the merging of the two peoples presented in the sources for the regal period, during the first centuries of the republic the Sabines remained a politically separate people who engaged Rome in many battles. They suffered a major defeat in 449 BC but were not conquered until 290 BC, when they were granted Roman citizenship.

Etruscans

Of all the peoples who inhabited the Italian peninsula during the early period of Rome's history, the Etruscans were the wealthiest and most powerful. They occupied the west coast of Italy north of the Tiber, and their territory stretched into the Po valley in the northeast of Italy. (The region of Italy today known as Tuscany takes its name from the Etruscans, who were *Tusci* in Latin.) While Rome was still a small hill-top community, the Etruscans were a major trading power in the Mediterranean. The most serious rival to Rome for dominance in central Italy, the Etruscans were the most influential on its culture. In fact, the famous Capitoline she-wolf, still the symbol of the city of Rome, has long been regarded as an Etruscan artwork. They are a constant presence in our sources for Roman history, though today they are best known from archeological remains such as elaborate tomb paintings, ornate sarcophagi, and intricately engraved bronze mirrors. The Etruscans had a reputation for luxurious living, and many of these items bear this out. Some paintings depict banquets in the manner of a Greek symposium (an aristocratic drinking party), while others portray musicians, dancers, and athletic contests.

The Etruscans were organized into a federation of twelve cities, sometimes referred to as the "League of Twelve Peoples." Like the so-called Latin League, it was a loose federation whose members shared a common religious site where they gathered to celebrate rituals and decide issues of common concern. Also like the Latin League, the members of this federation occasionally fought wars with one another. Nonetheless, during the sixth century, the Etruscans were the dominant power on the Italian peninsula and were a major threat to Rome's existence. Because Rome eventually conquered them, much about the Etruscans remains unknown despite all the material treasures they left behind ("mysterious" is an adjective often applied to them). Their language is not part of the larger group of languages known as Indo-European, to which Latin and many other Italic languages (as well as Greek and Sanskrit) belong, and so Etruscan has only been partially deciphered, mainly from inscriptions and religious calendars.

Close connections among the ruling classes of Rome and Etruria are evident in the traditional narratives of the regal period and the early republic. Moreover, in the lists of Roman consuls preserved by the Romans, Etruscan names can be found for the early years of the Republic. But whatever the reality of that political history, there were clearly close connections between the two peoples that extended into daily life. In fact, the earliest writing found on the site of Rome is Etruscan on pottery fragments. As the Romans themselves acknowledged, the Etruscans provided Rome with many institutions and practices that we now identify as Roman. Rome's

FIG. 2.7 An Etruscan dinner party, from the "Tomb of the Leopards" in Tarquinia (fifth c. BC), perhaps representing the banquet held by friends and family on the anniversary of the death of the person buried in the tomb. Note that women (the white-painted figures) dine with the men, which would not happen at a Roman banquet.

symbols of political power, such as the *fasces* that symbolized political authority, the purple-bordered togas of senators, and the curule chairs (the distinctive stools used by higher-ranking Roman magistrates) had their origins in Etruria. However, the most important way in which the Etruscans influenced Rome was religion. The Etruscans were considered experts in divine matters, and throughout the republic, Etruscan priests known as *haruspices* would be summoned when a prodigy or omen required interpretation. Tanaquil, Etruscan wife of the king Tarquinius Priscus, hints at this reputation, since she twice correctly interprets divine signs. The first case involves a bird that presages her husband's rise to the throne, and in the second she realizes the flames shooting from Servius Tullus's head mark him out for future greatness.

Despite the cultural borrowings and political connections, Etruscan society was very different from Roman in important ways. For example, women seemed to have possessed a higher status than in Roman society. Tomb inscriptions identify Etruscans by their mother's name as well as their father's, whereas the Romans used only the father's name. In tomb paintings, women seem to engage in the same activities as the men, such as the drinking parties favored by aristocrats.

Female spouses and family members would not be allowed at a Roman banquet. The elevated status of Etruscan women, at least in comparison to women at Rome, can be glimpsed again in the figure of Tanaquil, who spurs on her husband's ambitions and works behind the scenes to elevate Servius to the throne.

The Etruscans suffered a major military defeat in a naval battle in 474 BC at the hands of the Greek city of Cumae, on the Bay of Naples. They never recovered their former dominance, though they remained a major power in Italy until the Romans destroyed the Etruscan city of Volsinii in 264 BC. Nonetheless, their language, culture, and religion persisted throughout the Republic, and prominent Romans could be proud of their Etruscan heritage.

Beyond Italy

While much of Rome's early history concerns the peoples who inhabited the Italian peninsula, Rome had contacts, direct and indirect, with other peoples from the ancient Mediterranean world. As Rome expanded in the early years of the republic, these other peoples played an increasingly important role in Rome's history in different ways. It may sometimes appear that the first contacts with these peoples occurred only when Roman soldiers reached their territories, but in almost all cases Rome had some exposure to them long before the major conflicts that became defining moments in Rome's history. Too often we underestimate the extent to which people in the ancient Mediterranean moved around, especially as part of the trade networks that crisscrossed land and sea. In part, these movements are hidden to us because the everyday personal interactions and commercial contacts did not concern Roman historians as much as the glorification of "great men" and their military conquests.

Gauls

"Gaul" is a term used to designate a number of Celtic peoples who inhabited a vast area of Europe from northern Italy up to northern France and Germany, and along the coast of France to Spain. Gauls for the most part were nomadic tribes, though some settled in towns and small cities. The Romans generally thought of them as long-haired barbarians with the odd custom of wearing pants, and they did not have the cultural influence on the Romans as other peoples did, if only for lack of direct and prolonged contact. At some point during the early history of Rome, Gallic tribes crossed the Alps and occupied the area known as Cisalpine Gaul. (In contrast to "Transalpine Gaul," "Cisalpine" means "this side of the Alps," which from the Roman perspective is the south side and is today part of Italy that includes Milan and Venice. Milan, in fact, was founded by a Gallic tribe in the fourth century BC as Mediolanum.) The Gauls of northern Italy invaded and sacked Rome at the beginning of the fourth century, but they did not remain in central Italy and soon returned to their home territory. Gaul is perhaps best known because of Julius Caesar's ten-year military conquest of all its territory and peoples in the 50s BC, which put all Gaul under Roman administrative control.

Greeks

In Vergil's epic poem the *Aeneid*, Aeneas faced a war with the followers of King Latinus, and thus allied himself with a Greek king named Evander. This bit of legend symbolizes a long and sometimes uneasy relationship between the Greeks and Romans that continued throughout Rome's history. Greeks played an important role in the development of Rome, though direct military confrontation with any Greek power would not occur until the beginning of the third century BC, when a Greek king invaded southern Italy. In fact, southern Italy had been occupied by Greek settlers since the eighth century BC, and that region of Italy was known as Magna Graecia ("Great Greece"). In addition, the area around the Bay of Naples, on the coast of Italy south of Rome, had a Greek community that remained throughout the republic. (The name of Naples comes from *nea polis*, ancient Greek for "new city.") Recall as well that Rome's fifth king, Tarquinius Priscus, had a Greek father who emigrated to Etruria, and the Greeks and Etruscans interacted through trade long before Rome became a city to be reckoned with. The Greeks also had established an early presence on the island of Sicily, and its major cities, such as Syracuse, were originally Greek colonies that had grown into major cultural and commercial centers and would remain so for centuries.

Greece was the most influential culture on Rome, and Roman art, architecture, and literature are inconceivable without the Greeks. The very first Roman literature we know of, from the third century BC, is a translation of the ancient Greek epic the *Odyssey*, and as mentioned, the *Aeneid*, composed after the end of the republic, was modeled on both the *Odyssey* and the *Iliad*. It was not just poetry and other literature, such as lyric poetry, comic drama, and tragedies, that the Romans derived from the Greeks. Roman philosophy, the study of rhetoric (how to compose and deliver speeches), and even their own historical writings are rooted in the Greek tradition. In fact, the earliest Roman historians wrote in Greek. During the latter part of the republic, elite Romans would spend a year or two in Greece studying and polishing up their speaking skills, which was beneficial for a career in politics and in the law courts. Some prominent Romans kept educated Greeks, often as slaves, in their households to tutor their children and serve as intellectual companions and advisers. Wealthy Romans collected Greek statues in marble and bronze, as well as luxury items like engraved cups, and Romans hired Greek painters, craftsmen, and architects to build and decorate their temples and their houses. The Romans recognized Greek superiority in almost all areas of art and literature, summed up in a famous line by the Roman poet Horace in the first century BC:

> *Graecia capta ferum victorem cepit et artes intulit agresti Latio.*
>
> After it was captured, Greece captured its savage conqueror, and
> introduced the arts to rustic Latium. (*Epistles* 2.1.156)

The line highlights Rome's military conquest of Greece in the second century BC—Rome is the *victor*—but also portrays Rome, here represented by the region of Latium, as barbaric and uncivilized (*ferus* is related to English "feral," as in a wild animal, and *agrestis* is related to the word for field, as in agriculture, and is opposed to urban sophistication). Although the Romans brought their own originality to their cultural productions, it is not an exaggeration to speak of their culture as one of creative translation from the Greeks. Even though, as with so many other peoples, Greece would eventually fall subject to Roman military and political domination, the Romans held them in special regard. However, the Romans also had some disdain for the Greek cultural sophistication. In the eyes of some Romans, enthusiasm for Greek literature and art could lead to immoral and effeminate behavior, something no "true Roman man" would tolerate.

Phoenicians and Carthaginians

Among the numerous peoples and cultures of the ancient Mediterranean world with whom the Romans interacted, the Phoenicians and their descendants, the Carthaginians, deserve special mention. The Phoenicians, who came from the eastern shores of the Mediterranean around present-day Lebanon, were known as expert sailors, and engaged in trade along every coast. One of their most important colonies, founded decades before Rome in 814 BC, was Carthage, on the coast of North Africa in modern-day Tunisia. The name *Karthago* means "new city" in Punic, the language of the Phoenicians and the Carthaginians, who are sometimes called *Punici* in Latin. One notable contribution of the Phoenicians, who traded with the Etruscans and others on the west coast of Italy, was the alphabet. Their writing system, itself adapted from a script developed out of hieroglyphs by migrant workers in Egypt, was adopted and adapted by both the Greeks and Etruscans, and this became the basis for the Roman alphabet used in many languages today, including English.

Carthage became a wealthy and powerful city in its own right and played a prominent role in the history of the republic as a major rival to Rome. In the third and second centuries BC, Rome fought three major wars with Carthage, known as the Punic Wars, the second of which featured the Carthaginian general, Hannibal, who famously crossed the Alps with his elephants. After their final defeat in the second century BC, Carthage was razed to the ground, and their language and culture are all but extinct. Much as with the Etruscans, their memory is largely lost because of Roman conquests.

The meaning of "Roman" was thus very much in flux for centuries, and at first referred to little more than the inhabitant of a small town set among some hills along the Tiber river. It was through encounters with these other peoples that a sense of "Roman" began to emerge as a distinct identity. While Rome was shaped by these peoples, they in turn began to impose their own language, religion, and culture on them, by conquest as well as assimilation. These peoples would learn to speak Rome's language, worship its gods, participate in its festivals, fight in its army, and follow its authority. Yet even as these peoples became Roman, in different degrees and different respects, their own traditions did not always disappear. In fact, many of these peoples would recognize that "Roman" was often a rebranding of their own cultural traditions. Etruscan was still spoken in the last years of republic, and Etruscans maintained a distinct position as religious authorities. One of Rome's early poets from the second century BC, the first to write an epic poem on Roman history, was from a trilingual city in southern Italy and spoke Greek and Oscan as well as Latin. In the last century of the republic, peoples of Italy would rise in revolt one last time against Rome, and even issued coins in their own language. Rome was multicultural and polyglot from the beginning, and this did not change even as the republic grew in size and power, making the other peoples inhabiting the Italian peninsula and throughout the Mediterranean its subjects.

Credits

Fig. 2.1: Source: https://commons.wikimedia.org/wiki/File:François-Joseph_Navez001.jpg.

Fig. 2.2: Source: https://commons.wikimedia.org/wiki/File:Capitoline_she-wolf_Musei_Capitolini_MC1181.jpg.

Fig. 2.4: Source: http://penelope.uchicago.edu/Thayer/E/Roman/Texts/secondary/SMIGRA*/Fusus.html.

Fig. 2.5a: Source: https://commons.wikimedia.org/wiki/File:Rembrandt_van_Rijn,_Lucretia,_1664,_NGA_83.jpg.

Fig. 2.5b: Source: https://commons.wikimedia.org/wiki/File:Rembrandt_van_Rijn_-_Lucretia_-_Google_Art_Project_(nAHoI2KdSaLshA).jpg.

Fig. 2.6: Adapted from d-maps.com.

Fig. 2.7: Source: https://commons.wikimedia.org/wiki/File:Tarquinia_Tomb_of_the_Leopards.jpg.

CHAPTER 3

Growing Pains

Plebeians and Other Problems

FIG. 3.1 The Renaissance painter Botticelli (1445–1510) captured the entire narrative of Verginia in a single panel, with each scene representing a different point in time of the story.

Overview

After Rome conquered the Latin League at the Battle of Lake Regillus, struggles between the plebeians and the patricians threatened to tear the new republic apart. By withdrawing from the city and refusing to serve in the military, plebeians won political concessions from the patricians, including laws that provided them with greater access to political offices previously controlled by the patricians. The republic crafted its first law code, known as the "Twelve Tables," but another crisis between plebeians and patricians, dramatized in the story of Verginia, led to another secession by the plebs and further political reforms. The chapter concludes with an overview of Roman religion.

Timeline

509	Beginning of the Roman Republic
508	Lars Porsenna's siege of Rome
499 or 496	Rome defeats the Latin League at the Battle of Lake Regillus
494	First secession of the plebs
451–449	The Decemvirate; Verginia and Appius Claudius
450	The Twelve Tables
449	Second secession of the plebs; Valerio-Horatian laws
439	Spurius Maelius killed

Rome and the Latin League

As even the brief overview of the regal period and the republic's founding demonstrates, Rome engaged in almost constant warfare with its immediate neighbors. Over the course of its first two centuries, the Roman Republic gradually established itself as the dominant power over the peoples of central Italy. Early Rome was a militaristic society, as the census classes and organization of the Centuriate Assembly show. A male citizen was first and foremost a citizen-soldier, and the path to political power was paved by military success. The historical tradition focuses on glorious military deeds by exemplary individuals, but whatever historical truth there is to these heroic episodes, it is clear that the years following the foundation of the republic were ones of instability for Rome and the other peoples in the region.

According to the traditional account, the siege of Rome by Lars Porsenna ended in the retreat of Etruscan forces because of brave deeds performed by a few virtuous Romans. But even after Porsenna's "defeat," the exiled king Tarquinius Superbus was not yet finished with his attempt to return to the throne at Rome. Through a family connection, Superbus had roused the members of the Latin League to launch a concerted attack on Rome. Fear of this conflict led the Romans to appoint a dictator, and when it was discovered Superbus himself would be leading the enemy troops, and that his sons were also among the enemy, the Romans were eager for battle. The conflict came to a head in the Battle of Lake Regillus, ten miles southeast of Rome, in 499 or 496 BC. In a major victory for the new republic, Roman forces defeated both of these imminent threats to its existence, the Etruscan king Tarquinius Superbus and the Latin League. The importance of this battle for later Romans is highlighted by a story of divine intervention. According to the tradition, in the midst of the fighting two young men on white horses suddenly appeared, galloping across the battlefield. The Roman commander took this as a divine sign, and after he vowed a temple to the Dioscuri (the name for the twin gods Castor and Pollux, also known as the Gemini, the Latin word for twins), these mysterious young men led the Romans to victory. The twin gods were also said to have been the ones who first announced the victory back at Rome. They were seen watering their horses in the Forum before any mortal messenger could have arrived from the battle. As a result, a temple dedicated to them was built in the Forum, the remains of which can still be seen today.

FIG. 3.2 Remains of the Temple of Castor and Pollux (the Dioscuri) in the Roman Forum.

This victory led to the "Treaty of Cassius" of 493 BC, named after Spurius Cassius, one of the consuls that year (laws and treaties usually carry the name of consuls). This treaty, known in Latin as the *foedus Cassianum*, declared a lasting peace and set conditions for relations between Rome and the members of the Latin League. As described in the previous chapter, the Latin League was organized into a loose federation of thirty communities that shared a common language, culture, and religion, without any strict rules governing their relations to one another. Before the Battle of Lake Regillus, Rome might have hoped to become a member of this league, an equal to any other Latin community. The *foedus Cassianum*, however, established Rome as an independent state that was on its own the equal to the entire Latin League. In fact, the treaty served to confirm Rome's dominance over the other Latin communities and signaled how powerful a player it was quickly becoming in central Italy. According to the treaty, Rome would provide half of the entire army for any joint military campaign, meaning it alone was equal in military manpower to all thirty members of the Latin League. Rome also would receive half of all plunder taken in any war, with the other half going to all thirty members of the Latin League. Moreover, Rome on its own could make decisions to which all members of the Latin League were bound, while any single member of the league would need the support of all the other members. Even if the Latin League as a whole decided on a course of action, Rome seems to have had the authority to veto their decision. While this treaty brought to a conclusion the war between Rome and the Latin League, it did not create a lasting peace nor end tensions between them. A century and a half later, they will come to arms again.

After the Battle of Lake Regillus and the *foedus Cassianum*, the Roman Republic was safe from any immediate external threats, at least for the moment, since the peoples nearest them had been defeated. But Rome was still surrounded by other powerful peoples who would not long tolerate the republic's growing power, and feared, with good reason, that they might fall under Roman control just as the Latin League had. Rome's Latin and Etruscan neighbors had not been defeated for well, but at least the republic now had a secure foundation to defend itself and to extend its conquests, two aims that neither the Romans nor other peoples clearly distinguished.

The Secession of the Plebs

The security that Rome had won for itself in relation to its nearest neighbors did not mean all was well within the state itself. On the contrary, Rome's military operations, however necessary they may have seemed, created political tensions within the city, especially between the patricians and the plebs. The plebeians served as soldiers and provided the labor and manpower necessary for Rome's survival, yet despite their victories on the battlefield, they did not enjoy the fruits of their success to the same degree as the wealthy and powerful patricians and senators. The small farmers who provided the majority of the fighting forces faced economic difficulties, and many found themselves sinking into debt with no recourse from aggressive creditors. A farmer who fell into serious debt, even if due to an absence from his farm during his military service, was subject to imprisonment and beatings and could be kept in chains. There was even the possibility of being sold into slavery. As well, the poorer citizens were almost entirely shut out from political decisions, in particular the decision to go to war. But in our sources, the dire financial situation of the plebeians was the primary cause behind their breaking away from the state. The first troubles erupted shortly after the victory at Lake Regillus.

As often in the early history of Rome, the complex political situation is presented through the dramatic plight of a single individual. An old military veteran, dressed in filthy rags, appears in the Forum during a public meeting. He tells the crowd that while on campaign with the army, he lost his crops, his farmhouse, and all his possessions, baring his chest to display the scars from his battle wounds. Despite losing his property, he still had to pay a property tax, which was used to pay for the very wars he fought. He borrowed money to pay the tax, but the interest on the loan spiraled out of control until he lost all his family property. His lender had him thrown into prison, where he was whipped. He had scars on his back from this torture, in contrast to the battle scars on his chest (these proved his courage, since he never turned his back to the enemy). The public appearance of this brave old soldier and farmer, who had sunk to such a pathetic state, inspired other people mired in debt to come forward. Many of them still wore the chains their creditors had placed on them. Although these debtors had not been sold into slavery, they were subject to a Roman form of "debt bondage," known as *nexum*, in which a person could use his own body as collateral for a loan. Failure to repay meant the debtor became almost like his creditor's slave, and could even be placed in chains until the debt was repaid. While likely an exaggerated fiction, the story of the beaten-down veteran and the crowd of debtors in the Forum presents in a dramatic form the essential reasons for plebeian anger against the patricians and senators, who did nothing to address the problem of debt. Mandatory military service, debts and taxes, and loss of land and property with no means to recover it or receive compensation—all of this was enough to create social unrest. Added to this volatile mixture was the possibility of food shortages, with the threat of famine always looming. Despite some sympathetic proposals in the senate for debt relief, the sterner patricians resisted any reforms in the belief that a harsh response would subdue the unruly plebeians.

In 494 BC, Rome was still at war with the Latins, and when another order came down for the legions to march out of the city, the plebeians decided enough was enough. As a form of protest, they gathered together and occupied the Aventine, one of the hills of Rome, just outside the city boundary (the *pomerium*). This action is usually known as a "secession of the plebs".

Withdrawal to the Aventine was a drastic move, tantamount to rejecting the Roman state and their participation in it as citizens. In particular, it signaled a refusal to serve in the military and fight Rome's wars. It is not clear if the angry plebeians who seceded made up a majority or even a large a part of the infantry forces, or whether their refusal to serve would have crippled the army. The fact that this secession occurred while Rome was still engaged in a war that it still managed to win suggests that these plebeians were not an overwhelming majority, but any loss of manpower and any internal strife would present a clear danger to the republic over the long term. Even if Rome could manage a war or two without these plebeians, their withdrawal seriously weakened Rome internally. A later source describes this secession of the plebs as "two states created out of one."

According to the account found in the first-century BC Roman historian Livy, during this first secession, the senators sent to the Aventine one of their own members who was of plebeian background to negotiate. He used a parable of the human body to explain the proper relationship between the plebs and the patricians, at least from the patrician perspective:

> Once upon a time, all the parts of the human body did not work together as they do now. Instead, each body part had its own voice and followed its own plan. Some parts of the body complained that while they worked hard to provide everything for the stomach, the stomach sat quietly in the middle and did nothing but enjoy the delightful things they gave it. So they hatched a plot together, agreeing that the hands wouldn't give the mouth food, the mouth wouldn't accept it, and the teeth wouldn't chew it. Because of their angry desire to starve the stomach into submission, the individual body parts as well as the body as a whole began to grow weak. Then it became clear to them that the stomach, too, performed an important service, that it gave back as much food as it received, distributing to all the parts of the body the nourishment that gives us life and strength. The food we digest gives vigor to our blood, and this blood spreads into the veins in equal measures. (Livy 2.32)

In this analogy, the senatorial elite are the stomach, and the other body parts, representing the people, accuse it of doing nothing but enjoying the nourishment they work to provide. But, according to this speech, it is the stomach that keeps the entire body alive and strong, contrary to what the body parts think.

On the surface, this simple homespun fable appears to be a call for everyone to work together for the good of the whole. However, it might also be intended to deliver a harsh message to the plebeians: "Know your place!" Moreover, it suggests the plebeians do not really understand how the republic works. And since food shortages were a serious issue, framing the patrician message to the plebs with a story about feeding the body would carry an added punch. The parable had its intended effect of persuading the angry plebeians to end their secession, but they obtained some important concessions. They were allowed to form their own governing body, the Plebeian Assembly (*concilium plebis*), and created their own political offices, most notably the tribunes of the plebs. Both the Plebeian Assembly and the tribunes of the plebs play an important role in the history of the republic, and both were used to assert the rights of the plebeians against the patricians and the senators. At first, the Plebeian Assembly could only pass resolutions, known as *plebiscita*, which were recommendations subject to approval by the senate. Later, after further struggles, these *plebiscita* acquired the force of law.

Neither the story of the veteran nor the parable of the stomach can be treated as historical, but they do encapsulate the serious internal problems and tensions in the early Republic. And the fact that the senate's negotiator was a plebeian even if anachronistic, demonstrates an important point often forgotten in discussing the "Struggle of the Orders," as the conflicts of this period are sometimes called. The plebeians were not a monolithic, single-minded group, and some wealthy and ambitious plebeians might prefer to join the exclusive club of the wealthy elite rather than fight against it. Patricians would welcome into their ranks such individuals, who could be used to handle unruly plebeians, as in this instance. Moreover, the plebs as a whole did not necessarily think they were the equals of the patricians, or believe they deserved the same privileges and powers. So ingrained were the hierarchical social and political divisions at Rome that it would seem both natural and proper for the "betters" in society to make the important decisions and to govern everyone else. The senators and patricians, as the "fathers" of the republic, had an obligation to care for the people beneath them, if they at tmes needed to "discipline" them. The notion of equal rights for everyone is a modern idea, and we often forget how radical was the claim of the US Declaration of Independence, for all its shortcomings, that "All men are created equal." Nonetheless, the plebs were capable of recognizing unfairness and injustice within this accepted hierarchy. They could at least expect fair treatment and due consideration for their military service, even if they would not dream of complete equality. But how much was fair? This was the basic question for the plebeians and patricians in the early years of the republic.

Cincinnatus at the Plow

The conflicts between the patricians and plebeians over access to political offices and priesthoods were fundamentally about who really ought to have a voice in the governance of the republic. As we have already seen, early Roman history is replete with exemplary characters, whose existence as historical individuals is doubtful at best, but who nonetheless play an important role in the Romans' own understanding of their history. These are the individuals who captured the imagination of later generations and served as inspiring ideals for politicians and leaders in the Middle Ages, the Renaissance, and the modern world. Like many ideals, they could be used for evil as well as good, and a close reading of history often helps us to see how complicated these figures were in contrast to the simple uses to which they have been put. One of the most prominent of these model individuals from the first generations of the republic is Lucius Quinctius Cincinnatus.

In 458 BC, Rome was engaged, as it often was, in simultaneous wars against peoples in Italy, and each of the consuls had been sent out with his own army to fight against a different enemy. While the consuls were out on their campaigns, the Sabines launched an attack, and while one consul went to meet this additional threat, the other suffered a defeat and his army was pinned inside its camp. The situation was dire, and neither consul seemed able to meet the crisis, so the Romans appointed a dictator. The man they chose was Cincinnatus, and when a delegation from the senate was sent to announce his appointment as dictator, they found him hard at work plowing his fields on his small farm across the Tiber from Rome. Because this was official business, he was asked to put on his toga before hearing what the delegation had to say, so he sent his wife to their farmhouse to fetch his toga while he tried to clean up a bit, wiping off the sweat and dust. When he put on his toga, the delegation hailed him as dictator and explained the situation. Cincinnatus immediately headed for Rome, and though crowds of Romans came out to meet him, some plebeians, according to the traditional history, were not pleased to see him. They feared the absolute power of a dictator and believed the patrician Cincinnatus would use his authority against them. Nonetheless, Cincinnatus quickly assembled an army, defeated the enemy, and freed the trapped consul and his army from their besieged camp. In short order, he marched back to Rome, celebrated a triumph, then resigned as dictator, only sixteen days after his appointment. He could have held onto his office and all the power that came with it for the full six months, the standard term for a dictator, but instead he returned to his small farm and once again took up his work behind the plow.

The efficient and dutiful Cincinnatus is an idealized version of a Roman commander, and also of a Roman citizen. He lived a simple and frugal life, working his own land, unmoved by desires for luxury or ambitions for power. He carries out his duty to the state with dignity, treating his fellow Romans, including the plebeians, with firm justice and granting mercy to Rome's subdued enemies. When he was given a position of power with unquestioned authority over all Romans, he had no inclinations to stay in the position and use that power for other purposes. He thus eased the fears of the plebs and preserved the concord between the orders that a corrupt and overly ambitious individual would destroy.

While Cincinnatus's portrayal is likely not historical, it nonetheless carried a powerful message beyond the history of the Republic. Over two thousand years later, George Washington was compared to Cincinnatus. Because of the popularity and prestige he won as a military commander during the American Revolution, he was chosen as the new American Republic's first president. When his term in office was up, he did not succumb to the temptation to stay

FIG. 3.3 George Washington, copy of an original by Jean-Antoine Houdon (1792). Under his left hand are *fasces* and a sword, representing his political authority and military command, now covered by his cloak, symbolizing his retirement but readiness to serve. Note the plow behind his feet, associating him with Cincinnatus.

in office or assume the powers of a king, as some wished. Instead, much like a modern-day Cincinnatus, he resigned his command, left office, and returned to life at Mount Vernon in Virginia. The Roman dictator's name may look familiar because it lives on in the US city of Cincinnati, named for the "Society of the Cincinnati," an organization of veterans of the American Revolution founded in 1783, inspired by the actions of this early Roman soldier and farmer.

Law and Tyranny, Part I: The Twelve Tables and Verginia

Plebeian fears that Cincinnatus's appointment as dictator would lead to abuses of power were not unjustified, and the extreme injustices under the last king Tarquinius Superbus had not been forgotten. Moreover, the fundamental causes of the tensions between patricians and plebeians had not been directly addressed by the creation of plebeian magistrates and the Plebeian Assembly, won through their withdrawal from Rome. In addition, over the next few decades following the first secession of the plebs, there seems to have been an economic decline at Rome, which increased the financial hardships suffered by the plebeians.

Renewed internal strife led to the suspension of the constitution of the republic in 451 BC, and in place of consuls and tribunes of the plebs, governing authority was entrusted to an elected body of ten members, known as *decemvirs* (*decem* is Latin for ten, and *vir* means man). The purpose of this ten-man commission was to come up with a law code, something the plebeians had sought as a guarantee of fair treatment. Law in early Rome was in the hands of patricians, who acted as interpreters of the law and judges of legal cases. Some individuals may have had particular expertise in legal matters, but without a fixed code of laws that was made public, any individual who had a legal problem was essentially at the mercy of one judge's personal opinion. There could be no appeal to an established procedure or set rule, since these were known only to those with the power to enforce them. If there were questions about a case, only other senators would be consulted, and as a result, even if there was an attempt to be fair, the legal system remained in the hands of the elite. Law and justice were based on their perspective alone. A public law code would be a tremendous step forward in ensuring at least some protection from arbitrary decisions by corrupt politicians. The decemvirs, who were all patricians and former consuls, produced in 451 a draft of ten "tables" of laws, and in the following year another two tables of laws were added. The result was the Twelve Tables, Rome's first public law code.

The Twelve Tables

The laws of the Twelve Tables, as drawn up by the decemvirs, were inscribed onto bronze and set up in the Forum for all to see. Many Romans could neither read nor understand them, yet their permanent and visible presence in the Forum, the center of public life at Rome, was a powerful reminder to all citizens, regardless of their economic or social status, that some protection against the unjust exercise of political authority existed. The Twelve Tables and their publication represent a landmark in the history of Rome, especially in regard to the important ideal of equal treatment under the law. It was an important enough document that for centuries elite Roman schoolboys would learn it by heart. These laws did not, of course, bring about complete equality, or anything approaching it. In practice, elite Romans would not be subject to the same harsh treatment as the majority of uneducated and poorer individuals no matter what the laws said, and equal treatment applied only to Roman citizens. Nonetheless, these laws furthered the development of a type of liberty essential to the Roman Republic.

We do not have a physical copy of the Twelve Tables, and most of our knowledge of their contents comes from partial quotations by later authors. The Latin is archaic and condensed, making some of the quotations we have difficult to interpret, yet there is enough to shed some light on Roman society in the first generations of the republic. Each "table" seems to cover one general area of the law, with a number of individual statutes covering each area. The first table concerns basic legal procedures, such as how to bring somebody to court. Rome did not have a police force or lawyers in the modern sense, and if an individual wished to file a claim against someone, he had to do so himself and present his own case in person. There were individuals with expertise who could be consulted for legal advice, but a plaintiff or defendant was largely on his own. Nor did the Romans distinguish between civil law and criminal law in the way that we do. If someone stole something from you, you did not call the police, but summoned the individual to court yourself.

In Table I of the Twelve Tables, one law stipulated that if an individual was summoned to court and did not appear, the individual who filed a complaint could bring witnesses with him and try to bring the defendant in by force:

> If he calls to law, he shall go; if he does not go, he shall provide a witness;
> then, he shall seize him.

The law is confusing, not least because the subject constantly changes without any indication. It means "if [a plaintiff] calls [a defendant] to law, [the defendant] shall go; if the [defendant] does not go, [the plaintiff] shall provide a witness; then, [the plaintiff] shall seize [the defendant]." It is as confusing as modern law, but for the opposite reason: It is too short and simple rather than too long and complicated! The laws on procedure recognize that a defendant might have legitimate reasons for being unable to appear in court and specifies reasonable accommodations a plaintiff must provide in such cases. For example, if the person summoned to court is old or sick, the plaintiff is required to provide the person with a mule or horse as transportation to court, but not a more expensive wheeled carriage. This eliminates the possibility of the defendant claiming these as an excuse for failure to appear without placing an undue burden on the plaintiff.

Many of the laws exhibit the principle of "innocent until proven guilty," even though this is never explicitly stated. The Romans made other legal distinctions familiar today, such as between intentional murder (homicide) and an accidental killing (manslaughter). One law contains a clause that suggests a difference in criminal culpability based on intent: "if the weapon escapes his hand instead of being thrown." There are also provisions for self-defense and justifiable homicide, with the same confusing use of pronouns: "[I]f he [a thief] commits theft at night and he [someone else] kills him [the thief], he [the thief] is killed legally." There are also distinctions in penalties depending on status. Minors are punished with lighter penalties, while slaves are given much harsher treatment. According to the law on theft, if a slave is caught and found guilty, he will be whipped and then "hurled from the rock," a reference to the Tarpeian rock on the Capitol from which those condemned to die were thrown. A minor convicted of the same crime is whipped, but instead of a death penalty, he must repay his victims for any damages. The laws also provide for monetary damages when a person is injured, with specific rates for individual body parts, such as a broken limb or lost teeth. The bones and teeth of a slave were half the value of a free person's.

The importance of agriculture to Rome is clear from the laws, some of which call for compensation or punishment for damaged crops. For example, the owner of an animal that gets loose and wanders into someone else's field must pay compensation for the damage caused by the animal or give the animal to the owner of the damaged field. Intentional damage to or theft of someone else's crop is punishable by death. Many of the laws concern property in general, and in particular theft, ownership, and loans. The laws regarding debt show this was a serious problem, just as the secessions of the plebs suggest. As seen in the story of the poor veteran and farmer, a debtor who defaulted on his loan could be put in chains by his creditor, but the law specified that the chains could not weigh more than 15 pounds. If the debtor could not pay the creditor the amount owed within sixty days, the debtor could be sold into slavery. On the other hand, there were provisions in the law to make sure that debtors placed in chains were given food if they could not afford to provide their own. Several laws apply to burial customs and funerals. Burial or cremation within city limits was forbidden, but most of the laws on burial seem designed to restrict displays of wealth. For example, a funeral pyre could not be smoothed with a trowel, perfume could not be poured over a corpse, and no extra gold could be added to the body (unless, the law says, the dead person's teeth are held together with gold, evidence of early Roman dentistry). One fragment mentions ten flute players, and though the context is lost, this law may have set a limit on the number of flute players who could perform at a funeral.

Other laws concern the family, such as the rights of the *paterfamilias*, marriage, and wills. A law that will strike modern ears as especially inhumane says a father incurs no liability if he refuses to recognize a child born with physical handicaps as his. One of the more important of the laws is a ban on marriages between patricians and plebeians. While it often seems that all non-patricians are plebeians, this may not have been the case, even if the sources sometimes make it appear so. It is true that much of the social and political conflict in the early republic involved members of these two groups, but possibly many non-patricians did not identify as plebeian, or at least did not identify with those plebeians who agitated against the patrician monopoly on power. These non-patricians would be dependents of the patricians, in a patron–client relationship, in which they benefited from the protection and assistance of their patrons. For these individuals, access to political office or priesthoods, or even a greater voice in the political process, may not have been something desirable, and the status quo would be preferable to any change. This ban on intermarriage, therefore, might not have been intended to maintain the exclusivity of the patricians and to prevent social mobility, but rather to encourage wealthy and ambitious non-patricians to marry into the patrician order rather than the plebeian. In any case, this law remained in effect for only four years and was repealed in 445 BC.

One of the more notorious legal punishments in Rome was reserved for anyone who killed a parent or other blood relative (someone who committed this crime was known as a "parricide"). The murderer was sewed up in a leather sack together with a viper, dog, and monkey and thrown into the river. This law is only found in later sources, though there may have been an earlier version in the Twelve Tables in which the guilty party was sewn into a leather sack with his head wrapped with a cloth and then thrown into a body of water. While this punishment seems bizarre, there is a reason behind it. Killing a blood relative is such a monstrous crime that the killer is not only denied a burial, he is denied any contact with sky, earth, or water. The animals accompanying the guilty, which seems a strange group, were chosen because they were believed to kill their own parents.

The Story of Verginia

Despite this major step toward establishing equality under the law for all citizens, the decemvirs themselves soon became corrupt and began to behave in a tyrannical manner, following the pattern of the "cycle of constitutions." In fact, the two-year reign of the decemvirs in 451–450 BC is much like a condensed version of the overthrow of the monarchy, complete with another Lucretia at its center. The story of the young Verginia under the decemvirs parallels that of Lucretia and Tarquinius Superbus, told in the same dramatic manner and leading to a similar outcome. For the Romans, the laws and reforms that emerged from the turmoil caused by the brief rule of the decemvirs marked a major development in the history of the republic, and for them it was as important as the overthrow of the monarchy itself. The victimization of an innocent woman is again used to portray a major turning point in Roman history, but, unlike Lucretia, Verginia does not get to utter even a single word.

As befits the reputation of his *gens*, the patrician Appius Claudius was a haughty and overbearing aristocrat, but when the constitution was suspended and elections for decemvirs were imminent, he changed his tune and made himself popular with the plebeians. He was elected as the leader of the first group of decemvirs, and during this first year, there was political harmony at Rome, so much so that the plebeians did not concern themselves with the loss of the tribunes of the plebs. It seemed as if the office was no longer needed, since the decemvirs behaved as if they took plebeian concerns seriously. However, when the one-year term of the first decemvirs was coming to an end, and a new group was ready to be elected, Appius used his influence to block other candidates and had himself reelected with a group of lesser-known individuals who would not challenge his position of supremacy. This second group of decemvirs immediately began to behave like tyrants. They conducted business in secret, ignoring the senate and the people as well as the laws that had just been established. They even decided among themselves that there would not be another election so they could continue in office beyond their one-year term. One Roman even called them "ten Tarquins," comparing them as a group to the last tyrannical king of Rome, Tarquinius Superbus.

At this same time, Roman armies suffered a series of defeats, and there was fear that the Sabines would use this opportunity to attack the city. As an emergency measure, all the men still in the city capable of bearing arms were posted around the walls of Rome as guards. Appius Claudius, however, directed his energies in a different direction. He was consumed with lust for a plebeian girl named Verginia, whose father was a centurion in the army. Verginia was engaged to marry Lucius Icilius, a former tribune of the plebs and a strong advocate for the plebeians. Appius first tried to win over Verginia with gifts, but when these did not succeed, he had a friend of his make a legal claim that Verginia was his slave. Appius's plan was for his friend to bring his claim before the court, and Appius, because of his position as decemvir, would be the judge of the case. When Appius's friend seized Verginia in the Forum as she was on her way to school (a detail that hints at her young age), an outraged crowd of plebeians surrounded him. He ordered them to keep back, since Verginia was being summoned to court and he was following proper legal procedure. Just as they had planned, Appius's friend brought Verginia before the judge—Appius—and presented his sham case. Although Appius knew that according to the law Verginia should remain free until the case was decided, he claimed nothing should be done until her father Verginius returned to Rome, so Verginia would remain in his friend's possession. Verginius was on campaign with the army, at least a day's travel away, as Appius well knew. Verginia's fiancé Icilius tried to stir up the people against this corrupt and criminal abuse of power, but he was accused of trying to start a revolution for his own political purposes. Appius had attempted to have Verginius detained at his camp, but traveled as fast as he could and arrived on the day of the sham trial. His presence, however, did nothing to change the predetermined outcome. The lecherous Appius ruled in favor of his friend's fabricated claim, which meant Verginia would be his. Icilius and Verginius attempted to protest, but Appius threatened the use of armed force against them and the rest of the crowd, since, he claimed, they were creating a political disturbance. The threat of overwhelming force silenced the crowd, no longer willing to risk imprisonment or death to support Verginius and his daughter. In desperate straits, Verginius asked Appius for permission to question Verginia's old nurse in private, saying he hoped to discover if the story of her birth presented in court was true, which would mean he was not in fact Verginia's father. He led the nurse and Verginia away from the tribunal to an area of the Forum where there were shops and food stands. Once there, he grabbed a knife from a butcher's stall, and, plunging the knife into Verginia's heart, cried, "In the only way I can, my daughter, I set you free!"

The crowd of people who had come to witness the trial reacted with shock and horror when Verginia's corpse was displayed before them. In the ensuing turmoil, there was talk of taking this opportunity to free themselves from the tyranny of the decemvirs and recover their liberty. "Liberty," of course, is the catch-all political slogan used throughout the republic by different people with very different meanings. For the plebs at this time, "liberty" meant the reforms won by their earlier secession, in particular the office of tribune of the plebs and the right of appeal (*provocatio*), which provided them with safeguards against the actions of patricians such as Appius. When news of the patrician Appius's obvious injustice against the innocent daughter of a plebeian centurion reached them, Verginius's fellow soldiers prepared to march on Rome. Instead of an open rebellion, however, they decided to join the people of Rome in another secession of the plebs to the Aventine hill. The decemvirs who were in command of the military campaigns were forced to flee when the soldiers under them mutinied, and Appius himself fled from Rome.

The political importance of this drama is intensified by the combination of Icilius, a tribune of the plebs, and Verginius, an officer in the army. Together they represent the plebeian citizens and soldiers, both of whom had reasons to feel oppressed by the senatorial class. Not every senator supported the decemvirs, but the senate was complicit in their rule. Nonetheless, senators placed all the blame for the discord on the decemvirs. Two members of the senate, Lucius Valerius Potitus and Marcus Horatius Barbatus, were sent to negotiate with the plebeians. Horatius was a particularly good choice, since he had been openly critical of the decemvirs (he was the one who called them "ten Tarquins"). Their mission was two-fold. First, they were to try to reach a settlement with the soldiers and plebeians, who had now moved from the Aventine to the Sacred Mount (*mons Sacer*), a more serious secession since it was further away from the city and outside the *pomerium*. Second, they were also responsible for protecting the decemvirs from the anger of the people. In short, they were to restore political harmony. The plebeian demands were straightforward. They wanted a restoration of the rights they had lost under the decemvirs, as well as a promise that none of the plebeians would suffer any punishment for participating in the secession. However, one additional demand placed Valerius and Horatius in a tight spot: punishment of the decemvirs. Valerius and Horatius accepted the plebeians' demand for restoration of their rights but resisted the call for punishment of the decemvirs. They made an appeal to the plebeians for civic harmony: "Will our state never enjoy peace from the violent acts of senators against the plebs, or of the plebs against senators?" With this plea for unity, they brought the second secession of the plebs to a successful close, avoiding any acts of retaliation that would inflame tensions and lead to violence.

The Valerio–Horatian Laws

After the successful conclusion of their mission, Lucius Valerius and Marcus Horatius were elected as consuls for 449 BC. During their consulship, they passed a landmark set of laws that carry their name, the Valerio–Horatian Laws. As significant as the Twelve Tables for the future of Rome, these laws helped to bring the plebeians and patricians into a state of political agreement. They represented a formal recognition by the senate of the reforms for which the plebeians had agitated during the secession. The Plebeian Assembly was officially enshrined in law, and the resolutions it passed, the *plebiscita*, now had the force of laws. The special status of the tribunes of the plebs as "sacrosanct," meaning no one could lay a hand on them, was also affirmed. Finally, these laws granted all Roman citizens the right of appeal (*provocatio*), which gave any citizen the ability to appeal any action or decision by a magistrate before the people, which is to say the Plebeian Assembly. The people of Rome would now be the ultimate arbiter of justice. All citizens were, in theory, freed from the kind of tyrannical behavior associated with kings, but also seen in individuals such as Appius Claudius.

Despite the legal settlement of the conflict that arose in the aftermath of Verginia's death, the difficulty of maintaining the peace between the plebeians and patricians in practice was revealed by its sequel. While the plebeians refrained from seeking revenge against the decemvirs (one proposal was to burn them alive), they nevertheless demanded justice for their tyrannical behavior. They sought it under the Valerio–Horatian laws that had just been passed, and Verginius was selected to act as prosecutor of Appius, who was no longer in office. Appius entered the Forum to defend himself, surrounded by younger patricians. Despite all his misdeeds, Appius was charged only with illegally granting his friend custody of a free woman. As an official took hold of Appius so he could be taken before the court, Appius cried out "I appeal!" (*provoco*). Rather ironically, he makes use of this basic legal right now possessed by all Roman citizens thanks to the Valerio–Horatian laws, a right he himself had recently denied to Verginia and her father Verginius. Also ironically, when Appius tried to exercise his right of appeal, Verginius claimed that Appius should be denied this right because his case is an exceptional one. Even though Appius is a Roman citizen and should thus have the right to appeal, Verginius argues that his crimes were so outrageous that the law should not apply to him: "If there was one Roman who should not be allowed to enjoy this right, it was Appius!" And Verginius is not just any plebeian filing a complaint against an unjust patrician. He had suffered horribly because those very laws were being ignored by a wicked patrician (in the narrative, he is the one who suffers for killing his daughter). Appius was denied his right of appeal and led off to prison, not without some unease among the plebeians, who could recognize the dangerous precedent being set by Verginius's argument, especially since in this case a plebeian soldier was arguing against the principle of equality before the law. If exceptions to the law can be made, even when the justice of the exception seems clear-cut, who gets to decide the exceptions, and under what circumstances? More than likely, it would be plebeians who suffered the consequences.

Law and Tyranny, Part II: The Case of Spurius Maelius

The possibility of an overbearing aristocrat oppressing the plebeians may have been checked somewhat by the end of the decemvirate and the plebeian reforms in the Valerio–Horatian laws. Yet even though this "Struggle of the Orders" can often seem like a simple conflict between wealthy and powerful oppressors against the poorer masses yearning to be free, the social and political dynamics were not so straightforward. As we saw with Verginius's disregard for the basic citizen right of appeal in the case of Appius, the plebeians themselves could display tyrannical tendencies, either acting as a whole or in their support of individuals who could rally the masses against the senate or the upper class as a whole.

Yet another dramatic episode from the fifth century BC highlights the problem of popular agitation, and also reveals the difficulty of distinguishing between politicians who act for the greater good and those who only appear to do so to satisfy their own political ambitions. In 439 BC, a decade after the Valerio–Horatian laws, famine struck Rome, and the senators and tribunes of the plebs blamed one another for the calamity. To address the emergency, the plebs elected an official to oversee the grain supply. Even though this official attempted to procure grain from other peoples in Italy and overseas, he failed to obtain any, and instead imposed grain rationing and seized any extra grain held by Romans themselves. A wealthy plebeian named Spurius Maelius took matters into his own hands, and from his own resources began to hand out grain for free. This made him popular with the plebs but raised suspicions among the senatorial class. A private citizen acting on his own initiative, outside the constraints of political institutions, might have kingly ambitions, and Maelius did, indeed, have ambitions, or at least he was charged by his patrician opponents with having them. In fact, given his actions, he appeared to usurp the authority given to the public official appointed to supervise the grain supplies, even if that official had failed. As a plebeian, Maelius believed he could never become a consul, and thus, as the story goes, he decided to try to become king instead, which would mean the overthrow of the republic. The official in charge of the grain supply reported to the senate that Maelius was stockpiling weapons in his home in preparation to seize power for himself. In response, the senate decided to appoint a dictator to deal with Maelius's plot, and their choice was none other than Cincinnatus, now over 80 years old.

When a dictator was appointed, he would choose a second-in-command, known as "master of the horse" (*magister equitum*), to assist him. Cincinnatus selected Gaius Servius Ahala for the post and immediately sent Ahala to summon Maelius before the senate to answer the serious charges against him. Maelius refused to obey the summons, and Ahala killed him right then and there. Though the plebeians were in an uproar, Cincinnatus claimed Maelius had been rightly and legally killed, since he had refused a legal summons issued on the dictator's authority. Although the authority of a legally appointed dictator was absolute, there might have been a question whether Maelius could have exercised his right of appeal. However, echoing Verginius's argument when he denied Appius the right of appeal, Cincinnatus said that Maelius should not be treated as a citizen, since in aiming to make himself king, he had rejected the liberty Romans had won by driving out the kings. In other words, because Maelius had (allegedly) been preparing to make himself king, he had by his actions rejected the republic itself. In Cincinnatus's view, if a Roman citizen rejects the fundamental principle of the republic, he has rejected his citizenship, and therefore does not deserve the legal protections citizens possess. (Note that Cincinnatus unfairly assumed Maelius's guilt in making his argument.) Cincinnatus ordered Maelius's house razed, and all proceeds from his property were handed over to the public treasury. The plebs, who might be expected to react to Maelius's killing in a hostile manner, were placated by receiving at a very low price the grain Maelius had collected.

The dramatic histories of the struggles between the patricians and plebeians point to real social and political fractures in the republic. While the plebeians acquired protection under the law as well as the powerful defenses of their own assembly and their own political offices, the full effect of these changes will not be felt until the following centuries, after Rome confronts threats abroad.

Roman Religion

Roman religion on its own is a topic as broad, deep, and difficult as Roman history itself, and is of fundamental importance for understanding the history of Rome. One of the primary virtues the Romans saw in themselves was a religious devotion, as emphasized by the way the legendary Roman hero Aeneas is made to introduce himself in the national epic the *Aeneid*: *sum pius Aeneas* ("I am pious Aeneas"). In modern English, "pious" means devout and religious in a specifically modern sense, and it might be applied to someone who never misses a church service and prays frequently. The Latin word *pius* and the related noun *pietas* ("piety") include the sense of devotion and obedience to their gods, but since in Rome religion, politics, and social life were deeply intertwined in ways different from the modern world, Roman "piety" covers a much broader range of meanings. The Romans did not distinguish between religious and secular spheres of life, and thus, when we speak of "religion" in a Roman context, we have to take a much broader view of what "religion" means. In fact, religion was closely connected to the state, and for the Romans as well as other ancient peoples, a political community could not exist without some form of shared worship of the gods. Separating the two would not have occurred to the Romans, and the major figures of Roman history, whom we tend to think of primarily in terms of their political and military activities, also held priesthoods and other religious offices. Julius Caesar, for example, was also Rome's chief priest, the pontifex maximus.

Nearly every activity in Rome began with some form of religious observance or ritual in order to seek divine approval or ask for a god's assistance: birth, death, passage from adolescence to adulthood, marriage, elections, declarations of war and peace, buying and trading, eating and drinking, and most anything else. In short, the gods were everywhere, but if we speak of the Romans as a religious or pious people, we need to recognize that because of the way religion was interwoven into their everyday life, that their "belief" in it, and thus their "piety," would be very different. In fact, to speak of "belief" in Roman religion is tricky, because unlike major religions in the contemporary world, the Romans had no sacred scriptures (like the Bible or the Qur'an), no set of beliefs or teachings you had to follow. Even though Jupiter might be called on to protect guests or uphold treaties, and might be expected to punish wrongdoers, there was no specific moral code or set of commandments upheld by the gods. Even thieves had a protective god in Mercury, who was also the god of commerce and business. Even though all Romans were religious in the sense they participated in religious rituals, not all of them believed the stories about the gods. Nonetheless, most Romans believed there was something divine in the world, even if some thought the popular representations of the gods were false. Those of a philosophical bent who thought and wrote about the workings of the world and the universe deduced from the regular order of tides and seasons that there was a rational principle that governed the universe, which could be thought of as something divine.

No matter what one's belief, public forms of religious observance—festivals, sacrifices, prayers, and processions—were considered of utmost importance, if only for political reasons. Philosophers and intellectuals who were skeptical that Jupiter looked like a bearded man hurling a thunderbolt would nonetheless participate in these rituals, both public and private, and many of these individuals would be proud holders of priesthoods. All Romans recognized that a shared religion was fundamental to a political community, and none of these thinkers, even if they published books about the cosmos for other educated elite readers, would openly question the existence of gods or openly mock religious rituals.

A Roman scholar of the first century BC even laid out three categories of religion. The first he calls "poetic," which consists of the mythological stories about the gods found in poetry and represented in paintings and statues. This form is for popular consumption. Second is "philosophical," which he regarded as the true understanding of the divine forces at work in the universe; representing the gods in human form and acting in human ways (often badly) was a popular falsehood. Finally, there was "civic," which was an attempt to combine the best of the poetic and philosophic categories and made use of popular representations in art and literature as a means to keep the city unified under a shared system of beliefs and practices. So, for example, philosophical theology recognized lighting as a natural phenomenon that could be explained scientifically (e.g., as a result of clouds rubbing together), though it might still signal the divine will. In the poetic version, a lightning strike might be portrayed as Jupiter's anger, with a large bearded man casting a bolt much like a spear. The civic form presents a statue of Jupiter hurling a lightning bolt but was understood as a fictional representation of something divine at work in the universe, which poets, philosophers, politicians, and the people could all worship.

Communicating With the Gods

Religion was viewed as necessary not only for the founding of the city, but for its continued existence. As we saw, the second king Numa played the role of religious founder of Rome, but even the story of the founding of Rome itself occurs via a religious ritual. The twins Romulus and Remus disagreed on the site for the new city, and each of them went to a different hill, Romulus to the Palatine and Remus to the Aventine. To determine which of the two would be its founder, each sat at the top of his hill and watched for the appearance of birds, which would be taken as a sign of divine favor. Remus spotted a group of six vultures first, but then Romulus saw twelve. As it turns out, in one version of the story, this causes a dispute about whom the gods favored—was it Remus, who spotted the birds first, or Romulus, who spotted more birds? The dispute leads to the death of Remus, which settles the debate once and for all.

While watching for birds might strike us as a very odd way to settle an important question, to the Romans of the Republic this made perfect sense, and the scene would have been immediately recognizable to them. Both Romulus and Remus were "taking auspices," watching for the flight of birds to determine if the gods favored the time and place of an undertaking. Auspices is formed from the Latin words for bird, *avis*, and to watch, *specio*, and is the origin of the English "auspicious." This was an important form of religious divination for the Romans, and it remained in practice throughout the republic and the period of the emperors. Despite the word's roots, "taking auspices" did not always involve watching for birds, but was a ritual performed before almost any undertaking—an election, a meeting, a battle, a business deal—to determine whether the gods favored it. If the auspices were unfavorable, the action or event would be postponed and the ceremony repeated the following day. Not until favorable auspices were obtained could things move forward. A related procedure was "augury," in which divine approval was sought for a particular act, rather than just the time and place.

The relation between humans and the divine is one of exchange, as expressed by the Latin phrase *do ut des* ("I give so that you give"). Humans worship the gods in order that the gods treat humans well. We might use a more contemporary Latin phrase to render this exchange of favors, *quid pro quo* (literally, "something for something"). So, for example, Romulus vows a temple to Jupiter if Jupiter will give his troops courage to hold their ground against the enemy. Because of this exchange relationship, sacrifice was an essential component of Roman religious practice, especially a sacrifice involving the shedding of blood. The Romans regularly performed sacrifices and gave offerings to divinities, both at home and at public shrines and temples. The more formal and regular public sacrifices were performed on a large scale. There was a set procedure that had to be strictly followed, and any deviation or interruption meant starting over again from the beginning. The participants in a sacrifice, usually led by a priest of some kind, led an animal to the altar. The animal was always a domesticated

FIG. 3.4 A bull being led to an altar for sacrifice.

animal of use to humans, such as a pig, goat, sheep, or bull, though other animals, such as dogs, were sometimes sacrificed. The "victim," as the animal to be sacrificed is called, was purified with wine and salt, and then it was slaughtered. The animal's organs were examined to make sure there was nothing irregular, such as a deformed or missing organ, which would mean the sacrifice was not acceptable to the god, and the sacrifice would have to be performed again. After the victim was killed and its organs examined, some of the innards were burnt on the altar as an offering to the god; the rest would be cooked and eaten by the participants in the sacrifice at a banquet.

Probably the most serious offense against the gods was failure to perform the proper rituals and observances for them. The failure to carry out particular rites and sacrifices to obtain divine approval before any undertaking would result in disaster, if not immediately, then sometime in the future. Any sign of the gods' displeasure, which could be something as simple as a sneeze when beginning a sacrifice or a slip of the tongue when uttering a prayer, would bring any proceeding to a halt or prevent an action from being started. If a ceremony or sacrifice was interrupted by such an event, it was started again from the beginning. Disregarding a ritual or ignoring its outcome could prove disastrous, and the Romans took this very seriously. One famous example of a Roman ignoring auspices occurred during the First Punic War (264–241 BC), the first of three major wars Rome fought against Carthage, a powerful city on the north coast of Africa. The commander of a Roman fleet caught sight of Carthaginian ships, which were not expecting the Romans and were thus unprepared. It was a perfect opportunity to inflict a major defeat on the Carthaginians, who had a superior navy. Before attacking, however, the commander had to consult the will of the gods, for which purpose chickens were kept on board in one of the stranger forms of Roman divination. Cornmeal or other grain would be thrown before a chicken, and if it ate, the gods signaled their approval. The commander had the "sacred chickens" brought out and released from their cages; grain was thrown before them, but they would not eat. The commander tried again and again, and yet the chickens still would not eat, preventing him from launching an attack. In frustration, he exclaimed "If they won't eat, let them drink!" and tossed the chickens overboard. The surprise attack he expected would lead to a glorious victory for Rome as well as himself instead ended in failure and defeat. The story emphasizes the extreme importance of piety—even when a golden opportunity present itself in the middle of a war against a powerful enemy, the gods must be obeyed.

Religion in Space and Time

This story of the sacred chickens, the story of Romulus and Remus, and many others demonstrate how important religious observance was to Rome and its citizens, since the very foundation of their city could only be undertaken with divine approval. And once the gods did approve, the act of foundation itself was a religious ritual. The boundary of the city was marked out with a plow, and this boundary was known as the *pomerium*, which created a sacred space distinct from the surrounding area. No bodies could be buried within the *pomerium*, and no Roman consul could lead an army across it. The political authority of many political officials ended when they crossed this scared boundary. Spaces within the city were also marked out as sacred. A temple (*templum* in Latin, from a Greek root meaning "to cut") referred to any space made sacred by marking a boundary in a ritual manner, such as a plow cutting into the earth. A "temple" did not necessarily have to be a building, though it often was. The space where the senate met had to be a space inaugurated by a religious ceremony, and thus had to be a "temple" in this broader sense. The senate house, or Curia, was technically a "temple," as was the area in front of it where elections were held, though we do not usually think of them as "temples" in the usual sense.

Temples as we tend to think of them are buildings dedicated to a god or gods in which their cult statues were housed, and such buildings were integral to the city of Rome and everyday life. Most conspicuous of all was the Temple of Jupiter Optimus Maximus ("Jupiter Best and Greatest") on the summit of the Capitoline hill, sometimes referred to as the Temple of Capitoline Jupiter. In the Forum below it were numerous other temples, shrines, and structures dedicated to the gods. There were major temples such as the Temple of Jupiter Stator, by tradition vowed by Romulus during battle, the Temple of Castor and Pollux, built after the victory at Lake Regillus, as well as the House of the Vestals, where the Vestal Virgins lived and maintained the sacred fire. The intermingling of religious and political structures would have not been as noticeable to the Romans as it might be to us, and in fact they would not even speak of the buildings as two distinct categories (as we might note a courthouse across from a church). Individual houses also had shrines to household gods, the Lares and Penates, and families would also have shrines to their own ancestors.

Not only was the space of the city infused with religion, but the rhythms of daily life were also structured around religion. The calendar itself is a religious document. The history of the Roman calendar is a difficult and thorny topic, and though it is traditionally traced back to the king Numa, there is much dispute about its origins. Julius Caesar undertook a major reform of the calendar, and this Julian calendar remained in use until the introduction of the "Gregorian calendar," named after Pope Gregory XIII, in 1582 AD. Fragments exist of a few Roman calendars from the first century BC, and figure 3.5 is a partial reconstruction of the earliest extant Roman calendar, the only one that dates from before Julius Caesar's reforms.

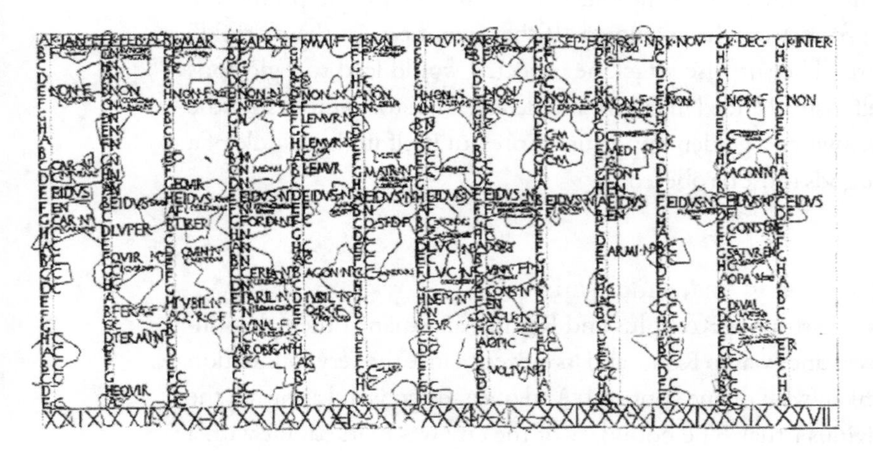

FIG. 3.5 A reconstructed calendar dating to ca. 60 BC, known as the Fasti Antiates.

Abbreviated month names are at the top, and the number of days in each month at the bottom, in Roman numerals. Days are listed by letters A through H, which represent the Roman eight-day market cycle. Note the months QUI, which stands for Quintilis ("Fifth"), and SEX, for Sextilis ("Sixth"), names held over from when the first month of the year was March. (Thus, the modern months September through December take their names from the numbers seven through ten.) INTER stands for "intercalary," a special month that would be inserted in some years to ensure the calendar remained in line with the seasons. NON and EIDUS stand for "Nones" and "Ides," two important markers in every month. The Ides were either on the 13th or 15th day of the month, and the Nones was nine days before the Ides. (The Romans counted inclusively, so they count nine days when we count eight. For example, the Ides of March are on the 15th day of the month, and the Nones are on the 7th, which is nine days earlier for the Romans.) Individual days were categorized as *fas* or *nefas*, indicating whether it was permitted to conduct business or hold meetings on those days. These restrictions were made for reasons of religion, though it is not always clear why. In addition, public festivals were held throughout the year, all of which had religious significance. Abbreviations in this calendar represent these annual religious festivals, such as LUPER midway down the column for February, which stands for the Lupercalia, and SATUR in the month of December, short for Saturnalia. By the end of the republic, these festivals and games took up over 150 days out of the year, though not all were a major event on the scale of the Lupercalia.

Religious Offices (Priesthoods)

Religious offices were as important as political offices, and, just as political offices had some religious functions associated with them, religious offices had political importance. In fact, officeholders frequently held religious offices at the same time, some of which were lifetime appointments. There were four major groups of religious officials, and these groups are normally referred to as "colleges," after the Latin *collegium*. There are four colleges of religious officials: pontifices, flamens, augurs, and haruspices (all are sometimes referred to as priests or priesthoods). There were numerous minor religious offices, but the most important ones are listed here.

Pontifex Maximus

The pontifex maximus was highest religious official of Rome, and, as the name implies, he was the head of a group of priests (*pontifices*). The "college" of *pontifices* eventually grew to 16 members. These priests oversaw all the religious activities at Rome, including holidays and rituals such as the Lupercalia. Originally, only a patrician could be a pontifex, but plebeians were eventually admitted. The priesthood was an office for life, and new members were first chosen by the other priests (a process called "co-optation), but later they were elected. Perhaps the most important role of the pontifex maximus was to advise the senate on all religious matters. Since most everything the Romans did had a religious component, including the opening of political meetings and voting assemblies, a pontifex had great influence. The title of pontifex maximus lives on today as the official title of the Pope, the "chief priest" of the Catholic Church.

FIG. 3.6 Flamens wearing their distinctive headgear, the *apex*.

Flamens

While the pontifices were charged with the oversight of religion in general, a flamen was a priest dedicated to a single god. There were fifteen in total, and the three most important were the *Flamen Dialis* (a priest of Jupiter), the *Flamen Quirinalis* (priest of little-known god Quirinus, sometimes associated with Romulus), and the *Flamen Martialis* (priest of Mars). These three "major" flamens had to be patrician, while plebeians could serve as any of the other twelve "minor" flamens. The flamens were not elected, but chosen by the college of pontifices, and held the office for life. These priesthoods came with restrictions that made military service or travel outside Rome impossible. For example, the Flamen Dialis could not look at people carrying weapons nor could he spend more than a night away from his bed. As a result, these priesthoods were not always desirable for an ambitious politician.

Augurs

Augurs were religious experts who provided advice and assisted with the taking of auspices. "Auspices" are the signs of divine approval or disapproval sought before any undertaking, such as a political meeting or military action. "Taking auspices" means watching the sky for birds as favorable or unfavorable omens, or observing a clap of thunder or flash of lightning. By the end of the republic, the college of augurs had 16 members, and new members were admitted for life. At first they were chosen by the college of augurs itself, and later by election at the Tribal Assembly from candidates nominated by the college of augurs.

Haruspices

Haruspices (singular *haruspex*) were experts in the interpretation of lightning bolts, unusual natural phenomena (such as a hail of stones), and the organs (such as the liver, heart, or intestines) of sacrificial animals. Haruspices were Etruscans, an ancient people from Etruria, the region north of Rome, famed for their expertise in religious matters. Haruspices would be summoned as a group by the senate to provide a remedy, usually through a religious ritual, for events such as famine, plague, or a major defeat in war.

Vestal Virgins

The Vestals are perhaps the best known of Roman religious officials, in part because it is one of the few positions of public importance for women. There were six Vestals, chosen as young girls between the ages of six and ten who then served for thirty years, under the supervision of the pontifex maximus. The chief duty of the Vestals was to maintain the sacred eternal fire inside the Temple of Vesta; to prepare the *mola salsa*, a mixture of grain and salt used in sacrifices; and to preserve sacred relics (such as the Penates) associated with the foundation of Rome and believed to be necessary to Rome's continued existence. Vestals were given some special legal privileges denied to all other women: They were not under the legal authority of their fathers and they could write their own will. After their service, they were free to marry, and they were provided with a dowry. (A "dowry" is the money or property given by a bride's family to the groom and was usually provided by the bride's family; the modern custom of the bride's family paying for a wedding is a holdover of this.) Vestals also had special seats reserved for them at the theatre and rode in a special type of carriage when they traveled in Rome. The punishment for Vestals who violated their vow of chastity is particularly cruel, though only ten or so instances are known. They were carried through Rome in a cloaked and muffled carriage, and then led down to a special underground chamber and buried alive.

Roman Gods

The gods were associated with different activities and areas of life, and sometimes a title or designation was added to the name of the god to indicate which particular aspect of the god was being honored or addressed, as in Juno Lucina (Juno of childbirth), Juno Regina (Queen Juno), and Juno Moneta (Juno who gives warning). Sometimes a local designation was added, such as Diana Nemorensis (Diana of the forest), who had a shrine near the Alban Mount. The Romans also built shrines and temples to abstract qualities, such as *Virtus* (Virtue), *Fortuna* (Fortune), and *Honos* (Honor). One of the more prominent temples in the Roman Forum was a Temple of Concord (*Concordia*), dedicated to political harmony.

The Roman gods cannot always be distinguished from their Greek counterparts, and in some cases they are also related to Etruscan and Phoenician deities. A sky god in one tradition would be viewed as the equivalent god in another, and thus they would be identified with each other in a process called "syncretism." Greek and Roman names for the same god may have originally referred to different deities, even if their characteristics and areas over which they had influence were very similar. Thus, Roman Venus and Greek Aphrodite (and Phoenician Astarte) are gods of love and sexual desire, and the Greek Dionysus and the Roman Liber (also known in both Greek and Latin as Bacchus) are connected with wine. There were also native Italic deities belonging to peoples such as the Latins and Sabines, but these were absorbed into the Roman–Greek pantheon. The syncretism of these gods and traditions was neither regular nor complete, but by the time of our sources, the traditions of these gods are so intertwined they cannot be untangled. For example, a set of three hammered gold sheets found at the site of Pyrgi, an Etruscan port northwest of Rome, records in both the Etruscan and Phoenician languages a temple dedication of the year 509 BC to "Uni-Astarte." Astarte is the Phoenician god of love, usually identified with Roman Venus and Greek Aphrodite, while Uni is the queen of the Etruscan gods, normally equated with Juno and Hera. The pantheons of the ancient Mediterranean were in fact a flexible system of gods, with no fixed identities and frequent intermixing. Ancient religions generally had nothing dogmatic in them, and for that reason there should be no dogma about them.

There was no set or fixed list of Roman gods, though the major gods of Roman religion can be closely identified with Greek equivalents, especially many of those known as the "Olympians." A list of some of the most important gods in Roman religion is as follows:

Roman	**Greek**	**Area of Influence**
Jupiter	Zeus	Sky, lightning, justice, king and father
Juno	Hera	Childbirth, marriage
Minerva	Athena	Battle strategy, wisdom, weaving
Neptune	Poseidon	Sea, horses, earthquakes
Mars	Ares	War and strife
Venus	Aphrodite	Sexual desire and love
Apollo	Apollo	Healing, prophecy, poetry and music
Diana	Artemis	Animals, hunting
Vulcan	Hephaestus	Fire, metalwork, craftsmen
Vesta	Hestia	Hearth and home
Mercury	Hermes	Business, trade, thievery, escort of souls
Ceres	Demeter	Grain, fertility
Liber	Dionysus	Wine, theater

At Rome, Jupiter, Juno, and Minerva form a group known as the "Capitoline Triad," because they were all worshipped in the Temple of Jupiter Optimus Maximus on the Capitol, considered the seat and symbol of Rome's power. These three replaced an earlier triad of Jupiter, Mars, and Quirinus, the last of whom may have been early Sabine deity, but at Rome was later associated with the deified Romulus. There was also a triad of Ceres, Liber, and Libera, who were worshipped on the Aventine, the hill to which the plebeians withdrew during a secession of the plebs. For that reason, both the hill and this triad of gods are associated with the plebeians.

Despite a reputation for conservatism, the Romans did accept foreign cults, though they did at times try to suppress them. The persecution of religious cults or sects was usually motivated by political concerns rather than hostility to foreign religions. At the beginning of the second century BC, the senate placed severe restrictions on a "Bacchanalian" cult, which carried out ceremonies in honor of Dionysus, also called Bacchus. However, shortly before this official action to suppress a religious practice, the Romans had with great ceremony imported a cult of the Great Mother (*Magna Mater* in Latin), also known as Cybele, from the coast of modern-day Turkey.

Credits

Fig. 3.1: Source: https://commons.wikimedia.org/wiki/File:VirginiaBotticelli.jpg.

Fig. 3.2: Source: https://commons.wikimedia.org/wiki/File:RomaForoRomanoTempioCastori.jpg.

Fig. 3.3: Source: https://www.publicdomainpictures.net/en/view-image.php?image=96266&picture=george-washington-capitol-rotunda.

Fig. 3.4: Copyright © by Wolfgang Sauber (CC BY-SA 3.0) at https://commons.wikimedia.org/wiki/File:Stockholm_-_Antikengalerie_Opferszene.jpg.

Fig. 3.5: Source: https://commons.wikimedia.org/wiki/File:Roman-calendar.png.

Fig. 3.6: Copyright © by WolfgangRieger (CC BY-SA 3.0) at https://commons.wikimedia.org/wiki/File:Ara_pacis_fregio_lato_ovest_2_A.JPG.

CHAPTER 4

Rome Rising

The Fourth Century

FIG. 4.1 Camillus arriving just in time to prevent the payment of a ransom to the Gauls, as imagined by an eighteenth-century artist.

Overview

Two watershed moments in the early history of Rome are the destruction of the Etruscan city Veii and the sack of Rome by the Gauls, representing the ups and downs of Rome's increasing power. In the aftermath of the Gallic invasion, further legislation benefitting the plebs altered the political landscape of the republic. Rome continued its subjugation of the Italian peninsula with the Samnite Wars and the final defeat of the Latin League, culminating in the Battle of Sentinum in 295 BC. At the end of the fourth century BC we encounter the first truly historical individual in Roman history, Appius Claudius Caecus. The chapter concludes with an overview of the Roman army.

Timeline

396	Defeat of Veii
390 or 386	Gallic sack of Rome
367	Licinio–Sextian Laws
343	Beginning of the Samnite Wars
338	Defeat of the Latin League
321	Roman defeat at the Caudine Forks
312	Censorship of Appius Claudius Caecus
295	Battle of Sentinum

The Destruction of Veii

The slow and painful development of the Roman Republic continued after the turmoil of the decemvirs in the middle of the fifth century BC. While Rome won numerous military victories, the wars with its neighbors were far from over. The cities of Etruria, home of the last kings of Rome, had in 474 BC suffered a major defeat at the hands of Cumae, a Greek city on the west coast of Italy. But Veii (pronounced vay-ee), a wealthy and well-fortified Etruscan town only 10 miles north of Rome, remained a major rival. In addition to general concerns about Rome's increasing power, Veii considered Rome a competitor for control of trade routes. Relations between the two were always tense, and Rome fought three major wars with Veii during the republic's first century, ending with Veii's destruction in 396 BC. The first of these wars (483–474 BC) was famous for a disaster that struck a single Roman family. An entire clan of 306 men, all with the *nomen* Fabius, went into battle, and only a single one survived to carry on the family name. The second war (437–435 BC) broke out when the tyrant of Veii, Lars Tolumnus, killed four Roman ambassadors. He claimed it was an accident, explaining to the Romans that during a game of dice, he uttered a curse at his bad luck, which his men misunderstood as an order to kill the ambassadors. The Romans did not buy this excuse and launched an attack. Romans remembered this war chiefly for an unusual event in their military history, something that occurred only three times in the history of the Republic. The Roman consul killed Lars Tolumnus in single combat, earning the rare honor of the *spolia opima* ("the best spoils"). It was common practice for a soldier to strip the armor and weapons from a defeated enemy, and these are called spoils (as in the phrase "the spoils of war"). Spoils, or a portion of them, were often deposited in temples as a dedication to the gods. The *spolia opima* were an honor earned when the commander of a Roman army, usually a consul, defeated the ruler of an enemy in single combat and took his armor. By tradition, Romulus had been the first to do so, and the only other Roman during the republic to be awarded the *spolia opima* was in 222 BC.

The third and final war with Veii was, by tradition, a ten-year siege (406–396 BC). It differed from the previous two in that Rome, now more aggressive, launched an attack first without any provocation by the Veians. Many historians believe the ten-year duration is not a historical fact, but this span of time was attached to this siege to make it comparable to the siege of Troy famous from the *Iliad*, giving Rome's victory over Veii an epic grandeur. The war also had omens and prodigies associated with it, including an inexplicable rise in the level of the lake at Alba. Following a prophecy that Rome would never take Veii until the water was drained, the Romans promptly emptied the lake by digging a tunnel. They would soon capture Veii, also by digging a tunnel. Much like the ten-year time span that elevated the siege to the level of the Trojan War, the divine signs connected to it served to highlight its importance for the Romans.

The victorious general who oversaw the fall and destruction of Veii was Marcus Furius Camillus, one of the leading Romans of the early fourth century. While still a semi-legendary figure, whose character and exploits are as idealized as a Cincinnatus, Camillus begins to show a complexity that earlier figures of Roman history did not possess. This is due in part to his lengthy military and political career. He was "consular tribune" six times and dictator a remarkable five times, the last in 367 BC (though this may be a later invention). His two major accomplishments, however, were bringing the siege of Veii to a successful close and leading the recovery of Rome in the aftermath of the Gallic invasion.

The siege of Veii did not proceed smoothly, less because of military difficulties than domestic tensions back in Rome, and for this reason Camillus was appointed dictator by the senate to bring the war to a close. Camillus began construction of a tunnel that would lead Roman soldiers to the citadel of Veii, but before doing so, he performed an *evocatio*, a ritual in which the protective deity of a city under attack is asked to abandon the city and come over to the Roman side. In this case, Camillus called on Juno, the patron goddess of Veii, to follow him to Rome. (The Etruscans would have called the goddess Uni.) As it turned out, the tunnel the Romans dug beneath the walls of Veii led the soldiers right beneath the temple of Juno at the very moment the king of Veii was performing a sacrifice there. Emerging from the tunnel, the Romans broke through the floor of the temple and took the city by storm, slaughtering the citizens of Veii or selling them into slavery. Once the fighting was over, a group of Roman soldiers went to retrieve the cult statue of Juno/Uni from the temple, but only after they had first ritually purified themselves by washing off the blood and gore from all the killing. As the story goes, the large statue of Juno/Uni was miraculously light and easy to carry, which was taken as a sign that the goddess had heard the *evocatio* and was glad to be taken to Rome. The statue was placed on the Aventine hill in a temple dedicated by Camillus.

All would seem to be well after this important victory over a major rival, but the wealth of Veii became a source of political troubles back at Rome. Camillus knew that Veii would provide plenty of plunder for his soldiers and for Rome, but he had doubts about the proper way to distribute all this newly won wealth. He thought if he were too stingy with the soldiers, they would be angry with him, but if he gave away too much to them, then the senators would be angry with him. He asked the senate how to proceed, and after some debate, the senators, in an attempt to make themselves popular with the plebs, decreed that any Roman who wanted a share of the

FIG. 4.2 A terracotta fragment from the Temple of Apollo at Veii.

plunder could go to Veii to take some. However, Camillus angered the plebs when he deposited into the public treasury the money earned from selling Veian captives into slavery. The plebeians attacked Camillus for taking money away from the amount that was supposed to be distributed to them. At the same time, they gave credit for the share of plunder they received not to Camillus, but to the senator who made the proposal that Camillus carried out.

When Camillus returned to Rome for his triumph, he further angered the plebs for celebrating it on a scale never seen before, even though Rome had never plundered a city as wealthy and powerful as Veii. In particular, Camillus used four white horses to pull his triumphal chariot, which to some people seemed like he was elevating himself to the level of a god. In addition, shortly before the final assault on Veii, when Camillus had taken the auspices and performed the *evocatio* of Juno, he also vowed a tenth of the plunder to Apollo, who also had a major temple in Veii. Even though this vow was a pious act by a dutiful Roman commander, it created a problem. Did the Roman people who went to Veii to receive a share of the plunder now have to return a tenth of it to fulfill this vow made by Camillus on behalf of Rome? There was also a dispute about whether the value of the Veian territory Rome had seized should be included in the calculation of the vow, which would add a significant amount to the total. The senate consulted the priests, and they concluded that the Romans should use the higher amount, including the value of the land. As a result, Rome needed to dip into the public treasury to meet the total sum required. However, even this was not enough money, so women of the upper classes, in a patriotic and pious act, contributed their own personal jewelry to the funds needed to fulfill the vow. (This scene was reenacted over two thousand years later during the French Revolution, when wives of the revolutionaries donated their jewelry to the cause.)

FIG. 4.3 An image from 1789 of French women donating their jewelry to the National Treasury during the French Revolution. The caption reads "Bravo, Ladies! Now it's your turn!"

Camillus's actions, both at his triumph and in the debate about the plunder from Veii, could be credited to his principled devotion to the state and its gods. His political enemies, however, used his actions to stir up popular resentment against him. Camillus, however, refused to yield to their attacks or to be concerned with his unpopularity among the plebs.

After the conquest of Veii, there was a proposal to resettle the city with Romans. Some suggested sending a combined group of senators and plebeians there to create a single Roman Republic consisting of two cities, Rome and Veii. The plebeians supported this proposal, and some tribunes of the plebs attempted to put it to a vote before the Plebeian Assembly. The proposal was vigorously opposed by the senators, and in particular by Camillus. Since any one of the ten tribunes of the plebs could veto any legislation, the senators only needed to convince a single tribune to use his veto, and this was often not difficult to do. A wealthy and ambitious tribune might very well wish to be on good terms with the senators and would be willing to do them a favor in the expectation of a future benefit from them. In the case of the settlement of Veii, two tribunes of the plebs vetoed the legislation, which so angered the plebs that they brought legal charges against these two tribunes and punished them with an enormous fine. Camillus, not attempting in any way to be diplomatic or conciliatory, blasted the plebs for undermining the authority of their own tribunes, since, by punishing the tribunes who exercised their veto power, they had in effect overturned a tribunician veto. This was the type of plebeian behavior that frustrated the senatorial class and which they used to justify their patronizing treatment of the plebs.

When the proposal to resettle Veii finally came up for a vote, those who opposed it appealed to the people's religious feelings and their emotional attachment to Rome. They begged the plebeians as Romans not to abandon the temple of Jupiter on the Capitoline hill and the Temple of Vesta in the Forum, the two physical structures that represented Rome as a seat of power and as an eternal home. The Temple of Jupiter Optimus Maximus, which towered above them atop the Capitoline hill, would remind Romans of the republic's founding, and of its destiny to become the capital of the world. In the Temple of Vesta burned the sacred fire tended by the Vestal Virgins, which made it the "hearth and home" of the entire city. As a result of this plea, the proposal to settle Veii was defeated, but just barely. The senators, pleased with their victory, immediately passed a decree that small plots of land be given to the plebs, a signal the senators would reward them for loyalty and obedience.

Despite what seemed to be a peaceful resolution to an issue that caused great domestic turmoil at Rome, Camillus was not spared from the anger of the plebs. He stood firm on his principles, and let it be known to all. He seemed uninterested in playing nice with the plebs or engaging in the compromises that are sometimes necessary in the political arena. In fact, he was as critical of the senators as of the plebs when he felt it necessary. In addition, he did not attempt to maintain a network of political support, which provided necessary defense against political attacks. Because of the way he handled the distribution of the plunder of Veii, and because of his demand that the religious vow he made before Veii's destruction be properly fulfilled, he opened himself up to the charge of being hostile to the poorer citizens at Rome. A tribune of the plebs brought a legal charge against him, claiming he took some bronze doors from Veii for use in his own house. The truth behind the charge was a secondary concern, and legal charges in Rome are usually more about politics than justice. His friends, we are told, offered to help pay any fine imposed on him, but they could not vote for his acquittal, since this would anger the plebeians (their votes would not depend on his actual innocence or guilt). The fact that Camillus ended up in exile suggests he did not have powerful friends willing to expend political capital to help him, which is quite something for the triumphant conqueror of Veii. Camillus bid farewell to his friends and family, and as he left Rome, he turned around and uttered a bitter prayer to the gods: If they agreed he had been treated unjustly, he asked them to make the Romans soon regret what they had done to him and soon realize how much they needed him. With that, the conqueror of Veii turned his back on Rome.

The Gallic Sack of Rome

At the same time Camillus was sent into exile, a plebeian reported to the senate that in the middle of the night he heard a voice, which did not sound human to him, commanding him to tell the senate that the Gauls were coming. The senators did not take the man's report seriously, in part because he was just a common plebeian, and in part because no one knew who the Gauls were. But the Gauls were coming.

The capture of the Capitol in 390 (or 386) BC by a band of marauding Gauls under the leadership of their chieftain Brennus is one of the most dramatic episodes from the first centuries of the republic, in part because later Roman historians presented it as such. Many historians, both Roman and modern, view the sack of Rome as a dividing line in Roman history, not because of any serious damage it did to Rome itself, but because of the changes it brought to the writing of earlier Roman history. It has been presumed the Romans' own historical records were destroyed during the Gauls' occupation of the city, leading to much of the confusion about dates, events, and people from the first two centuries of the republic (including the date of the sack itself). Yet, as with many major events, there is still some question about whether this "sack of Rome" was truly a serious invasion, and how much damage it actually caused. This debate is also fueled by the hints that the Romans did not drive off the Gauls through a dramatic nighttime raid, as in the traditional account, but by a massive payment in gold, essentially a ransom to recover control of their city. Such a conclusion to the Gallic invasion would not sit well with Rome's self-image.

Another question is why the Gauls traveled so far south into Italy, and why they chose Rome as their target, if indeed it was an intentional choice. One story places the blame on an Etruscan man angry that his wife had cheated on him. He had taken in a young orphan and raised him in his home, only to see this young man steal his wife away from him. Seeking to avenge this act of betrayal, he went north to visit the Gauls, whom he had recently heard about, in the hopes of convincing them to attack his city. He introduced the Gauls to wine, and they developed such a liking for this intoxicating beverage that they soon crossed over the Alps and headed south into Italy in search of where it came from. While this story seems too silly to be true, many such stories carry a grain of historical truth within them. In most versions of the Gallic invasion, the Gauls first attacked Clusium, an Etruscan city 90 miles north of Rome (and hometown of Lars Porsenna), though it is not clear what brought them there. The story of the angry husband is sometimes associated with the Gauls' attack on Clusium rather than an earlier migration into northern Italy. Underlying the story may be internal political strife at Clusium, leading one faction (represented by the angry husband) to hire the Gauls as mercenaries in order to defeat the other faction. The family strife of the story substitutes for civil discord.

Frightened by the appearance of the Gauls at their doorstep, the Clusians sent an embassy to the senate at Rome to ask for help, a testament to Rome's preeminence in central Italy after the defeat of Veii. The Romans sent three brothers to the Gauls on a diplomatic mission, and these young ambassadors warned the Gauls not to resort to war, since, if they did, the Romans would come to the aid of Clusium. They suggested that the Gauls and Clusians should instead find a peaceful settlement. The Gauls agreed and asked only that the people of Clusium provide them with some land, since Clusium possessed more territory than its citizens could use. According to an account by the later Greek biographer Plutarch, the Roman embassy asked the Gallic leader Brennus what the Clusians had done to the Gauls to cause them to threaten the city. Plutarch puts in the mouth of Brennus a speech responding to the question, and though the speech is obviously fiction, he makes a compelling case, using Rome's own behavior as part of his argument.

> The Clusians treat us unjustly, because even though they can only farm a small amount of land, they're determined to possess a lot of it and refuse to share any with us, a large band of poor strangers. This is the injustice once committed against you, Romans, by Alba, Fidenae, and Ardea, and also now by Veii, Capena, and many of the Faliscans and Volscians. If they refuse to share with you any of their possessions, you wage war against them, enslave them, plunder them, and raze their cities to the ground. There's nothing wrong with that—you're only following the oldest of human customs, according to which the property of the weaker is given to the stronger. This custom holds true for all, from the gods all the way down to the animals. Even among them it's natural for the stronger to try to possess more than the weaker. Stop feeling sorry for the Clusians we're besieging. Otherwise, you might teach us Gauls to show some sympathy for the people you're oppressing! (Plutarch, *Camillus* 17)

The barbarian Brennus is suspiciously well informed about Roman history, including the conflicts with Alba, Fidenae, Ardea, and the very recent conquest of Veii. He also seems well educated in philosophy, law, and rhetoric. Giving enemies a speech is a common technique in ancient history, aiming not at historical accuracy, but at a presentation of issues the historian considers important to both the past and his own times. In fact, a speech given by an enemy of Rome can serve as a form of indirect criticism of Rome's policies and practices. In this speech, Brennus offers a defense of the Gauls' hostile actions against Clusium using Rome's own aggressive expansion against other peoples. He begins with a philosophical appeal to natural justice, based on the principle that those who have more than they can use should share with those who have less than they need. He claims that the Clusians are violating this principle, and because of this injustice, he argues that the Gauls are in the right to take land from Clusium, since in accordance with another law of nature, the strong dominate the weak. The Romans, he says, also act in accordance with this principle when they oppress others and are not wrong to do so. For this reason, he criticizes the Romans for coming to the defense of Clusium against the Gauls, suggesting it is hypocritical given the Romans' own past actions. He concludes with a veiled threat, suggesting that if the Romans chose to fight on behalf of Clusium because they believed the Gauls would be wrong to attack, then the Gauls would likewise fight Rome in defense of the cities Rome had wrongly attacked. A Roman presented with this speech might find some uncomfortable truths, and perhaps sense in Brennus's words a warning about the consequences of an overly imperialistic policy. Were the Romans, as they extended their powers throughout Italy (and beyond), behaving like the Gauls? And if the Romans believed the Gauls were uncivilized barbarians, were the Romans acting like uncivilized barbarians? This is the type of perspective that history can provide, and Brennus, as a fictionalized historical figure, makes effective use of it.

The behavior of the three Roman ambassadors bears out the underlying message of Brennus's speech. As ambassadors on an official diplomatic mission, they had no authority to engage in any hostile acts. To fight in a war would require the senate's approval, and any hostile action would need to be sanctified by the proper religious ritual. However, in defiance of Rome's own policies and procedures, and contrary to the widely accepted protocols of international diplomacy, the three Romans took up arms in the ensuing battle between Clusium and the Gauls. One of them even kills a Gallic commander. In the words of the Roman historian Livy, they "acted more like Gauls than Romans." Nonetheless, the reaction of the Gauls to this affront was quite civilized. Instead of attacking Rome in anger at their violation of diplomatic norms, they sent their own envoys to Rome to demand that the young Roman ambassadors be handed over to them. The senate believed the Gauls were justified in their demand, and deeply disapproved of the behavior of the Roman envoys. However, because these three brothers were from a prominent family at Rome, the senate issued no decree of its own. Instead, the senate referred the matter to the Plebeian Assembly, which promptly elected the three guilty ambassadors to be military tribunes for the following year. As for the senate, they could at least claim they should not be blamed for the coming war with the Gauls.

Outraged that the young ambassadors not only escaped punishment but were rewarded with election to high political office, the Gauls quickly marched on Rome. At the approach of the Gauls, some Roman troops stationed along the banks of the Allia, a small river that joined the Tiber about 10 miles from Rome, fled in fear with their commanders, not back to Rome, but to Veii. "No one behaved like a Roman," in the words of a Roman historian. The Gauls carried out a massive slaughter of the Roman soldiers who remained. So devastating was the defeat that its anniversary was marked in the calendar as *dies Alliensis*, the "Day of the Allia," and was considered an ill-omened day (*nefastus*) on which no public business could be conducted. Later Romans also knew the phrase *Gallicus tumultus* ("Gallic tumult"), which referred to the declaration of a military emergency when soldiers are conscripted immediately without the usual procedures.

After this catastrophic defeat, the Romans decided to evacuate the city, taking with them the sacred objects from the Temple of Vesta. Younger soldiers, along with their wives and children, formed a garrison atop the Capitol, abandoning the rest of the city below to the invaders. Only during an extreme crisis did the Romans seem to be able to put aside their political wrangling, and at this moment, the older patrician senators and former consuls who could no longer bear arms decided to remain in Rome, prepared to die together with the elderly plebeians. The Gauls entered the near-empty city, wary of the ghostly quiet and fearing an ambush. The elderly nobles, wearing the regalia of their former offices and commands, sat in silence on their ivory chairs, the doors to their houses left open. One story tells of a Gaul entering a house and marveling at the figure seated before him in stony silence, wondering if it might be a statue. To see if this figure was real, he slowly reached out toward this dignified elder statesman and touched his beard, at which he received a bonk on the head from the Roman's ivory cane. With that, slaughter and destruction ensued throughout the Forum as the Romans camped on the Capitol looked on.

Rome's Second Founder: The Return of Camillus

The Gauls were unable to attack the Roman forces on the Capitol given its steep cliffs, so they decided to mount a siege and starve the Roman garrison into submission while they plundered the territory around the city. To obtain supplies, some of the Gauls headed for Ardea, the city that had been besieged by the last king, Tarquinius Superbus. As luck would have it, Ardea was where Camillus had chosen to spend his exile. He told the men of Ardea he would repay their kindness to him by leading them to victory against the Gauls, promising that in battle the Ardeans would slaughter them like lambs, since the Gauls, although fearsome in appearance, were undisciplined. He quickly made good on his promise.

Meanwhile, the Romans who fled to Veii at the arrival of the Gauls had repelled an attack by Etruscan forces hoping to take advantage of Rome's misfortunes and recapture Veii. The Romans' successful defense improved their morale, and their numbers increased as volunteers came from Latium to meet the threat of the Gauls. What they were missing was a proven leader, especially since the older men with experience had been killed in Rome. They decided they needed Camillus, and, just as he had prayed would happen when he left Rome, they sent messengers to Ardea to ask for his help. Camillus agreed to lead the Romans against the Gauls, but since he still held true to his principles, he thought it of utmost importance to follow the proper legal procedures, even in these most dire of circumstances. He was still legally an exile, and the law required that his appointment as dictator be confirmed by the Senate of Rome, which at that time was under siege on the Capitol, surrounded by a horde of Gauls. In order to fulfill the letter of the law, the Romans sent a daring young man on a night-time mission through enemy lines, crossing the Tiber river on cork floats and scaling the heights of the Capitoline hill. The senate then had the Curiate Assembly formally recall Camillus from exile so the senate could legally appoint him a dictator. Then the brave young man had to make it back safely through the Gallic forces to report the decree of the senate to Camillus.

More than anything, this episode is meant to demonstrate the critical importance to Rome's survival of adherence to traditional forms of decision-making and respect for the proper performance of religious and political rituals, even when it might seem foolish to do. It also serves as a warning against deviating from established norms, since doing so creates grave dangers for the entire community, no matter how much an individual may benefit in the short term. Religious and political institutions exist in part to curb the unruly ambitions of both patricians and plebeians, as individuals as well as groups. In this traditional version of the Gallic sack of Rome, extreme measures are taken to ensure all proper legal procedures were followed so Camillus could save Rome. This stands in stark contrast to the behavior of the three young ambassadors, whose disregard of proper procedure sets off the Gallic invasion.

For the Romans, the Gallic invasion was one of their darkest hours as well as one of their greatest comebacks. As a result, the histories of it contain many of the best-known legends of Rome. The end of the Gauls' occupation of Rome under the leadership of Camillus ranks among the most famous. Before Camillus can muster troops to rescue Rome, the Gauls discover a way up to the Capitol, and under the cover of night struggle their way up to the summit. Neither the sentries nor guard dogs notice, but some geese who lived on the Capitol honked and beat their wings at the arrival of the Gauls, alerting the Romans to trouble. The geese were sacred to Juno, and for this reason had not been eaten even though food was in short supply. (Unfortunately, the dogs who failed to sense the intruders were slaughtered as punishment.) The Romans beat off the Gauls under the leadership of Marcus Manlius, earning him the honorific *cognomen* Capitolinus. Yet neither side could declare victory in what was a stalemate, and famine and disease began to affect both sides.

The climax of the Gallic invasion comes when the Romans, unable to hold out against the siege, strike a bargain with the Gauls to pay a large sum of money in exchange for their departure. As the gold is being weighed out on a pair of scales, a Roman complains that the weights do not seem fair. The Gallic chieftain Brennus utters the immortal Latin phrase, *Vae victis*! ("Woe to the conquered!") and throws his sword onto the scale, adding to the weight of gold the Romans must pay. The message is that the conquered should not argue matters of justice with their conquerors. At this moment, Camillus makes a theatrical entrance and saves the Romans from themselves as much as from the Gauls. Camillus stops the payment of the ransom, and when the Gauls protest that an agreement had already been made, Camillus reminds them that only he, as dictator legally appointed by the senate, has the authority to make any binding agreements. In the end, his strict adherence to the laws pays off. He sends the Gallic representative away and orders his men to win back Rome "with iron rather than gold." The Gauls are defeated and killed in quick order, and Camillus is hailed as a second Romulus, founder of Rome and father of his country.

With the existential threat to their city eliminated, the Romans quickly return to political squabbling, and given the condition of Rome after the Gallic occupation, the earlier proposal to abandon Rome and move to Veii resurfaces. Camillus again rises to the occasion, delivering a stirring speech to convince the Romans to hold on to their native city, which includes beautiful praise of the city of Rome (composed by a historian in the first century BC):

> Does the soil of our fatherland and this ground we call our mother mean nothing to us, do our feelings for our native land depend upon its walls and buildings? I take

> no pleasure in recalling the injustice you did to me, but I admit that when I was an exile, every time I thought of my home country, what came to mind were the hills, the fields, the Tiber, this land so familiar to our eyes, this sky under which I was born and raised. Love for all this, Romans, should stir you to remain here where you are, rather than to be tortured with longing for it after you leave. The gods and men chose this place to found a city for good reasons—health-giving hills, an advantageous river that brings us grain from inland and trade from overseas, close enough to the coast for commerce, but not so close that we are exposed to the dangers of foreign fleets, in the center of Italy, a place uniquely created to grow a city. (Livy 5.54)

Camillus's speech carries the day, and the Romans set to work rebuilding their city. According to the traditional account, the construction was undertaken without any planning or coordination, and so the city of Rome took on a jumbled appearance, without any regular layout. In reality, whatever damage the Gauls did to Rome may have been more psychological than physical. No archaeological traces of a Gallic sack have yet been identified. Some may one day be discovered, but Rome did seem to recover remarkably quickly, engaging in major military campaigns within a few years after the Gauls left. Once Rome had taken possession of Veii and its territory, it would have been one of the most powerful cities in all Italy, and the "sack of Rome" did little to stop that, as the rest of Italy was soon to discover.

As important as the sack of Rome is to the history of the republic, the portrait of Camillus that emerges from its history is equally important. He is a Roman leader caught between the plebs and patricians, unable to satisfy either. As a result, he goes into exile rather than compromise his principles. Camillus's exile can be read as criticism of Roman politics in first century BC as well as the fourth century BC. Different groups of citizens—wealthy conservatives, poorer plebeians, arrogant commanders, and aristocratic reformers—can all be criticized for their behavior. From the senatorial perspective, only when Romans find themselves in the most dire of situations—almost too late—do they realize that Rome cannot survive, much less prosper, without leaders such as Camillus. Or, as so often, the story is a reminder to the plebs of their place in the hierarchy and a message to the patricians never to yield.

New Nobles and New Men: The Licinio–Sextian Laws

Camillus's career, according to the traditional account, lasted for another twenty years after the Gallic sack, during which time he was still called on even as an old man to lead the Romans to victory. In one instance, he jumped up from his sickbed where he lay close to death to inspire Roman soldiers who, under the command of a younger man, were fleeing from the enemy. In the last year of his life, still facing intense hostility from the plebs, he prayed to the gods for an end to all the political strife and vowed to build a Temple of Concord. Lo and behold, the next day, despite all the heated arguments between the people and the senate, a compromise was reached. In celebration of this moment of agreement, the people who the day before had been calling for

Camillus's arrest instead voted to build the temple he vowed, cheering him as they followed him home. A Temple of Concord is a nice gesture, but the need to vow one suggests that discord more often has the upper hand.

The issue that created the turmoil and discord in Rome was part of a major reform brought about by the Licinio–Sextian laws of 367 BC. This legislation was the result of agitation that had begun ten years prior, when two tribunes put forward a proposal that at least one of the consuls be a plebeian (there is some debate whether the law meant one consul *had* to be a plebeian or *could* be a plebeian). The patrician senators vehemently opposed this reform, but the people refused to give in. They continued to reelect the two tribunes who made the proposal, Gaius Licinius Stolo and Lucius Sextius Lateranus. Their persistence paid off, and in 367 BC, the legislation was passed. In the year following the passage of the laws, Sextius himself became the first plebeian consul. Like the Valerio–Horatian laws some eighty years earlier, these laws brought about reforms that benefited the plebeians. The earlier laws allowed the plebs some form of representation and protection through the creation of the office of tribune of the plebs and the formation of the Plebeian Assembly. The plebeians had a political voice, one separate but not equal. The Licinio–Sextian legislation, on the other hand, was a first step in opening up existing offices and priesthoods to the plebeians, so that by the end of the fourth century BC, plebeians had access to the structures of power over which the patrician nobility had maintained a firm grip. It was a significant change in the constitution of the republic and altered the make-up of the ruling class at Rome.

Following passage of the Licinio–Sextian laws, several other major pieces of legislation were passed in the last decades of the fourth century, granting plebeians access to the censorship and some of the priesthoods, including the augurs. New offices were created as well, such as the praetor urbanus (initially restricted to patricians) and curule aediles, providing more outlets for ambitious individuals, and increasing the opportunities for advancement into the political elite. Up to this date, appointment to the senate had been made by the censor, who made an official list of the senators every year, and was thus ultimately responsible for senate membership. In practice, this likely meant the same individuals were selected every year, since the censor, as part of the ruling elite, would not want to endanger his own future in the senate by angering anyone in this exclusive club. Near the end of the fourth century BC, however, a law was passed that granted automatic lifetime membership in the senate to anyone who won election to the office of quaestor. At that point, a senator could only be removed by the censor for failure to maintain the requisite level of wealth or for some other failing, moral or criminal. Along with this was the development of the *cursus honorum*, the "ladder of offices," which required that a Roman work his way up through a series of political offices, beginning with the lowest office of quaestor and leading to the consulship. (This law was often ignored, especially for extraordinary individuals, and was reestablished in the first century BC.)

The path was now open to plebeians to join the upper echelons of the Roman aristocracy, and because of this a new plebeian nobility was created. You may recall that "noble" has a specific meaning in Roman history, referring to someone who had an ancestor who had reached the consulship. Now, with the ability to become consul, plebeians could create their own nobility. However, it is worth considering whether this new nobility was drastically different from the old one. Even though plebeian-patrician political conflict is rampant in the opening centuries of the Roman Republic, the plebeians who could realistically aim for election to a political office and membership in the senate, not to mention the rarefied air of the consulship, would already be part of the wealthy elite. These plebeians would likely have more in common with their new patrician colleagues in the senate than they would with the people who worked in the city or on farms and served in the lower ranks of the army. This new nobility was still very restrictive, and it was extraordinarily difficult to be the first member of a family to gain admittance to the senate, much less win election to the consulship. The Romans even had a special term for individuals who were the first in their family to enter the senate, *novus homo* ("new man"), and such individuals were unusual enough throughout the republic to deserve a special term.

Since the Romans liked to consider themselves traditional conservatives, "new" always carried sinister undertones. There was always some concern that a "new" man, who did not have a family history of adherence to traditional norms, might create political disturbances, including *res novae*, "new things," which meant "revolution" to the Romans. The episode of Spurius Maelius discussed in the previous chapter continued the theme of anxiety about monarchy that runs through the republic, but also demonstrates the fear of a wealthy individual acquiring power by means outside the customary political and military channels. The motives of politicians who sought to solve a problem by assisting the plebs always came under suspicion, and they often found themselves accused of acting like Maelius, even if they were not stockpiling weapons. On the other hand, the story of Spurius Maelius also served as a warning to the patricians. If wealthy plebeians could not find an outlet for their ambitions within the framework of the republic, they might attempt to find alternative means to satisfy them.

As the traditional history of the early Roman Republic reveals, the primary tension at play in Roman politics was between a small ruling elite and the rest of the citizen body. Even if the ruling nobility expanded to include plebeians as well as patricians, the fundamental divide remained. In one sense, the creation of a patrician-plebeian nobility in the fourth century BC was a means by which the more powerful plebeians were coopted into the elite and could be used to further maintain a rigid hierarchy rather than break it down. In the traditional view of the Romans and the ancient world in general, the upper classes, in addition to being wealthier, were unquestionably wiser and more suited to be the leading members of society. It was, in this view, simply a matter of "better" birth. On the other hand, these individuals were more prone to corrupt and arrogant behavior, particularly in their treatment of the lower classes. The plebeians were recognized for their important service to the state, and as valuable citizens who deserved fair treatment—though what was considered fair was a matter for debate. At the same time, the common people were considered fickle and emotional, easily swayed from one extreme to another, especially by unscrupulous nobles who wished to use them for their own political ambitions. In the view of many patricians, most plebeians could not take a long-term view of things, and complex realities were simply beyond their understanding. The poor masses of Rome, in the eyes of patricians, only considered the short term, and were unable to consider the consequences of political decisions. In short, they were not to be trusted because of their inconstancy. It was better for Rome if they obeyed their superiors. Their attitude was one of condescension, but we must remember, as repugnant as it might sound to our ears, it was the world into which they were born and raised. That some people are better than others by birth seemed normal, natural, and traditional, to the extent that even the institution of slavery went unquestioned for centuries.

Appius Claudius Caecus

One of the major figures of this period deserves special mention, not only for his accomplishments and character, but because to many scholars he is the first genuinely historical personality in Roman history. A descendant of the wicked decemvir in the story of Verginia, this Appius had a much different reputation. Despite his patrician background, he is known as a reformer, who went so far as to enroll the descendants of freed slaves into the senate. This is likely an exaggeration, something his political opponents would accuse him of in order to magnify the dangers of his reforms to the traditional order. He became censor in 312 BC, which was somewhat unusual since he had not held any other high office, but his censorship was notable for some remarkable accomplishments. He exercised his authority to extend the influence of the plebeian lower classes in elections and excluded some individuals of higher status from the senate, judging them on the basis of merit rather than family background. He was also revered by later Romans for his stern morality, and as an example of proper Roman conduct. However, though Appius is a historical figure, he is nonetheless prone to being romanticized as a democratic reformer and champion of the plebs. Despite the efforts he made on behalf of plebeians and the lower classes, he also opposed plebeian eligibility for some priesthoods.

FIG. 4.4 A section of the Via Appia.

As the censor who oversaw their construction, his name was attached to two major public works, the famed Via Appia (or Appian Way), remains of which can still be traveled today, and the Aqua Appia, the first aqueduct in Rome. While both of these works were of great benefit to the city of Rome, the Appian Way in particular had a strategic use. It was likely part of a larger policy advocated by Appius of establishing colonies elsewhere in Italy. These settlements offered poorer Romans the chance to obtain their own land in a new community, and also served as an extended buffer of military garrisons throughout Italy.

While Appius can be lauded for the material benefits he brought to the larger population of Rome, he still upheld the expansionist view of Rome's power, for which the plebeians were a necessary foundation. He may have had Roman glory more in mind than the quality of life of the plebeians, but he recognized more than others their role in contributing to Rome's military glory. He earned the *cognomen* Caecus ("Blind") because he was carried into the senate as a frail and blind old man so that he could argue against Rome's making peace with a Greek king who threatened an invasion into southern Italy.

Appius's importance to the history of Rome is as much about what he became as what he truly was. His intentions and motivations are deduced by reasoning backward from his actions, a slippery process that allows him to be claimed by both democratic idealists and traditional conservatives. Appius could in one view be regarded as a reform-minded politician who supported popular causes, but others might see in his actions an underlying conservative view of the Roman plebs as useful instruments for Roman expansion. In reality, he was likely a thoughtful and complex individual, but real historical figures are often reduced by later historians to simplified versions of a political platform.

Rome's Continued Conquest of Italy: Samnites and Latins

While the reforms of the fourth century BC brought drastic changes to the landscape of political life at Rome, conflicts with other peoples of Italy did not cease. Over the course of the last decades of the century Rome gradually brought the rest of central Italy under its control. During this period, Rome engaged in a series of wars with some of its fiercest enemies. In the 340s BC, Rome renewed the treaty it made in 509 with Carthage, the powerful trading city on the north coast of Africa, and also came to terms with the Samnites, a people related to the Sabines who inhabited the mountains of central Italy. In terms of territory and population they were more than Rome's equal. While we often consider a treaty a sign of the end of hostilities, often it instead indicates that serious tensions exist, and the treaty merely delays the outbreak of open warfare—a peace treaty is sometimes war by other means. This is certainly the case with the Samnites and Carthaginians, who were two of the greatest military threats to Rome. War with the Samnites broke out almost immediately after their treaty with Rome, while the first war against Carthage would come later, in part because it lay across the sea at some distance from Rome. The opening of hostilities with the Samnites coincided with the final defeat of the Latin League in 338 BC. As mentioned, Rome had made a treaty with the Latin League shortly after the founding of the republic. Whether the treaty had lapsed or Rome simply ignored it, war soon broke out, perhaps because the Latins had felt a sense of betrayal when Rome concluded a peace treaty with the Samnites in 341 BC. The result of this brief war was the end of the Latin League. Henceforth

FIG. 4.5 Italy in the fourth c. BC.

the Latin communities had to make individual agreements with Rome and were forbidden from making agreements with one another. All of their dealings had to go through Rome.

The next obstacle in Rome's expansion into southern Italy were the Samnites, who were organized into a federation of four tribes, sometimes known as the Samnite League. Rome fought a series of wars against them, lasting from 343 until 275 BC, when the Samnite League was dissolved by Rome. Aside from marking a major development in Rome's conquest of Italy, the wars are best known for Rome's humiliating defeat at the Battle of the Caudine Forks in 321, during the Second Samnite War, sometimes known as the Great Samnite War. On their march into Samnite territory, without any guides, the Romans found themselves trapped in a narrow ravine surrounded by Samnite troops. There was no escape. Recognizing the hopelessness of their position, the Roman commanders decided after some hesitation to surrender, since they believed if their army was completely annihilated, then Rome itself would soon be lost as well. The Samnites themselves were unsure what to do with their overwhelming advantage, so they asked the aged father of their general for advice. He advised them to let the Romans go away unharmed. They rejected this surprising suggestion, and so they asked him again. This time, he responded that they should kill every single Roman, leaving no survivors. Baffled, they asked him to explain why he proposed two completely opposite courses of action. The general's father explained there was no middle course with the Romans. If the Samnites forced the Romans to surrender and come to terms, it would only be a matter of time before the Romans, filled with shame, would return to make the Samnites pay for their humiliation many times over. The only other option was to wipe them out completely. Ignoring his advice, the Samnites forced the Romans to surrender in a degrading way. Every single Roman soldier, from the consul down to the lowliest foot soldier, was stripped of everything except a single piece of clothing. Each one of them was then "sent beneath the yoke." This was a recognized form of surrender, used by the Romans as well as other peoples, in which two spears were set in the ground with a third placed horizontally between them. This was the "yoke," and defeated soldiers were then forced to pass through it with nothing but the single garment they were left with.

The father of the Samnite general was correct, of course. After the consuls and soldiers returned to Rome in shame, they attempted to make good their disgrace with a proposal to the senate. They offered to be sent back to the Samnites bound and naked and would accept the blame for agreeing to a surrender that the senate did not officially recognize. Rome could then resume the war without violating any formal agreement with the Samnites. The consul in command of the Roman forces had given the Samnites a formal promise, for which he himself was responsible. If the senate did not agree to the terms of surrender he had personally accepted, he would be expected to keep his promise and give himself up to the Samnites as a prisoner. This consul actually argued that the senate should not to accept the surrender he had negotiated, and in accordance with his own proposal, he was escorted bound and naked back to the Samnite general by a fetial priest (fetial priests were responsible for making treaties as well as declarations of war and peace). As he was being handed over to the enemy, he cried "I am a Samnite citizen!" and with his hands still tied behind his back he kneed the Roman priest in the thigh. This was a feeble attempt to provide the Romans with a justification to restart the war against the Samnites, since an assault by a Samnite against a Roman priest on a diplomatic mission would be an unacceptable violation of protocol and grounds for war. Though the consul was now a prisoner of the Samnites, he certainly was no citizen, and the Samnite general was having none of it. He even accused the Romans of never keeping their word in defeat, using the Gallic sack of Rome as an example. He claimed that after the Romans had agreed to pay the Gauls to leave Rome, they instead cut the Gauls down as the gold was being weighed. (A very different history from the Roman one!)

Armed conflict with the Samnites would continue for another forty years. Finally, in 295 BC the Romans handed them a major defeat at the Battle of Sentinum, from which the Samnites never fully recovered. The defeat was all the more deflating because the Samnites had allied themselves with Gauls, Etruscans, and the Umbrians, an Italian people of central Italy just north of Samnium. The ability of the Romans to defeat the combined forces of these peoples on different fronts was proof of their power and strength. Appius Claudius Caecus was one of the Roman commanders in this war and fought the Etruscans in the north, but the hero of the Battle of Sentinum was Publius Decius Mus, who sacrificed his life during the battle in a ritual known as *devotio*. "Devotion" in this context means to offer oneself as a sacrifice to the gods by rushing headlong into the enemy lines, where death is certain. The spoken formula necessary to carry out a ritual "devotion" is preserved by a Roman historian:

> Janus, Jupiter, Father Mars, Quirinus, Bellona, Lures, new gods, native gods, gods who have power over us and our enemies, and gods of the Underworld! I bow down and worship you, I ask for your favor and beg you: Make prosperous the conquering power of the Roman people, the Quirites, and strike the enemies of the Roman people, the Quirites, with terror, dread, and death! As I have uttered this prayer, on behalf of the Republic of the Roman nation of Quirites, and of the army, the legions, and auxiliary troops of the Roman nation of Quirites, I hereby devote myself and together with me the legions and auxiliary troops of our enemies to the gods of the Underworld and to Earth. (Livy 9.3)

This ritual self-sacrifice is an act of political and religious piety that guarantees a Roman victory and serves as a future example of placing the greater good above one's own self-interest, even above one's life. Publius Decius Mus was not the first example of a Roman soldier carrying out a *devotio* in battle. In fact, his ritual devotion at the Battle of Sentinum is a suspicious repetition of his father's a generation earlier during the war against the Latin League. But even though the historical truth of these "devotions" is questionable, the extension of Roman control over Italy is not. The incorporation of Samnite territory in particular brought Rome into contact with the Greek communities of southern Italy (the area known as Magna Graecia), which will lead shortly to Rome's first military conflict with forces from mainland Greece, a major step in its military and political involvement with states across the waters of the Mediterranean.

Colonies and "Romanization"

As Rome extended its influence over the rest of Italy, they certainly did not have the manpower to place military garrisons throughout the Italian peninsula. However, by enlarging their territory through conquest and incorporating defeated communities into the republic, they also increased the number of citizen soldiers available to them. One way of increasing the size of their military forces was to grant citizenship to conquered peoples, bringing these new members into their state. These individuals would thus identify, at least in a legal sense, as Romans. While grants of citizenship may sound like a nice gesture to a conquered people, it was not always welcome to the communities that received it, and in some cases citizenship was forced on them. Aside from the obligation to serve in the military, there was the additional burden of taxation, which helped to pay for the wars the citizens had to fight in. Moreover, the grant of citizenship and incorporation into the Roman state meant a loss of independence. These new Roman communities might in practice still govern themselves on a day-to-day basis, but they were ultimately subject to the authority of the senate and people of Rome.

At the same time, Roman citizenship carried many advantages, not least the protection under the laws and the right of appeal, even against a Roman senator. As a result, a local official might think twice about engaging in corrupt practices, since there was at least a chance he might have to suffer the consequences from a higher authority in Rome. There were a few different forms of Roman citizenship, and full Roman citizenship came with the right to vote. Of course, the practical matter of travel to Rome to vote during an election would make this right meaningless in the majority of cases, especially for a member of one of the lower property classes, for whom the vote would count for very little. But wealthy and ambitious individuals from Italian communities that acquired Roman citizenship could, in theory, seek their fortunes in Rome, and perhaps even climb their way up the *cursus honorum*.

In addition to converting existing communities, Rome also created colonies, by sending out citizens to found a new community. Colonies were often placed in strategic locations, serving as a defensive outpost against any encroachment into Roman territory. In fact, one of the sources of friction between Rome and the Samnites was Rome's establishment of colonies on the border of Samnite territory. These colonies not only helped to secure Roman interests throughout Italy, they also provided an outlet for disaffected plebeians at Rome, who would be given a plot of land to farm. In addition to providing an economic benefit to these colonists, the problem of plebeian unrest at Rome itself would be diminished. Many of these colonists would also be military veterans, useful in the case of military conflicts far from the city of Rome.

Both grants of citizenship and the establishment of colonies promoted Roman interests throughout Italy. Since all of the paths to power and prestige eventually led to Rome, the culture of these areas, especially among the elite, would become more and more Roman, in a process known as "Romanization." In some cases, this would occur through assimilation, since Italians who hoped to benefit from Roman power and prestige would try to look and act more like those in power at Rome. They might hope that their children would be educated at Rome, speak "proper" Latin, and maybe even one day become someone important in the great capital. A young man from a town in central Italy with a good education might become a prominent lawyer or a Roman senator, elevating himself and his descendants. Such individuals, of course, would be all the more willing to assimilate themselves to Roman ways of thinking and behaving, and might even lose their native accent to sound less rustic when speaking at Rome. Others, of course, would not be so eager to adopt Roman forms of behavior and might resist having to conform to a people they saw as an occupying power. "Romanization" would eventually predominate, but under the surface remained powerful resentments. These would one day explode into a revolt.

The Roman Army

One of the images that first springs to many minds upon hearing "Ancient Rome" is a bare-armed burly man wearing a crested helmet and gold-chased breastplate, a broad sword hanging along his thigh atop a skirt of leather armor, shod in standard-issue Roman sandals. This image, found in many movies and television shows, is not representative of a typical soldier of the republic, but neither is it completely false. The reason for its prevalence in the popular imagination is the fundamental importance of the military to Roman history, which can sometimes seem like little more than a long catalog of wars and battles. The arts of war (and occasionally peace) were essential to the Romans' view of themselves. In the *Aeneid*, the legendary hero Aeneas has the opportunity to visit his deceased father in the underworld. His father gives him a glimpse of Rome's future, and tells him what will define the Romans:

> Other people will hammer out bronze
> that seems to gently breathe, bring life
> to faces of marble. They will
> excel us as lawyers, map with
> better skill a planet's movements,
> predict the risings of heaven's stars.
> But remember, Roman, you will
> rule over nations with might—
> these are your arts: to make peace the law,
> show mercy to the defeated,
> and battle down the arrogant. (*Aeneid* 8.847-854)

The Romans are willing to yield pride of place in the arts and sciences—sculpture and painting, law and rhetoric, mathematics and astronomy—to other peoples, especially the Greeks. But the particular "Roman arts" will be those of war and peace, and for these the army was essential. For the Romans, peace (Latin *pax*) came through strength, and *pax* often meant forceful pacification through overwhelming military might rather than a condition of harmonious coexistence. A Roman historian of the first century AD puts in the mouth of a Briton fighting against Rome a devastating comment on Romans as "peace-makers." As often, it sounds better in Latin:

> *ubi solitudinem faciunt, pacem appellant.*
>
> They create a wasteland and they call this "peace." (Tacitus, *Agricola* 30)

Rome was in many ways a militaristic society, and though this can often be exaggerated, there can be no question that the military was one of the bedrocks of Roman civilization. Every male citizen was obligated to serve, and military service was a formative education, and sometimes their only education. Each year there would be a levy of soldiers on the Capitol at Rome, and as Rome expanded levies would be held in cities elsewhere. Eligible citizens would show up for the possibility of being selected for service. Once selected, the soldier would swear an oath (*sacramentum*) "to follow the consul wherever I am called, to neither desert the standard nor do anything contrary to the law." The maximum length of required service was 16 years for infantry and 10 years for cavalry, though it is better to speak in terms of the number of campaign seasons, rather than calendar years. When wars were fought closer to Rome, the campaign season was March to October, and thus soldiers could return home for the winter and take care of the harvest and planting if need be. When wars were fought farther afield, soldiers would remain in winter quarters. For much of the republic, a soldier could expect to spend six continuous years in active service, and soldiers could volunteer to serve more than the required number. Young men from elite families would often be assigned to serve an internship of sorts with a commander, who was usually a friend, relative, or political associate of the boy's father. Most of our information about soldiers comes from the upper classes, who were commanders and officers, so the life of the poorer foot soldiers who carried out most of the fighting and suffered the majority of casualties is not well known.

For most of the republic, a Roman citizen-soldier was expected to provide his own equipment, and the wealthier an individual, the more he was expected to provide. The census attributed to the king Servius Tullius, which divided Romans into property classes for voting, is based on the original military classifications of the armaments an individual could afford. The highest class was the cavalry, the "equestrian order," because owning and maintaining a horse was expensive, and only the very wealthy could afford them. The other classes were based on the pieces of armor used by a typical soldier. A member of the first property class, just below the cavalry, was required to provide a bronze cuirass (breastplate), a spear, a sword, a shield, and greaves (shin guards). The second class provided all the same equipment except the breastplate, then the third also omitted the greaves, and the fourth only had to provide spear and shield. The fifth class only used slingshots. The poorest Roman citizens, the *capite censi* ("counted by head," since they had no wealth to count), were exempt from military service, except in extreme emergencies, often following a catastrophic defeat. In such an emergency, slaves might be offered freedom in exchange for serving in the infantry. Within each class were the *juniores* (younger), aged 17–45 and *seniores* (older), 46 and older, though Romans were generally exempted from military service at age 60. However, there are examples of commanders serving beyond that age, and the general Marius, whom you will meet later, was still active in the military in his 80s. The *juniores* went out on campaign, while *seniores* would remain in Rome as a reserve force to defend the city.

Sources claim pay for soldiers was first introduced at the siege of Veii (406–396 BC), though this is uncertain. However, a soldier's pay, called a *stipendium*, was initially meant to cover expenses rather than provide a salary. Cavalry, the wealthiest members of the army, were paid three times the infantry, to cover the cost of maintaining a horse. Soldiers could expect a share of plunder from a victory, and later some Roman commanders offered additional pay from their own pockets to secure loyalty. A major change occurred near the end of the first century BC, when the property qualification to serve was removed, a change attributed to the Roman general Marius. The minimum level had already been reduced significantly, so it is difficult to gauge the true effect of this change, and the professionalization of the army, making the army a viable career, had begun around 200 BC.

The army was organized into legions, from a Latin word meaning "to select" (*lego*). A legion was between 3000–6000 soldiers, with 4500 being a standard number. Even these numbers can be misleading, however, since soldiers provided by Rome's allies (known as *auxilia*, "auxiliaries") would often be attached in units of 500 soldiers to a legion, adding to their size. For a legion of 4500 men, 3000 would be infantry from the first four property classes, and 1200 would be the light-armed skirmishers from the lowest class. There were an additional 300 cavalry. The consuls were usually commanders, and sometimes praetors, since these were the offices that possessed *imperium*. Anyone who did not hold these offices would have to be given consular or praetorian authority, as a "proconsul" or "propraetor," in order to command an army. At first, the Roman army consisted of two legions, one for each consul. By the end of the fourth century BC, this was doubled to four, and as Rome increasingly fought wars outside of Italy and across the Mediterranean, the legions gradually increased in number, reaching 28 in total by the end of the republic.

FIG. 4.6 A coin from 32 BC showing legionary standards, with the eagle (*aquila*) in the middle.

Each legion had a standard, which consisted of a banner and other decorations placed atop a long pole to be visible to others. Metal discs may have been used to identify the number of the legion, and standards often displayed one of five animals at the top: boar, horse, lion, wolf, or eagle. By the first century BC, the eagle (*aquila*) was the norm, and the soldier responsible for carrying the standard was the *aquifer*, "eagle-bearer." These standards were treated with peculiar reverence, and to lose them was a major disgrace. Note that the military oath quoted above specifically mentions deserting the standard. If the standards were lost, the Romans would sometimes go to great lengths to recover them. At the Battle of Lake Regillus, the commander is said to have hurled the standards into the enemy in an act of desperation, knowing that the soldiers would charge into the enemy line to recover them. Near the end of the republic, the Romans suffered a catastrophic defeat at the hand of the Parthians, a people from modern-day Iran. The commander, one of the most prominent Romans of his age, was killed along with his son, but the real disgrace was the capture of the legionary standards by the enemy. Twenty years later, it was considered a great achievement when these were recovered through negotiation.

The tactics, organization, and equipment of the army changed over the centuries, and much of our evidence comes from the imperial period. During the early republic, we are not well informed about the organization of a legion, but we have evidence that by the third century BC, perhaps as early as the years following the Gallic invasion, Rome had developed a system of "maniples." A maniple was a group of soldiers consisting of one or two "centuries." Despite its name, a century was usually 60 men. These maniples were deployed in three lines, each line consisting of ten maniples. In the front line were the *hastati* ("armed with a spear"), who were younger and less experienced soldiers. The second line was made of soldiers in the prime of life, late twenties to mid-thirties, called the *principes*. In the last line were the older and more experienced troops, the *triarii*. Survival to that age was no easy task for any Roman, much less a soldier. Apart from these three battle lines were the *velites*, the youngest of the soldiers. Equipped for speed, they had no armor except a small wicker shield and a helmet covered in wolf skin. They carried throwing javelins and a short sword. Cavalry units would be placed on either side of the legion, and for this reason were referred to as *alae* ("wings").

As they did in other areas, the Romans adopted military equipment and techniques from other peoples. The earliest forms of the famous Roman legions were probably borrowed from the Greeks, likely via the Etruscans. Early on, no later than the end of the third century BC, they also adopted the shorter "Spanish sword," which remained standard equipment for Roman soldiers throughout the republic. As Rome grew from an Italian power to a Mediterranean one, they also made use of the particular skills of peoples who were their allies. Our sources frequently refer to Cretan archers, Balearic slingers (from islands off the coast of Spain), and Numidian cavalry (from North Africa).

Roman soldiers could be awarded various military decorations, usually in the form of a wreath worn as a crown (*corona*). The laurel wreath was worn by victorious commanders and became on its own a symbol of victory. Other wreaths were awarded on the basis of acts of bravery, such as being the first to scale the walls of an enemy city, being the first to board an enemy ship, and saving a citizen's life. There were also a variety of minor military awards, such as a gold choker (*torques*), armbands (*armillae*), and metal disks attached to breastplates (*phalerae*), all forerunners of modern military insignia, ribbons, and medals.

Credits

Fig. 4.1: Source: https://www.nationalgalleries.org/art-and-artists/140798/furius-camillus-liberating-rome-brennus.

Fig. 4.2: Copyright © by rjdeadly (CC BY-SA 4.0) at https://commons.wikimedia.org/wiki/File:-Temple_of_Apollo,_Veii.jpg.

Fig. 4.3: Source: https://gallica.bnf.fr/ark:/12148/btv1b69440859.item.

Fig. 4.4: Copyright © 2014 Depositphotos/cafelab.
Fig. 4.5: Adapted from d-maps.com.
Fig. 4.6: Copyright © by Classical Numismatic Group. Reprinted with permission.

CHAPTER 5

Troubles Next Door

Rome in the Mediterranean

FIG. 5.1 Pyrrhus, king of Epirus. The image on the right is a lightning bolt, though it does not look like one. The Greek text, BASILEOS PYRROU, means "of king Pyrrhus."

Overview

After the Battle of Sentinum in 295 BC, Rome was the preeminent power on the Italian peninsula and exerted control over most peoples south of the Alps. But their military dominance did not pass unnoticed by others around the Mediterranean. Rome endured an invasion from one of the Greek kingdoms that arose following the death of Alexander the Great in 323 BC, and engaged in two difficult wars with Carthage, the great commercial power on the north coast of Africa, including their first military campaign outside the boundaries of Italy. Their wars with Carthage presented a serious threat to their existence, especially the second, when the great general Hannibal crossed the Alps and invaded Italy. After their hard-fought victories brought new territories under their control, the Romans developed a system of provinces to govern its growing empire. This chapter concludes a description of the Roman triumph.

Timeline

295	The Battle of Sentinum
280–275	Pyrrhus invades Italy
264–241	First Punic War against Carthage
237	Sardinia and Corsica become the first Roman province
218–201	Second Punic War and the invasion of Italy by Hannibal

Greece Comes to Italy: The Invasion of Pyrrhus

Rome's dominance of Italy after the defeat of the Samnites and the victory over the combined forces of Gauls, Etruscans, and other peoples of Italy at the Battle of Sentinum in 295 BC did not result in a period of peace. On the contrary, it merely brought Rome into closer contact with more powerful and well-established cities and kingdoms beyond the borders of Italy. This is a process that will continue over the generations to come, as Rome's military expansion never results in a settled state of fixed boundaries, but draws Rome further into the complex politics of the Mediterranean. (The drawing of national boundaries is a much later development.) As Rome's military reach extended outward, there is a corresponding flow back to Rome of wealth and culture from the conquered regions, and the influences from abroad will present Rome with a challenge to its identity.

The Greek cities of southern Italy, the area known as Magna Graecia, had much closer ties to the Greek mainland, which was a short sail across the narrow opening of the Adriatic Sea that separates the east coast of Italy, the heel of the "boot," from the coastline of modern-day Albania and Greece. These independent cities, originally colonies founded by mainland Greek cities, had their own conflicts with one another, but they had not engaged in any serious dealings with Rome itself until Rome's conquest of the Italic peoples who were their immediate neighbors. Once Rome came into prominence in southern Italy, however, it was almost inevitable that Rome would get drawn into the politics of Magna Graecia, mainland Greece, and beyond.

In 282 BC, one of the major cities of Magna Graecia, Thurii, was under attack by the Lucanians, an Italic people who spoke the now extinct language of Oscan. The Thurians appealed to Rome for assistance, probably something they would not have done prior to Rome's victory over the Samnites at Sentinum. The other cities of Magna Graecia were wary of Rome's military involvement right next door and would understandably be concerned that Roman help for Thurii would be a first step to further Roman encroachment on their independence. One of these cities, Tarentum, was a former colony of Sparta founded in the eighth century BC, not long after Rome's own founding. It was a major commercial port and had grown into the wealthiest and most powerful of the Greek cities in southern Italy. In fact, in the fourth century BC, the powerful north African city of Carthage had formed an alliance with some Etruscan cities to check Tarentum's increasing power. Tarentum itself had engaged in military conflicts with neighboring Italic peoples, including the Samnites and Lucanians, and on occasion sought help for these wars from Greek rulers in Sicily and western Greece. A Roman military presence in Thurii, located across the Gulf of Tarentum (the instep of the boot of Italy), would be unwelcome to the Tarentines. It would also draw Rome into the complex political situation of the region. When Rome decided to support Thurii and placed military garrisons both there and in other nearby cities, Tarentum sought to avoid all-out conflict by signing a nonaggression pact with Rome. This pact set defined limits within which each state could operate without posing a threat to the other. One of the provisions of this treaty was that Roman ships would not sail into the Gulf of Tarentum. However, not long after the treaty was signed, a Roman commander sailed into

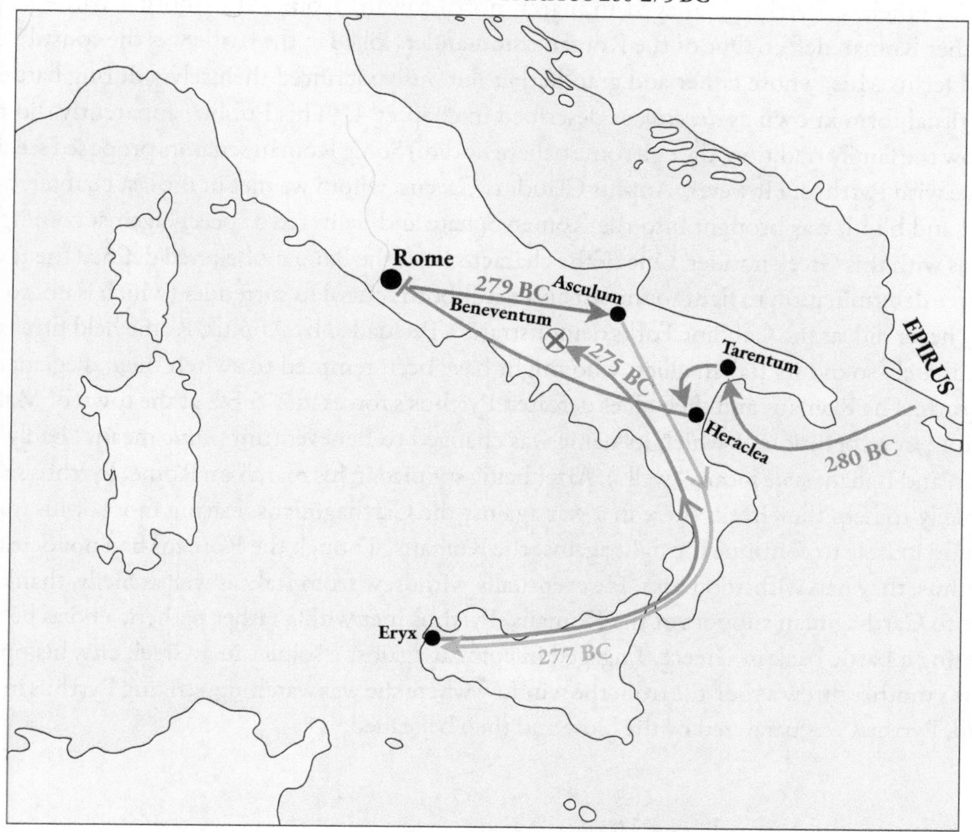

FIG. 5.2 Map of Pyrrhus's invasion.

the gulf with a small force. The Tarentines attacked it, sinking four ships and killing the Roman commander. For good measure, they also expelled the Roman soldiers from Thurii. Recognizing that the Romans would respond in kind, the Tarentines did as they had done in their previous conflicts with neighboring peoples and sought help from a Greek ruler. In this case, they called on Pyrrhus, king of Epirus, a land on the coast of the Adriatic (now part of modern-day Albania and Greece). Pyrrhus was a distant relative of Alexander the Great, a relationship he advertised, and ruled over one of the kingdoms that contended for supremacy and survival in the eastern Mediterranean after Alexander's death. Pyrrhus had his own ambitions to expand his empire, and thus readily answered the summons from the Tarentines. He set sail for Italy in 280 BC with a military force that included elephants—the first time the Romans would encounter them on the battlefield. Pyrrhus fought the Romans in several fierce battles, and though he emerged as the victor every time, his losses were so heavy that he supposedly exclaimed, "One more victory like that and we've lost!" His sentiment lives on today in the expression "Pyrrhic victory," meaning a victory that comes at such a heavy cost it is really more of a defeat.

Nonetheless, Pyrrhus managed to march north toward Rome, and another battle led to another Roman defeat. One of the Roman commanders killed in the battle was the consul Publius Decius Mus, whose father and grandfather famously sacrificed themselves during battle in the ritual form known as *devotio*, as described in chapter 4. (This Publius apparently did not follow the family tradition, though some believe he did.) Some Roman senators proposed seeking peace with Pyrrhus. However, Appius Claudius Caecus, whom we met in the last chapter, now aged and blind, was brought into the Roman Senate and delivered a speech against coming to terms with this Greek invader. One of the characteristics the Romans believed defined them was a fierce determination to fight to the last and a stubborn refusal to surrender (which is not to say they never did, as the Caudine Forks demonstrates). Persuaded by Appius, Rome held firm, and fortunately so did its Italian allies, who might have been tempted to switch their allegiance to Pyrrhus. The Romans and their allies defeated Pyrrhus's forces in 275 BC at the town of Maleventum, in recognition of which its name was changed to Beneventum (*male* means "badly" in Latin and Italian; *bene* means "well"). After being stymied in his march on Rome, Pyrrhus sailed to Sicily to help the Greeks there in a war against the Carthaginians, leaving most of his forces behind in Italy to continue the fight against the Romans. Though the Romans had not defeated Pyrrhus, they had withstood him. He eventually withdrew from Italy as well as Sicily, thanks in part to Carthaginian support of the Romans. Pyrrhus met with a rather pathetic end as he was fighting a battle back in Greece. Engaged in combat against a soldier in a Greek city, his opponent's mother threw a roof-tile from the window where she was watching, striking Pyrrhus in the head. Pyrrhus was paralyzed by the blow and then beheaded.

Carthage and the First Punic War

Nothing brings people together like a common foe, and even the bitterest of enemies will sometimes cooperate, at least temporarily, if it is in their mutual interest. As Rome was drawn into deeper engagement with other Mediterranean powers, such shifting political and military allegiances, based on temporary advantage, will play an important role in the relations between Rome and other peoples. Carthage, a port city on the coast of North Africa at the site of modern-day Tunis (capital of Tunisia), had been founded as a Phoenician colony in 814 BC. Over the centuries it had grown into an independent and powerful city, the dominant commercial power in the western Mediterranean. It was a short sail to Sicily and southern Italy, but the Carthaginians had inherited the Phoenician expertise in sailing, and their trading contacts extended throughout the Mediterranean and beyond, reaching as far as England, and likely down the west coast of Africa. We know the form of their government, at least as it was constituted in the fourth century BC, because the Greek philosopher (and tutor of Alexander the Great) Aristotle provides a brief account of it. Similar to the Roman Republic, Carthage had both a senate and a popular assembly, along with elected generals and other magistracies. The highest elected officials were two *suffetes*, elected annually, just like Rome's consuls. There was also a "supreme court" with 104 members. Like Rome, their government was dominated by a small group of wealthy families who competed for power and prestige. Unlike Rome, however, Carthage had not extended its citizen body through grants of citizenship and did not have a large base of manpower to supply its army or navy, and it thus had to rely on mercenaries, many of whom were from overseas, including Italy.

Carthage was no stranger to Rome, and we know of a treaty between the two dating from 509 BC, the year the republic was founded. There are records of other treaties, including one from 279 BC when Carthage assisted Rome in the war against Pyrrhus. Carthage had a particular interest in Sicily, so this agreement with Rome was at the moment beneficial to both parties, who wanted to drive out of the island a Greek force that had designs on Italy as well as Sicily. Once the threat of Pyrrhus was eliminated, the Carthaginian claim to Sicily would eventually bring them into conflict with Rome. Just as Rome was forced to confront Pyrrhus when drawn into a conflict between two smaller powers in southern Italy, so too would a minor struggle in Sicily lead them to war against Carthage.

A group of mercenaries from Campania, the region in Italy just south of Rome, had fought against the Carthaginians in Sicily for the Greek city of Syracuse, one of the wealthiest and most powerful cities in the western Mediterranean. These mercenaries, however, went rogue and took over the city of Messana on the tip of the east coast of Sicily, separated from the toe of Italy by a narrow body of water, the Straits of Messana. They expelled the citizens from Messana, executing some of them, and began to conduct raids on the surrounding communities. Syracuse was not from far Messana, and its king did not look on these raids favorably. He thus sent a force to drive the mercenaries away. The mercenaries, calling themselves Mamertines, were apparently of two minds about how to confront the forces sent from Syracuse, and so sent delegations to both Rome and to Carthage to ask for help. The Carthaginians acted first, since they already had a naval force in the area, and stationed their own soldiers in Messana to help defend it against the Greek forces sent by Syracuse. In the meantime, the Roman Senate was deliberating whether to send their own troops in response to the Mamertines' plea for assistance. Opposed to sending aid were senators who thought the Mamertines had acted unjustly by seizing Messana and committing other crimes. To lend them military support would not be in accordance with Roman ideals. In favor were senators less concerned with the possible stain on Rome's reputation, and instead gave more weight to the strategic value of Messana's location. Moreover, if the Carthaginians moved first and took control of Messana, they would pose a serious threat to Roman interests in Sicily, and a major rival of Rome would have a foothold just off the coast of Italy. Carthage already had control of Corsica and Sardinia, the two large islands off the west coast of Italy, as well as a strong presence along the southern coast of Spain, whose natural resources, including silver mines, supplied Carthage with revenue. It would not be unreasonable for Rome to feel as if they were slowly being surrounded from the west and south by the other major power in the region.

The Romans were also in a bind because at this same time a similar situation had arisen in the town of Rhegium, situated on the toe of Italy directly across the narrow strait from Messana. The people of Rhegium had feared an attack by Pyrrhus on land and by Carthage from the sea, and had thus appealed to Rome for help. The Romans sent a force of some 4000 soldiers,

Campanian allies under the command of a Campanian. However, this force took control of Rhegium, expelling or executing its citizens. The Romans at first did not react, occupied as they were with fighting Pyrrhus, but eventually they recaptured Rhegium. Most of the allied soldiers who had unjustly seized Rhegium died while fighting against the Romans, knowing that their punishment would be severe, but three hundred were captured. The Roman consuls had them brought to the Forum, where they were flogged and beheaded. As the second-century BC Greek historian Polybius reports, the Romans inflicted this harsh punishment in order to recover "their reputation for keeping good faith with the allies." Since the Mamertines had now done the same thing, the Romans might be expected to treat them with the same standard of justice. At the very least, they should not help them.

As so often, the harsh political, military, and economic realities of the situation won out over any appeals to ideals of justice and honor. The Romans, as so many other peoples, liked to think of themselves as upholding a strict moral code in all that they did, and integrity and loyalty were particular to Roman ideals. (They even disdained the Greeks as smooth talkers who could never be trusted to keep their promises.) When compelled to act contrary to their principles, Romans were often at pains to justify their actions. In one way of looking at Roman history, the Romans were frequent hypocrites, always ready to use their ideals to paper over the harsh and unjust things they did to expand and maintain their empire. In a more sympathetic view, their internal struggles and debates about their policies and their principles were very real, and their stated desire to act justly and honorably signals at least a recognition of their failures to do so consistently. The pressures of empire at times forced them to compromise their values, but there may be something positive, if not forgivable, in their unwillingness to abandon those ideals and simply admit to their brutal exercise of power.

Although Rome had only recently recovered from their struggle against Pyrrhus, the Roman people voted to support the Mamertines, in contrast to their treatment of the allies who seized Rhegium. Rome sent a force to Messana, led by the grandson of Appius Claudius Caecus. Among the Mamertines, however, there was a difference of opinion about whether to favor Carthage or Rome. The Mamertines who favored Rome over Carthage managed to convince the Carthaginian commander to depart Messana, a decision for which he was later crucified by the Carthaginians. The Romans then defeated the Greek forces sent against the Mamertines from Syracuse and next attacked the remaining Carthaginian forces. In the kind of turnabout that happens so often in international diplomacy, the king of Syracuse negotiated a 15-year peace treaty with the Romans, part of which was his promise to be Rome's ally against the Carthaginians. At this point, Rome and Carthage were declared enemies, and the First Punic War, a struggle that would last for the next 23 years, had begun.

This would be the first of Rome's three wars with Carthage, the last of which was only a desperate struggle against Rome that had little chance of succeeding, ending in 146 BC with the total destruction of Carthage. The second would be one of Rome's greatest challenges, when they came closest to defeat and destruction because of the leadership of one of world history's greatest generals, Hannibal. All this was still in the future when Rome first fought Carthaginian

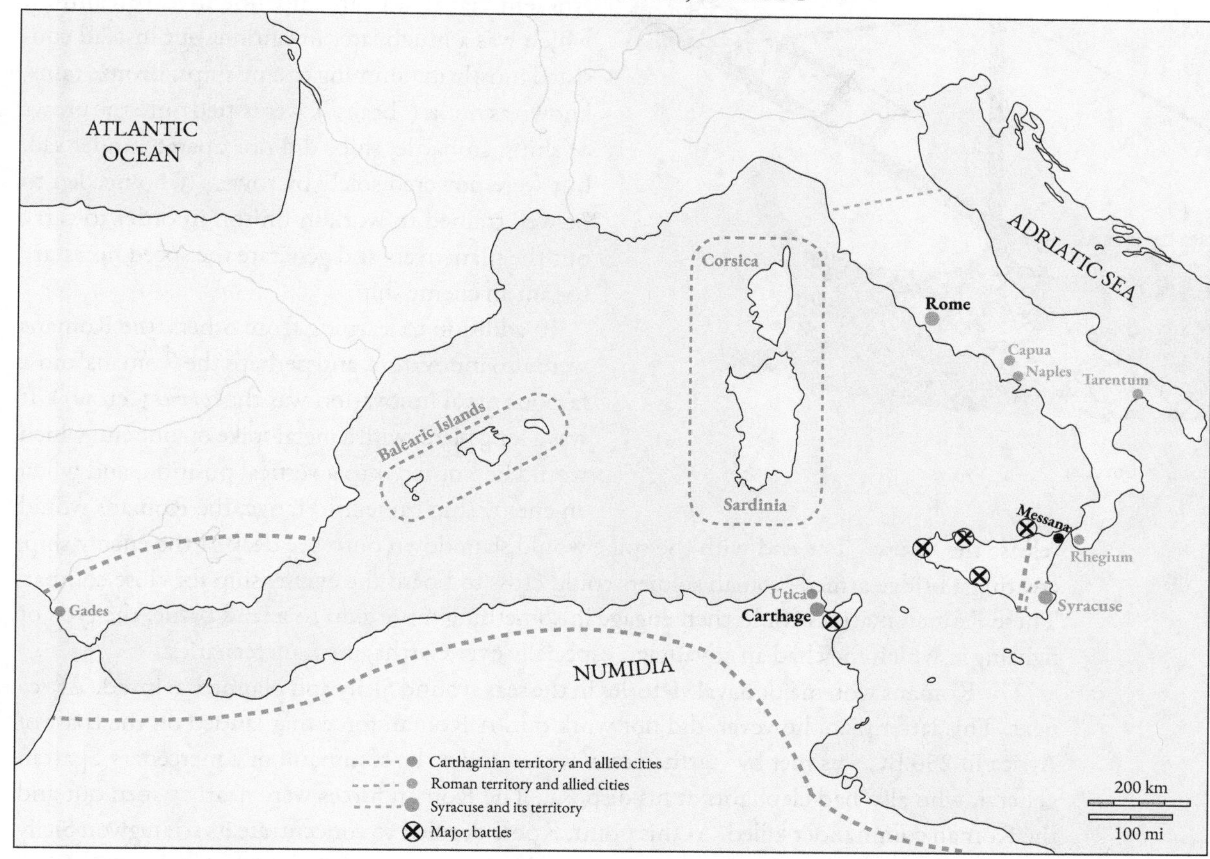

FIG. 5.3 The First Punic War.

forces in Sicily. With hindsight, it seems inevitable these two powers would fight for supremacy in the western Mediterranean and also inevitable that peace would come only with the extinction of one of them. Unlike the later two wars, the First Punic War is not well represented in our sources, and it is difficult to gain a sense of the long, hard slog it must have been for both sides. However, it is clear that Rome was confronted with a significant disadvantage in this first conflict with Carthage.

While the Carthaginians were excellent sailors with a massive fleet at their disposal, the Romans were relatively inexperienced in naval warfare and did not have the type of warship that Carthage possessed. By the end of the fourth century BC there were two Roman officials who each commanded ten warships, though Rome often relied on allies to provide warships. However, according to the sources, a Carthaginian warship had washed up on the coast of Italy, and the Romans, never shy from adopting improvements from other peoples, copied its design and built a fleet on this model. They also trained rowers on dry land in mock-ups of rowing benches.

FIG. 5.4 Corvus.

Ancient naval warfare did not involve cannon, which was a much later invention, but instead consisted mostly in ramming enemy ships. Bronze rams, known as *rostra* ("beaks"), were fitted onto the prows of ships. In battle, ships did not operate under sail, but were powered solely by rowers, who needed to be well trained to work in unison in order to carry out the maneuvers and generate the speed necessary to ram an enemy ship.

In addition to learning from others, the Romans were also innovators, and perhaps the Romans' most famous naval innovation was the *corvus* ("crow"). It was a long plank with a metal spike on one end which would be hoisted into a vertical position, and when an enemy ship came into range, the Romans would release the "crow." The end with the spike would slam down onto the deck of the enemy ship, creating a bridge armed Roman soldiers could cross to board the enemy ship for close combat. These Roman marines could then engage in something more akin to a land battle, the type of fighting at which they had an advantage, especially over Carthaginian mercenaries.

The Romans won major naval victories in the seas around Sicily and planned to invade Africa next. This latter plan, however, did not work out. A Roman force that landed on the coast of Africa in 256 BC was met by Carthaginian forces under the command of a mercenary Spartan general, who also had elephants at his disposal. The Roman forces were nearly wiped out and the Roman commander killed. At this point, Rome decided to concentrate its strategy on Sicily itself. Rome then suffered some setbacks, including a major defeat in which they lost 93 of 120 ships—this was the famous incident when the Roman commander, attempting to take auspices before attacking, grew frustrated with the sacred chickens and threw them overboard. In Roman eyes, his impiety caused this disaster.

After this defeat, the Carthaginians seemed poised for victory under the command of their general Hamilcar Barca, a member of one of Carthage's leading families and now better known as the father of Hannibal, the great general of the Second Punic War. Rome itself was in such desperate straits that they asked wealthy citizens to contribute funds for ships in order to rebuild their navy. Fortunately for Rome, internal politics back at Carthage intervened, and a faction came into power that was opposed to both the Barca family and continued involvement in Sicily. With weakening support at home and a newly recovered Roman navy, the Carthaginians suffered a massive defeat and were now prepared to seek peace on Rome's terms. In the treaty that ended the war, Carthage was required to abandon Sicily, return all Roman prisoners, and pay a massive sum of money to Rome every year for twenty years. Even after they agreed to the peace terms demanded by the Roman people, Carthage's troubles were not over. Tens of thousands of their mercenary soldiers began a violent uprising in north Africa and on the island of Sardinia, demanding the pay they had been promised for their service in Sicily. Hamilcar Barca took command against these former mercenaries and eventually subdued them after three years of bloody fighting. However, when Carthage attempted to resettle Sardinia, the Romans protested that this would be a violation of the peace treaty and seized control of Sardinia and of the neighboring island of Corsica as well. This aggressive move by Rome, based on a rather expansive understanding of the treaty that ended the First Punic War, was not something Carthage would forget.

In reading history, one often encounters phrases such as "Rome decided" or the like. These shorthand phrases often cover over contentious internal debates, and though the Roman people and the senate did often act with a single purpose after a course of action had been decided, there was often much debate and wrangling leading up to the decision. Rome's decision to help Carthage subdue the former mercenaries in Sicily is no different. Some senators would have wanted to begin a phase of better relations with Carthage, though in a relationship in which Rome's superiority would not be questioned. Moreover, defeat of Carthage by the mercenaries, or Roman support of the mercenaries against Carthage, might result in Carthage's inability or refusal to pay the large sum of money owed to Rome, which some senators would not want to risk losing. However, there were also senators who viewed Carthage as an enemy who might play nice in the short term but would eventually threaten Rome again once its strength had been restored. This fear of Carthage would never go away until the final destruction of Carthage a century later, which was motivated by this fear as much as anything else.

Roman Provinces

To maintain control over Italy, Rome had established colonies throughout the peninsula, distributing land to veteran soldiers and other Romans, who then possessed varying degrees of citizenship with different rights. As Rome's influence spread beyond the boundaries of Italy, a model based on the establishment of individual colonies would not be sufficient, especially in controlling large areas. To administer their newly acquired territories outside of Italy, Rome created "provinces," the first of which was Sicily in 241 BC, and the other in 237, consisting of Corsica and Sardinia together. At first, Romans would send out a quaestor to govern a conquered territory, but as a low-ranking magistrate, a quaestor lacked the authority to act on his own and would need to communicate with Rome before taking any serious actions involving military action or deciding issues of law and order. The increasing distances of Rome's conquests from Italy made this an unworkable system. The situation demanded a magistrate who possessed *imperium,* which is to say a praetor or a consul, who had the authority to give independent commands without reporting to a superior back in Rome. Thus, not long after the acquisition of their first overseas territories, Rome began to elect praetors to govern these provinces on an annual basis, though the term could be extended by the senate if necessary. (The Roman official in charge of a province is usually called a "provincial governor," though the term "governor" was not used by the Romans.) As the number of provinces increased over time, instead of holding elections of minor officials to govern the provinces, the Roman Senate began to appoint individuals who were given the authority of a praetor or consul. In that capacity, the individual would be called "propraetor" or "proconsul." In these terms, the prefix *pro-* means "standing in for, in the capacity of," and such *pro-* magistrates were used in other situations. For example, a consul or praetor could continue performing duties overseas beyond his term of office as a proconsul or propraetor, or in a military emergency, a senator might be sent out on a special military command as a proconsul.

"Province" (*provincia*) originally meant the duties assigned to a particular magistrate, but came to refer specifically to the geographical area over which a Roman magistrate had authority. Governing a province in general meant maintaining order, but in particular involved supervising the collection of taxes, resolving legal disputes involving Roman citizens, and keeping the local population under control. The governor also commanded any military forces in the province, which provided the opportunity to engage in skirmishes that might earn the governor the glory of a triumph back in Rome. Many also saw a provincial governorship as an opportunity for enrichment,

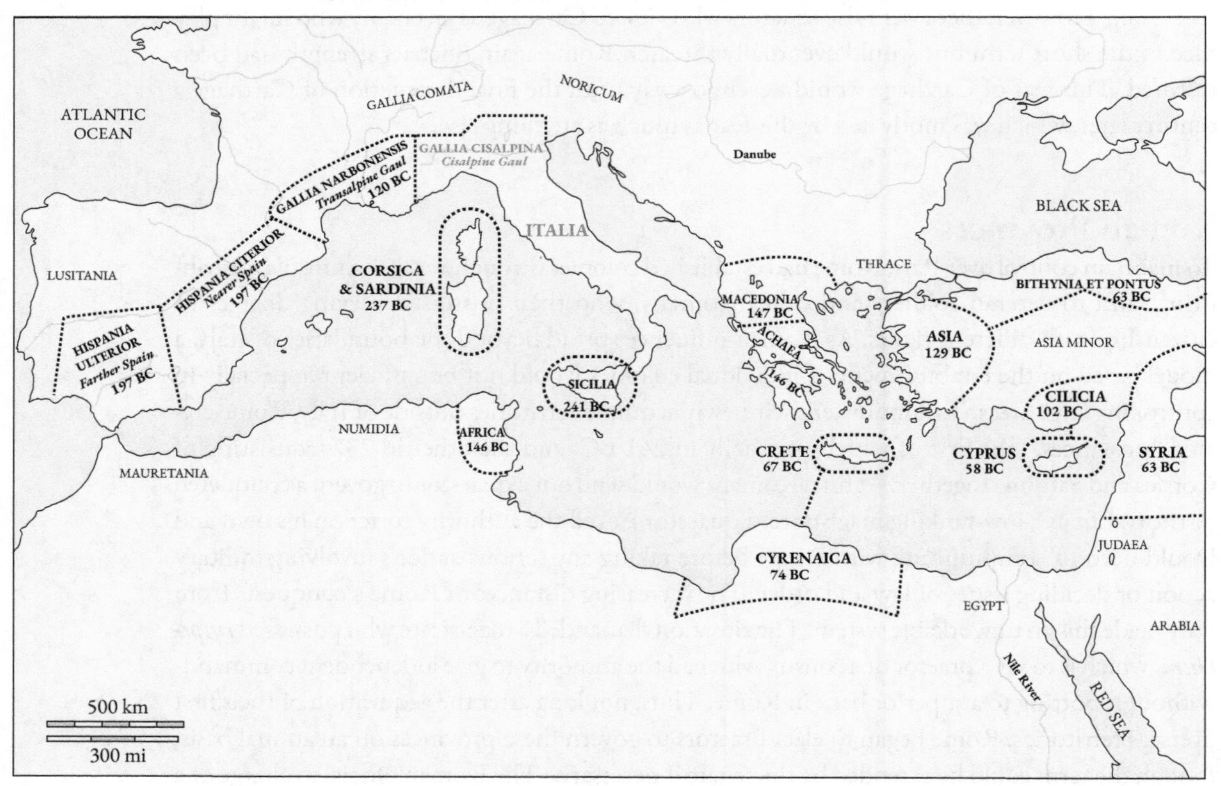

FIG. 5.5 Roman provinces.

through gifts (often really bribes) from local officials or Roman businessmen, embezzlement of public funds or skimming revenues, or even through outright theft and plunder of temples and the homes of wealthy provincial inhabitants. A governor would take along a staff, usually consisting of one or more quaestors, who served as treasurers and accountants (particularly important for the collection of taxes and other revenue), as well as three "legates" (*legati*) appointed by the senate. Friends and close relations often accompanied the governor during part or all of his year of service, in part to provide advice and assistance as well as friendly company, but these individuals would also expect to enrich themselves. Because of this, many senators used their influence to obtain provinces that would be especially lucrative. In the last decades of the republic, laws were passed to control the assignment of provinces in order to prevent the political jockeying and corruption that went into obtaining particularly desirable provinces, but these had little effect.

The creation of the provincial system was an important step in Rome's growth into a major empire, especially as their conquests began to occur farther from Rome. Yet it was also a system ripe for abuse. A provincial governor essentially had all the authority of a consul without any of the checks he would have to face back in Rome. There were no tribunes of the plebs to veto legislation, no opposing faction in the senate to exert its influence and stymie any actions. There were laws and regulations that governors were obliged to obey, and the inhabitants of the provinces did have the right to bring charges against Roman provincial administrators, but in practice these were often ignored or circumvented. A non-Roman citizen who suffered any wrongdoing at the hands of a provincial governor or his staff would have a difficult time seeking justice. To bring legal charges, he would need important connections at Rome, since these charges would have to be brought before the senate back at Rome, and any trial would have to occur there. Some Roman politicians recognized that unjust abuses of power occurred, and special law courts were established to deal with issues of corruption, but prosecutions were rare, and convictions even rarer. Many senators who hoped to benefit from a year as governor of a province, or who themselves had already engaged in some of the same criminal behavior when they had been governors, would not be eager to convict a fellow senator, whose support they might need one day. It is not surprising that relations between Roman authorities and the inhabitants of the provinces were often strained at best, and many people in the provinces would understandably feel they were living under a harsh authority that did not have their best interests in mind. On the other hand, some would benefit from Rome's presence in their territory, which offered a protection and stability they had not enjoyed before. As well, provincials who assimilated to Roman customs might find business opportunities, or even a path to upward mobility within the Roman system, perhaps at Rome for the more ambitious.

This model of provincial administration, followed by later colonial powers, obviously created tensions. Aside from the simple fact of being occupied by a foreign power, the behavior of Roman officials often led on occasion to revolts and rebellions, which would then be ruthlessly suppressed. Such unrest was not always unwelcome to a Roman provincial governor, since it might lead to a triumph. More importantly, a provincial governorship would allow an individual Roman to acquire influence among the wealthy elite of a province, and these personal bonds sometimes came into conflict with Rome's larger interests. The situation is not unlike a major US corporation with extensive and valuable holdings in a country that might begin to act contrary to the wishes of the US government—even in the best of circumstances, conflicts of interest and corruption are unavoidable.

Other Peoples and Other Problems

Rome's victory in the First Punic War, while establishing it as a major Mediterranean power, did not mean an end to conflicts elsewhere. The Gauls in the north of Italy, beyond the Po river just south of the Alps, were still a problem (they were known as "cisalpine" Gauls, opposed to the "transalpine" Gauls north of the Alps). Though Rome came to a truce with the cisalpine Gauls in 232 BC, they did not maintain a firm grip on the area until they seized the land from one of the tribes there and distributed it to Roman colonists. The resentment of these Gallic tribes at the loss of their land and their independence caused many of them to join the side of Carthage in the Second Punic War. A more serious problem confronting Rome in the aftermath of the First Punic War were pirates at sea, who disrupted the imports of grain essential for the city's population, and also posed a threat to Roman citizens, who would be kidnapped and sold into slavery. Piracy was a constant problem in the Mediterranean, and Rome would be forced to deal with it constantly over the coming centuries.

In 231 BC, Queen Teuta, a ruler of Illyria on the eastern shore of the Adriatic Sea, appeared to the Romans to be supporting pirates in their harassment of Roman vessels. When the Romans sent a delegation to complain as well as to threaten, pirates killed one of the envoys. In response, the Romans sent a fleet against Queen Teuta, who was prepared to meet the Romans with her own naval force. Unfortunately, the commander of her navy, a Greek by the name of Demetrius, betrayed her and cut a deal with the Romans (for which he was rewarded with his own territory to rule). Teuta was allowed to remain on the throne as queen, but under the yoke of Roman authority. This method of indirect control became a standard Roman policy, especially when dealing with the numerous monarchs in the eastern Mediterranean. Rather than establish provinces under the direct control of a Roman official, the Romans would exert indirect control by keeping friendly monarchs on the throne—some might call them puppets of Rome. As long as rulers acknowledged Roman authority and answered whatever demands the Romans might place on them in terms of financial payments or military assistance, they could be assured of Roman protection from any threats, whether within their own territory or from a neighboring kingdom. Friendly rulers were a useful means for Rome to maintain its presence in distant regions without expending manpower or resources, and these client kings and queens also served as useful buffers between Rome and other powers. In addition, these monarchs could be played off one another, and Rome became quite adept at political manipulation, though they were also prone to being manipulated by some skillful monarchs in the East. These complicated political maneuverings also drew Rome into further conflicts, and while Rome might sell out a friend or ally if a better offer came along (or a different faction in the Roman Senate exerted its influence), just as often,

Rome would find itself betrayed by a once-friendly ruler, forcing it to retaliate if it were to maintain its prestige and power. Such was the case with Teuta's unfaithful commander Demetrius, who after he received from Rome his own territory to rule proceeded to attack other territories under Rome's protection. He was forced to flee but found safe harbor with King Philip V of Macedon, a descendant of Alexander the Great, and soon to be a thorn in Rome's side during the next war with Carthage.

Elephants Over the Alps: The Second Punic War

After the mercenary revolts had been put down and Carthage accepted the harsh terms of surrender to Rome at the end of the First Punic War, Hamilcar Barca did not retire. He moved on to Spain, the area long dominated by Carthage and whose mines provided much of its wealth. To many Carthaginians, Spain was a far more important territory to Carthage's future than Sicily. The indigenous inhabitants of early Spain are not well known to us, but it is clear they did not welcome control by foreign powers. Hamilcar met with fierce resistance as he attempted to extend Carthage's control in the region, and eventually drowned trying to cross a river during a battle in 229 BC. His son-in-law, Hasdrubal, replaced him as general, testifying to the continued preeminence of the Barca family back at Carthage. Hasdrubal was an able general and succeeded in establishing a new city in Spain, named "New Carthage" (today known as Cartagena). Further east along the Mediterranean coast was an old Greek trading colony, Massillia (modern-day Marseilles in France), an ally of Rome and hostile to the neighboring Gauls as well as to Carthage. The founding of "New Carthage" would be alarming news to Massillia, since this Carthaginian settlement would be an economic rival and military threat. Their unease was shared by Rome.

In the aftermath of the First Punic War, Rome had been dealing with the Gauls in the north and Queen Teuta to the east. As a result, Hasdrubal's activity in Spain had not met with any resistance, but in 226 BC Rome and Carthage signed a treaty setting limits on Carthage's activities in Spain. The river Ebro was fixed as the boundary between the two powers: Carthage could do as it pleased south of the river, and Rome had control north of it. Shortly afterward, in 221, Hasdrubal was assassinated, which opened the door to another member of the Barca family, Hamilcar's oldest son Hannibal, to take control of Carthaginian operations in Spain. Almost all of what we know of Hannibal comes from Roman sources, since as a result of Carthage's ultimate destruction at the hands of Rome, the language of Carthage, Punic, is extinct and no writings exist. Yet even Roman sources treat him with respect and admiration, though praise of his abilities increases the magnitude of Rome's victory and the glory of the general who received the credit for his defeat. Even if we had no admiring depictions of him in Roman historians, his accomplishments speak for themselves, despite his ultimate failure. He managed to lead an army (many if not most of whom were mercenaries) over the Alps, then spent over ten years fighting in Italy, defeating Roman armies and some of their best commanders, all without suffering a major defeat or defection. This is an astounding achievement, and only a leader of extraordinary ability could have carried this off. In a famous story of questionable authenticity, when Hannibal was a young boy, his father took him to an altar and made him swear to the gods that he would always treat Rome as an enemy. The story makes Hannibal an implacable enemy of Rome who must be defeated at all costs, and who would never accept peace with Rome. Yet at the end of the war, it is a defeated Hannibal who urges the Carthaginians to accept the peace terms offered by the Roman victor.

At the time of his arrival in Spain, Hannibal was still a young man, but he already possessed the qualities of a great leader. He quickly brought all of Spain up to the Ebro under Carthaginian control, including the town of Saguntum, which was on the coast of Spain within the territory granted to Carthage in the treaty with Rome. Although our sources are confused, Saguntum seems to have had some kind of political relationship with Rome, but it is unclear exactly what kind. If it had been a formal ally recognized by the senate, it might well have been an exception to the treaty. However, it is possible later Roman sources made the relationship appear more binding than it was at the time in order to justify Rome's actions there, and to blame Carthage rather than Rome for the outbreak of the Second Punic War. Later Romans would want this war, one of Rome's greatest victories, to be a "just war," and unwarranted Roman aggression would spoil the story. Hannibal, for his part, accused the Saguntines of attacking nearby peoples who would have been under Carthaginian protection, and wished to attack the city in retaliation. The Saguntines sent ambassadors to Rome, pleading for protection, and they may have pledged themselves as an ally to Rome at this point. Hannibal warned the Romans to keep their hands off Saguntum in accordance with the treaty, but Rome sent a mission there in response to the plea for help. There would have been both pro-Roman and pro-Carthaginian factions at Saguntum, and the visit by the Roman delegation resulted in the execution of some leading citizens. These were most likely leaders of the faction sympathetic to Hannibal (or at least hostile to Rome), and their deaths would ensure the city would not be betrayed to Hannibal from within.

From the confusion in the sources, it cannot be determined who was in the right, if anyone was, but it is clear that fear and suspicion on both sides was as much a cause of war as anything else. Whatever the cause, Hannibal besieged Saguntum, capturing it in 218 BC. Rome felt it could not ignore this outcome, whether because Saguntum was an ally or because they feared an advance by Hannibal across the Ebro. The Romans first sent an embassy to Carthage to demand the surrender of Hannibal to them, a shrewd move since there would be a faction there hostile to Hannibal that would like to see him recalled. The first-century BC historian Livy preserves the dramatic scene when the Roman delegation, led by a former consul Quintus Fabius Maximus Verrucosus (the *cognomen* means "warty"), stood before the Carthaginian senate and presented the Roman demands. At the end of his speech, he gathered in the folds of his toga, and declared, "We bring you either war or peace—take the one you want!" Carthage had been humiliated enough by Rome after the First Punic War, with the payment of huge sums of money and the loss of significant territory, including Rome's insulting seizure of Sardinia and Corsica. The Carthaginian senators thus gave a spirited answer: Rome could give them whatever they wanted, and they would gladly accept it. So began a 17-year struggle in which Rome came close to defeat and total

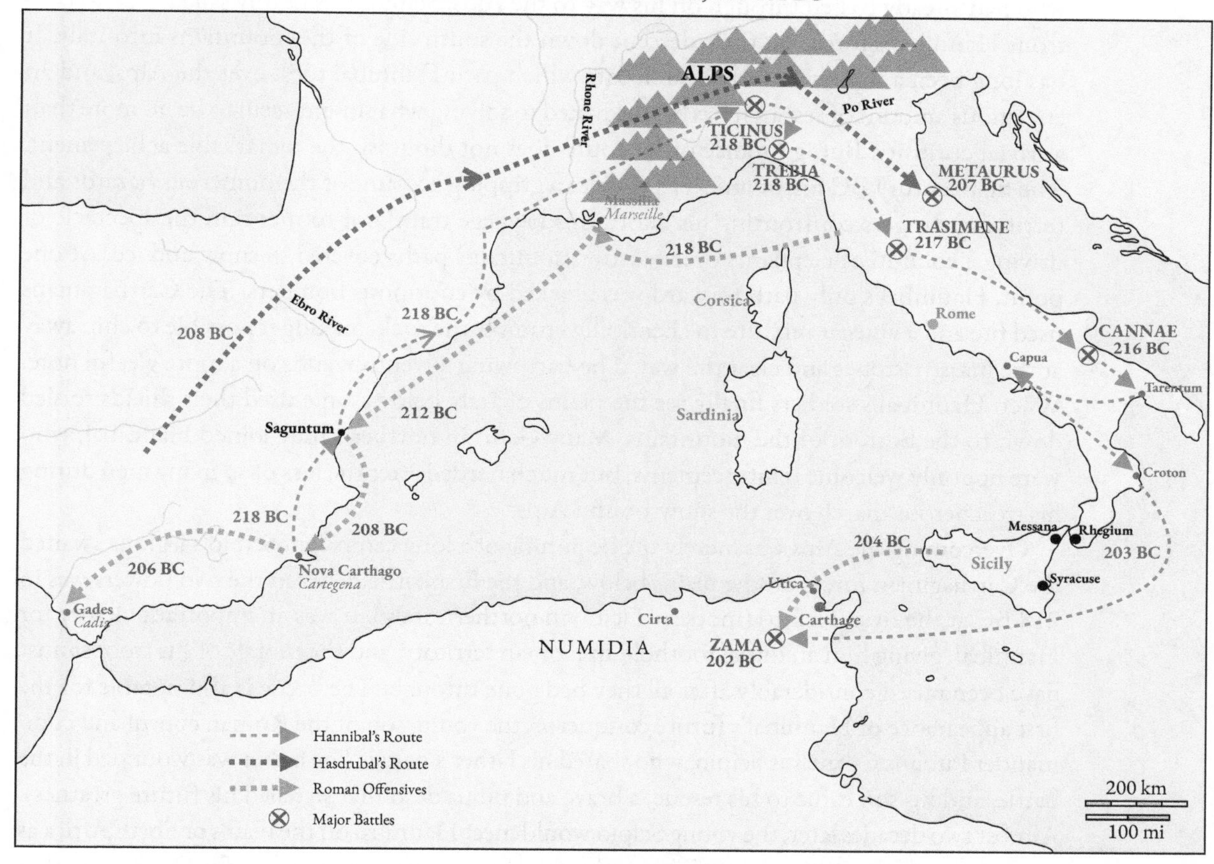

FIG. 5.6 Second Punic War.

destruction, suffering some of its most memorable and crushing losses and winning its greatest victory. The fact that the Romans managed not only to survive this war, but ultimately prevail, is a testament to their determination, even if it is played up in later sources.

In contrast to the First Punic War, Rome now held the upper hand at sea, and with their naval superiority, Hannibal could not rely on supplies to reach him by sea. For this reason, he decided to attack Rome by land, marching along the Mediterranean coast and crossing the Alps in the north. Though this was a far more difficult and risky path to Rome, it did present the possibility of recruiting to his side the Gauls in northern Italy, who had only recently come to terms with Rome and had suffered loss of their lands.

Rome initially decided on a two-pronged strategy: to stop Hannibal before he reached the Alps and to invade Africa from Sicily. As for the first, Rome dispatched the consul Publius Cornelius Scipio to Massillia in order to intercept Hannibal on his march along the coast of modern-day France. As it turned out, Scipio arrived in Massillia too late to confront Hannibal, who had already passed through on his way to the Alps. Scipio thus hastily sailed back to confront Hannibal's forces on their descent down the south side of the mountains into Italy. It has long been a matter of historical debate which path Hannibal took over the Alps, and an enormous amount of research has been devoted to solving what might seem to be no more than a trivial curiosity. But ignorance of his route does not diminish the remarkable achievement. The first-century BC historian Livy provides a gripping account of the numerous hazards and terrifying dangers confronting his enormous baggage train, not to mention the spectacle of driving a column of elephants over narrow mountains paths covered in snow and ice. At one point, Hannibal's only path forward was blocked by enormous boulders. The Carthaginians used fire and a vinegar mixture to chemically crumble the rock, making it possible to chip away at the massive stones and clear the way. The harrowing adventure ends on a more gleeful note. When Hannibal's soldiers finally see the plains of Italy below, some used their shields to sled down to the bottom of the mountains. Many Gauls in northern Italy joined Hannibal, who were not only welcome reinforcements, but much needed after the loss of so many men during his treacherous march over the snow-bound Alps.

Overcoming the Alps was merely the beginning of a long campaign. Scipio's legions awaited the Carthaginian forces on the plains below, and the first battle between the two powers was in 218 BC at the river Ticinus (modern Ticino in northern Italy). It was an important victory for Hannibal, giving him an initial foothold in Roman territory, and the morale of his troops must have been raised considerably after all they had gone through. The battle is also notable for the first appearance of Hannibal's future conqueror, the young son of the Roman consul and commander Publius Cornelius Scipio, who shared his father's name. The father was wounded in the battle, and his son came to his rescue, a brave and pious deed that signaled his future greatness. Almost two decades later, the young Scipio would meet Hannibal on the plains of north Africa as commander of the Roman army. The battle at the Ticinus was also a success for Carthage in that it forced Rome to cancel the second part of their initial strategy, the planned invasion of Africa. Instead, they sent that army north to confront Hannibal on land. Rome's strategy of conducting the war on two fronts immediately collapsed, and for the next decade the war would be fought on Italian soil.

Hannibal's victory in his first engagement with the Romans was assisted by the addition of Gallic soldiers, though he did not place a great deal of trust in them. At the end of 218, shortly after the battle at the Ticinus, Hannibal inflicted a more serious military defeat on the Romans at the river Trebia, luring the Roman consul who had come to join forces with the consul Scipio into a trap. Hannibal's study of the terrain and superior tactics gave him an advantage, but he was greatly assisted by the rashness of the Roman commander, Tiberius Sempronius Longus. Sempronius is portrayed as impatient and impulsive, hoping for a quick victory to boost his chances in the upcoming elections. However, he may have worried that failure to take immediate action would cause Rome's allies, especially the Gauls, to lose confidence in Rome and turn to Hannibal. Both sides had concerns about the loyalty of the Gauls, and in some accounts, they quickly deserted Hannibal and joined the Romans. In one of our sources for the battle at the

Trebia, Sempronius makes a patriotic appeal for battle in his attempt to convince the other consul to take swift action. Standing at the bedside of Scipio, still recovering from the wounds suffered at the Ticinus, he appeals to the glories of the First Punic War, not without some exaggeration:

> Our fathers once fought before the walls of Carthage—they would groan if they saw us, their descendants, two consuls with consular armies, cowering in fear behind walls in the very heart of Italy, while this Carthaginian has taken the lands between the Alps and the Apennines! (Livy 21.53)

The desire to live up to the standards of past glories achieved by one's forebears always exerted a powerful influence on aristocratic Romans. Sempronius, like so many of them, fell prey to this desire, and Hannibal exploited it.

Hannibal had sent a small force with some cavalry to harass the Romans while he hid other forces among some thorn bushes and brambles. In response to this initial attack, Sempronius decided to send his men, not well trained or experienced in battle, across the Trebia river (modern Trebbia) on a cold and snowy morning, intending to attack the Carthaginian and Gallic forces, just as Hannibal anticipated. During the river crossing, the Roman army was massacred when Hannibal launched his ambush against the Romans' undefended rear. By some estimates, fewer than 10,000 of the original 40,000 soldiers, both Romans and Italian allies, survived. As is common in traditional accounts of Roman warfare, the rash behavior of a Roman commander was severely punished.

The defeat raised an alarm at Rome, and new consuls were elected to replace the disgraced Sempronius and the wounded Scipio. One of the armies was ordered to march back toward Rome to defend the city. Hannibal began to devastate the surrounding territory, both to show Rome's Italian allies that the Romans were powerless to protect them, and to draw the consular army under the command of the new consul Gaius Flaminius into battle. While Flaminius held out longer than Sempronius did, he too was eager for battle. Hannibal lured the Roman army onto a narrow path with Lake Trasimene on one side and steep hills on the other, where he had stationed his troops. At Hannibal's signal, the Carthaginian forces, assisted by a fog that reduced visibility, swept down from the hills in another ambush. Before they realized what was happening, the Romans were surrounded on three sides, with Lake Trasimene on the fourth. The Romans did not even have a chance to draw up into a proper formation, and in a matter of hours were slaughtered, some drowning in the lake in a desperate attempt to escape. The consul Flaminius himself was killed by a Gaul serving in Hannibal's cavalry. Recognizing the consul, he charged after him and shouted, "Here's the man who killed our soldiers and ravaged our cities and our land—I offer him as a sacrifice to the spirits of all my fellow Gauls he so wickedly murdered!" The Gaul first cut down a Roman soldier attempting to protect the consul, then plunged his lance into the consul's chest. The Romans and allies who survived were captured and sold into slavery.

While the defeat at Trebia was certainly cause for worry at Rome, the disaster of Lake Trasimene, including the ominous death of a consul, created a panic. To meet the crisis, the Romans decided to appoint a dictator, which they had not done in decades. The senate selected Gaius Fabius Maximus Verrucosus (the "warty" we met earlier). Fabius had twice been consul, the second time in 228, and was also censor in 230. He has also earned the honor of a triumph. More recently he had been a member of the delegation sent to Carthage to offer peace or war. It was Fabius, in fact, who spoke before the Carthaginian senate and dramatically unfolded his toga with the "gift" of war. He was an elder statesman and a respected patrician, exactly the kind of man the nervous Romans would turn to for stability in a crisis. Though he would often come under harsh criticism for his conduct of the war, the senate's confidence in him was not misplaced. He initiated a strategy of slow attrition against Hannibal, avoiding pitched battles and hoping over time to wear down the Carthaginian forces, who were essentially trapped in Italy. His tactics, though not always popular with the people or more ambitious Roman commanders, turned out to be the right choice. The resolve of Rome to see this strategy through, however, would be tested on more than one occasion.

The ultimate victory over Hannibal in the Second Punic War would go to Publius Cornelius Scipio, son of the consul wounded at the Ticinus, and he would earn the honorific *cognomen* Africanus for his defeat of Hannibal in Africa. Yet it was Fabius's delaying tactics that deserve as much credit for allowing Rome to survive Hannibal's invasion and ultimately prevail. For his service during the war, he earned the *cognomen* Cunctator, "the delayer," memorialized in a line by one of Rome's earliest poets, Ennius, who was a young man at the time:

> *unus homo nobis cunctando restituit rem*
>
> one man, by delaying, restored our republic

The "Fabian strategy," as it is called, had to survive not only Hannibal's countermoves, but also the recklessness of another Roman commander, who happened to be Fabius's *magister equitum* during his year as dictator. Normally, a dictator would be permitted to choose his own second-in-command, but in this instance, the senatorial faction eager for a swift victory over Hannibal seems to have forced him to accept Marcus Minucius Rufus, who had been consul in 221.

After Fabius suffered a slight setback and Minucius won a victory against the Carthaginians, a tribune of the plebs back at Rome had the Plebeian Assembly pass a law that elevated Minucius from Fabius's second-in-command to Fabius's equal as dictator. Minucius was puffed up with pride and thought of Fabius rather than Hannibal as his real rival. The sober Fabius reminded him who his and Rome's true enemy was. Even Fabius's own troops, eager to prove themselves, had begun to hold him in contempt for his inaction. Minucius criticized Fabius for keeping to the hills and mountains, among the clouds and mist, where he could safely keep an eye on the Carthaginians. Fabius would restrict Hannibal's movements, but never descended from the safety of the hills to engage in battle on open ground. Minucius cruelly joked that Fabius was giving his soldiers excellent seats to watch the spectacle of Italy's destruction by a foreign enemy, and also mocked him for trying to lead his troops up into the heavens, since he did not seem to care for what was happening down on earth. No longer Fabius's second, but his equal, Minucius took sole command of part of the Roman forces and soon fell into one of Hannibal's traps. Fabius had expected as much, and thus had stationed his troops nearby. When he saw the dire straits into which Minucius and his troops had fallen, he rode to the rescue and forced Hannibal to withdraw. In our sources, Hannibal is said to be the only one who recognized the wisdom of Fabius's strategy. After Fabius swooped down from the heights to save Minucius, Hannibal remarked to his troops:

> Didn't I tell you that the cloud we've seen hovering over the mountain tops would one day burst out into a raging storm? (Plutarch, *Fabius Maximus* 13)

To his credit, Minucius finally recognized the wisdom of Fabius's strategy and apologized before all their soldiers. Despite Minucius's failed attack and change of heart, many Roman senators, and many of the plebs, still believed Rome simply needed to bring its full force to bear against Hannibal to chase him from Italy once and for all. The consuls elected for 216 were Gaius Terentius Varro and Lucius Aemilius Paullus. Both of them marched out to confront Hannibal, who was now in south central Italy where he occupied an important supply depot at a place called Cannae. Both Roman consuls were present with the army, which meant that they took turns in command of the combined forces, alternating every day. Once again, the rashness of one military commander, in contrast to the caution of the other, proved the Romans' undoing and led to a disaster even greater than the previous ones.

Aemilius Paullus was the more prudent consul of the two and had promised Fabius Maximus that he would adhere to his strategy of avoiding battle with Hannibal. Terentius Varro, on the other hand, possessed the same headstrong character as the other consuls who had been defeated by Hannibal. On his day to be in command, despite warnings from his colleague, he led the Roman soldiers forward to meet Hannibal and his troops at Cannae. When the battle lines met, the Roman army fell into a classic pincer movement as the Carthaginian center fell back, drawing the Romans forward until Hannibal's cavalry, stationed on the wings, wheeled inward and crushed the Roman army from both flanks. Many of Rome's leading men perished in the battle, including Aemilius Paullus, who had fought bravely even though he warned his colleague against the attack. As the Romans fled in confusion, a member of the Roman cavalry saw Aemilius Paullus sitting on a rock, covered with blood. He offered Paullus his horse, since he knew it was not this consul's responsibility for the crushing defeat. Paullus, however, refused the offer, not wishing to expose himself to the accusations that would be flung against him back in Rome. Instead, he asks the young soldier to deliver a message for him:

> Don't waste the little time you have left to escape the enemy on useless pity. Go, tell the Senate to fortify Rome and defend it with troops before the victorious enemy arrives. But take Fabius Maximus aside and tell him that Lucius Aemilius Paullus lived and now dies remembering his strategy. Now let me breathe my last breath among my men, the victims of this massacre. In this way I can avoid standing trial after my consulship is over, and avoid defending my innocence by blaming my colleague. (Livy 22.49)

Such was the disgrace of Cannae that the soldiers who managed to survive were sent to Sicily to fight for the duration of the war, and Rome refused to pay a ransom for those who surrendered and were taken captive. It was the Battle of Cannae above all that would leave the deepest scar on Roman memory, in part because Hannibal's victory came closest to depriving Rome of important allies in Italy. A serious blow to Rome was the defection of Capua, a large city in Campania just north of Naples and 120 miles south of Rome. After the tide of war turned in Rome's favor, however, they would pay dearly for their decision.

In reaction to news of the massive defeat at Cannae, Rome went into full panic mode and first consulted the gods about possible remedies. They consulted the Sibylline Books, an odd collection of oracles to which the Romans would turn at moments when they felt the gods were punishing them. They also sent a delegation to seek advice from the famous oracle at Delphi in northern Greece. Even more drastically, they resorted to human sacrifice, burying four individuals alive. As for more practical measures, they opened up service in the army to all, eliminating the property qualification and even offering slaves and criminals their freedom in return for serving in the ranks. The situation was desperate, yet Rome refused to surrender and would continue the fight for another twelve years. Hannibal, for his part, may have helped Rome to survive. In one of the few decisions he made over the course of the war that can be criticized, he decided to let his soldiers rest after the overwhelming victory rather than head straight for the enemy capital. Rome was crippled, demoralized, and had lost important allies. If there was a moment to march on Rome, this would seem to be it. Hannibal's second-in-command, Marharbal, urged him to do so at once, claiming he himself would race ahead with the cavalry, and in four days' time Hannibal would hold a victory banquet on the Capitol. Hannibal, however, replied he needed to think over the idea, to which Marharbal replied:

> It must be true that the gods do not give all gifts to one man—you know how to gain a victory, Hannibal, but you do not know how to use it! (Livy 22.51)

After Cannae, there was no longer any debate about the wisdom of Fabius Maximus's strategy of delay, and Rome adopted it for the remainder of the war, out of necessity as much as anything else. A slow and steady recovery followed. Allies who defected were brought back under Rome's authority, including the Greek cities in the south. In 211, Rome recaptured Capua, which Hannibal's troops had used as winter quarters. Some believed the Carthaginians had grown soft enjoying the pleasures to be found in this wealthy city and were now less able to endure the hardships of war. Rome abolished Capua's government and executed all its senators, then after depriving its citizens of all rights and sending them into various small communities, made Capua's territory public land under the control of Rome. Disloyalty was a sin Rome would not forgive.

As the war in Italy had its ebbs and flows, Rome also had to deal with issues on other fronts. Philip V of Macedon, who had given refuge to Queen Teuta's disloyal admiral, formed an alliance with Hannibal in 215, presenting to Rome the threat of an invasion of southern Italy, much as Pyrrhus had carried out years before. The Romans were not capable of meeting this threat militarily, but instead handled it through skillful diplomacy. They turned to other Greek states who felt threatened by Philip's ambitions and created an anti-Macedonian coalition by allying themselves to a group of Greek city-states known as the Aetolian League. This league would keep Philip occupied in Greece and prevent him from launching an expedition against Italy. Much to Rome's displeasure, the Aetolian League eventually made a truce with Philip instead of continuing to fight him, but their diplomatic maneuver was still a success, as it kept Philip from bringing assistance to Hannibal. In Spain, the elder Publius Cornelius Scipio had recovered from the wounds he suffered at Trebia and joined his brother Gnaeus in Spain to fight against Hannibal's brother Hasdrubal. The Scipio brothers achieved some success, including the capture in 212 of Saguntum, the town that had been the cause of the war. However, Hasdrubal eventually destroyed the Roman army, and both Scipios perished. Nonetheless, their efforts had delayed Hasdrubal from making his journey to Italy to join Hannibal.

Lastly, Rome also undertook a campaign against Syracuse in Sicily, led by a survivor of Cannae, Marcus Claudius Marcellus. The city eventually fell to Rome in 212 after a long siege, and shortly afterward Rome retook control over all of Sicily. While the capture of Syracuse was an important military event, it is better remembered for the role of the Greek scientist Archimedes in defending it. He is credited with inventing clever devices to fend off the Roman ships attacking the city's coastal walls, including a primitive laser that used curved mirrors to concentrate the sun's rays into a powerful beam and set Roman ships aflame. (Recent research suggests that Archimedes's "secret weapon" may have been a steam cannon rather than some kind of laser.)

FIG. 5.7 Archimedes's laser, as imagined by a 16th-c. artist.

When the Romans finally captured Syracuse, the Roman commander Marcellus is said to have wept over its fate, pondering the fact that such a prosperous and magnificent city would be utterly ruined within a few hours. But nothing distressed Marcellus as much as the death of Archimedes and the loss of his great intellect. As the Roman soldiers were ransacking the city, one of them came upon Archimedes, who was deep in thought over a math problem. He was so engrossed in the diagram he was drawing to demonstrate a theorem that he was unaware that the city had fallen. The soldier ordered Archimedes to come with him, but Archimedes refused to move until he had worked through his problem. The soldier killed him on the spot. Marcellus's tears for Syracuse and hatred for the soldier who slew Archimedes might seem odd, even unpatriotic, for a Roman military commander, but his reactions represent the growing appreciation and admiration aristocratic Romans had for Greek culture. This high esteem for Greek culture is known as "philhellenism," from the Greek words for love (*philia*) and Greece (*Hellas*). Indeed, an understanding and appreciation of Greek literature and philosophy was taken as a mark of worldliness and sophistication. However, such studies were not to detract from the serious and practical matters of war and politics, and not all elite Romans shared in this philhellenism. Some, in fact, thought it a dangerous threat to Rome, weakening the Roman moral character. Yet such was the respect aristocratic Romans had for Archimedes's intellectual achievements that the first-century BC orator and politician Cicero searched for Archimedes's tomb in Syracuse when he visited Sicily. He knew what it looked like—it was a sphere inside a cylinder, because Archimedes had demonstrated that the volume of a sphere is two thirds that of a cylinder that contains it. Cicero discovered it hidden underneath bushes that had grown over it, since it had been neglected for so long.

Publius Cornelius Scipio Africanus

The Roman recovery from Hannibal's invasion continued, and though the Fabian tactics slowly tilted the balance of the war in favor of the Romans, it would take a daring departure from this strategy to bring the war to an end. We have already met this Publius Cornelius Scipio before, when he rescued his wounded father at the battle of Trebia. He was also a survivor of Cannae, where he was credited with urging the Romans to continue to fight (perhaps a fiction to preserve his image given the general dishonor attached to survivors). His father and uncle, who had both perished in Spain, were distinguished consuls and commanders, and young Scipio would be expected to attain the same heights. After the defeat at Cannae, the Romans sought new leaders for the Roman forces and turned to this popular young man from an aristocratic family. In 211 BC, even though he was only 25 years old and had not been elected to any lower offices, the Romans gave him consular authority to take command of the military in Spain, following in the footsteps of his father and uncle. He justified the confidence placed in him by soon capturing New Carthage, the colony founded by Hannibal's father, and then defeating Hasdrubal, who had inflicted a crushing defeat on the Roman army led by his father only a couple of years earlier. He won over the local population by releasing the Spanish hostages that the Carthaginians kept to guarantee good behavior. As a result of his success, Carthaginian influence in Spain was brought to an end, a decisive factor in the outcome of the war. After his defeat in Spain, Hasdrubal headed for Italy to join forces with his brother, which would have certainly turned the tables on Rome. The Romans, however, managed to prevent the Carthaginians from joining forces, keeping Hannibal pinned in southern Italy while defeating Hasdrubal in the northeast near the Metaurus river.

Scipio was elected consul for 205, which was somewhat irregular given his age, but Romans were always willing to break with tradition in order to accommodate extraordinary individuals, especially at critical moments. As a consul from a prominent family with a distinguished record of service, and with a reputation for feats of bravery and filial piety, Scipio carried an authority among the Romans well beyond his years. His record also shows that if he was daring, he was not reckless. Now as elected consul and respected commander, he proposed a major change to Rome's war strategy: He would invade Africa and take the war to Carthage. Some Roman senators resisted his plans, including Fabius Maximus Cunctator, "the delayer." In their view, Scipio's bold and daring proposal seemed too much like the rash behavior of the Roman commanders at Trebia, Trasimene, and Cannae. Scipio was thus not allowed to carry out his proposal and was instead given Sicily as his theater of operations. However, he was granted permission to invade Africa, but only if the opportunity presented itself.

This slight qualification opened an indirect way to carry out his plan, and in 204, he sailed from Sicily with his forces and landed at Utica on the north coast of Africa, just northwest of Carthage. He did not immediately march on Carthage, however. He first formed an alliance with Massinissa, ruler of the kingdom of Numidia. Massinissa had been deprived of his kingship by a rival Numidian, Syphax. To add insult to injury, Syphax had also stolen Massinissa's future bride, Hasdrubal's daughter Sophonisba. Syphax had earlier been a friend to Rome and had even trained his army in the Roman manner, but in 206 he became an ally of Carthage and also Hasdrubal's son-in-law by his marriage to Sophonisba. Scipio took advantage of this personal and political rivalry, joining forces with Massinissa, who sought revenge against Syphax. Scipio then opened peace negotiations with Syphax, but with no intention of reaching an agreement. Instead, he used the negotiations to lull Syphax and his army into a false sense of security. One night, he had some of his soldiers set fire to the Numidian camp where Syphax and his army were sleeping peacefully, without any worry that the peace-seeking Romans would engage in any hostile action. When the Numidian soldiers were awakened by the flames and ran out of the camp unarmed, Scipio's soldiers cut them down. Through this underhanded ploy, Massinissa regained his throne as well as his bride Sophonisba, who had a reputation for Carthaginian patriotism and hostility toward Rome. In fact, Scipio had some concern that she would use her influence over Massinissa to turn him against Rome, and Scipio also wanted to take Sophonisba back to Rome to be displayed in his triumph. When Scipio demanded Massinissa hand her over, Massinissa was torn between loyalty to Scipio and love for Sophonisba. In the end, instead of giving her to Scipio to be led in chains in a Roman triumph, he gave her a cup of poison to drink, sparing her from disgrace (or at least solving his dilemma).

Carthage now found its own walls threatened with imminent attack and opened up peace negotiations with Rome, though with the same false intentions as Scipio. To begin with, they recalled Hannibal from Italy, itself a major achievement for the Romans and a validation of Scipio's strategy. In 202, Hannibal and Scipio then drew up their armies across from one another outside of Carthage on the plains of Zama, which gave the battle its name. As so often in the writings of Roman historians, an enemy of Rome delivers a speech full of importance for future Romans, and here Livy has Hannibal speak rather philosophically to Scipio before the final battle of the Second Punic War:

> You should have the least amount of confidence in the greatest of luck. At this moment of your success, and in our uncertain situation, you will earn honor and glory by granting peace, while we seek peace out of necessity, not as a matter of honor. A guarantee of peace, which is in your hands, is better and more secure than a hope of victory, which is in the hands of the gods. Do not risk all Rome's success over these many years on the outcome of a single hour. ... It is in war that outcomes are least likely to be what everyone expects. You might gain more glory by a victory in battle than by granting peace, but however much more it is, it is still not as much as you would lose in defeat. A single hour can wipe out all the honors you've won, and all the honors you hope for. With a peace treaty, Publius Cornelius, you are in control of everything. If you risk battle, you must submit to the luck that is in the hands of the gods. (Livy 30.30)

Contrary to the legend of Hannibal's childhood oath to be an unwavering enemy of Rome, here he encourages Scipio to accept a peaceful resolution to the long and bloody conflict, which had claimed the lives of so many on both sides, including both of their fathers. The speech sounds very much like something Fabius Maximus Cunctator would say, not only to Scipio, but to future Romans (the speech, in reality, was written at the end of the first century BC, after the end of the republic). Needless to say, Scipio spurns Hannibal's wisdom about the uncertain fortunes of war and commits to battle.

Hannibal is defeated and urges Carthage to accept the peace terms offered by Rome, however harsh they might appear. Carthage was required to surrender all territories outside of Africa, to reduce its fleet to a bare minimum, to recognize Numidia as an independent ally of Rome, and to pay a massive sum of money in annual installments for fifty years. Hannibal himself survived, and we find him playing a leading role in Carthage's government in the years after Zama. He was elected to high office and undertook reforms of the government and taxation. These seem to have been so successful that Carthage offered to pay back the entire sum of money owed to Rome early (Rome refused the offer). Nonetheless, he still had political enemies and was eventually forced to flee Carthage. He found refuge with his earlier ally Philip V of Macedon, from whom Rome demanded his return. Hannibal then constantly sought out other friendly monarchs to shelter him, sometimes offering them advice on how to deal with the Romans. Various Romans continued to hound him for years, as much for their own personal glory as for vengeance for Rome. In 183 BC, nearly

20 years after the end of the Second Punic War, Hannibal was taken in by a Greek king in Asia Minor (the traditional name for the area corresponding to modern-day Turkey). Fearing his host would betray him and turn him over to the Roman consul pursuing him, he committed suicide.

The Roman Triumph

The Roman triumph is one of the better-known spectacles from ancient Rome, and numerous depictions exist in painting and film. A triumph was a ritual celebration of a victory in war, and a general who was awarded one would be elevated into elite company. The celebrations were of such importance that they were recorded in official calendars from the early days of Rome, and also resulted in the addition of an honorific title to one's name, such as Africanus or Macedonicus, which could be passed down to sons and descendants. The word "triumph" seems to derive from *io triumphe*, a Greek exclamation used in the cult of Dionysus to call for the god to appear, and the victorious Roman commander would in many respects be treated as a divinity. A triumph celebrated the return of the victorious army and was the only time military weapons were allowed within the sacred boundary of the city (the *pomerium*). The general, however, lost his authority to command, his *imperium*, as soon as he crossed the city limit, and thus needed to apply to the senate for a triumph while still outside the *pomerium*.

Only the senate could award a triumph, and certain conditions had to be met. First, the war in which the Roman commander had won his victory must have been a "just war" (*iustum bellum*). A "just war," in Roman terms, meant that it was properly declared in accordance with the ritual performed by the fetial priests, and at least had the appearance of being undertaken for the right reasons, either to punish wrongdoing against Roman interests or to defend a Roman ally. Wars waged against slaves, such as the suppression of a slave revolt, or victories in civil wars, fought against fellow Romans, would not normally qualify for a triumph. The victory also had to be large enough, measured in part by the number of enemies killed (5000 was the minimum), and the senate also had to determine that the war involved a serious conflict. An "easy" victory over a weak foe would lessen the likelihood that the senate would grant a triumph. Lastly, the Roman commander had to possess *imperium* at the time of the victory, which would mean a praetor, consul, or dictator, or someone granted praetorian or consular authority (e.g., a propraetor or proconsul governing a province). The award of a triumph, as with many things at Rome, was more a matter of politics than the commander's performance. If the senate did not approve of a triumph, a general could instead celebrate an *ovatio*, which was a lesser form of a triumph and not nearly as prestigious. For example, the victorious commander had to walk on foot rather than ride in a chariot. A Roman could also celebrate a triumph at his own expense on the Alban Mount, outside of Rome, if he so chose.

The central feature of a triumph was, of course, the procession of the victorious commander, the *triumphator*, and his troops through the city of Rome toward the temple of Jupiter Optimus Maximus on the Capitoline hill. On the morning of the triumph, this parade would gather outside the city walls, entering through the "Triumphal Gate" (*Porta Triumphalis*, its exact location is unknown.) From there, the procession passed along the Circus Maximus and made its way into the Forum, where the triumphant commander halted before Jupiter's temple. At the front of the procession were wagons carrying displays of the plunder taken from the conquered, including valuable works of art as well as piles of weapons and armor. War captives were also led in chains, and especially notable captives, such as the enemy monarch or his family members, were put on special display. Signs with the names of the captives would be carried alongside them, and also large paintings depicting notable scenes from the war. Senators and magistrates came next in the procession, walking before and alongside the *triumphator*, who rode in a special chariot. The *triumphator* was dressed in a purple robe decorated with gold thread (known as the *toga picta*) and wore a laurel wreath symbolizing victory. Some believe his face was also painted with cinnabar, a reddish pigment, to make him look like the statue of Jupiter in the temple on the Capitoline. The triumphant general would thus be marked out as above the mortals around him and assimilated in some form to a divinity. To ensure that the *triumphator* did not entertain any notions he was truly divine, a slave rode behind him in the chariot, constantly whispering in his ear the reminder that he was only a mortal (*memento te hominem esse*). Behind the triumphal chariot, and bringing up the rear of the procession, were the soldiers of the victorious commander, who behaved very differently from the solemn figures who preceded the chariot. Wearing laurels of victory like their commander, they chanted insults and sang dirty songs about their commander. A bawdy three-line verse sung by Caesar's soldiers, in which they mocked their general for allegedly performing oral sex on an eastern king, is quoted in a later biography of Caesar:

> *Gallias Caesar subegit, Nicomedes Caesarem:*
> *ecce Caesar nunc triumphat qui subegit Gallias,*
> *Nicomedes non triumphat qui subegit Caesarem.*
>
> Caesar brought Gaul to its knees,
> and Nicomedes brought Caesar to his:
> now Caesar triumphs because Gaul went down,
> but Nicomedes doesn't, though Caesar went down.
>
> (Suetonius, *The Deified Julius Caesar* 49.4)

At the conclusion of the triumphal procession, the triumphator would offer his laurel wreath to Jupiter Optimus Maximus, ending his brief stint as a god, and then host a banquet for elite Romans. There would also be festivities and games for the people of Rome, as well as gifts of money and other rewards for the soldiers, making a triumph a welcome holiday for all of Rome.

While the triumph never lost its religious character, it did transform over the years as Rome grew more wealthy and powerful, and became, like so much else in Rome, a political spectacle. The celebration of a triumph became an opportunity to further elevate an individual Roman's status and influence, and the more lavish and generous the celebration of the triumph, the greater the victory for the general. By the end of the republic, the celebration of a triumph could last

FIG. 5.8 A representation a Roman triumph on a triumphal arch from the first c. AD.

for more than a day and involve enormous outlays of money and resources, much of it taken from the wealthy kingdoms of the east that Rome continued to add to its empire. Pompey the Great, for example, celebrated a "triple triumph" in 61 BC, in which he introduced the spectacle of having a chariot led by elephants rather than horses. Unfortunately, the elephants could not squeeze through the *Porta Triumphalis* and had to be replaced by horses at the last minute.

Credits

Fig. 5.1: Copyright © by Classical Numismatic Group (CC BY-SA 3.0) at https://commons.wikimedia.org/wiki/File:Pyros.jpg.
Fig. 5.2: Adapted from d-maps.com.
Fig. 5.3: Adapted from d-maps.com.
Fig. 5.4: Copyright © by Gabriel Rodríguez Alberich (CC BY-SA 2.5) at https://commons.wikimedia.org/wiki/File:Corvus.svg.
Fig. 5.5: Adapted from d-maps.com.
Fig. 5.6: Adapted from d-maps.com.
Fig. 5.7: Source: https://commons.wikimedia.org/wiki/File:Archimedes-Mirror_by_Giulio_Parigi.jpg.
Fig. 5.8: Source: https://commons.wikimedia.org/wiki/File:Arch_Titus,_relief_triumph,_Forum_Romanum,_Rome,_Italy.jpg.

CHAPTER 6

"Our Sea"

Rome Conquers the Mediterranean

FIG. 6.1 *The Sack of Corinth*, by Thomas Allom (1870).

Overview

After Scipio's defeat of Hannibal, Rome had established itself as the preeminent power in the Mediterranean, and by the middle of the second century BC had razed Carthage to the ground and completed its conquest of Greece. During this period, Rome found itself entangled in further political and military conflicts throughout the Mediterranean, and increased contacts with peoples around the Mediterranean added to the internal turmoil in the republic. One of the most important Romans from this period, Cato the Elder, exemplifies the growing divide among the ruling elite between those claiming to uphold the traditions of the republic and those embracing the increase in wealth and overseas influence, especially from Greece. The suppression of a "foreign" cult of Bacchus, dramatized in an incident known as the "Bacchanalian conspiracy," reveals the tensions between the old and new, and the different ways these two notions are framed. The chapter concludes with a brief survey of Latin literary culture, with a focus on borrowings from Greek literature.

Timeline

201	End of Second Punic War
198	Flamininus proclaims "freedom" for Greeks
188	Defeat of Antiochus III ("the Great")
186	"Bacchanalian Conspiracy"
168	Defeat of Perseus of Macedon
149–146	Third Punic War
146	Destruction of Carthage and Corinth
154–134	Wars in Spain

Entanglements in the East

As we saw in the last chapter, Rome had become increasingly involved in the complicated politics of the eastern Mediterranean following the invasion of Pyrrhus and the interference of Philip V of Macedon in the Second Punic War. Their use of a coalition of Greek states to oppose Philip V was merely a preview of political maneuverings to come. In the western Mediterranean, Rome tended to rely more on the creation of provinces to administer and control conquered territories, though there were also client rulers in the west. Scipio's alliance with Massinissa in the Second Punic War, described in the previous chapter, is a good example of a king who enjoyed Rome's protection but was also subject to its authority. In the eastern Mediterranean, Rome initially turned to indirect forms of control rather than provinces. All this would gradually change, however, and much of the eastern Mediterranean would eventually come under provincial administration by the end of the republic. One major disadvantage of indirect control is that the ruler who became a friend and ally of Rome could never be fully trusted. Provincial administration, for all its faults, was less prone to the double and triple dealings of rulers in the eastern Mediterranean. But the use of political alliances and diplomatic maneuvering instead of the imposition of a Roman provincial governor was not simply a choice Rome made. The cities and kingdoms of the eastern Mediterranean, including Greece, Egypt, Syria, and Asia Minor, had their own long histories of organized states and political traditions, and many had impressive military resources at their disposal. Wealthy, powerful, and independent, many of them would see Rome as a rude upstart, lacking civilization and culture—and they would not be wrong to think so, even after the Second Punic War. The Romans, in fact, would admit as much, even if they considered themselves superior in morals and military might.

Rome's involvement in the eastern Mediterranean, beginning with figures like Queen Teuta and Philip V of Macedon, would often lead to the same results as their involvement in the disputes of Magna Graecia or with the Mamertines of Sicily. Small disputes would lead to larger conflicts and draw Rome into even deeper involvement in the politics of the eastern

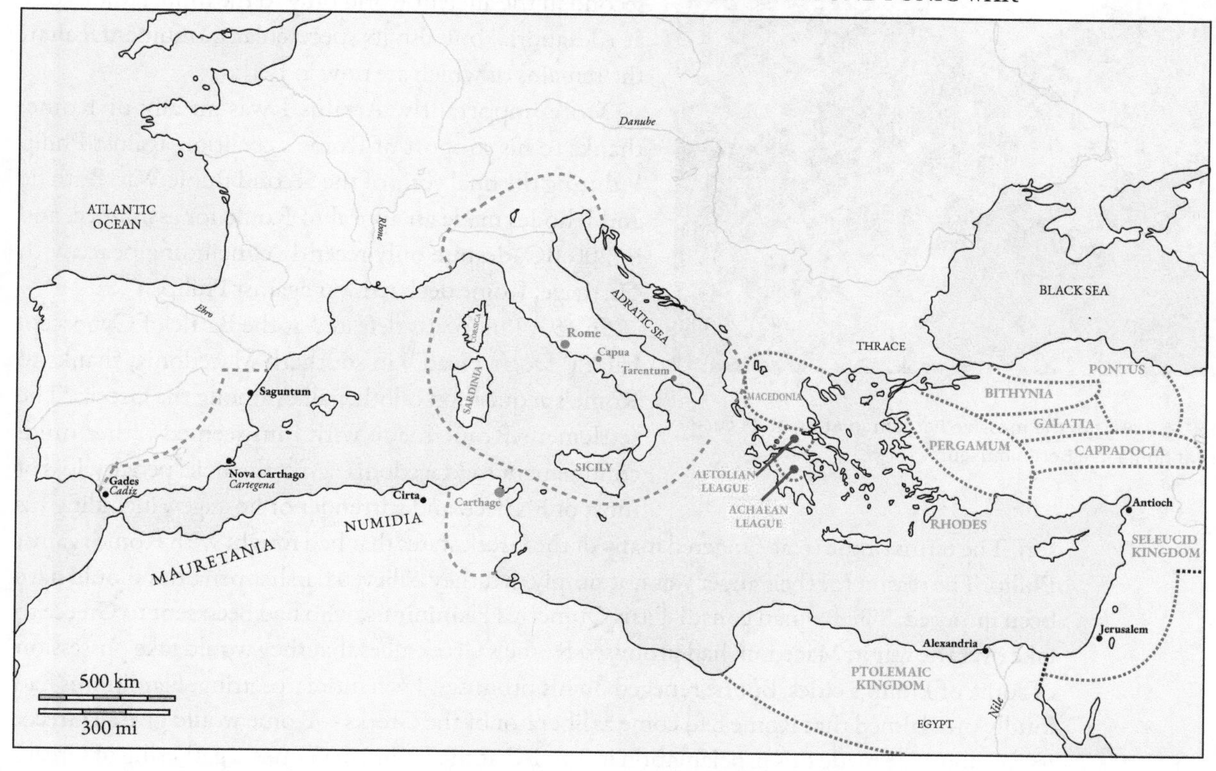

FIG. 6.2 After the Second Punic War.

Mediterranean, eventually necessitating military action. In fact, in the aftermath of the Second Punic War, Rome's conflicts with Philip V and Greece were just beginning, leading to a series of military engagements often known as the Macedonian Wars (of which there are three in the traditional accounting).

Philip V of Macedon

After Hannibal's defeat, Philip sought to expand his influence across the Aegean and into Asia Minor, and turned his attentions away from Italy to the east, across the Aegean Sea to Rhodes, an island off the southwest coast of modern-day Turkey. Possessing several good ports and a strategic location in the Mediterranean, Rhodes was a major commercial center with an excellent fleet to keep pirates at bay and protect trade. As might be expected, Philip's designs on Rhodes alarmed other rulers in the area, particularly Attalus I of Pergamum (or Pergamon), a small kingdom on the central coast of modern-day Turkey that emerged out of the feuds following the death of Alexander the Great. Pergamum was wealthy and powerful, famed not only for its library,

FIG. 6.3 Part of the massive Pergamon Altar, at its current home in a Berlin museum.

second in the ancient world only to the more famous one at Alexandria, but also its spectacular monumental altar, the remains of which are now in Berlin.

More importantly, Attalus I was an ally of Rome, thanks to his support of Rome's coalition against Philip V during the final years of the Second Punic War. Both he and Rhodes made an appeal to Rome for assistance, and in 200 BC, despite only recently concluding peace with Carthage, Rome declared war against Philip.

In 197, Philip was defeated at the Battle of Cynoscephalae ("Dog's Head") in southern Macedonia, thanks to Rome's acquisition of other allies among the Greeks. The settlement Rome made with him seemed rather mild: confinement to Macedonia, a stiff financial penalty, loss of most of his fleet, and surrender of hostages, including his son. The terms of the treaty angered many of the Greek states that had fought with Rome against Philip. The reason for their anger was not simply that they believed harsher penalties should have been imposed. The Roman consul Titus Quinctius Flamininus, who had been sent to Greece to take over the war in Macedon, had promised Rome's Greek allies that they would take possession of some of Philip's cities, but he reneged on his promises. Even more upsetting, Flamininus had loudly proclaimed that Rome had come as liberator of the Greeks—Rome would give all Greece its freedom! He made this proclamation in 196 BC at the Isthmian Games, a gathering of Greeks to compete in athletic games and dramatic performances, equivalent to the Olympics. According to some reports, his announcement was greeted with such a resounding cheer that passing birds dropped to the ground, killed by the burst of sound. Despite his proclamation of freedom, the Greeks were left with Philip at their doorstep, and what was worse he actually became an ally of Rome. Moreover, because of the helpful military service he provided to Roman armies, he was freed from having to pay the remainder of his fine.

Greek city-states (*poleis*; in the singular, a *polis*) had a long tradition of political autonomy, one of the reasons why they never really managed to unite into a larger political coalition for long, unless faced with a common external enemy, such as during the Persian invasions at the beginning of the fifth century BC. Even then, their unity was fragile at best. Following in his father's footsteps, Alexander the Great brought the *poleis* together only because he placed them all under his yoke, and, after his death, the territories he claimed to rule broke apart into smaller kingdoms ruled by his former companions and commanders, who competed with one another in a dizzying series of political intrigues. Greek city-states were especially prone to support anyone who claimed to support their freedom. Though they were often disappointed in the results, they never seemed to tire of hearing the promise. They may have expected something different from Rome, but it was not to be. In fact, within a few decades after Flamininus declared Greece free, Greek cities would find themselves subjugated to this new power from the western Mediterranean rather than enjoying their independence. It would be easy to accuse Flamininus and the Romans of hypocrisy, but again, larger strategic issues overwhelmed any pretense that Rome could simply free the Greeks and let them be. In fact, Rome's first military engagement in the eastern Mediterranean was only a first step to permanent involvement, which would culminate in Roman soldiers reaching the borders of modern-day Iran.

FIG. 6.4 An eighteenth-c. medal representing Flamininus restoring liberty to Greece. He places the felt cap worn by freed slaves on female deities representing Greek city-states.

Antiochus the Great

After Flamininus returned to Rome, another Greek ruler and heir to Alexander the Great's conquests supplanted Philip V as the thorn in Rome's side. For the first time, Roman forces would be sent beyond Greece and across the Hellespont, the narrow strait linking the Aegean Sea to the Black Sea that served as the traditional boundary between what the ancients called Europe and Asia.

Antiochus III (also called "Antiochus the Great") was king of the Seleucid Empire, which stretched from the eastern shores of the Mediterranean to present-day Iraq. When his childless brother was assassinated, he was summoned from the great ancient city Babylon to the city of Antioch in modern-day Syria, where he would assume the throne of the Seleucid Empire. While Rome was engaged in its long war with Hannibal, Antiochus was busy dealing with rebellions throughout his kingdom. Once these were settled, he began to pursue his own imperialistic ambitions, which would soon come into conflict with Rome's. In 194 BC, he first secured an alliance with Egypt, after defeating them militarily, by marrying his daughter Cleopatra I to the ruler of Egypt, Ptolemy V, a young man who was a poor excuse for a king. Rome had just finished coming to terms with Philip when Antiochus moved his forces into Thrace, the region west of the Hellespont and north of Macedonia, largely corresponding to modern-day Bulgaria. This territory had traditionally been considered part of the Seleucid Empire, at least by the Seleucids, and thus his entry there could be justified as a recovery of lost territory rather than an invasion. In his journey from Asia Minor into Greek lands, he won over to his cause many cities that had become disgruntled with Rome, in part by giving them his own hollow promise of freedom. Flamininus warned Antiochus to keep his hands off independent Greek *poleis*, but since these cities had not enjoyed the fruits of the liberty the Romans had supposedly granted him, they were more than happy to try their luck with Antiochus.

FIG. 6.5 Antiochus III on a coin issued around 200 BC. The figure on the right is Apollo, seated on the *omphalos* representing the oracle at Delphi, where Antiochus proclaimed freedom for Greece in 192.

Before he set out on his campaign to the west, Antiochus had supposedly received some sage advice on how to deal with the Romans from a familiar source—Hannibal. The Carthaginian general told him that in order to have any chance of victory he would need to bring together all of Rome's enemies in an alliance to confront Rome with a unified front. Antiochus either ignored the advice or realized it was an impossibility, since unity was rarely a feature of kingdoms in the eastern Mediterranean. Instead, it was the Romans who made common cause with Philip V of Macedon, other Greek states, and even Carthage to defeat Antiochus. Forced to flee, Antiochus headed east toward Syria with the Romans in pursuit. Roman forces crossed over the Hellespont from Europe into Asia under the command of Lucius Cornelius Scipio (Africanus's brother). The Romans defeated his armies at Thermopylae (191 BC) in Greece and at Magnesia (190 BC) in Asia Minor, and after he suffered a naval defeat as well, Antiochus's ambitions came to an end with the Treaty of Apamea (named after a town in Syria) in 188 BC. Rome offered Antiochus the standard peace terms of surrender of territorial possessions and payment of a large fine, and Rome divided up Antiochus's lands among its allies. Antiochus went east to the Persian city of Susa (in modern-day Iran) and was killed while robbing the Temple of Baal in an attempt to acquire money.

After Hannibal: Scipio on Trial

While Rome's victory over Carthage in the Second Punic War would be one of its greatest triumphs, the contrasting positions that were evident in the approach to the war—the daring and sometimes reckless pursuit of conquest and glory opposed to a cautious and deliberate strategy—manifested themselves in the domestic politics of the republic. The opposing factions managed to act with some semblance of unity during the war, but at its conclusion broke into open conflict on the domestic front. Although these conflicts were in some sense normal political differences found within any government, they also represent a more fundamental opposition. On the one hand, there was a hesitation to depart from the traditional behaviors and ideals believed to have led Rome to great heights. On the other hand was a demand for recognition that Rome's position in the world had changed, and Rome must change with it. In our sources, usually representing the traditional senatorial perspective, this tension often arises from the impetuous and rashness of the plebs, always eager for quick action and easy solutions and always opposed to the more prudent counsels of the senate. Many senators, however, would agree with the plebeian demands for action, even if only for their own advancement.

This opposition is exemplified in the debate at the end of the Second Punic War over the young Scipio's desire to take the war into Africa. The elder statesman Fabius Maximus Cunctator opposed it, claiming it was a risky enterprise undertaken by a hot-headed young man. (Hannibal is made to express a similarly cautious approach in his battlefield speech to Scipio.) Yet Fabius's concern was not only for Rome—he also wished to protect his own standing (*dignitas*) at Rome and feared losing prestige and glory to this young upstart from a distinguished family. In fact, if

Scipio carried out his plan and succeeded, then many who had criticized Fabius's strategy of delay could claim they were right all along. It was not the wrong strategy to bring to the battle, they could say; they had only chosen the wrong commanders. In Roman politics, it is often difficult to untangle personal ambitions from political strategies, and a clear line between the two cannot always be drawn.

Fabius almost certainly believed his strategy was the correct one, as difficult as it was to maintain while Italy was slowly being devastated by Hannibal's troops and the people of Rome grew impatient for victory. Yet there are good grounds to believe that behind Fabius's opposition to Scipio was the desire to preserve his status and dignity, loss of which was extremely serious to elite Romans, to a degree that sometimes is difficult for us to understand. When a deep concern for one's own personal interests influences the way one approaches an issue of vital importance to the state, we often regard this as wrongful bias. In this view, personal interests should be separate from discussions of the public good, and to impute to Fabius a personal motive in his actions puts a stain on an otherwise heroic character. For the Romans, to defend one's personal *dignitas* as part of a political debate on war strategy would make perfect sense, and Fabius's opposition to Scipio on personal grounds would not undercut his arguments for his strategy. On the contrary, he would be expected to do so. Fabius died shortly before Scipio's defeat of Hannibal at the Battle of Zama in 202 and thus did not live to see the eclipse of his standing by the young general now endowed with the honorific title Africanus, which to most Roman ears would have a more glorious ring than Cunctator ("the delayer"). For all the deserved accolades Fabius earned over his own glorious career, his strategy did not lead to the summit of glory for a Roman commander, a triumph. He might well consider this a personal failure.

Scipio Africanus's career after the Second Punic War was not free of turmoil, even though he could claim to be the most popular and prestigious man in Rome. His military victories overseas, in fact, paved the way for political battles back at Rome. He was viewed by some as something more than mortal, and both his success at such a young age and his own behavior did little to discourage this belief. Early in his career during his command in Spain, when he captured New Carthage, he had told his troops that the god Neptune had come to him in a dream promising to help him (specifically him, not his soldiers or Rome itself). Whether or not he meant to elevate himself in the eyes of the soldiers as someone under the special protection of the gods, it was certainly taken that way in many quarters. Following his defeat of Hannibal, he was elected consul twice in the 190s and was also made *princeps senatus* ("first man of the senate"), formal recognition of his preeminence among the senatorial elite. Nonetheless, his prominence and popularity, especially among the soldiers and the plebs of Rome, alarmed many among the nobility, who would have been fearful of the power he might wield in Rome.

In 190 BC, his brother Lucius Cornelius Scipio was involved in the war in Greece against Antiochus. Scipio volunteered to assist him as a legate, a subordinate position that conferred no real authority, but his presence would have caused a stir among both the Roman soldiers and their enemies. The campaign ended in a peaceful settlement, which Scipio presented to the Roman Senate, and this would have been a dignified end to a distinguished career. However, in the twilight of his career, Scipio's political enemies in Rome chose this moment to launch an attack. In republican Rome, political attacks frequently involved legal prosecution, often against family members. In 187, a tribune of the plebs demanded that Scipio's brother Lucius provide an official accounting of the vast sums of money he had received from Antiochus when they had come to terms with him. Lucius replied that this money was not paid as part of the peace treaty, but was instead plunder from the war, and thus not subject to review by the senate. Scipio Africanus gave a more dramatic response when he ripped up the account books before the eyes of the senators. A tribune of the plebs imposed a fine on Lucius, but he avoided paying it when one of the other tribunes vetoed it. A few years later, however, another tribune of the plebs launched another accusation about the funds the Scipio brothers received from Antiochus, this time against Scipio Africanus himself. Instead of addressing the charges, Scipio spoke of all his achievements. The tribunes pressed their case, using rumor and innuendo to accuse him of corruption, and spoke until evening when the trial was adjourned. As the trial was about the resume the following day, Scipio went up to the rostra followed by a huge crowd. He delivered a dramatic speech reminding all those present of the glorious victory he had won just over a decade earlier:

> Tribunes of the plebs and the citizens of Rome, today is the anniversary of my victorious battle against Hannibal and the Carthaginians in Africa, a day when there should be no trials or legal wrangling. So I will leave this assembly and go to the Capitol to pay my respects to Jupiter Optimus Maximus, to Juno, to Minerva, and to the other gods who stand guard over our Capitol. I will thank them for giving me the desire and the ability to perform distinguished service for my country, on this day and on many others. Follow me, citizens, if you can, and pray to the gods for leaders like me. From the time I was seventeen until my old age [he was 49!], you have always elected me to offices before I reached the minimum age, and I have always exceeded your expectations in all the offices you have given me. (Livy 38.51)

At the end of his speech, he walked out of the trial before it even started. All those present followed him, even the clerks and messengers working the trial, leaving the tribunes who accused him standing alone.

Although a moral victory for Scipio, he had no illusions about what awaited him the next day and the days after. He knew that he would not escape more accusations and legal wrangling about his conduct. He refused to appear at the trial to defend himself and instead left Rome. His brother gave the excuse that he was ill—he was certainly sick of the politics at Rome. Though the tribunes intended to continue with the trial, and openly criticized Scipio for his absence, one of the other tribunes, who had been on bad terms with Scipio, unexpectedly put an end to the entire affair with a brief speech justifying Scipio's refusal to appear on account of his extraordinary achievements. The tribune concluded his speech with a rhetorical question, which was meant to apply not only to Scipio, but to all outstanding individuals:

> Are there any accomplishments, any honors you grant, citizens, that would allow exceptional citizens to reach a place beyond mortals cares, where they can be free of worry in their old age, where they can finally rest, and where, if they can't be treated with respect, can at least be free from political attacks? (Livy 38.51)

Scipio died shortly afterward, having never set foot in Rome again. This was the rather disappointing end of one of the most glorious careers of the republic.

Our information about these trials is often confused, and it usually impossible to achieve a clear understanding of them. More important, however, is the way the trial is presented in our sources—less a question of Scipio's guilt or innocence than a debate over the preeminence of a single individual. To what degree is such an individual allowed to deviate from traditions and laws, even when in doing so he performs valuable services to the state? While it is easy enough to claim that no one should be above the law, as some Romans did, individuals such as Scipio had often been granted leeway in the past. To deny them the privilege of acting more freely and independently than other Romans could reasonably be viewed as a personal attack rather than a sincere concern with equal treatment under the law. The trial of Scipio reflects a fundamental tension between the personal and political that would eventually split Rome in two.

Strange Gods? The Bacchanalian Conspiracy of 186

While Roman soldiers were fighting battles in the eastern Mediterranean and the Scipio brothers were legal combatants in the courts, a sensational scandal hit the city of Rome. In 186, Rome was struck by a panic over the discovery of a secretive cult within the city. It was believed to involve thousands of people engaged in sordid initiation rituals. The first-century BC historian Livy gives a dramatic account of this so-called "Bacchanalian conspiracy," which in his telling contains all the elements of a tawdry *telenovela*. Fortunately, this incident provides one of those rare instances when we possess a contemporary piece of evidence to compare to the narrative histories, in this case a bronze inscription of a senatorial decree, discovered in the seventeenth century in southern Italy. Livy's description of the decree closely matches the version on bronze, so he can be trusted in that regard. The narrative he constructs of the events that lead to the decree, however, is difficult to accept as historical truth.

According to Livy, the origins of this "clandestine conspiracy" lay in Etruria, where a low-born Greek arrived as something of a religious huckster, conning people into joining a secret night-time cult. There were secret initiation rituals, but also a fair amount of drinking and eating, which made this cult attractive to a growing number of men and women. The drinking parties, which contrary to Roman norms included women as well as men, turned into sexual orgies, leading to further outrageous immoral behavior, including cult members poisoning their family members. Many of these complaints were exaggerated, and hyperbolic accusations were often lodged against long-standing religious practices from around the Mediterranean, especially religious practices associated with the Greek god of wine, Dionysius, known in Rome as Bacchus or Liber. (Thus, the English word for a wild drinking party is known as a Bacchanalia, the same word used in the senate's decree, known as *De Bacchanalibus*.) In time, this secret cult made its way to Rome.

A young man named Publius Aebutius, whose father had died, was being raised by his mother and stepfather. To help his stepfather to steal Publius's inheritance, his mother informed Publius that she had made a vow to Dionysus when he was still an infant, and now it was to time to fulfill her vow by initiating him into the cult. Publius was in a relationship with a neighbor, a former slave and prostitute named Hispala. In her earlier life as a slave, she had been introduced to this cult and all its horrors, which she related to Publius, even revealing that the clashing of cymbals was to drown out the screams of initiates being sexually assaulted. On hearing this, Publius refused to go along with his mother's wishes, and reported what he heard to the consul, who wished to question Hispala. Overwhelmed at first with panic and trembling, she finally managed to divulge all she knew about the cult. In fear of her life, she asked to be sent away to live outside of Italy, far from the reaches of the cult leaders, but the consul provided her assurances that she could live safely at Rome.

In Hispala's telling, the cult's shrine had first been off limits to men, and married women took turns serving as chief priestess. Their initiation rituals lasted for three days and were held during the day. Then a chief priestess from Campania had instituted radical changes, lengthening the initiation by two days, holding them at night, and, more notably, admitting men. The initiates now began to engage in sexual orgies, with no distinction between male and female. Men in convulsions uttered prophecies, and women would rush to the Tiber carrying torches, where they would dip them into the river and raise them again, still burning. (Oddly, no one in Rome seemed to take notice of all this.) Perhaps most terrifying to the consul was Hispala's revelation that a vast number of individuals were involved, including members of the nobility—almost a "second city," in her words. When the consul presented his findings to the senate, they were gravely concerned not only that this cult might grow into a conspiracy against the state, but also that some of their own family members might be involved. They authorized the consul to uproot this threat to the moral order of Rome, and other officials were tasked with hunting down the priests and priestesses and ensuring secret nighttime meetings were no longer held. The senate also decreed that all Bacchic sites of worship were to be destroyed, not just in Rome, but throughout Italy, and all future Bacchic worship was forbidden. As news of the senate's decree became public, many of those associated

FIG. 6.6 A fifth-c. BC representation of a maenad or bacchant, a female worshipper of Bacchus/Dionysus. In her right hand she carries a thyrsus, a staff made of a fennel plant wound with ivy at the top, associated with worship of Bacchus/Dionysus.

with the cult tried to flee, and some committed suicide. According to Livy, more than seven thousand people were involved.

This narrative includes many elements straight from a script written for the stage: the prostitute with a heart of gold, the wicked step-parent, and the naive young man caught up in trouble. Yet the basic facts are real enough, as confirmed by the copy of the actual decree of the senate. The main body of the decree is as follows:

> No one is to possess a place where the festivals of Bacchus are celebrated. If anyone claims it is necessary to have such a place, they must appear before the praetor urbanus at Rome. After their claim has been heard by at least 100 senators, the Senate will make a decision. No man, neither a Roman citizen nor a Latin nor any ally of Rome, is permitted to be a Bacchant, unless they appear before the praetor urbanus, and the Senate grants him permission by decree when at least 100 senators are present.
>
> No man is permitted to be a priest; no one, either man or woman, is permitted to be an official; nor is anyone of them permitted have charge of a common treasury; no one shall appoint either man or woman to be master or to act as master; henceforth they shall not form conspiracies among themselves, stir up any disorder, make mutual promises or agreements, or exchange pledges; no one shall observe the sacred rites either in public or private or outside the city, unless he appears before the praetor urbanus, and the Senate grants him permission by decree when at least 100 senators are present.
>
> No one in a company of more than five persons altogether, men and women, shall observe the sacred rites, nor in that company shall there be present more than two men or three women, unless in accordance with the opinion of the praetor urbanus and the Senate as written above.

The decree is sometimes portrayed as evidence of Rome's religious and cultural conservatism and abhorrence of foreign religion, though a close examination of the evidence presents a more nuanced story. The aggressive reaction against the Bacchic cult was not because it was foreign, and also likely not because it was new and strange, as Livy's narrative suggests. It is unlikely that the worship of Bacchus was anything new, and in fact Livy's description of the decree states that anyone who considered Bacchic rituals "traditional and an essential part of his religious observance" could appeal to the senate. The senate acknowledged there might be people for whom this worship was traditional, which suggests some form of Bacchic worship predated the events of 186 BC. Moreover, the call for suppression not just in Rome, but throughout Italy, also suggests a well-established religious practice. The decree itself, as preserved in both Livy and the original inscribed on bronze, hints at the real reasons for the suppression of the cult. In the second section of the decree, the worshippers are forbidden "to form conspiracies among themselves," or "to make mutual promises" or "exchange pledges." These actions in themselves have nothing to do with religious practice or belief but suggest a type of social and political bond that takes place outside of the state and the family. Even in Livy's narrative, the reaction of the senate is telling.

There is no mention of strange gods or foreign influence, only fears of sedition against the state and possible family involvement, which follows Hispala's hint at a secret "second city" within Rome itself. The final section of the decree also points to this direction, in limiting the size of the meetings. This also suggests that the senate believes the rites will continue to be practiced following the strict guidelines they have set down.

In fact, Rome was not opposed to the importation of foreign cults, as is often claimed. Near the end of the Second Punic War, Rome had followed the instruction of the Sibylline Books and the Delphic Oracle to import the cult of Magna Mater ("Great Mother," also known as Cybele) from Asia Minor. The cult image of the goddess was a black stone, likely a meteorite, and a new temple was built for it on the Palatine hill at the center of Rome. A relative of Scipio Africanus was charged with the mission to retrieve the stone image, and a woman of a noble family, Claudia Quintia, is said to have miraculously freed the ship carrying the cult object when it ran aground before it reached Rome. This foreign cult was welcomed, with the full and even enthusiastic support of the senate and the ruling elite, even though it too could be described in the same exaggerated way as the Bacchic cult in Livy. The followers of the Magna Mater were known to dress in bright clothes, beg for money, and worship the goddess with what are described as "wild Phrygian rituals" (Phrygia was a region in western Turkey, the home of Cybele). The male priests of Cybele even castrated themselves. However, the cult was sanctioned by the state, and its apparent wildness remained within its control.

The Romans liked to think of themselves as conservative adherents to traditional practices, but what exactly counted as traditional was fluid and always open to debate. The Romans, in fact, were always willing to innovate, even if at times they tried hard to disguise the fact. In the case of the "Bacchanalian conspiracy," tradition dictated that religious practices remain under control of the state, or at least any large-scale forms of worship that might grow to constitute a "second city." Rome's attitude to "foreign" imports, religious or otherwise, is not always as straightforward as it appears. It must be remembered that the distinction between Roman and non-Roman itself was always fluid, and from the beginning Rome gladly borrowed from other cultures. However, the increasing contacts with more peoples, ideas, and practices, leading to the importation of these back to Rome, created a hostile reaction among some Romans. They began to draw a distinction between what was acceptably Roman and what was not. Yet the reaction may not have been simply due to foreignness, on the basis of coming from elsewhere, but due to elements perceived as contrary to Roman ways. Just because something came from elsewhere did not automatically mean it was un-Roman. We must be careful not to let an oversimplification of Roman attitudes create an oversimplified portrait of Rome.

Everything Ends: Greece and Carthage

Perseus of Macedon and the Sack of Corinth

Although Philip V of Macedon died in 179 BC, Rome's wars with Macedon were not yet over. His son, Perseus, who had fought alongside his father both against the Romans and with the

Romans, succeeded to the throne of Macedon. He renewed the treaty his father made with Rome, but he was not a friend of Rome by any means. Through a series of adept diplomatic and military maneuvers, he became increasingly popular throughout central Greece and extended his influence by forming family connections, including his own marriage to a Seleucid princess. It is unlikely that he had any idea of defying Rome or confronting them militarily and instead only wished to improve the conditions of the Greek cities and lighten the burdens of Rome's authority. Nevertheless, Rome became suspicious of his actions, especially when a rival of Perseus named Eumenes, heir to the throne of Attalus I at Pergamum and an ally of Rome, complained about him. This provided the Romans with the grounds they needed, and, in 171, Rome declared war against Perseus.

Perseus rather foolishly accepted Rome's challenge. After holding out for three years, in 168 he was defeated at Pydna in Macedonian territory. Taken to Rome as a captive, he was displayed in the triumph of the Roman consul Lucius Aemilius Paullus, who earned the honorific title Macedonicus for his victory. Perseus was kept in prison at Rome, where he died. His son, named Alexander after his famous ancestor, was also taken to Rome; he learned Latin and eventually became a clerk. Macedon itself, a source of troublesome rulers for some time, was now divided into four "republics." Restrictions were placed on the Macedonians, who were not allowed to trade or intermarry with Macedonians in the other "republics," equivalent to the way Rome treated members of the Latin League earlier in its history. Rome also imposed payment of a tribute and took control of the mines, which were a major source of revenue. So great was the bounty for Rome from this conquest that Roman citizens were no longer required to pay taxes.

There was one last gasp of Macedonian resistance to Rome twenty years later, when a man who claimed to be Perseus's son led an uprising against Rome. It was soon crushed, and the four "republics" became the province of Macedonia. The home of Alexander the Great was now an administrative unit in the burgeoning empire of the Roman Republic. The loss of independence was devastating for Greece, but even more so was the utter destruction of Corinth, an ancient city located on the isthmus between the Peloponnese and Attica. The Isthmian Games, the occasion for Flamininus's declaration of Greek freedom, had been held at Corinth for centuries, but when a Roman consul was sent there to punish it for participating in the revolt against Rome, he allowed his troops to plunder it at will. The city enshrined as "wealthy Corinth" in the poetry of ancient Greece was burned to the ground.

The Third Punic War

The year Corinth was destroyed also saw Carthage razed to the ground, at the end of the Third Punic War in 146 BC. Carthage had upheld the terms imposed on it by the treaty that concluded the Second Punic War almost fifty years earlier, and had even supported Rome in its campaigns against Antiochus in the eastern Mediterranean. However, Rome's old friend from Numidia, Massinissa, decided to take advantage of the restrictions placed on Carthage, in particular the prohibition against engaging in war without Rome's permission. Massinissa began to seize parts of Carthage's territory, until Carthage, acting in accordance with the terms of the treaty, complained to Rome. In 153, the Roman Senate sent a delegation to investigate. While the Romans could not fail to acknowledge the injustice of Massinissa's actions, what disturbed them far more was the flourishing condition of Carthage, awakening their fears of the return of their greatest foe. In one story, at the conclusion of his report on Carthage before the senate, a member of the delegation shook his toga so that some Libyan figs brought from Carthage fell to the floor. When the senators admired their freshness and fine quality, he reminded them that the city from which they came was only three days' sail from Rome.

Carthage was frustrated with Massinissa's incursions into their territory and equally frustrated with Rome's refusal to intervene. Although there were members of the Carthaginian senate who would have preferred to remain on Rome's good side, an opposing faction took control and urged Carthage to take military action against Massinissa, even if it meant violating the terms of their treaty with Rome. The attack on Massinissa failed, and thus their transgression of the treaty gained them nothing but the anger of the Romans. The Carthaginians attempted to make amends and sent an embassy to beg for peace, but given what they had already seen, the Romans were more than eager to declare war. It could easily be deemed a "just war" given Carthage's actions. Carthage made a last-ditch plea for peace and agreed to destroy all their weapons, send three hundred hostages to Rome, and obey the Roman consuls in all matters. But when Rome further insisted that the Carthaginians abandon their city and build another at least 10 miles from the sea, they decided they might as well fight.

The Third Punic War, unlike the previous two, was no large-scale conflict fought over large swaths of territory, no back and forth struggle lasting over a decade, but a three-year siege in which the Carthaginians hunkered down and fought to the last. The Roman commander of the siege was Publius Cornelius Scipio Aemilianus, the biological son of Lucius Aemilius Paullus, who had defeated Perseus in 168. He had been adopted by the son of Publius Cornelius Scipio Africanus, the victor over Hannibal. The "Aemilianus" was added to his name to indicate his adoption from Aemilius Paullus. Adoptions of adult males sometimes occurred between aristocratic families when one of them had no male heirs. This adopted Scipio would, like his adoptive grandfather, earn the honorific *cognomen* Africanus (and is sometimes known as "Scipio the younger" or "Africanus the younger"). Also like his grandfather, he was elected consul and given command of Roman forces before he was old enough to hold the office. Despite the determined resistance of the Carthaginians, this younger Scipio captured Carthage and burned it to the ground. The Carthaginian general in charge of the defense of the city begged for mercy, but his wife, made of sterner stuff, mocked his cowardice, then grabbed their two sons and leapt into the flames. All Carthaginian survivors were sold into slavery, the site of the city was cursed, and, according to tradition, the land was sown with salt. (This is sometimes thought to render the soil unable to grow crops, but it was more likely that a small amount of salt was used ritually, and the soil itself would not have been harmed.) Carthage and its territory also became a Roman province, the first in Africa.

Much like Marcellus at the fall of Syracuse in the Second Punic War, Scipio is said to have wept as he looked upon the ruins of Carthage. There is a moving account preserved by a later Greek historian that can be traced back to Polybius, a Greek historian of the second century BC, who was taken to Rome as a captive but became a friend and teacher of Scipio:

> They say that Scipio, as he watched Carthage fall into ruins and neared its final destruction, shed tears, openly weeping for the enemy. It had prospered for 700 years, ruling over land and sea, abounding in with troops, ships, elephants, and money, as rich and powerful as the mightiest kingdoms, but greater than them in courage and pride. He stood there for some time deep in thought, thinking how every city, and every nation and kingdom, must perish, just like every human being. He knew this was the fate of Troy, once a glorious city, and the fate of Assyria, Media, and Persia, in their days the greatest of empires. This was even the fate of Macedonia, so recently made glorious. Either intentionally or unconsciously, this line escaped his lips: "A day will come when sacred Troy will fall, and Priam and his people be slain." (Appian, *Punic Wars* 8.132)

At this moment of Rome's final conquest over its greatest enemy, Scipio sees in the fall of Carthage not as a glorious moment for Rome, but a vision of its future. The legendary Troy had fallen, the mighty Carthage now fell, and one day so too Rome would fall. Notably, he quotes from Homer's epic the *Iliad* to express his sympathy, revealing that he, like Marcellus, is a philhellene. While the moment is one of great emotion and imbues Scipio with a humanity that is touching, there is also implicit in this portrait a dark side. His cosmopolitan perspective, which transcends the boundaries of Rome, also represents a threat to the more traditional morality of Rome and the ideal of patriotic duty. If ultimately even the greatest of empires will fall, why fight wars on behalf of Rome? Why try to live up to the glories of one's ancestors, if in the end all turns to dust?

The political back and forth between Rome and the various kingdoms of the Greek East is confusing, with the same names and different numbers for the monarchs and ever-shifting alliances and loyalties. This is but a small sampling of the major players, but the result is clear: The Roman Republic has become the dominant power throughout the entire Mediterranean, and everything that happens around it now must be its concern. While Rome may have still felt some sense of a cultural inferiority to the civilizations of the eastern Mediterranean, their confidence in their military superiority, and their way of life, remained undiminished. To others, their growing confidence began to appear more like arrogance. Flamininus may have been greeted with cheers when he proclaimed Rome the liberator of Greece, but many must have thought it presumptuous for a Roman to claim that title rather than a Greek successor of Alexander the Great. One episode preserved in a Roman historian's account provides a snapshot of this Roman attitude, be it confidence or arrogance. Gaius Popillius Laenas, consul in 172, was sent to Egypt on an embassy to the Seleucid king Antiochus IV, son and heir to Antiochus III ("the Great,"), whom the Romans had defeated in 188. Laenas was there not to conduct diplomacy as much as to deliver an ultimatum that Antiochus IV must evacuate Egypt immediately. Antiochus, who would see himself as heir to Alexander the Great and would regard himself as one of the most powerful, wealthy, and important individuals in the ancient Mediterranean, hesitated to reply. Laenas drew a circle in the sand around Antiochus and told him he must make a decision before stepping outside of the circle. Remarkably, Antiochus not only endured this humiliating treatment, but agreed to evacuate Egypt. Whatever the truth of the story, that it was even found the least bit credible in antiquity serves to demonstrate how fear of Roman might now pervaded the Mediterranean. It also explains why what some might understandably regard the attitude of Rome as intolerable arrogance.

Back West: Wars in Spain

Near the end of the Second Punic War, the elder Scipio had brought Carthage's dominion over Spain to an end, and shortly after the end of the war, in 197, Rome created two provinces out of the conquered territory with the helpful names of Farther Spain (*Hispania Ulterior*) and Nearer Spain (*Hispania Citerior*). These provinces proved somewhat difficult to manage, and the indigenous peoples of these Spanish provinces, such as the Lusitanians and the Celtiberians, frequently resisted any authority placed over them. In the early years of the provinces, Rome was fortunate that the first two governors, Marcius Porcius Cato and Tiberius Sempronius Gracchus, managed them with some prudence and honesty. Tiberius, for example, had defeated the Celtiberians in 178 but did not impose harsh terms on them. He even founded a city for them, named Gracchuris after himself. However, the greed and ambition of later governors led to revolts against Roman authority, and two major military campaigns, beginning in the 150s and lasting more than a decade, were required to subdue the people there. In one notable instance, a Roman praetor invited the Lusitanians, a people who inhabited an area within modern-day Portugal, to peace talks, but when the Lusitanians arrived in good faith, suspecting nothing, they were massacred. Unsurprisingly, the Lusitanians decided to wage war against Rome and its allies, and one of the survivors of the massacre would soon become the leader of the long and bloody struggle against Rome. Cato, who had a reputation for honesty and upholding traditional Roman values, attempted to bring legal charges against the Roman commander responsible for the betrayal and murder of the Lusitanians, but senators always found it difficult to condemn one of their own. Not only was Cato's prosecution unsuccessful, the defendant was elected consul a few years later.

The second phase of this war, lasting from 143 to 133 BC, is often simply referred to as the Numantine War, after a Celtiberian settlement named Numantia. The survivor of the earlier massacre, named Viriathus, proved a capable commander and popular leader, and later historians regard him as an early expert in guerilla warfare. In one daring raid, he rescued a group of Lusitanian fighters who had been surrounded by Roman legions. He reminded these fighters not to accept any terms of surrender offered by the Romans, given how dishonorably the Romans had behaved. He even managed to bring together several of the usually uncooperative tribes into a coalition against Rome. Since the Romans had little military success against

Viriathus, they resorted to other means. Three members of an allied Spanish tribe were offered payment to assassinate him, and one night in 139, they slit his throat as he lay sleeping. The Romans refused to pay the assassins, however, since, in the words of one senator, "Rome does not pay traitors."

Even after the elimination of Viriathus, the war dragged on, and the Romans continued to send out commanders each year in the hopes of finally capturing Numantia, but without any lasting success. In 136, Gaius Hostilius Mancinus arrived, and despite several attempts, he not only failed to take the city, but himself was surrounded by the enemy. The only possibility of survival was to negotiate a surrender, and a young soldier named Tiberius Sempronius Gracchus, son of the earlier governor with the same name, was sent to conduct the negotiations. He was chosen because the Numantines would trust him, given his father's earlier fair treatment of them. The terms Tiberius managed to receive were quite reasonable, but these had to be formally ratified by the senate back in Rome. The senate, however, refused to accept the terms of surrender, and instead sent Mancinus back to the Numantines as a prisoner. The experience undoubtedly left a bitter taste in Tiberius's mouth, and helped to shape his attitude of distrust toward the senatorial elite. (As we shall see in the next chapter, his conflict with the senate will make him one of the foremost and famous Romans of the late republic, and a martyr for populist causes to this day.) The war did not come to an end until the following year, after another lengthy siege of Numantia by the Romans. Trapped within their strongly fortified city, the Numantines began to suffer from famine and disease, but rather than surrender, they all committed suicide.

Cato the Elder

One of the most prominent Romans of this time was Marcus Porcius Cato, often identified as Cato the Censor or Cato the Elder, to distinguish him from his great-grandson, whose suicide in 46 BC punctuated the last civil war of the republic. The elder Cato's importance to the history of the republic is as much for what he came to symbolize as much as for his actual life.

Born in 234 BC, he spent his childhood in the territory of the Sabines, the people east of Rome who had a reputation for frugal hardiness and piety. These attributes would become part of Cato's character, especially in his criticisms of the growing wealth and luxury he saw as a threat to the traditional Roman way of life. He came from an undistinguished family, and thus had to make his own way in the political arena of Rome without the benefit of important connections. He not only trained physically to endure the hardships of a soldier's life, but developed his speaking ability as well, becoming a legal advocate in the towns surrounding Rome. As a young man of 17, he fought in the Second Punic War under Fabius Maximus Cunctator and was a quaestor on Scipio Africanus's staff as he was preparing for the invasion of Carthage. In one account, Cato openly chastised Scipio for his lavish expenditures, particularly for the high pay he gave his soldiers, which Cato believed would corrupt them. This would be a shocking criticism for a lowly quaestor to utter directly to a consul, and not just any consul, but the charismatic and popular Scipio. Cato's comments were not well received by his commander, so

FIG. 6.7 A portrait bust from the first c. BC, once thought to be Cato the Elder.

he left Scipio's army and returned to Rome. According to our sources, during the debates between Fabius Maximus and Scipio about the proposal to take the war against Hannibal to Carthaginian soil, Cato worked with his former commander Fabius to undermine Scipio by bringing charges of wasteful spending against him. In fact, some sources claim Cato also worked against Scipio in the trials he underwent with his brother in the 180s, though there is no evidence for that. Nonetheless, the two men clearly represent different perspectives on Rome, and their mutual dislike for each other reflects one of the fundamental tensions in Roman republican history.

Thanks in part to the support of a patrician patron, Cato was elected consul in 195, a remarkable achievement for a "new man" (*novus homo*), someone without any ancestors who had reached that office. In the same year, he became one of the first governors of the new province of Nearer Spain. His military campaigns were a success, for which he was awarded a triumph in 194. He rewarded his soldiers with silver, but true to his reputation for frugality, took none of the spoils of war for himself. He did not retire from military service after his triumph but served as a staff officer in northern Greece as well as a military tribune in the war against Antiochus III.

Cato also had a reputation for resistance to the growing influence of Greek culture on Rome, supposedly considering it a sign of decadence and weakness. A later biographer tells us he did not learn Greek until late in life, which has served to bolster this reputation as someone who rejected Greek culture, in contrast to philhellenes like Scipio. Yet one might wonder why he bothered to learn it all if he was so hostile to it. Another story, from the Greek biographer Plutarch, presents a different image. Cato, as a young soldier on campaign under Fabius Maximus in Magna Graecia, was lodged with a Greek philosopher and follower of Pythagoras (best known today for the Pythagorean theorem, though Babylonians had known of it earlier). He was curious about Pythagorean teachings, and his host discussed with him the rejection of bodily pleasures, which were an incitement to wickedness, and the purification of the soul. These ideals of simple living and self-discipline were attractive to Cato, even though they came from a Greek school of thought. Moreover, the later Greek biogrpaher Plutarch claims he studied the Greek historian Thucydides and the Greek orator Demosthenes to improve his own speaking abilities, and that many of his own sayings are translated from Greek. As evidence of his disdain for Greek culture, some will point to the report that when he gave a speech in Athens, he chose to have an interpreter translate his Latin into Greek. However, this was a common practice among educated elite Romans to speak in Latin before Greek audiences even when they knew Greek well. Disparaging remarks about the Greeks themselves are attributed to Cato, and it is likely he found many faults with them, particularly those with whom he would have had personal experience in the political machinations in which Rome became entangled. But he also recognized that Greek culture had much to offer, if handled in a proper (which is to say, Roman) way. While not a philhellene by any stretch of the imagination, Cato was not so simple-minded to reject what he found useful simply because it was Greek.

His identification as "censor" not only signals that he held this office in 184 BC, but that he exercised its functions with uncommon strictness and severity. One of the censor's most important duties was to maintain membership in the senate, as well as to make sure members of different orders met the minimum financial qualification for their census class, and also upheld moral and physical standards. This last qualification was widely ignored, unless a senator committed an egregious crime. However, in contrast to most other holders of the censorship, Cato applied the regulations about physical and moral fitness rigorously, without apparent regard to the status of some of those he branded with the disgrace of removal. For example, he expelled from the senate Lucius Quinctius Flamininus, brother of his former commander Titus, even though Lucius himself was of consular rank, and this disgrace would affect Titus as much as his brother. In this case, the grounds for expulsion seem quite justifiable. The story goes that Lucius had a young boyfriend who accompanied him on his military campaigns and to his province. At a dinner party, the boyfriend coyly stated that he came to see Lucius even though he had to leave a gladiatorial show, which saddened him since he still had never seen a man killed (suggesting that the boyfriend had never been in combat). Lucius immediately ordered a condemned prisoner to be brought to the dinner party and had him executed on the spot to satisfy his boyfriend's wish. Cato expelled another senator for a far less disturbing offense. The senator had passionately kissed his wife in broad daylight in the presence of their daughter. He also removed from the equestrian order Lucius Cornelius Scipio, brother of Scipio Africanus, even though he had celebrated a triumph for his victory over Antiochus III. In doing so, Cato could claim he was maintaining the traditional values of Rome with strict regularity, no exceptions allowed. Such an attitude would certainly not win him friends, if it got him admirers. Though he acquired some prominence as a speaker in law courts, and involved himself in the prosecutions of those he thought deserved it, he was forced to defend himself in court 44 times—a sure sign of the hostility he aroused among the senatorial elite. He maintained a lifelong commitment to frugality and simplicity, which he believed upheld Rome's moral character, and fought against the luxury and decadence he saw as a threat to Rome, much of it imported from the Greek east.

Near the end of his life, he was one of the members of the delegation sent from Rome in 153 to investigate Carthage's complaints about Massinissa encroaching on their territory. When he saw how Carthage was flourishing, he returned to the senate and attempted to rouse Rome to war against Carthage, since he believed Carthage was preparing to attack Rome. (It was Cato whose trick with the Libyan figs was described in the previous chapter.) He is perhaps most famous for adding the phrase "Carthage must be destroyed," or more precisely, "It is my opinion that Carthage must be destroyed" (*censeo Carthaginem esse delendam*), to the end of every speech he gave in the senate, no matter what the topic. Less well known is that another leading Roman would retort, "It is my opinion that Carthage must be *spared*." Dying in 149, the first year of the Third Punic War, he did not live to see his wish come true with the final destruction of Carthage. However, he was not always a proponent of aggressive Roman military action, and earlier in his career he gave speeches against military involvement in the East.

In addition to his achievements as a soldier and politician, Cato was also an important figure in the development of Latin literature. He published over 150 of the speeches he delivered over the course of his career in law and politics, and his straightforward and unadorned manner of speaking became a model for future Roman orators. He also wrote a history of Rome, called the *Origines*, which can claim to be the first history of Rome written in Latin. The only work of his that survives complete is the *De agricultura*, a manual on farming and a guide for wealthy Romans on how to manage their agricultural estates, including instructions on how to handle slaves. One of the more infamous passages offers a bit of advice that strikes a modern ear as incredibly inhumane:

> Sell old oxen, unhealthy cattle, unhealthy sheep, wool, hides, an old wagon, old tools, an old slave, a sick slave, and anything else superfluous. (*De agricultura* 2.1)

This attitude toward slaves, as simply one item in a list alongside rusty tools and worn-out cattle, was even criticized in antiquity as excessively cruel. It perhaps best represents Cato's commitment to principles and ideas over actual human beings. While Cato in many ways could be regarded as conservative, and certainly was less flexible in terms of moral standards and legal duties than many other aristocratic Romans, he was not the cartoonish curmudgeon as often portrayed. He was a complex figure, as most notable figures from history are.

Roman Literary Culture

The Romans developed over time a vast body of literature in Latin that would be enormously influential on the intellectual traditions of the Western world, especially as Latin became the language of Christianity and the educated elite through the Middle Ages and the Renaissance and into the modern world. It is not an exaggeration to say that European literature is built on a bedrock formed in Rome. As in so many other areas, the Romans borrowed heavily from other peoples, and for culture the people they looked to more than any other were the Greeks. In fact, Latin literature is inconceivable without the vast body of Greek literature from which it sprang. It developed later than one might expect, emerging shortly after Rome's military conquests in Magna Graecia and Greek-speaking Sicily. The timing is not coincidental. When the Romans begin their rise to prominence in the Mediterranean, their neighbors already had a well-established and highly esteemed literary culture, which set the standard to which they aspired. Even though Rome would have had its own traditions and forms of writing previous to its engagement with the Greek world, the deeper contacts between aristocratic Romans and Greek culture spurred elite Romans into a cultural competition. Romans had a desire to elevate their own culture to the heights which the Greeks, in their eyes, had already attained.

Greek literature possessed both the origin and perfection of many literary forms, including the epic poems *Iliad* and *Odyssey* attributed to Homer and the lyric poetry of Sappho and Pindar. In drama, the Greeks could boast of the great tragedians of the fifth century BC, Aeschylus,

Sophocles, and Euripides, as well as the comedies of Aristophanes and the later Menander. In history as well, the Greeks led the way with Herodotus and Thucydides, and in one of the most important fields of study for an ambitious Roman, the Greeks could boast of great speechwriters such as Lysias, Isocrates, and Demosthenes. Lesser-known authors had produced numerous manuals for instruction in different types of rhetoric. Philosophy had a long tradition in ancient Greece, including the masters Plato and Aristotle from the fourth century BC, each of whom were credited with founding a "school," the Academy in Plato's case, and the Lyceum of Aristotle. (Followers of Plato were thus identified as "Academics," while followers of Aristotle were known as "Peripatetics.") There were also the later philosophical schools that developed from the time of Alexander the Great, including the Stoics and Epicureans, both of which had devoted followers among aristocratic Romans. Moreover, there were numerous mathematical and scientific treatises, such as Euclid's on geometry and Eratosthenes on geography, as well as work on astronomy, medicine, biology, botany, and countless other subjects. While much of "classical" Greek literature dates from the fifth and fourth centuries BC, the establishment of the famous Library of Alexandria in Egypt at the beginning of the third century BC by a successor to Alexander the Great, who founded the city he named after himself, ensured that many of these works were preserved and studied, and new ones were produced by the scholars and poets who worked at the library.

Given all this, it should not be a surprise that the earliest Latin literature we know of was produced by a former Greek slave named Livius Andronicus (Andronicus is a Greek name). We know very little about him, and what is known is disputed. In some accounts, he was from Tarentum, a city in Magna Graecia, and was captured in the Second Punic War. However, he seems to have already composed a drama in 240 BC, a year usually considered the beginning of Latin literature. His plays were based on Greek originals, and fragments of his Latin translation of the *Odyssey* survive. In all likelihood, he was a slave who belonged to an aristocratic Roman, whose children Livius tutored and under whose patronage he would have written and performed his plays. Another important early poet in Latin was Ennius, whose home was also Magna Graecia. He was apparently trilingual—he spoke Greek, Latin, and Oscan—and was brought to Rome from Sardinia in 204, likely as a war captive. In addition to plays, he wrote an influential epic poem about Rome's history known as the *Annales*, and in its opening lines he claims to be possessed by Homer's soul. Thus, Rome's first stirrings in the field of literature were produced by Greek speakers made captive to Rome, who wrote Latin translations and adaptations of Greek works. The earliest Roman comedies we have, by the playwrights Plautus and Terence, date from the second century BC and are also adaptations of Greek comedies. The first attempt at writing history at Rome was made by Quintus Fabius Pictor, a patrician who covered in his work the early foundations of Rome up until the Second Punic War. He wrote in Greek, perhaps in part to present the Greek-speaking world a view of Roman history from the Roman perspective. Latin poets of the first century BC imitated different types of Greek poetry while attempting to surpass it, or at least give it a distinctive Roman touch. The first-century BC poet Catullus, for example, most famous for his "Lesbia" poems, translated a poem by Sappho, and shortly after him Horace produced very Roman versions of Greek lyric poetry. This rivalry of sorts culminates in the *Aeneid* of Vergil. Composed after the end of the republic, it is an epic poem the draws on Ennius, but is also a combination of the *Iliad* and the *Odyssey*, making Vergil into the "Roman Homer," as his contemporaries would say. This emulation of Greek models would remain a feature of Rome's literary culture throughout the republic and beyond, even as Romans developed their own ideals in each of the genres mentioned.

The earliest Latin literature now survives only in small bits and pieces, usually called fragments. Later authors would quote from an earlier work, which was then lost. Only the quotation survives, often without any context or even a title of the book from which it was taken. Sometimes not even the author's name is mentioned. In fact, only about 10 percent of Latin literature from the Roman Republic survives. In order for a piece of literature to be passed down through the ages, it had to be copied by hand. Most early writings were on papyrus, a reed plant that grows along the Nile in Egypt. It was cut into thin strands, then formed into long rolls by pasting these strands in a crisscross pattern. When these were rolled up, they formed scrolls, and this was the form in which literature was preserved. Later, dried and smoothed animal skins, known as parchment, were used as writing material. Books as we think of them did not come into existence until the first or second century AD, in a form known as a *codex*. Printing as we know it was not developed until over a thousand years later, first in China. Printing using moveable type, which made mass production of books possible, was not invented until 1450, by Johannes Gutenberg of Germany. (Today there are 21 complete "Gutenberg Bibles" in existence, each of which is worth around $30 million.)

Papyrus, which is essentially a dried plant, makes a good writing surface, but is subject to decay and destruction, especially by moisture. As a result, most surviving papyri come from Egypt, where the dry climate made survival of papyrus much more likely. A library filled with papyrus scrolls was discovered in a house that had been buried by the eruption of Mt. Vesuvius, but these had been carbonized into hardened and blackened chunks. Only recently has technology allowed us to recover some of the text on these papyri, which are rare examples of original writings from the Roman Republic. In the vast majority of cases, the earliest physical copies we have of a work written at any time during the republic

FIG. 6.8 A portrait of a young man reading a papyrus scroll, from the first c. AD.

FIG. 6.9 A portrait of a young woman with wax tablets bundled in a *codex*. She holds a *stylus* (writing implement) to her chin.

would be a manuscript from the Middle Ages, several centuries or more after the author first wrote it. This means the text had been copied by hand for at least a thousand years, and more like 1500 years, escaping fire, flood, insects, or even reuse. Sometimes a text on papyrus or parchment was erased and reused, and now using visual imaging technology the erased text can be recovered, which is known as a "palimpsest." For less permanent writings, the Romans used small wax tablets placed in wooden frames. They used a stylus with a sharp end to write in the wax and a flattened end to smooth out the wax to erase the writing.

What should be remembered, but is all too easily forgotten, is that Rome's literary culture was primarily oral, and all texts, not just plays, would be read aloud. Reading in silence, as nearly everyone does today, was still an oddity in the fourth century AD, when Saint Augustine thought it strange that Saint Ambrose read without moving his lips or making a sound.

Credits

Fig. 6.1: Source: https://commons.wikimedia.org/wiki/File:The_Sack_of_Corinth_by_Thomas_Allom.jpg.

Fig. 6.2: Adapted from d-maps.com.

Fig. 6.3: Copyright © by Nigel Swales (CC BY-SA 2.0) at https://www.flickr.com/photos/nigel321/4982460330/in/photolist-8AhpSs-byuqsg-bXxB8U-bXx2JG-bXwQMN-bXxDLw-bXuFQy-byuhVR-VMZVif-6khXDv-98AHAT-hd3QLr-6ozfa1-a22yab-98ALqZ-6khZ3T-8AhqtY-6khYit-3oHTQc-3oHV7V-3oNtJ3-JMYcG3-3oNyod-8AhnKw-67cZnb-3oNtbh-3oNt6q-dNM2jq-3oNtPd-3oNsHU-8AhhXy-3oHUuM-3oHUf4-3oHUyz-98DHQ1-8Ahhky-3oHTV4-8AeimX-8Aej3v-aAYG2G-98AP5R-98DLjC-ofYzjJ-6tG316-zk1N1U-6tG3cX-98E3C1-98DA9u-98AWST-6ov3oV.

Fig. 6.4: Copyright © by Classical Numismatic Group. Reprinted with permission.

Fig. 6.5: Copyright © by Classical Numismatic Group (CC BY-SA 2.5) at https://commons.wikimedia.org/wiki/File:Antiochos_III_the_Great,_Tetradrachm,_222-187_BC,_HGC_9-447u.jpg.

Fig. 6.6: Source: https://commons.wikimedia.org/wiki/File:Mainade_Staatliche_Antikensammlungen_2645.jpg.

Fig. 6.7: Source: https://commons.wikimedia.org/wiki/File:Patrizio_Torlonia.jpg.

Fig. 6.8: Source: https://commons.wikimedia.org/wiki/File:Busto_maschile.JPG.

Fig. 6.9: Source: https://commons.wikimedia.org/wiki/File:Herkulaneischer_Meister_002.jpg.

CHAPTER 7

When Did the End Begin?

FIG. 7.1 In a seventeenth-century painting, Cornelia, mother of Tiberius and Gaius Gracchus, refuses a crown—and marriage proposal—from Ptolemy VIII, ruler of Egypt.

Overview

Following the military conquests of Carthage, Greece, and Spain, Rome controlled the Mediterranean, but political turmoil and violence created a challenge to the institutions of the republic. Difficulties in finding new recruits to serve in the army and labor shortages that affected agricultural production threatened the stability of Rome. Two brothers, Tiberius and Gaius Gracchus, attempted to address these problems by using the office of tribune of the plebs to push through land distributions and other reforms. Though they took different approaches, they were both met with aggressive opposition by the senatorial elite, and both were killed during violence instigated by their opponents. The reforms they proposed, the means by which they sought to institute them, and the senate's resistance to both opened a deep divide in the Roman state. The chapter concludes with an overview of Roman food and dining.

Timeline

134	End of the Numantine War
133	Tribunate of Tiberius Gracchus
131	Death of Tiberius Gracchus
125	Destruction of Fregellae
123–122	Tribunates of Gaius Gracchus
121	Death of Gaius Gracchus

A Changing Future

When a censor at Rome finished conducting the census, he would perform a special sacrifice known as a *suovetaurilia*, named for the animals sacrificed: pig (*sus*), sheep (*ovis*), and bull (*taurus*). Then the censor would utter a prayer following a traditional formula: "May the gods make the state of the Roman people better and greater!" (*populi Romani res meliores amplioresque faciant*). In 142 BC, only a few years following the destruction of Carthage, Scipio Aemilianus was a censor. When he completed his census and performed the *suovetaurilia*, the official who assisted him read out the traditional prayer for him to recite. But Scipio replied that the Roman state was already great and good enough and changed the prayer to his own version: "I pray that the gods forever preserve it from harm!" This story is given in a collection of famous deeds and sayings written by Valerius Maximus, an author of the first century AD. We do not know if it really happened, but it serves as a reminder that for all Rome's past success and military glory, its greatest dangers were just ahead. Scipio's prayer might be taken to express the view that Rome's empire had reached the greatest extent it possibly could without weakening itself. Further growth and expansion, such as into Britain or into the Near East, would be in this view a grave mistake. The change to the traditional prayer by Scipio reflects a recognition that now that Rome's foreign adversaries had fallen, the real dangers were at home. In fact, it was fitting to have Scipio Aemilianus, under whose command Carthage was destroyed, signal this worry in his prayer. Tiberius and Gaius Gracchus, who received the credit for attempting to solve the problems facing the republic, also received the blame for fatally weakening it, especially in the views of Romans such as Scipio Aemilianus. The Gracchi brothers had family ties to Scipio, so the danger was close to home.

When Romans themselves later looked back on their history and wondered when the end of the Republic had begun, many would date it to the end of the Third Punic War and conquest of Greece in 146. The destruction of Corinth and Carthage eliminated major foreign enemies, and the fear of a major enemy, some Romans thought, forced Rome to keep in fighting shape, and to maintain the traditions and way of life that had given them the ability to defeat so many peoples and nations. Once there was no longer a powerful external enemy, Romans would become lazy, decadent, and corrupt. Instead, they would spend their time enjoying the luxuries their military conquests had brought them, rather than work to maintain the discipline and morality that had made their victories possible. (This theory is sometimes referred to with the Latin phrase *metus hostilis*, "fear of an enemy.") In addition, a foreign enemy forced Romans with different political views to work together, and without one, political opponents became bitter enemies and attacked one another.

Other Romans would pinpoint the beginning of the end to events twenty years after Scipio's supposed prayer, when in 133 BC a young man named Tiberius Gracchus won election as a tribune of the plebs and attempted to bring about major social and political reforms. In the violence that followed his attempts to push his reforms through, he would be killed by his fellow citizens. A decade later, his brother Gaius also became a tribune and attempted to implement his own program of reforms. Like his brother, he was killed by his political opponents. A Roman scholar writing around the time Julius Caesar first came into power said that the Gracchi brothers had made Rome *biceps*, "two-headed." Exactly what he meant is not clear, since we do not have the context for this quotation, but it seems he believed that the Gracchi, along with their supporters and the senatorial elite who opposed them, formed two distinct factions. The republic was no longer a single unified state. Each side had a mind of its own, seeing with its own eyes and speaking with its own mouth.

Of course, Romans looking back from the years after the assassination of Julius Caesar, or even later from the time of the emperors, might very well see the origin of the republic's final collapse in any number of events, but making the case that one particular event was the actual cause of its fall requires more than linking one historical event to a later one. There is always the danger of falling into the logical trap of *post hoc ergo propter hoc* (Latin for "after this, therefore because of this"), which is the mistake of believing that an event that follows an earlier event in time is also a direct result of the earlier event. Common sports superstitions are an everyday example of this kind of error. When I wear a certain pair of socks, then my team wins, and thus I begin to believe my team's victory is a result of my wearing of those socks. In writing history, one has to do more than describe a series of events to develop a theory that explains why things turned out the way they did, and this requires interpretation, imagination, and evidence.

Whether or not the final defeat of Carthage or the actions of the Gracchi were causes of the republic's downfall cannot be proven as a scientific fact, but they can be argued for. For our purposes, what is important is that some Romans who lived shortly after these events certainly thought the events surrounding the Gracchi and their attempts at reforms marked a critical turning point in the history of the Roman Republic. They had good reasons to believe it was.

Optimates and *Populares*

In the politics of the Roman Republic, there were no political parties with platforms that party members were expected to support. Rather, there were shifting factions, and even the term "faction" may imply too much rigidity in the shifting loyalties and allegiances that determined who gained the upper hand on any particular issue. Political groupings were not formed simply around differences in policy or political views. Family connections, through blood or marriage, were also important, and exerted more influence on politics than they do today. However, one broad division of politicians was between *populares* and the *optimates*. These terms did not come into use until the last century of the republic, but the basic division began to appear much earlier, and in some ways is the evolution of the early divisions between patricians and plebeians. Of course, it must be remembered that Roman historians, who often viewed the past in terms of their present, would often project this division back into earlier history.

A *popularis* politician, as the word implies, advocates for the causes important to the plebs, such as land reform, debt relief, or subsidized distributions of grain (essentially food welfare). It is important to note, however, that these *populares* were not necessarily from the lower classes, or even plebeian. It would be almost impossible for someone not born into wealth and prestige to acquire any political influence, much less win election to an office and gain admittance to the senate. If these individuals were plebeian, they were usually members of the plebeian nobility. While they may see greater good in advocating for the people of Rome, they were still part of the ruling elite and would not usually argue for drastic changes to the status quo. In fact, politicians who espoused *popularis* causes often did so not for any common good, but for their own political purposes. The plebs were often no more than a convenient excuse to increase their own power and a useful tool to employ against their political opponents. A *popularis* politician would often make use of the Plebeian Assembly to advance his causes, at times in direct opposition to the authority of the senate.

Optimates, meaning "the best," is the label for politicians who upheld the traditional role of the senate as the governing authority at Rome. They tended to oppose any reforms that favored the plebs. Of course, these politicians saw themselves as the best people in the state, the ones who naturally should be in charge. While far fewer in number than the plebs, they believed that by virtue of their own preeminence they should decide what was best for the whole. It was, in their view, the natural and proper order of the state, and any threats to that would be attacked to preserve their elite position, but also in the sincere belief that such threats would create disorder and endanger the republic. Patricians for the most part would be *optimates*, but many *optimates* would be from a plebeian background. However, they allied themselves with the ruling nobility and often looked on the masses of the plebs as uneducated and unable to take a proper view of things. From the period of the Gracchi until the end of the republic, many politicians can be classified as *optimates* of *populares*, but it must always be remembered these were not permanent labels. Any individual politician might hold positions that at times aligned with *optimates*, and at other times with *populares*.

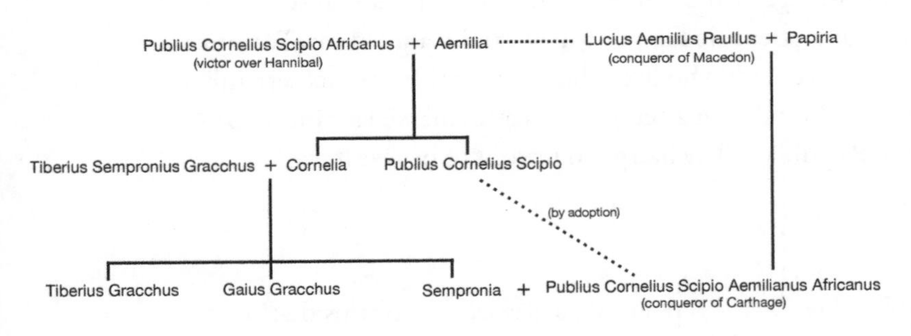

FIG. 7.2 A family tree (known as a *stemma*) of the Gracchi.

Are Two Heads Worse Than One?

Even though the conquests of 146 BC established Rome's unquestioned dominance over the Mediterranean, there were still serious challenges to Rome abroad. The wars in Spain, mentioned in the previous chapter, proved difficult and bloody, requiring a permanent military force stationed far from Rome. Soldiers, most of whom would have been drawn from small farms in Italy, did not have the opportunity to return to their homes during these campaigns. Unable to tend to their harvests, they and their families fell into financial hardship and ruin. As well, many of the soldiers were allies of Rome from Italy, and thus would not receive the same rewards for service upon discharge, such as grants of land. Much of the Italian countryside had been devastated during Hannibal's invasion only a few generations earlier, and agriculture had only slowly begun to recover. When Rome had retaken possession of land in Italy after their victory in the Second Punic War, the government had leased out this farmland on a permanent basis. However, most of it did not end up in the hands of small farmers, who served as soldiers, but went to senators and other wealthy Romans, their commanding officers, who acquired large-scale estates. And even though a law had been passed two centuries earlier to limit individual landholdings to 500 *iugera* (350 acres, or about 270 football fields), this law had not been enforced and was widely ignored. In effect, even though it was technically state-owned property, land-owners treated it as their own private property. Thus, instead of a large number of small farmers owning lands throughout Italy, a smaller number of wealthy men possessed large estates. Moreover, much of this land was used for grazing and pasturing rather than growing crops, forcing Rome to depend even more on imports of grain from elsewhere in the Mediterranean. These large-scale estates tended to use slaves for labor rather than hire freeborn Romans. Even when free Romans and Italians were hired, they would in many cases still be too poor to qualify for military service. On the other hand, the wealthy landholders had made investments in their land, and had sometimes sold it or used it as collateral for loans. This is understandable, since such land had been treated as private property for a long time and treating the land as one's own had become an accepted and normal practice.

The combination of the squeeze on small farmers and the drawn-out wars in Spain led to serious difficulties with the recruitment of Roman soldiers. The number of citizens who met the minimum property requirement to be eligible for military service was decreasing, and those who did possess the minimum amount of property were increasingly unwilling to serve. The stories coming back from Spain would have persuaded many to seek an exemption from service, which a tribune of the plebs could grant. One brief passage from a Greek historian of Rome's war in Spain paints a bleak image of a difficult siege, led by a consul who is described as "eager for glory and in need of money":

> The Roman soldiers grew sick from guard duty and lack of sleep, and also because they were not used to the food of that country. They didn't have any wine, salt, vinegar, or

> oil, but had to live on wheat and barley, as well as deer and rabbit meat boiled without salt. This caused dysentery, from which many died. (Appian, *Wars in Spain* 6.54)

This consul, when he attempted to levy soldiers in 151, was said to have been very strict in his enrollment of new recruits and did not grant exemptions from service to those who requested it. As a result, tribunes of the plebs had him and his colleague imprisoned. Though this may seem like the tribunes were standing up for the soldiers, they may have been angry that the consuls would not allow them to use the exemptions from service as political favors. In other words, they may have been more concerned about themselves than the soldiers, just like the consuls. As well, while these two consuls might be portrayed as overly harsh and cruel, they may have felt forced to be strict and rigid in their enlistment of soldiers, since if they allowed exemptions they may not have been able to head to Spain with an adequate force. For their part, the tribunes may have only been trying to protect their ability to do political favors, but at the same time, it would have been accepted practice to release men from service as a political favor, as the consuls well knew. In their view, the consul was stepping on the tribune's authority. Everyone had his own explanation for acting as he did, and his own reason for being angry at the other party.

There were competing and conflicting needs of the Roman state, but the upshot was that it was becoming difficult to fill necessary military posts. A brief summary from a lost book by the Roman historian Livy clearly describes the difficulty, but also praises an individual from an aristocratic family who stepped forward to serve, inspiring others to volunteer:

> Since so many battles ended in failure, the war in Spain created turmoil in the Republic—nobody would serve as a military tribune, or even accept a position on the commander's staff. However, Publius stepped forward and declared that he would undertake any kind of military service assigned to him. His example made everyone eager to serve in the military. (Livy, *Summaries* 48)

This Publius is, of course, Scipio Aemilianus, who would go on to fight bravely in Spain as a military tribune under the greedy and strict consul who had been imprisoned by the tribunes of the plebs. Scipio was awarded the military decoration known as the *corona muralis*, given to the soldier who is first to scale the walls of an enemy city. When he returned from Spain, he married Sempronia, sister of Tiberius and Gaius Gracchus. A few years later, he would be the victorious commander of the Third Punic War.

Scipio Aemilianus's actions reflect the more traditional and conservative view of Rome's problems and their solutions. The aristocratic and noble citizens should, in this view, be exemplars of patriotic duty and express proper scorn for those unwilling to step forward for the good of the state. Part of this outlook would be a belief that the lower classes should know their proper place, and any sign of yielding to their demands would only weaken the *mores* that had made Rome great. Of course, the aristocratic perspective might also entail a certain blindness to more serious conditions that would make poorer individuals hesitate to serve in the army. Underlying it was a belief in every Roman's personal responsibility and duties as a citizen, even when many now labored under conditions that made an adherence to public duty all but impossible.

The tensions created by the wars in Spain were not solved by Scipio's example and were still causing problems a decade later. In 140 BC, a tribune of the plebs attempted to prevent a consul from leaving for Spain to take up his military command, and in defiance of the tribune's authority to veto any action by a magistrate, the consul made his way there. This consul gained a reputation for cruel treatment of the soldiers under his command. Angered at their jokes about him, he decided to punish them in an underhanded way. He commanded six hundred men, including officers, to cross a river to gather wood from a mountain occupied by the enemy, which was equivalent to sending them on a suicide mission. Though he would not have ordered them to go if they had apologized, the soldiers apparently decided to face death rather than give him any satisfaction. After they gathered the wood (accompanied by allied cavalry to protect them), they piled it around the consul's tent and set it on fire.

Two years later, in 138, the consuls were said to have publicly flogged deserters, and at least in one case sold a deserter into slavery, suggesting desertion had become a problem and a stern example needed to be set. These two consuls were thrown into prison by a tribune of the plebs, since as in the earlier case they did not allow the tribunes to grant exemptions from service. Again, the tribunes may have been more interested in defending their privilege of granting favors than protecting individuals from being compelled to fight in a brutal and unrewarding war far from Rome. Nonetheless, there was a serious political tension between the consuls, who represented the senate's authority, and the tribunes of the plebs, who represented the people's.

One of these imprisoned consuls was Publius Cornelius Scipio Nasica, whose name should look somewhat familiar, since he was a cousin of Scipio Aemilianus. He was involved in another conflict with a tribune over another serious problem for plebeian Romans at this time, the grain supply, which was an essential source of food for many Romans. The agricultural problems, as well as the increased population of the city of Rome, meant that Rome depended more and more on imports of grain. A shortage of grain or a spike in the price created a very real hardship for many of the city's inhabitants. During Scipio Nasica's consulship, a tribune of the plebs used his authority to force Nasica to appear at a public gathering, where the tribune publicly pressured him to take steps to purchase grain. (The tribune also gave Nasica the nickname Serapio—"pointy nose.") Facing the large gathering, Nasica spoke openly in opposition to this proposal, and when the crowd began to shout him down, he said, "Please, citizens, keep quiet! I know better than you what's good for the Republic!" While this may sound today like an arrogant aristocrat speaking down to his inferiors, it is a good example of the elite view of the plebs. A noble rightfully reminds the plebeians both of their proper place in the republic and of his natural-born right to decide for them. Our sources for this story reflect the elite senatorial perspective, and thus the people did not react angrily when Nasica tells them to shut up. Instead, they fell silent out of respect for his authority and his status, which at least in the historical narrative had greater power over them than their hunger.

Change Begins at Home

Scipio Nasica, Scipio Aemilianus, and other elite Romans from prominent families represent one of the two heads into which the Roman Republic was split. The other was represented by Tiberius Gracchus and his younger brother Gaius, Scipio Aemilianus's brother-in-law. We should remember that they too were also elite Romans from prominent families, and the same family as some of their political opponents. Tiberius and Gaius Gracchus were the two surviving sons of Tiberius Sempronius Gracchus, a man of distinguished political and military service who we met in the previous chapter as the prudent governor in Spain. But it was their mother, Cornelia, who provided them with a truly noble lineage, since she was the daughter of Publius Cornelius Scipio Africanus, who defeated Hannibal, and also the niece of Lucius Aemilius Paullus, conqueror of Macedon in 168. Mothers are not always identified in biographies of famous Romans, and even when they are, it is often to supply a connection to another famous man. Cornelia herself is best known as the mother of the Gracchi, and the evidence we have of her life and her views are chiefly concerned with the influence she had on her sons, both of whom she would outlive. A Roman biographer of the first century BC quotes from letters she wrote, though whether they are really by her is disputed. Nonetheless, they were believed to be hers not long after her death, and even if they are not by her hand, they provide a glimpse of how she was viewed by other Romans a generation after her death. One letter is addressed to her younger son Gaius after Tiberius has been killed:

> I would readily swear that no enemy, except for the murderers of Tiberius, has given me as much trouble and worry as you have. You're the only child I have left, and you should have taken on the role of all the others, to make sure my old age was free of worries, to desire my approval for everything you do. You should consider it impious to do anything important against my advice, especially since I do not have long to live. Can't this brief span of life left to me stop you from opposing me and bringing ruin to your country? And where will this end? Will our family stop behaving madly, is there no limit to this? Can't we stop causing problems, when we already have enough of them? Is there no shame in creating disturbance and disorder to the Republic? If none of this possible, then at least wait until after I am dead to seek the tribunate. (Nepos, fragment 1.1)

In this letter, Cornelia is presented as advising her younger son Gaius not to seek the office of tribune of the plebs, since she knew he would use the office to push for reforms like his older brother Tiberius. This would, in her view, lead to the same uproar and the same deadly outcome. It is easy to believe that Cornelia would have felt this way, but her letter sounds suspiciously like what an opponent of Gaius would want her to say to him. Other sources, in fact, suggest she was supportive of the policies of both her sons, and she is said to have spurred her sons to reach the heights of glory attained by their grandfather Scipio Africanus and other members of her illustrious family. In the life of Tiberius Gracchus by the Greek biographer Plutarch, the blame for his fateful decision to seek the office of tribune of the plebs in order to push forward his reforms was placed on Cornelia, who supposedly complained that she was known as the mother-in-law of Scipio Aemilianus, and not yet the mother of the Gracchi.

The differing views of Cornelia tend to reflect attitudes about her sons, as happens with many other women who appear in the pages of Roman history. The letter quoted, genuine or not, provides a glimpse of the reaction to the efforts made by the Gracchi to improve conditions at Rome, especially by their opponents. For them, the traditional order must prevail, even if this meant forgoing necessary reforms that might address current problems and prevent violence later. It says something about the state of the republic that the reforms proposed by the Gracchi, which will strike most modern ears as rather reasonable and not all that radical, would create such chaos in the political situation at Rome. In fact, the opposition may well have been more about the way the Gracchi pursued their reforms than the reforms themselves. To their opponents, the Gracchi awakened the fear of a *popularis* politician seeking monarchical power, which was a greater threat to the republic than the problems they tried to solve.

Tiberius Gracchus: Revolutionary or Reformer?

Romans from both sides recognized there were serious problems in the republic and that one of the root causes was the increase in large-scale landholdings by the wealthy at the expense of the small farmers. There was even a move by a member of the senatorial elite toward invoking an earlier law of 367 BC limiting landholding to 500 *iugera*. Gaius Laelius, an older friend of Scipio Aemilianus and one of the consuls of 140 (not the one hated by his soldiers), put forward a proposal to improve the conditions for farmers in Italy, likely relying in part on the older law. However, his proposal met with fierce resistance from other senators and wealthy landowners, and rather than create a more serious disturbance by pushing the proposal forward, he withdrew it. For this reason, according to some sources, he earned the nickname Sapiens ("wise").

Although it is not clear when Laelius made his proposal for land reform, there is no question that following his failed attempt, Tiberius Gracchus took up the cause for which he won his reputation as a popular reformer, and also his reputation for splitting the Roman Republic in two. Born in 162 BC, Tiberius received an elite education, including the study of Greek rhetoric and philosophy, as befit his family's status, and married into an equally aristocratic family (his father-in-law was consul in 143 and censor in 136). At the age of 16, Tiberius took part in the sack of Carthage at the end of the Third Punic War, accompanying Scipio Aemilianus, the consul and commander as well as his brother-in-law. Tiberius also served in the wars in Spain, and, as described in the previous chapter, because his father had earlier dealt fairly with the people there, he was the only one whom the Numantines trusted to conduct negotiations when the Roman consul Mancinus was forced to surrender. However, the senate rejected the terms Tiberius managed to negotiate, even though it would save the lives of Roman soldiers. The Roman people, especially the friends and relatives of the soldiers, praised Tiberius for what he had done, but some senators opposed the treaty, perhaps as much for the way it was made as what the terms were. Some senators even declared that Tiberius, along with Mancinus and the other officers, should be handed back unarmed to the Numantines to do with as they pleased. In the end, the treaty Tiberius had negotiated was declared invalid, but only the consul Mancinus was turned over to the enemy. One of those who rejected Tiberius's treaty was his brother-in-law, Scipio Aemilianus, one of the most influential and powerful leaders of Rome. This would not be the last time they opposed one another.

Tiberius was elected as a tribune of the plebs for 133, apparently with the plan to pursue land reform legislation. Why Tiberius, in contrast to Laelius, pushed his plan forward in the face of serious opposition is not a question that has a final answer, and many theories have been put forth, beginning in antiquity. Ancient writers quote a story told by his brother Gaius, in a letter or political pamphlet he supposedly published, probably in support of his own reforms. According to the story, as Tiberius was traveling north through Italy on his way to Numantia in Spain, he noticed that there seemed to be few people in the fields. When he did see people farming or tending flocks, they were foreign slaves. The story offers a reformer's view of the problem, and a reason why land reform was so important. And even though the affair of the treaty with Numantia may have made Tiberius hostile to the "old guard" of the Roman Senate, he had the support of many prominent senators, including his father-in-law. But the rejection of his treaty, as well as the opposition to Laelius's earlier attempt at land reform, must have revealed to him the forceful resistance he would have to confront. On the most sympathetic interpretation, he saw land reform as the only solution to the serious economic, social, and military problems facing Rome. Drastic measures were called for to save the republic. A less generous reading of his actions would attribute to him overbearing pride and a powerful desire for glory. There is probably some truth to both readings.

Following the normal procedure for new legislation, Tiberius first introduced his law to the senate in order to seek its approval before a vote in the assembly. When he presented his proposed law to the senate, he offered them practical reasons to support it:

> Wasn't it fair for public property to be distributed to the public? Wasn't a citizen always more Roman than a slave, and a man who is a soldier more useful than one who isn't? Doesn't someone who has a share in the state care about it more? ... Romans acquired most of their land by force, and hoped to possess all the habitable land left in the world. The critical question now is whether we will take possession of the lands that remain because we have plenty of brave men or will we lose to our enemies the lands we already have because of weakness and envy. (Appian, *Civil Wars* 1.11)

Given the problems with the recruitment of soldiers and desertion, his point that his land reform bill would strengthen the military would certainly appeal to the senators who served as commanders. But his final point is a clever appeal to the senators who might oppose the deal because they feared the law would mean the loss of lands they possessed. Tiberius flips this fear on its head. There are only two options, he says: either Rome will acquire even more territory through military strength or lose what they already have because of military weakness. As he presents it, passage of the law would strengthen the military and ultimately allow Rome (and particularly the senators) to possess even more land. If they opposed his land reform, then Rome (and, again, the senators) would in fact lose what they already had.

Moreover, the issue of slave versus citizen would appeal less to a senator's patriotic sentiment and more to an actual fear. The image from Tiberius's journey through Italy of foreign slaves working large estates, often not under direct supervision, would call to mind a slave revolt that had broken out in Sicily in 135, two years earlier. It was led by a Syrian named Eunus, who claimed to be a divine prophet and even blew fire from his mouth (skeptical Romans said he used a nut filled with sulfur for the trick). Yet he had more than magic tricks up his sleeve, and he managed with a band of slaves to capture several cities. He crowned himself king under the name Antiochus, which was the name of the line of kings from his native Syria, and even issued a coin with an image of himself as King Antiochus. It took the Romans three years to subdue Eunus and his thousands of followers. Tiberius, in his speech to the senate, made sure to remind them of this danger at their doorstep.

FIG. 7.3 An idealized modern statue of Eunus in Sicily.

Following his speech, Tiberius had his law read out to the senate. The essential point of the law was the enforcement of the 500-*iugera* limit on the amount of state land a Roman could possess. This land, known as *ager publicus*, was the land Rome had acquired through its military conquests in Italy or had seized from cities after the Second Punic War as punishment for their support of Hannibal. To ease the concerns of those who feared they would not have enough land to pass down to their heirs, Tiberius's law added that an additional 250 *iugera* (about 135 football fields) could be held for each child. Anything more than this would be redistributed to poorer Romans in plots of 30 *iugera* (about 16 football fields). His law would also forbid the resale of these allotments to prevent the wealthy from reacquiring their large estates. A three-man commission would be set up to oversee the process.

Despite his appeal to the senators' anxieties about their own wealth and security, and despite modifying his initial proposal to meet some of their concerns, there was still resistance to his proposal in the senate. A later Greek historian gives a summary of the complaints from the wealthy landholders:

> The wealthy found the proposed law extremely upsetting, since the three-man commission meant they could no longer ignore the law as they had in the past, and they wouldn't be able to buy the land given to others. ... They pointed out to the poor that these lands had since long ago been *their* farmlands, *their* vineyards, and *their* homes. Some pointed out that they had paid good money to their neighbors for land—would they lose their money along with the land? Others said the graves of their ancestors were on this land, which they had inherited from their fathers, while yet others had spent their wives' dowries on their properties,

> or had used the land as a dowry for their daughters, and moneylenders had made loans to people who used this land as collateral. (Appian, *Civil Wars* 1.10)

These complaints are not unreasonable, since land that was long believed to be a family inheritance would now be taken away. But the focus is entirely on the problems the upper-class landowners might face rather than the larger and more serious problems that the republic as a whole faced. These individuals could rightly be criticized for placing their own self-interest above the public good, and the speech of Tiberius quoted could be seen as an attempt to persuade these men that the land reform was, in fact, in their own interest as well as that of Rome's. Yet he failed to do so, and perhaps in the belief he could not make these men see beyond their personal interests, he pushed ahead with his plan for what he and others saw as the greater good.

Gaius Laelius had earlier earned his nickname Sapiens for withdrawing his land reform bill in the face of senatorial opposition, but Tiberius chose a different, and fateful, path. He took his proposed law directly to the Plebeian Assembly. This was a perfectly legal move, since the approval of the senate was not technically necessary for the passage of a law, but it was against the long-held traditions of Roman governance. The senate was still the center of authority, and to continue with legislation contrary to the wishes of the senate drove a deep wedge between the senate and the people of Rome, even if Tiberius did have the support of some prominent senators, including Publius Mucius Scaevola, one of the consuls in 133. Another prominent supporter had the long name Publius Licinius Crassus Dives Mucianus. He had already been praetor, and shortly after the tribunate of Tiberius would be both pontifex maximus in 132 and consul in 131; his daughter was married to Tiberius's brother, Gaius.

To the people, Tiberius delivered an even more moving speech, clearly designed to rouse the people to his side rather than to convince aristocrats of the benefits of his reform:

> Wild animals that roam throughout Italy have at least a den or some lair where they can find shelter, but the men who fight and die for Italy don't have a share in anything except the air and the sun—without homes, without a place to stay, they roam about with their children and wives. Their commanders urge them during battle to defend their family tombs and shrines from the enemy, but it is all a lie. Not one of all these Roman soldiers has an ancestral altar, not one has a tomb that goes back generations. Instead, they fight and die for someone else's wealth, someone else's luxury. They are called "masters of the world," but possess not a single clod of earth. (Plutarch, *Tiberius Gracchus* 9.4)

It is a speech filled with stirring imagery and phrases calculated to tug at the heartstrings, but certainly not a speech designed to convince a conservative Roman senator. Tiberius clearly knew the two sides well and tried to appeal to both of them in the manner he thought best for each. In a speech before the people, this more emotional appeal would not only rouse the people to fervent support, it would also serve as a warning to the senators who opposed the law, since they might fear a widespread popular reaction that would lead to public disorder.

However, when Tiberius began to read his law to the assembly prior to the vote, another tribune of the plebs, Marcus Octavius, stepped forward and used his veto to put a stop to the proceedings. The assembly was called off, so Tiberius made a second attempt the following day. Once again, Marcus Octavius used his veto to prevent any vote on the law. Octavius was said to be a friend of Tiberius, and the reasons for his opposition are not clear. It was said he himself possessed a great deal of land that he feared losing, and in one story Tiberius offered to pay him for his land out of his own pocket if he allowed the vote on the law to go forward. More likely, Octavius was influenced by more powerful and influential senators, though one could not rule out the possibility that he simply opposed it out of principle. Whatever the case, Tiberius persisted, using his own powers as a tribune to prevent any other public business from being carried out until there was a vote on his law. He even closed up the public treasury so none of its funds could be used, essentially causing a government shutdown. There were rumors that assassins had been hired to take out Tiberius, and it was said he carried a dagger concealed under his toga for protection. Another attempt was made to hold a vote, but the large urns in which Romans cast their votes had been stolen. Tensions were running high, and as the many supporters of the law were gathering, two former consuls came to Tiberius and begged him to stop. Tiberius attempted one last time to appeal to the authority of the senate so he could proceed with the vote, but once again, he could not make any headway with them.

At this point, Tiberius took a drastic step, and although it may not have been technically illegal, it was unprecedented and guaranteed to create a constitutional crisis. He decided to have Octavius removed from office by the Popular Assembly. Octavius was a duly elected magistrate, and had done nothing illegal, so Tiberius made the case for stripping him of the tribunate in a way that set a dangerous precedent:

> If a tribune of the plebs changes and begins to harm the people, weaken their power, and rob them of their vote, by his own acts he has deprived himself of his office, since he is not living up to the promises for which he received it. If a tribune cannot disqualify himself for office in this way, then nothing can be done against a tribune, even if he tries to tear down the Capitol or set fire to the navy's ships. A tribune who does these things is a bad tribune, but if he takes away the power of the people, he is no longer a tribune. Wouldn't it be outrageous if a tribune has the authority to throw a consul in prison, but the people can't take away a tribune's authority when he uses it against the people who gave it to him? After all, both consuls and tribunes are elected by the people. ... So is it right for a tribune who causes harm to the people to keep that sacred authority, when that authority was given to him in order to serve the people? Such a tribune destroys the very power which is the source of his own power! And if it's right for him to become a tribune by a majority of the vote, then it must be even more right for him to lose the office of tribune by a unanimous vote. (Plutarch, *Tiberius Gracchus* 15)

Translated from Plutarch, *Tiberius Gracchus*.

Tiberius claims a tribune of the plebs can do many awful things, including commit acts of sacrilege or sabotage, and still be a tribune—a very bad one, to be sure, but a tribune nonetheless. However, if he does anything that brings harm to the people, he should no longer be considered a tribune, since the fundamental duty of a tribune of the plebs is to defend the plebs. This is a logical argument, and certainly sounds persuasive, but it also opened the door to domination of the government of Rome by the people. A senator would reasonably see this as an attack against the senate, and also against the constitution of the republic. Who, for example, would determine what counts as harm to the people? In Tiberius's speech, he simply assumes that opposition to his proposal is a serious wrong committed against the people. The other part of his argument is also dangerous. He claims that if the people voted a tribune into office, then they have the authority to remove the tribune by a vote before his one-year term is up. It is easy to understand why *optimates* would find the argument terrifying. At the same time, if the *optimates* were stubbornly resisting any reforms that would alleviate serious problems, did the people have any choice?

Tiberius, in the eyes of his opponents, had become the kind of *popularis* politician they feared most, one whose power and influence was based on an ability to sway popular opinion with emotional appeals and promises to please them. Such individuals are known as "demagogues," from the Greek words for "people" (*demos*, as in democracy) and "to lead" (*ago*), and the word always carries a negative sense. The senators and other traditional-minded Romans believed Tiberius crossed the line from a popular leader who had the public good in mind to a demagogue who was usurping power by manipulating the masses. Even if their opposition was originally to the law, now they began to oppose Tiberius himself.

Tiberius managed to pass his law and to have Octavius removed from office by the same vote. Then there were a few practical matters that had to be dealt with. First, there would have to be a survey of lands and an account of individual landholdings. Tiberius had thus included in his law the establishment of a three-man land commission that would be responsible for taking care of these administrative details. He would be a member, of course, and so would his younger brother, 20 years old at the time. The third member of the commission was Tiberius's father-in-law Appius Claudius Pulcher, consul of 143, censor, and *princeps senatus* in 136. Second, to confiscate land from individuals who had come into possession of land in a way they believed was legal and fair, and who had made improvements on the land or used it as collateral for loans, not only seemed unjust, but also might create serious economic problems for everyone. However, Tiberius did not propose simply taking the land away. He offered landowners compensation, and the commission would arrange payment from public funds for any lands seized, much in the way that "eminent domain" works today in the United States.

Of course, paying all these landowners for thousands of plots of land would require an enormous sum of money, and some resistance to his law might reasonably arise from the costs associated with it. However, Tiberius met with a great stroke of luck. In 133, Attalus III died. Ruler of Pergamum, a kingdom on the east coast of modern Turkey, he had been a friend and ally of Rome and was once even introduced to the Roman Senate. In his will, he left his lands and his treasury to Rome, a huge financial windfall. Tiberius thus proposed that this new revenue be used for his land reform. Tiberius's plan to use this windfall for the people only confirmed his opponents' suspicions of his demagogic motives. Since the senate traditionally supervised public finances and foreign affairs, some senators began to accuse him of seeking to undermine the authority of the senate in order to bolster his own power. One senator, a neighbor of Tiberius, even claimed that the representative of Pergamum who brought news of Attalus's will to the senate had presented Tiberius with a purple robe and a diadem, the royal headgear of eastern kings. The story is meant to suggest that Tiberius had ambitions to become a king, and as has been made clear, Romans suspected of aiming at kingship were killed. Tiberius did nothing to dispel this suspicion when he sought to be reelected as tribune of the plebs for the following year. To run for the office again was not unprecedented, and Tiberius would rightly believe that he needed to remain a tribune in order to complete the work of his land reform. Moreover, as long as he was a tribune of the plebs, he could not be prosecuted on legal charges, and the office would provide him with a measure of safety and security. He feared for his life, but to kill a tribune would be unthinkable—almost. From the perspective of his opponents, his decision to seek another term was another step toward his goal for absolute power, and if that were the case, his life was in danger, even if he was a tribune.

The voting for the following year's tribunes was contentious, and Tiberius was not assured of victory. But during the election, a senator who supported Tiberius approached him. He had just left a meeting of the senate, at which a group of senators had decided to send some of their friends and slaves to kill Tiberius, even though the consul, Gaius Gracchus's father-in-law, did not support this. Tiberius and his supporters immediately prepared for a fight, breaking up pieces of wood to use as weapons. The attack came, and in the noise and confusion of the fighting Tiberius pointed to his head, supposedly as a signal to his supporters that his life was in danger, but his opponents instead saw it as a gesture that he was asking for a king's crown. This latter version was reported to the senators, including the pontifex maximus, Publius Cornelius Scipio Nasica, the "pointy nose" we met earlier and Tiberius's cousin. Scipio Nasica demanded that the consul declare a state of emergency so he could eliminate the "king." The consul replied he would not put a Roman citizen to death without a trial, but if Tiberius persuaded the people to vote for anything illegal, he would not regard it as valid. Scipio Nasica rejected this conciliatory approach and called for all senators who believed in the rule of law to follow him to the Capitol to confront Tiberius and his supporters. Nasica covered his head with his toga, likely as a sign that as chief priest of Rome he was carrying out a religious duty and left the senate house. Those who followed him reached the Capitol, where they attacked Tiberius and his supporters with clubs and broken-off chair legs. As Tiberius tried to flee, he stumbled. One of the other tribunes struck him the head. Other blows followed, and soon Tiberius and a few hundred of his followers were dead. Their bodies were thrown into the Tiber, including Tiberius's, even though his brother Gaius had asked for his corpse in order to give it a proper burial. The followers and allies of Tiberius who survived were either banished from Rome or put on trial and executed.

Aftermath

The aftermath of this bloody civil war in miniature is not what one might expect. Tiberius's land reform legislation was not overturned, and two new members of the commission were elected for the following year, while Gaius Gracchus stayed on. One of the new members was Marcus Fulvius Flaccus, who had warned Tiberius of the impending attack against him. As for Scipio Nasica, the senate sent him off on a diplomatic mission in the province of Asia (the western part of modern Turkey), and he died shortly afterward in Pergamum.

During the turmoil and violence surrounding Tiberius's year as tribune, his brother-in-law Scipio Aemilianus was far away in Spain. He had become consul again in 134 and took command of Roman forces still involved in the wars there. Like other Roman commanders at the time, he had difficulty raising troops from Italy and even had to rely on his personal clients to serve. Nonetheless, he finally brought an end to the war by besieging Numantia and starving its inhabitants into submission. He returned to Rome in 132 to celebrate a triumph. It is interesting to speculate whether events would have turned out differently had he been present in Rome during Tiberius's tribunate, since he would have represented a powerful and popular opposition to Tiberius and his reforms. It is said that when news of Tiberius's death reached him in Spain, he recited in a loud voice, so everyone could hear him, a line from the Greek epic poet Homer: "May all who attempt such evil perish!" When he returned to Rome, he successfully worked to strip the land commission of its authority and transfer it to the consuls. He also spoke against an effort to allow tribunes to run for reelection, while Gaius Gracchus gave a speech in favor of it. In 129, however, only a few years after his return to Rome, he suddenly died. There was a widespread belief that he had been poisoned, and many suspected his wife, the sister of Tiberius and Gaius, had murdered him to avenge Tiberius's death, while some thought the killer was their mother, Cornelia.

Tensions between popular reformers and more conservative politicians continued, and the issues of land reform did not go away. One effort made during this time was to rent out plots of land along new roads being built throughout Italy, and to make those who lived on this land responsible for maintaining the part of the road along their property. One of the consuls of 132, who had overseen the punishment of Tiberius's supporters, undertook such a scheme, which suggests even those who were the most hostile to Tiberius recognized a need for a solution to the land problem. However, another issue created new conflict.

Rome's allies throughout Italy had been unhappy with the program of land redistribution since many of them were affected by it. Some had earlier asked Scipio Aemilianus to represent them in the senate, which he had done when he weakened the land commission. But Marcus Fulvius Flaccus, the man who had warned Tiberius and later served on the land commission, became consul in 125. In an attempt to continue the land program, he sought support from these Italian allies and proposed giving them the opportunity to become Roman citizens. The offer would convert them into a more powerful political force at Rome. The aristocratic element of the senate opposed the law, but this time it was the assembly that rejected the law. Since their votes would not carry the same weight as before, the people of Rome would have viewed this extension of citizenship as weakening their own political influence and lessening the value of their citizenship. The senate managed to deal with Flaccus in a rather tidy way by sending him off to fight the Gauls in the southern part of modern-day France.

However, the rejection of citizen rights for allies did not sit well with some inhabitants of the town of Fregellae, about 70 miles southeast of Rome. Established as a colony with "Latin rights" in the fourth century BC, Fregellae had long been a loyal ally, standing with Rome against both Pyrrhus and Hannibal. But in 125, the town rose in rebellion. A Roman army under the command of the praetor Lucius Opimius was sent out to subdue it. After the city was betrayed from the inside and its gates opened to the Roman army, the Fregellans surrendered. Opimius razed the city to the ground, and its territory was placed under a curse. Opimius sought a triumph, but was denied, since he had not added to Rome's territory, only restored what had been temporarily lost. In the following year, a new colony was founded on land next to the former site of the city. The harsh treatment of Fregellae was not simply punishment for their rebellion, but also a warning to other Latin allies. It worked, in the short term, but the issue of Italian citizenship that led Fregellae to revolt continued to simmer and would soon erupt into a full-scale war between Rome and its allies.

His Brother's Keeper: Gaius Gracchus

Gaius remained active in the years after his brother's murder and continued to speak out for popular reforms in the senate. Although he was in Sardinia during the revolt of Fregellae, he returned to Rome in 124 and was elected as tribune of the plebs in 123. He immediately set to work to continue the program of the reformers and introduced several laws to that end:

- The penalty for killing a Roman citizen who had not been convicted by a court set up by the people was death.
- Reelection of tribunes was explicitly made legal.
- Grain would be provided to the people of Rome at a low, fixed price.
- The state would provide soldiers with their clothing.
- Colonies would be founded where poorer Romans would receive plots of land.
- New roads and public granaries would be built.

While the last four the laws were addressed to solving the economic ills plaguing the republic, the first two were more for his own political purposes. Gaius's law on the killing of Roman citizens without a trial was aimed directly at the murderers of his brother and supporters, but also had a larger political purpose. In Rome, someone could be charged with a crime even if the law making their act a crime postdated their act. Such a law would be useful in seeking revenge against political enemies for past acts and would make aristocrats think twice before doing to Gaius or his supporters what they had done to his brother and his followers a decade earlier. The second law paved a clear path to his own re-election. This was an ambitious program, but Gaius proceeded much more carefully and shrewdly than his brother had. At the same time, Gaius proposed no measures to directly threaten the authority of the senate, which made it more difficult to justify the use of violence against him than against Tiberius.

In order to pay for many of the changes he introduced, he passed another law that granted businessmen the right to enter into contracts with the Roman government to collect taxes in Asia. These tax collectors, known as *publicani*, would bid on government contracts to collect a certain amount of tax revenue for the state, and they would keep a percentage of what they collected as their profit. A *publicanus* was basically a government contractor, and tax collection was a lucrative business. As one might imagine, *publicani* could behave rather badly in their efforts to collect, as their profits depended on it. They developed quite a bad reputation in the provinces. In the first century AD, Roman tax collectors were singled out as wicked individuals in the New Testament, and Jesus shocks his followers when he agrees to have dinner with one. Politically, however, Gaius's proposal was a smart move. The most prominent *publicani* were members of the equestrian order, who were very wealthy but had little interest in running for political office or becoming a senator. But even if *equites* did not care to enter the senate, they were still politically influential. By giving them access to a huge market, Gaius could use them as leverage against the senate.

Gaius did the equestrian order another favor, which was another blow to the senatorial elite. He passed a law excluding senators from serving as jurors on trials that involved corruption and extortion. A court had been established in 149 BC to prosecute Roman government officials, especially governors of a province, on charges of corruption, which might involve requiring provincials to pay bribes or seizing the possessions of wealthy provincials. Anyone found guilty in this court would be forced to pay back double what he had taken. Most of those charged in this court were senators, but a jury of senators would not be eager to convict one of their own, especially since they were likely guilty of the same crime. *Publicani* would also likely fall afoul of this law, given that their business model was essentially trying to squeeze as much money as possible out of provincials. If members of the equestrian order were now jurors, they could protect their own interests to an extent not possible before, and senators would be less willing to interfere with their business.

Thanks to his legislation, Gaius was reelected as tribune for 122 and 121. Instead of attempting to revive his brother's controversial legislation and land commission, he instead directed his energies to establishing colonies, both in Italy and overseas. He revived the question of citizenship for Italian allies, even though this had failed miserably when Flaccus proposed it a few years earlier, since neither the senatorial elite nor the plebs supported the idea. Their opposition had not diminished, and Gaius started to tread in dangerous waters. Moreover, his attempt to establish an overseas colony at the site of Rome's former enemy Carthage did not go well. According to one story, every time stakes were planted to mark out the boundaries of the new settlement, wolves would come and take them away—clearly a bad omen.

Despite his careful political maneuvering, the push to give voting rights to the Italian allies went too far for many of his supporters. The consul of 122 had supported him initially but switched over to the opposition. But Gaius still had plenty of support among the people, and if he could continue to hold the office of tribune, he could use the office's extraordinary power as a weapon against the senate. His opponents, however, were not without some political skills of their own, and while Gaius was away at Carthage overseeing the foundation of the new colony, they persuaded another tribune, Marcus Livius Drusus, to put forward even more radical proposals before the people. These were never intended to be put into effect. Instead, their purpose was to undermine Gaius's popularity by offering the plebs far more than Gaius had. Drusus proposed 12 new colonies in Italy with rent-free plots of land for 3000 new settlers in each colony, far more than Gaius would offer, since Gaius was attempting to pass actual legislation. To win over the Italian allies, Drusus put forward a law that would make it illegal for Roman commanders to physically punish allied soldiers. The political gamesmanship was successful, and Gaius lost his bid for reelection upon his return to Rome. There was also a new consul for 121, Lucius Opimius, who a few years before had destroyed Fregellae and was determined to undo Gaius's reforms. In the same year, another tribune attempted to repeal the law that called for the foundation of the colony at Carthage. However, Gaius's term of office was not yet over, and he continued to defend his reforms.

The stage was set for another violent conflict. In one version of what happened, both Gaius's supporters and the opposing faction gathered on the Capitol on the day of the vote to repeal Gaius's laws. After the consul had performed the necessary sacrifice to begin the voting, one of his lictors, while pushing his way through a crowd of Gaius's supporters, yelled out, "Make way for decent citizens, you scum!" Someone in the crowd stabbed him, and his violent death provided Opimius with an opportunity to take more serious action against Gaius and his supporters. The body of his lictor was taken to the senate house, where it was used as a political prop to generate outrage among the senators. The senate promptly issued, for the first time in Rome's history, the *senatus consultum ultimum*, the "final decree of the senate" (often abbreviated SCU). This was a formal declaration of a state of emergency, similar to a modern-day declaration of martial law. The SCU directed the consul to take any measures necessary in order to maintain the safety and security of the Roman state. Once this "final decree" was issued, Opimius wasted no time in carrying out his task. He ordered senators as well as members of the equestrian order to arm themselves and to bring armed slaves with them. Gaius, Fulvius Flaccus, and their supporters headed for the Aventine hill, much as the plebeians had done generations earlier in their conflict with the patricians. As Gaius left his home for the Aventine, his wife tearfully pleaded with him not to go, and she gave a speech as moving as Gaius himself could have given:

> I'm not sending you off to the rostra, as I once did, to be a tribune and lawmaker, nor off to a glorious war. If you died in battle, my grief would at least have some honor. But you are exposing yourself to the murderers of Tiberius, and though it is right for you to go unarmed, so that you will only suffer wrong instead of committing any, your death won't do any good for the Republic. The worst men have finally won, and arguments are now settled with violence and weapons. If your brother had died in Numantia, we would have been able to bury his body, recovered under treaty. But I fear I will have to

beg some river or sea to return your body to me. After the murder of Tiberius, why should anyone have faith in the laws or the gods anymore? (Plutarch, *Gaius Gracchus* 15)

Flaccus sent his son to the senate in an attempt to settle the conflict peacefully, but Opimius instead took him hostage and launched his attack. It is said Gaius did not participate in the fighting, but instead withdrew into the Temple of Diana on the Aventine hill, where he prayed that Rome might forever be kept in slavery for their thankless treachery against him. (Quite different from the prayer uttered by Scipio, and likely a later invention to make Gaius look bad.) Eventually he fled on foot, accompanied by a single slave. No one dared to give him a horse or help him in any way. He and his slave stopped in a grove of woods sacred to the Furies (goddesses of vengeance), where the loyal slave first killed Gaius, then committed suicide over his master's body. Gaius's corpse was beheaded, since there was a reward equivalent to its weight in gold. His body, along with the corpses of three thousand of his followers, were thrown into the Tiber.

To mark the end of the conflict and the return to peace and order, Opimius restored the Temple of Concord that Camillus had dedicated centuries before. This gesture infuriated the people, who viewed it as Opimius celebrating the murder of fellow citizens. It is said that sometime during the night, someone tagged the temple with a bit of graffiti to highlight Opimius's hypocrisy: "An insane act of discord creates a Temple of Concord." The people performed their own act of reverence by putting up statues of the Gracchi brothers, placing offerings before them almost every day. They also turned the spots where each had died into sacred places. Their mother Cornelia supposedly said these were worthy tombs for her sons. She lived out her life on the coast, not far from Rome, and it is said she would tell her many visitors about the life of her famous father Scipio, but also would speak of the accomplishments of her two sons without tears.

Roman Dining

The basic elements of the Roman diet were grain (wheat and barley for porridge and bread), olives (to eat and to make oil), and grapes (for wine). These three items are sometimes referred to as the "Mediterranean triad," since they formed the basic diet of many peoples in the region. Beans such as chickpeas and lentils were an important source of protein, especially for the lower classes, and Romans ate a fair amount of chicken, but otherwise meat was a luxury. Oysters were a prized delicacy, though fish and shellfish were not part of the everyday diet of most Romans. And while Romans enjoyed cheese, milk and butter were considered uncivilized foods.

Wine was the main drink, second only to water, and there were different types, including a wine and vinegar mixture known as *lora* (for laborers and preferred by old women), a raisin wine known as *passum*, and higher quality vintages of *vinum*. Particularly prized were Falernian wines from Campania, and Caecuban wines from Latium. Wine was stored and aged in amphoras, large vessels with two handles on either side of a narrow neck (*amphora* is Greek for "two-eared" from the appearance of the handles), and the years of the vintage were denoted by the consuls. One prized vintage was Opimian, from the consulship in 121 BC of Lucius Opimius, destroyer of Fregellae and consul responsible for the death of Gaius and his followers. According to some ancient writers, it was illegal for women to drink wine, and their husbands had the right to kiss their wives (the *ius osculi*) to find out if they had been drinking. Beer (*cervisia*) was not a Roman drink and was found only among peoples where grapes were not grown.

Though we normally think of bread or noodles as a standard type of food made from grain, early Romans ate their grain in the form of a porridge called *puls*, essentially grain cooked with water or milk. In fact, *puls* was such a staple of the Roman diet that they could be identified as "porridge-eaters" (*pultiphagi*). By the end of the Second Punic War, when so much else changed at Rome, bread began to supplant *puls* as a staple of the Roman diet. In fact, a later source claims that the first bakery in Rome was in 171 BC, but this seems questionable. However, later Romans did attribute major changes to the Roman diet around this time, and Livy claimed this was when cooking at Rome became an "art."

There may be some truth behind Livy's statement, since eating habits and attitudes about food seemed to change at this time, at least among the elite. During the Second Punic War, Rome instituted an emergency measure limiting displays of personal wealth, or against what might be called "conspicuous consumption." This was followed in 182 BC by passage of a law that set a limit on the number of dinner guests, the first "sumptuary law" ("sumptuary" is from the Latin word for expense or spending, the root of "consumption"). Cato the Elder argued against its repeal the following year. Then in 161, a *lex Fannia* also set various limits on dinner parties, including the number of guests and the types of food that could be served, and we know of several other sumptuary laws over the following century, usually extending or reaffirming the *lex Fannia*. Sulla passed a law in 81 that allowed 300 *sestertii* to be spent on dinner for certain holidays and festivals, but otherwise the limit was 30 *sestertii* (roughly a couple of weeks pay for a soldier). Another law passed a few years later limited the types of food that could be served rather than the expense. The repeated passage of laws on the same subject suggests that they were ineffectual, but it is clear that "fine dining" of a certain kind had become prevalent among the elite following the Second Punic War.

A cookbook with almost five hundred recipes survives, which is attributed to a first century AD author named Apicius, but the recipes are likely from much later. The book is organized, like many modern cookbooks, into sections based on the main ingredients, such as meat, vegetables, beans, poultry, and seafood. The dishes are clearly aimed at the upper classes, though some of the recipes are quite simple:

> Slice beets and leeks; add ground coriander and cumin, boil down in raisin wine. Remove beets and serve with oil and vinegar.

Another recipe is for Lucanian sausage, which can still be purchased today:

> Grind pepper, cumin, savory, parsley, laurel berries and place in a broth. Mix with finely chopped pork and mix with the broth. When his mixture thickens, add whole peppers and nuts. Fill sausage casings with mixture, then hang the sausage to smoke.

One of the more infamous Roman food products was a condiment known as *garum*, also called *liquamen*, which seems to have been produced by placing anchovies, sardines, or other fish (or parts of fish) in a barrel and letting them rot until they fermented. It must have had a powerful smell and an incredibly pungent taste.

Romans usually ate three meals a day, though, as might be imagined, there was a big difference in the way the upper classes and lower classes ate, and since most of our sources reflect the upper classes, our view of dining is necessarily skewed toward them. The first meal of the day, the *ientaculum*, corresponds to breakfast, and was usually taken upon first rising in the morning. *Prandium* was a meal in the middle of the day, equivalent to lunch. These meals seemed to have been very light, consisting of only cold foods—mostly bread or cheese, though sometimes there might be some cold meats or vegetables washed down with a bit of wine. The main meal of the day was dinner, known as *cena*. Since most of our evidence comes from upper-class sources, these meals can seem like elaborate dinner parties, and for elite Romans they sometimes were.

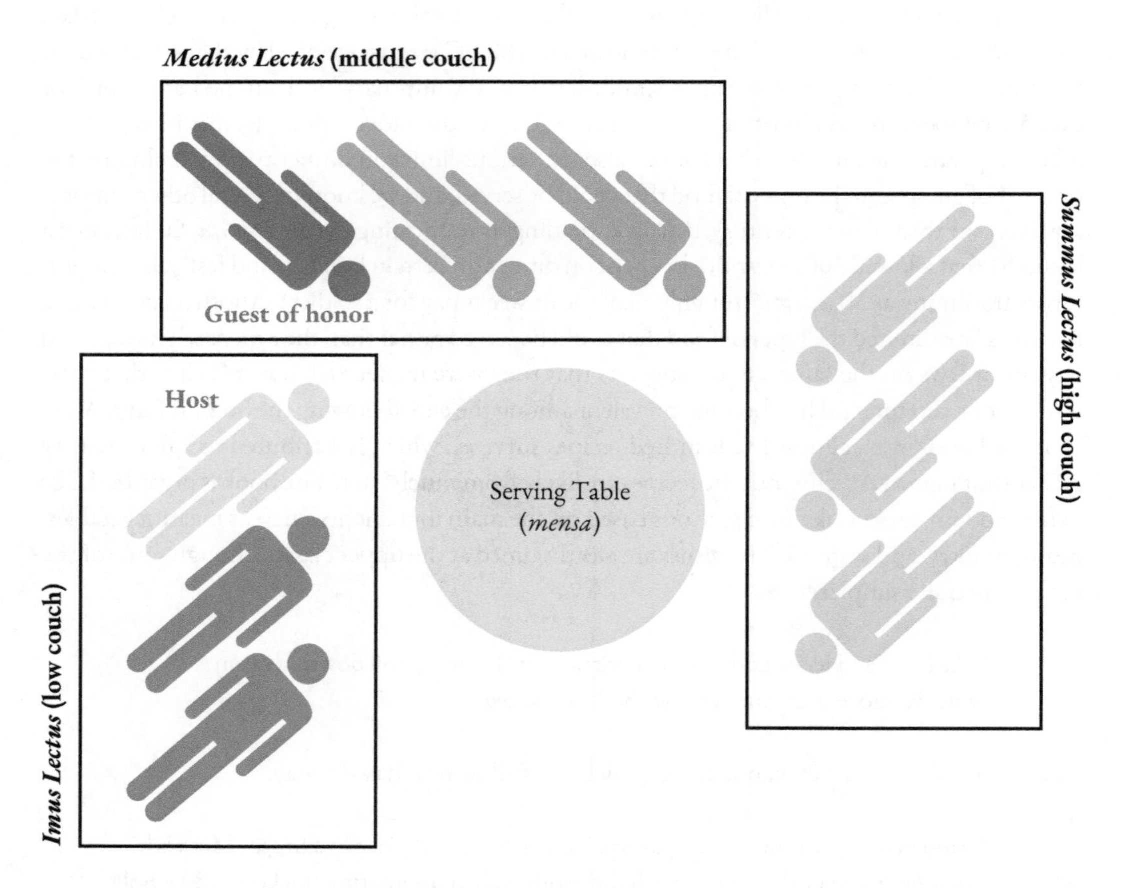

FIG. 7.4 The seating arrangement for an elite Roman dinner party.

The wealthier Romans had a special dining room in their house, known as a *triclinium*, formed from Latin words for "three" and "recline." Instead of sitting on chairs, the Romans would eat while lying down on their sides on one of three large couches, usually with three persons per couch. The couches were arranged in a U-shape around a square table on which the food would be served. In keeping with the Roman concern for status and hierarchy, the bottom position on the middle couch was the *locus consularis*, reserved for the guest of honor, while the host reclined on a separate couch, in the position that put him next to the guest of honor.

FIG. 7.5 A dining establishment in Pompeii. The basins sunk in the counter contained hot or cold foods.

Many people, of course, grew their own vegetables in gardens, though there were also markets and shops, as well as places one could grab a meal or a drink. Examples of these have been preserved in Pompeii, the city in the bay of Naples that was buried by the eruption of the volcano Mt. Vesuvius in 79 AD. A counter in the front contained several small wells from which both hot and cold foods could be purchased. There were also places to eat out, the *taberna* (usually translated as "tavern") and the *popina*, a kind of restaurant associated with the lower classes.

Credits

Fig. 7.1: Source: https://commons.wikimedia.org/wiki/File:Laurent_de_la_La_Hyre_001.jpg.

Fig. 7.3: Copyright © by Eannutum (CC BY-SA 3.0) at https://commons.wikimedia.org/wiki/File:Euno22009si.jpg.

Fig. 7.5: Copyright © by Jose Goncalves (CC BY-SA 4.0) at https://commons.wikimedia.org/wiki/File:Pompeii_2004_(6).jpg.

CHAPTER 8

All Roads Lead to War

Commanders and Corruption

FIG. 8.1 A coin issued by the confederation of Italian allies during their war against Rome. On the left is ITALIA, Italy represented as a goddess. On the right, representatives of the eight allies take an oath before a standard. The person in the center holds a pig, which will be sacrificed to seal the oath.

Overview

In the aftermath of the Gracchi, political tensions continued to build among groups with competing interests, including most fundamentally between the people and the Senate of Rome. Two major wars, against tribes from Germany and a king in north Africa, brought one of Rome's greatest generals, Gaius Marius, to the fore, but the period ends with the outbreak of war between Rome and its Italian allies. At the end of the chapter is an introduction to the roads, bridges, and aqueducts of Rome.

Timeline

121	Death of Gaius Gracchus
113–104	War against the Germanic tribes
111–105	The war against Jugurtha
107	First consulship of Marius
100	Sixth consulship of Marius
91–89	The Social War

Divided Loyalties

The bloodshed that ended the lives of the Gracchi brothers and their followers was confined to the city of Rome, even though the issues concerned the allies throughout Italy, as Fregellae's revolt and its destruction showed. Yet it was only a small step from fighting over soldiers to fighting against them, and within another generation, the factional strife that convulsed Rome would lead first to a war against the allies and eventually to a full-blown civil war.

Even if the methods by which the Gracchi pursued their reforms could be criticized, the reforms themselves were needed. Yet some among the senatorial aristocracy appeared unwilling to take any major steps in that direction. In part, reforms meant a threat to their grip on power, which entailed governing the people of Rome and its empire but included opportunities to acquire power, prestige, and wealth by governing provinces or in military commands.

Tiberius and Gaius Gracchus, as well as Scipio Aemilianus, had been charismatic leaders. While they had their personal ambitions, they all maintained a sense of a greater good, even if they had different ideas about how to attain this good. Rome's political system functioned best when personal interests aligned with the public good, even if imperfectly, but such an alignment was possible only when there was some collective idea of a republic from which everyone derived some common benefit. While there had always been glory-seeking individuals, the violence that erupted around the Gracchi seemed to demonstrate that a shared belief in SPQR, the Senate and People of Rome, no longer existed. Political opponents were now assumed to be working primarily for their own benefit, and republican politics was treated as a zero-sum game: What is good for you is bad for me. A greater public good, shared in by all, was no longer conceivable. No longer did political opponents have competing ideas about how to govern the republic—opponents now had incompatible visions of the republic itself. The opposition of the senatorial elite to land reform seemed to reveal a lack of concern for a greater good, and so too did the people's rush to accept any proposal that benefitted them most, without consideration of the consequences of those proposals. In such a state, both sides seemed unable or unwilling to compromise, and opposition to policies was seen as a direct assault against individuals rather than a difference of opinion. In some ways, the period of the Gracchi opened a "cold civil war," with only brief outbursts of political violence. In time, this division would lead to actual civil war in which Roman soldier fought against Roman soldier.

The two sides that emerged in this turbulent period were given the names *populares* and *optimates*, discussed in the previous chapter. Land reform and the grain supply were two issues always closely identified with the *populares*, but not all *populares* were genuinely interested in helping the people of Rome. Instead, they saw the people as a useful means to achieve their own personal ambitions. Likewise, *optimates* were not all opposed to reforms that benefitted the people, and many were simply opposed to the growing political power of the people at the expense of the senate. For example, after Gaius's death, some *optimates* helped to institute land reforms, and not all of the Gracchan reforms perished along with their authors. In fact, *optimates* would at times pursue policies that managed to address the same problems *populares* wished to address. However, they often seemed to do so only as a means to weaken political support for their opponents, or to prevent an outburst of popular discontent. Just as many *populares* reasonably believed that many *optimates* were concerned only with maintaining their own positions of influence and power, and not with the people as a whole, so too did many *optimates* understandably suspect *populares* politicians of manipulating the people for their own personal ambitions. The terms were as much about political style as substance, and the conflicts between *optimates* and *populares* were often less about the laws and reforms than the authority behind them.

The Afterlife of the Gracchan Reforms

In the aftermath of Gaius's death, the reforms first instituted by his brother were not completely undone. The land commission, which had been weakened, was finally abolished, and a provision that prevented the sale of distributed lands was overturned. Yet a major land reform law was passed in 111, and this law upheld the distributions already made by the Gracchan law and converted some of the land that was technically leased by the state to private property. An important reform passed by Gaius, the transfer of the juries in criminal trials from senators to members of the equestrian order, also managed to outlive him. In the tensions between the senate and the people, the members of the equestrian order (*equites*) were something of a wild card, who could extract concessions from both sides who wished to have their political support. Even if many of the *equites* had little interest in a political career in the senate, preferring to engage in lucrative forms of trade and business that were legally off limits to senators, they nonetheless wielded considerable political influence thanks to their economic activities and their personal wealth. Moreover, their sons would often have political ambitions, and their entry into political life at Rome would only strengthen the connections of this order to the senate.

The senate, the people, and the equestrians constituted three important elements of Roman politics and society in this period, and much of the turbulence and turmoil resulted from competition among the three groups, in the never-ending quest to balance their own interests with the others. Some decades later, the famous orator and politician Cicero put forward the political ideal of a "harmony of the orders" (*concordia ordinum*), by which he meant that senators and the *equites* worked together for the mutual benefit of the republic. In this aristocratic and optimate perspective, the people are protected by the orders above them, governed by their betters:

> The senate was established to be the guardian, leader, and defender of the Republic. Our ancestors wanted the authority of the senatorial order to guide the magistrates, who should act as if they served the senate. They also wanted the senate to have the support of the members of the prestigious order [the *equites*] that came second to it, and it should always be ready to protect and magnify the liberty and interests

of the plebs. If anyone, no matter what order he belongs to, defends these principles to the best of his ability, he is an optimate. (*In Defense of Sestius* 137-8)

This idea of the "harmony of the orders" never gained much traction in practice. Instead, it eventually transformed into a broader ideal that abandoned the orders and, as the last sentence in the passage suggests, aimed for the "agreement among all good men" (*consensus omnium bonorum*), no matter their order. Cicero, a "new man," attempted to redefine "nobility" into a matter of political outlook rather than family history. Anyone who shared in his vision of a well-ordered Rome based on a shared conception of the common good would count as a member of this new nobility. Cicero's vision was optimistic, idealistic, and doomed. The "orders" as a whole could not seem to find any harmony, and as it would turn out, neither could the "good men." The period of the Gracchi and its aftermath helps to explain why.

Another group that rose to political prominence during this time were the Italian allies. They had not received the political or financial rewards that corresponded to their crucial role in supplying manpower for the Roman military, and as we saw in the last chapter the idea of granting citizenship in some form to the allies had become important. The destruction of Fregellae in 125 might have prevented any further drastic action by allied communities throughout Italy for the short term, but the issue certainly did not go away and would rear its head soon enough.

A City for Sale: Jugurtha Comes to Rome

In the past, Rome had seemed able to discover moments of political unity when faced with a serious threat from an external enemy, but the two major foreign wars that occurred in the last decade of the second century BC revealed that even those times of togetherness were no more. Because of the wars with Carthage, Rome had long been involved with Numidia, a north African kingdom whose territory spread across parts of modern-day Algeria, Tunisia, and Libya. The Numidians, famed for their skill in horsemanship and archery, were valuable military allies, especially as cavalry. They were instrumental in Rome's victory at the battle of Zama in 202 BC, which ended the Second Punic War. As well, it was Carthage's complaint to Rome about the incursions into their territory by a Numidian king, Massinissa, that eventually led to the Third Punic War. Massinissa was generally pro-Roman, in part no doubt because he was hostile to Carthage and saw Rome as useful in that regard. In 148, Massinissa died, and his kingdom was divided among his three sons, usually a recipe for disaster, but in this case it was a grandson named Jugurtha who stirred up trouble.

Jugurtha was born in 160 BC to Mastanabal, the youngest son of Massinissa. Handsome and intelligent, he devoted himself to physical training, preparing himself to be a soldier, a commander, and eventually a king. He was raised not by his father, who died when Jugurtha was a young boy, but by his uncle Micipsa. Because of the close relations between Rome and the Numidians, and because his adoptive father was concerned about his growing popularity among the Numidians, Jugurtha was sent at the age of 26 to command the Numidian forces (including elephants) supporting the Romans in their war in Spain. Jugurtha had learned to speak Latin and became quite popular with the elite Romans. Earning recognition during the siege of Numantia for his bravery in combat and sound military advice, he became friends with Scipio Aemilianus. In the telling of the Roman historian Sallust, Scipio gave young Jugurtha some advice before he returned to Numidia:

> Scipio advised the young man to go through public officials, not back channels, to cultivate friendly relations with the Roman people, and he warned him about resorting to bribery. To buy from a few men what belonged to the people was risky, he said, and if Jugurtha could remain true to himself, he would find fame and the power of a king without looking for it. But, Scipio warned, if tried to take the easy way, his own money would be the cause of his ruin. (Sallust, *The Jugurthine War* 8.2)

The advice is suspiciously prescient, since it was written after Jugurtha had revealed himself to be a troublesome foe of Rome, because of the massive bribes he doled at Rome and his crafty tactics on the battlefields of north Africa. Scipio also wrote a letter praising of Jugurtha to his uncle Micipsa, who was now the sole ruler in Numidia. The letter caused Micipsa to change his attitude toward Jugurtha, and rather than try to eliminate him as a potential rival, he decided to adopt him as his own son. Micipsa already had two of his own sons, so when he died in 118, there were again three brothers who ruled Numidia, but as it turned out, Jugurtha had his own ideas about who should be king.

To eliminate one of his stepbrothers, Jugurtha sent men to break into his house and behead him. There was no doubt about who was behind this and what it meant, so the other brother, Adherbal, quickly prepared for war and sent ambassadors to Rome. Jugurtha wasted no time

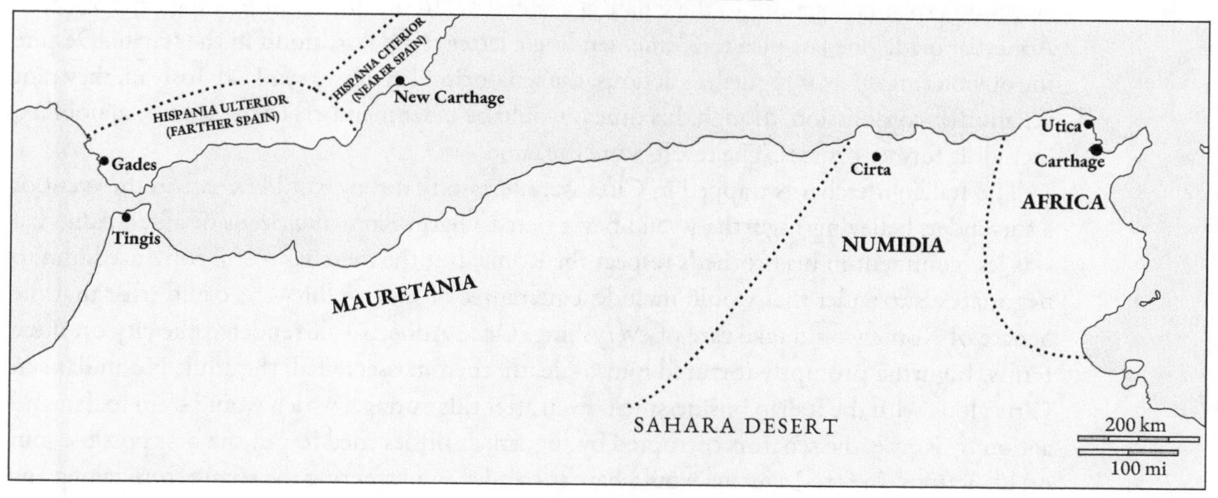

FIG. 8.2 North Africa and southern Spain.

in defeating Adherbal in battle, who then fled to Rome to seek assistance. Jugurtha was well acquainted with the ways of Rome, and knew he had little chance of fending off a Roman force should it come to open war. Instead, he sent his own ambassadors to Rome, well supplied with gold and silver to pay off the Roman nobles he already knew and to make new "friends" among the senatorial elite. Adherbal delivered a speech before the Roman Senate, appealing to the long-standing ties of friendship between his ancestral kingdom and Rome, and to Rome's sense of justice and fairness. (He clearly did not understand Rome as well as his brother Jugurtha did.) Because of Jugurtha's widespread bribery, only a few senators spoke in favor of giving aid to Adherbal, while the majority praised Jugurtha. Still, a commission of ten senators was sent to Numidia to divide the kingdom between Jugurtha and his brother, but Jugurtha used bribery again to win over most of the commission to his side. When he was in Spain Scipio had given him advice befitting a virtuous noble, but Jugurtha realized that what he heard from his other friends in Rome was true: Everything at Rome was for sale.

Despite receiving the better half of the kingdom in the senatorial commission's allotment, Jugurtha nonetheless brazenly invaded his brother's half. Adherbal sent another embassy to Rome and again prepared for battle, though he had little confidence he could defeat his brother. After Jugurtha launched an attack, Adherbal retreated inside the walls of Cirta, the main city of the kingdom and an important port from which Rome received shipments of grain. When Jugurtha first attacked, numerous Roman and Italian merchants had taken part in the fighting. They were now trapped inside the city along with the Numidian followers of Adherbal. In response, Rome sent an embassy consisting of three young men, not considered important enough for Roman historians to name, and their age suggests the senate was only making a show of concern about Jugurtha's actions, likely because of his bribery. (Members of the earlier ten-man commission, in contrast, were leaders of the senate.) The three men spoke only to Jugurtha, who promised he would explain his actions to the senate at a later date. In the fifth month of the siege of Cirta, Adherbal made one last plea to Rome, sending a letter to be read aloud in the senate. Despite the obvious injustice of Jugurtha's actions, the senate decided not to send aid. Instead, they sent yet another commission, though this time it would be older members of the senatorial nobility, including former consuls. The results were the same.

The Italian merchants trapped in Cirta were certain that they would be safe in the event of a surrender, believing Jugurtha would never dare to harm Roman citizens or allies. Adherbal was less confident in his brother's respect for Rome, but the merchants still convinced him to negotiate a surrender that would include a guarantee of his own life—he could trust that the Senate of Rome would take care of everything. Once Adherbal surrendered the city on these terms, Jugurtha promptly tortured him to death, then massacred all the adult Numidians in Cirta along with the Italian businessmen. Even after this outrage, which would seem to demand action by Rome, the senators corrupted by Jugurtha's bribes tried to put the best possible spin on his actions. In fact, Jugurtha would have succeeded in preventing the senate from taking any action if Gaius Memmius, a tribune of the plebs in 111, had not roused the anger of the people and threatened to expose the rampant corruption among the senators. As a result, the consul who was assigned Numidia as his province was given command of an army and the funds to pay for it, with the mission of bringing Jugurtha to heel.

However, without engaging in any battles, the consul accepted a surrender negotiated by Jugurtha, who used the greed of the Romans to ensure he gave up nothing except some war elephants, some cavalry horses, and a small amount of silver. The people of Rome, undoubtedly under the influence of *popularis* politicians, were outraged, while the senate hesitated whether to approve of the terms of the surrender. Memmius, the tribune who had already spoken out, delivered a blistering speech against senatorial corruption—at least the historian Sallust has him deliver one. His speech, as crafted by Sallust, goes beyond the issue of Jugurtha's surrender. In one part, he turns on its head the charge of tyranny often leveled by *optimates* against *populares*:

> What hope is there for good faith or harmony? Those men [*optimates*] want to be tyrants, you only want liberty; they want to cause harm, you want to prevent it. In short, they treat our allies like enemies and our enemies like allies. Can peace and friendship co-exist in the minds of men who hold such contradictory attitudes? I urgently warn you, don't let their wrongdoing escape unpunished. This is not just embezzlement from the treasury, not just money extorted from our allies—these are serious crimes, but now so common no one thinks twice about them. Instead, the Senate's dignity has been sold to profit a ruthless enemy, and so has your authority. Both here at Rome and overseas, your country's interests have been put up for sale. If a tribunal does not investigate these actions, if the guilty get off scot-free, all that will be left to us is to spend our lives as the slaves of those who do all these things. To do whatever you want without punishment is to be a king. (Sallust, *The Jugurthine War* 31.24-5)

In Memmius's view, it is not a single *popularis* politician swaying the masses who is accused of aiming a kingship, but the entire senate, and it is the senate that now subverts the traditional order of Rome. In selling out to Jugurtha and doing his bidding, they act like oppressive tyrants, and they do all of this contrary to the wishes of the people. If they are not punished, they will succeed.

The senate could not ignore this open attack on their corruption, and since Memmius disavowed any use of violence, it would be difficult to accuse him of promoting political unrest. He proposed only that Jugurtha be compelled to appear before the senate and give testimony, with the hope he would expose corrupt senators. Those guilty of corruption would then be prosecuted in a court of law. Jugurtha was sent for and agreed to appear after receiving assurances of protection from a Roman praetor in Numidia. For good measure, he also won over a tribune of the plebs with a massive bribe. When Jugurtha appeared before the senate, he was not dressed as a king, but wore clothes of mourning, something Romans typically did when they were being prosecuted in a court of law to arouse the pity of the audience and the jurors. Memmius ordered him to speak, but just as he began, the corrupt tribune of the plebs used his authority to command him to be silent and brought the session to a close. There was anger and shouting, but the meeting ended. Jugurtha had won the day again.

Translated from Sallust, *Bellum Jugurthinum*.

Another Numidian, also a grandson of Massinissa, was in Rome at this time, having fled north Africa after Jugurtha captured Cirta. Because of his family lineage, he would be a suitable replacement for Jugurtha on the throne, and a Roman consul urged him to put forward a claim to it. Jugurtha recognized that this Numidian prince, a relative of his, presented a problem. He handled it by sending one of his men to kill the prince. Unfortunately for Jugurtha, the assassin was captured and made to stand trial, where he was expected to implicate Jugurtha (even though it was quite obvious to everyone who was behind the murder). Fifty of Jugurtha's Roman friends put up a huge amount of money as bond to ensure the accused assassin would not flee Rome before the trial, yet Jugurtha spirited him away back to Numidia. A few days later, Jugurtha left the city. It is said that as he departed, he looked back to Rome and exclaimed, "A city for sale, and soon to fall—if someone will buy it!"

Patricians and *Populares* at War: Metellus and Marius

There was no longer any question that Rome would go to war against Jugurtha, but the first consul sent to conduct it met with little success, thanks to Jugurtha's delaying tactics both in battle and in diplomacy. The time for elections back in Rome drew near, so the consul returned from the war in Numidia to oversee them. Political wrangling delayed the elections, however, so the consul's brother, who had been left in charge of the Roman troops, decided to take matters into his own hands. Jugurtha sent envoys to him as if to negotiate, but it was only a ruse to disguise a surprise attack on the Roman camp. It is also said he bribed a number of the Roman officers to look the other way as his soldiers approached. As a result of this raid on the Roman camp, Jugurtha forced the consul's brother to accept a disgraceful surrender.

The next consul assigned to take command of Numidia for the year 109 BC was Quintus Caecilius Metellus, a competent commander and under no suspicion of having been corrupted by Jugurtha's bribery. Given the state of the Roman forces there, many of whom could not be trusted, Metellus enlisted new soldiers, including allies from Italy and even troops supplied by client kings in the eastern Mediterranean. He also took a patient and prudent approach to the war, bringing discipline to the soldiers under his command. Jugurtha, realizing he now faced a Roman commander he could not corrupt, offered to surrender on the condition that his life and the lives of his children be spared. While openly suggesting he was open to peace, Metellus prepared for war, taking a page from Jugurtha's playbook. He sent envoys to various Numidians with offers of a reward if they would betray Jugurtha to him, dead or alive, but found no takers. He then engaged Jugurtha's forces in difficult combat. While the Romans were often successful, thanks to Jugurtha's clever tactics Metellus could not force the enemy to submit. Eventually, Metellus's persistence left Jugurtha few options, so he fled to the neighboring kingdom ruled by his father-in-law, Bocchus. Some months earlier Bocchus had tried to become an ally of Rome but had been refused either because he did not offer sufficient bribes or because Jugurtha already had. Both Metellus and Jugurtha appealed to Bocchus, the one reminding him of the advantages of friendly relations with Rome, the other warning him of the Romans' unbridled lust for conquest. Bocchus dithered and delayed, but it seemed only a matter of time before the war with Jugurtha would be over.

One of Metellus's officers was Gaius Marius, an ambitious man born around 157 BC. He came from a small town in northeastern Italy, where his father belonged to the equestrian order. He was by no means from a poor or humble background, but he did not have the status or connections of the senatorial aristocrats at Rome. A career in politics, rising up through the *cursus honorum*, was mostly unthinkable, though there was the example of the "new man" Cato the Elder, who had reached those heights a few generations before. Military service, however, provided Gaius with an outlet for his ambitions, and he could use both the equestrian order and the people as leverage for his self-promotion. He would go on to become one of Rome's greatest military leaders, and his career would make a deep impact on the last generations of the republic.

Like Jugurtha, Marius had fought under Scipio Aemilianus during the siege of Numantia in 134–132, and also like Jugurtha, his distinguished service brought him to Scipio's attention. In one story, Marius was sitting next to Scipio at a dinner in the commander's tent. When Scipio was asked where he might find someone who could fill his shoes, he gave Marius a pat on the shoulder and said, "Maybe right here." Marius developed other personal connections to the political elite of Rome, and his family had long been clients of the Metellus family, which included the consul of 109 who was finally making progress in the war against Jugurtha. Thanks to these connections, he was elected as a tribune of the plebs in 119, an office in which he would have been expected to defend the interests of his aristocratic patrons more than defend the plebs. Marius, however, preferred to acquire power and influence on his own terms, rather than as a subservient client to an established noble family. As tribune, he proposed a law that would weaken the influence patrons exercised over their clients in elections, almost as if he were attempting to declare his own independence from those who helped him to the office. Naturally, the senatorial elite opposed the bill, and Marius threatened to arrest the consuls, one of whom was a Metellus, the brother of the consul of 109. Unsurprisingly, Marius lost the election for the office of aedile, which would have set him on a course toward the higher magistracies. Undaunted, he expended all the resources at his disposal, partly in the form of bribes, to win election to the praetorship in 115, which in itself is a remarkable accomplishment. This office gave him his first opportunity for military command, which was in the province of Farther Spain. And whatever offense he may have caused to the family of the Metelli, Quintus Caecilius Metellus managed to overlook it, since he made Marius a member of his staff when he took command of the war against Jugurtha as consul in 109. Marius seemed to have learned a lesson about how to deal with Roman aristocrats, but Metellus had not yet learned about Marius.

FIG. 8.3 A bust thought to be of Marius in Munich, Germany.

Marius performed admirably in Numidia under Metellus's command, but his ambitions would not long tolerate playing second fiddle. Despite his unquestionable bravery, hard work, and military skill, a consulship would normally be out of reach because he did not come from the "right family." In some accounts of his life, a fortune-teller told him that he was destined for great things, and he should not hesitate to take risks, since the gods would ensure all would turn out well. Whether or not this is true—different sources put the event at different times in his life—after several months of fighting in north Africa, Marius asked Metellus for permission to leave for Rome so he could be a candidate for the consulship of 107. Metellus was somewhat surprised, and in his response revealed an attitude shared with many nobles about those from "lesser" families:

> Pretending to give friendly advice, he told Marius not to attempt anything improper, or to think of anything above his proper place. Not everybody can aim for everything, and each person should be satisfied with his own lot in life. Finally, he warned him not to want something the Roman people would rightly refuse him. (Sallust, *The Jugurthine War* 64.2)

When Marius persisted, Metellus finally told him he should not rush things. In time, he said, Marius could be consul together with his son. Metellus's son was around 20 years old and would not be eligible for the consulship for more than 20 years, while Marius was already close to 50.

Marius, of course, did not take this refusal lightly. He began to complain to the Roman and Italian businessmen in North Africa about the way Metellus was conducting the war, and even bragged that if he were in command Jugurtha would be in chains in a matter of days. These businessmen, members of the equestrian order, would want the war to come to a speedy end, since it was hurting their bottom line. They communicated Marius's complaints about Metellus as well as his boasts about himself to their friends back in Rome. Metellus finally allowed Marius to return home just before the elections, in part because their relationship had soured. The reports from the equestrian businessmen in North Africa provided ample ammunition for *populares* politicians in Rome, especially the tribunes of the plebs, to turn the people against Metellus and in favor of Marius. In a severe blow to the *optimates*, Marius rode a wave of popularity to victory and was elected consul. Command of the war against Jugurtha would be transferred from Metellus to Marius, despite the efforts of the senate to keep Metellus in charge.

Before setting out, Marius delivered a speech to the people in the hope of making men eager to enlist in his army. He took the opportunity to criticize the Roman nobility, contrasting his upbringing and character with theirs:

> Now, citizens, compare me, a "new man," to those arrogant nobles. What they only hear or read about, I have seen with my own eyes, and in some cases done myself. What they have learned from books, I have learned from service on the battlefield. Judge for yourselves which is worth more, words or deeds. They scorn my lack of a noble family, I scorn their worthlessness; I am criticized for my lot in life, they for their scandals. For my part, I believe all men are the same by nature, but the best sort of men are those that are bravest. (Sallust, *The Jugurthine War* 85.13-15)

His claim is in part for advancement based on merit rather than birth, but is framed more as a direct attack on the senatorial elite like Metellus. After plenty of other criticism directed against the senatorial elite, Marius gathered his troops and supplies and set sail for Numidia. When he arrived, Metellus avoided the customary meeting with the incoming commander. He had his deputy hand over command of the army to Marius while he returned to Rome.

FIG. 8.4 A coin issued by Sulla's son in 56 BC. Bocchus on his knee offers an olive branch to a seated Sulla. Jugurtha is on the right, a captive with his hands tied behind his back.

Through a combination of careful preparation and daring action, Marius had great success in Numidia, further enhancing his reputation. Eventually Jugurtha and Bocchus, who had joined forces, were at the point of defeat. Bocchus requested to speak with Roman envoys in order to arrange for a truce between Rome and himself, but not with Jugurtha. Marius sent a young cavalry officer, Lucius Cornelius Sulla, who would later be one of the chief instigators of civil war at Rome. In this moment Sulla revealed something of his own future ambitions. Since he was the intermediary in negotiations with Bocchus, Sulla had earned his trust and gratitude. However, one could never be certain whether Bocchus would ultimately betray Jugurtha to the Romans, or Sulla to Jugurtha. In secret negotiations, Sulla demanded that Jugurtha be handed over as the condition for any agreement between Rome and Bocchus. At the same time, Jugurtha told Bocchus to take Sulla prisoner in order to use him as a bargaining chip with Marius. Bocchus set up a meeting with Sulla, but also made sure Jugurtha was nearby. Both Sulla and Jugurtha expected to take the other prisoner, and Bocchus himself seemed unsure which path to take until the last minute. In the end, he put an unsuspecting Jugurtha in chains and handed him over to Sulla, who then took Rome's great enemy to Marius. The war was over.

On January 1, 104, Marius celebrated a triumph back at Rome. Jugurtha was put on display in chains as part of the triumphal procession, and after being led through the streets of Rome was strangled to death. Though Marius was the triumphant general, Sulla did not let people forget he was the one who captured Jugurtha. He is said to have made a signet ring with an image of Jugurtha's surrender (a signet ring is used to make an impression on wax seals as a kind of official signature). Sulla's supporters, and Marius's enemies, also made sure Metellus received credit for laying the groundwork for the victory.

The Germans Are Coming!

However, there was no time either for further celebration or for political bickering, as Rome faced a serious threat from the north, which presented a greater military danger than Jugurtha. Tribes from northern Germany and Scandinavia made their way south into Gaul, threatening an invasion of Italy. These tribes were not well known to the Romans, and it is not clear why they decided to migrate south. The most prominent of the tribes were the Cimbri and Teutones (the latter giving us the English word "Teutonic," meaning "German."). In 112 BC, other tribes in northern Germany had been overrun and asked Rome for assistance. The Cimbri and Teutones, however, inflicted a series of defeats against the Roman legions sent to help. They next invaded a Roman province in southern France, and victories at the sites of modern-day Bordeaux and Aix-en-Provence put them within shouting distance of Italy. The greatest blow to Rome, however, came in 105, as Marius and Sulla were finishing the war against Jugurtha. In order to put an end to the Cimbrian threat, a consul was sent out together with an ex-consul at the head of one of the largest armies Rome had assembled since the days of Hannibal, said to number around eighty thousand men. The consul, who held supreme authority, was, like Marius, a "new man," while the proconsul who accompanied him was a member of the senatorial nobility. Out of jealousy, pride, or both, the aristocratic proconsul was unwilling to submit to the authority of the "new man." As a result, the Roman forces were split in two and encamped on opposite sides of a river, which led to a catastrophic defeat at the hands of the Cimbri near the town of Arausio, close to modern-day Orange, France. Out of the eighty thousand Roman soldiers, only a few hundred managed to survive the Battle of Arausio.

Panic set in at Rome, and though Marius had not yet returned from Numidia, he was elected consul for 104. This was his second consulship, three years after his first, and he was not in Rome for the election. For both of these reasons, his election might be considered illegal, but it was certainly contrary to the norms of Roman governance. But to the people, Marius was the answer to Rome's prayers, and in continued defiance of tradition, he would be elected to the consulship every year for the next five years, until 100. The people had begun to exert their authority more and more, which could be justified in part by Marius's successes, but their behavior also justified the *optimates*' fear of an irrational and emotional mob reacting hastily and foolishly to any crisis of the moment. The people also began to use the courts to bring charges against commanders who had not achieved the success they wished, partly because they were now suspicious that any failure was a result of bribery and corruption. The behavior of the senate with Jugurtha gave them ample grounds for their suspicions.

Marius, however, demonstrated that the people were right to put their trust in him, and following the disaster at the Battle of Arausio, he took command of the armies as consul in 104. Fortunately, the Cimbri had not followed up their overwhelming victory with a march across the Alps into Italy, but instead turned west toward Spain. This provided Marius the time to whip his soldiers into shape and make other preparations, and he did not undertake any rash movements or attack before he felt the time was right. His soldiers, on the other hand, continually clamored for battle, especially since the Germanic tribesmen would occasionally taunt them with remarks such as "What message do you want us to deliver to your wives?" In 102, Marius defeated one of the Germanic tribes in southern France, but in 101 the Cimbri passed over the Alps, since the other Roman commander had failed to adequately guard the passes. The Cimbri were now in Italian territory, just north of the Po river in the northwest, while the other Roman commander stationed his troops just south of the river. The Cimbri took their time plundering the territory, allowing Marius to bring his forces from southern Gaul as reinforcements. The Romans repelled this threat, which was a great

THE CIMBRIAN WARS 112-101 BC

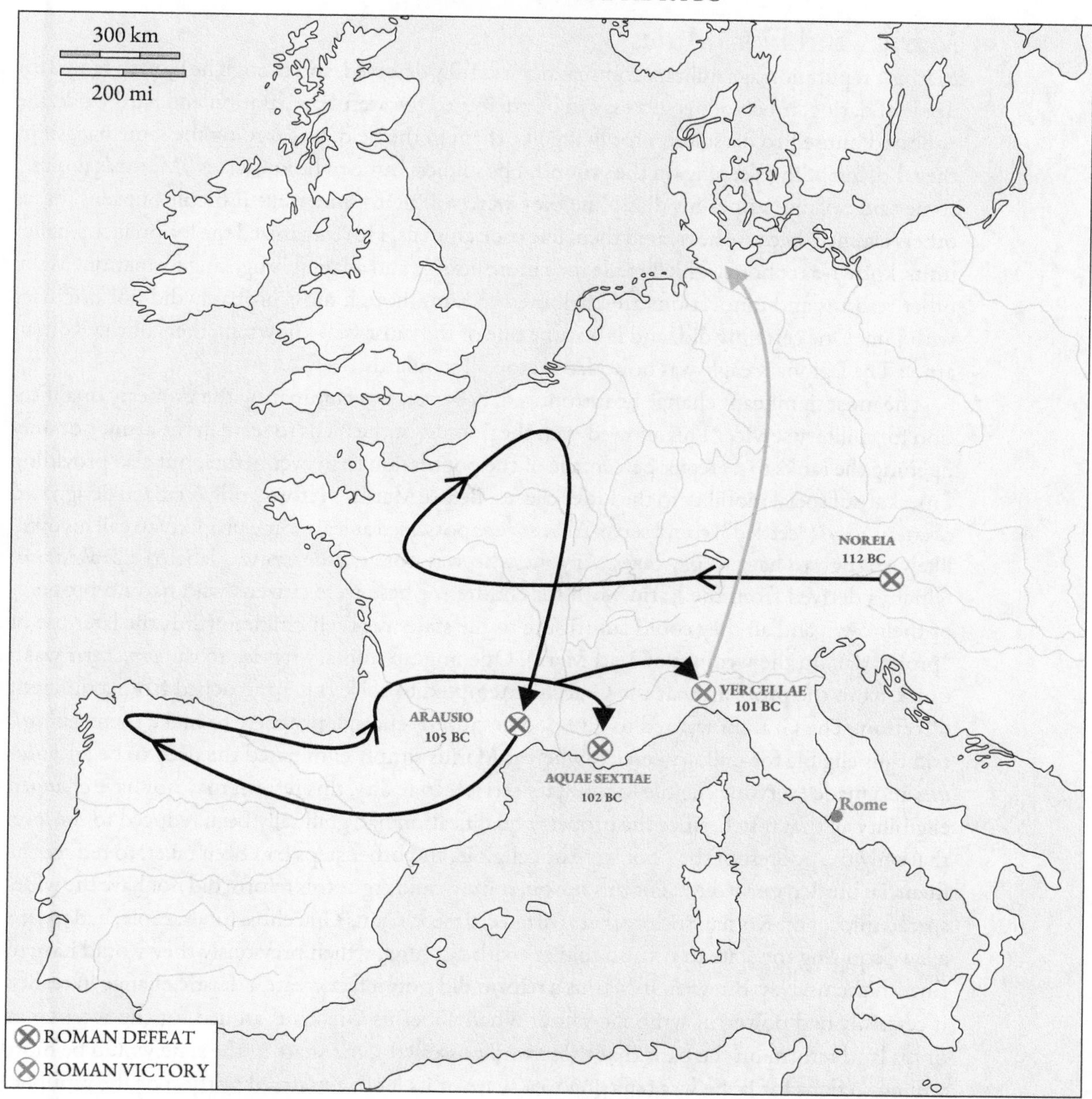

FIG. 8.5 Cimbrian War.

relief to people throughout Italy, but the two victorious Roman commanders could not agree to share in their glory. They argued over who deserved credit for the victory and became bitter enemies.

Marius and His "Mules"

Marius's reputation as a military commander was fully deserved, and though he is often famed for deeds of daring, much of his success can be attributed to careful preparation and hard work. He endeared himself to his soldiers for living like them in the field, undergoing the same hardships they did, including sleeping on the ground. His soldiers came to be known as "Marius's mules," some said because under his discipline they were willing to undertake difficult burdens, or, as others claimed, because he treated them like pack animals. He reorganized the legion into smaller units, known as cohorts, which made for a more flexible and adaptable fighting formation. Many other reforms and innovations are attributed to him, though most probably did not originate with him. One certainly did, and it became one of the most well-known markers of the Roman army: The legionary eagle was now placed atop all standards.

The most significant change he introduced, however, was eliminating the property qualification for military service. This allowed even the poorest of the plebs to serve in the army, not only opening the ranks to a greater percentage of the population than ever before, but also providing a measure of social mobility to the lower classes. Before Marius's reform, only a citizen designated as an *assiduus* ("settled") could serve. An *assiduus* possessed at least some property to call his own, likely enough to have to pay taxes. Anyone who was not an *assiduus* was labeled a *proletarius*, which is derived from the Latin word for children. These were citizens who had no property of their own, and all they could contribute to the state was their children (thus the later use of "proletariat" in the writings of Karl Marx). Opening up military service to the *proletarii* was a quick fix to the problem that the Gracchi attempted to solve but approached from a different direction. The Gracchi wanted to give poorer citizens enough property to make them *assidui*, and thus eligible for military service, whereas Marius simply eliminated the need to be an *assiduus* and made everyone eligible for military service. In reality, this reform may not have changed eligibility all that much, since the property qualification had gradually been reduced to the level that only the poorest of the poor were not eligible, and other steps had been taken to reduce the financial burden on soldiers. For this reason, some would argue this reform did not have the widespread impact on Roman society that is often claimed. Gaius Gracchus, for example, had passed a law requiring the state to furnish soldiers with clothing, which previously they would have to furnish themselves. But even if Marius's reform did not in fact create a drastic change in reality, it certainly had powerful symbolic value. When Tiberius Gracchus argued for the acceptance of his land reform on the basis that those who possessed some share in the state would be more willing to fight for it, he was referring to a share of its land, a material portion of the republic. With the change instituted by Marius, a propertyless individual could claim an equal "share" in the republic as a soldier, and hope to receive his share of land after service.

Marius undertook this reform when he started to recruit soldiers for the war against Jugurtha. According to Sallust, some saw a personal motive behind it:

> Some say he made his reform since not enough recruits met the property qualification for service, others said it was because he wanted to make himself

> popular, since the poorest class had given him his offices and raised his political standing. For someone who wants power, the poorest man is very useful, since he doesn't have any property, doesn't worry about his possessions, and believes that anything that provides a salary is an honor. (Sallust, *The Jugurthine War* 86.3)

This criticism may sound snobbish, almost something that a proud noble like Metellus or Scipio Aemilianus might say. Yet Marius's bid for personal popularity as the basis of his political power did create dangerous conditions for the future, since the poorest soldiers might be more thankful to their individual commanders than to the republic. If the senate decided to replace a popular commander whose troops were devoted to him, would they obey? And if their commander decided to march on Rome toward a civil war, would they fight for him and against the senate and people of Rome?

Marius at Peace?

Whatever credit his fellow commander may have deserved in the victory over the Germanic tribes, it was Marius who was hailed as Rome's savior and compared to Camillus, who had saved Rome from the Gallic invasion almost three hundred years earlier. Marius had attained unparalleled heights of popularity and prestige, but his victories on the battlefield would be difficult to translate back into the political arena of Rome. Although the senatorial elite would hesitate to attack Marius openly, given his outstanding military success, they would certainly have serious concerns about his individual preeminence. He had supported popular legislation early in his political career, but since then had devoted all his energies to military conquest. Now he was faced with different foes on a different kind of battlefield. Though he had engaged in some shrewd political maneuvering before, such as his campaign to unseat Metellus, his real opponents might now be more difficult to recognize.

Now close to sixty years old, Marius was elected consul for the sixth time in 100 BC, and there were at present no longer any military campaigns that required his services. He did need to ensure that his soldiers were properly rewarded with grants of land and to make sure his supporters throughout Italy and among the equestrian order were taken care of. Yet it was not senatorial opposition that would create trouble for Marius. At the height of his success, those who did the most to elevate him created the conflicts that would lay him low.

In 103, shortly after Marius's triumph over Jugurtha and during his campaign against the Cimbri, Lucius Appuleius Saturninus was a tribune of the plebs. He introduced a law granting land in Africa to some of Marius's veterans. The law was vetoed by another tribune, who was then attacked by a mob, forcing him to withdraw his veto and allow the law to pass. This was just the kind of "settlement" Gaius Gracchus's wife had predicted. Saturninus then proposed a far more dangerous law, making it a crime to harm the *maiestas* of the Roman people. *Maiestas* is where the English word "majesty" comes from, and it is sometimes translated that way, but a better word might be "dignity" or "greatness" (*maior* in Latin means bigger or greater). It is hard to define exactly what it would take to harm the *maiestas* of the Roman people, and that is the point. The vagueness allowed almost anything to count, as long as the people, or one of its representatives, believed it did. Under the Roman emperors, a criminal charge of *maiestas* was equivalent to a charge of treason, the penalty for which was death, and this was freely applied to "crimes" such as writing a poem the emperor did not like or cracking a private joke at the emperor's expense, which might be overheard by the wrong person. Saturninus's law was just as dangerous and would be useful for the *populares* against their political enemies. In fact, both of the commanders at the Battle of Arausio were prosecuted on the basis of this law and were forced into exile. The vague meaning of the word made it a powerful weapon; the only question was who got to wield it.

Despite an attempt by Marius's former commander Quintus Caecilius Metellus, who was censor in 102, to use the authority of that office to expel Saturninus from the senate, Saturninus was again elected as a tribune of the plebs for the year 100, during Marius's sixth consulship. (Marius's colleague in the consulship that year was another member of the Metellus family, a cousin of Quintus). Saturninus proposed a series of laws in line with *popularis* concerns, much of which would benefit Marius's soldiers: grants of land from territory recaptured in Gaul, the foundation of overseas colonies, and a revival of Gaius Gracchus's law for the distribution of grain at a fixed low price to the poor citizens in Rome. He also proposed giving Marius command against the pirates who were disrupting trade in the eastern Mediterranean with the support of Mithridates VI, king of Pontus, a region in north central Turkey. (Mithridates himself would soon prove to be a troublesome enemy for Rome.) Saturninus's proposed laws would not have been welcome to the *optimates*, but it was a specific provision that created a serious uproar. Saturninus added to his laws a requirement that all senators swear an oath to uphold these laws or be expelled from the senate. This would, in effect, make it impossible for his laws to be altered or repealed after he left office. With this provision, it probably would not have mattered to the *optimates* what his laws actually proposed. Although much of Saturninus's legislation would appear to be in support of Marius's aims, the provision about the oath placed the *popularis* consul in a bind. In fact, it is quite likely Saturninus had used Marius's popularity for his own ambitions and was now prepared to undercut him.

When the assembly began to gather to vote on the laws, the intense opposition created an unruly scene. Some of the people of Rome, who thought the law benefitted the Italian allies more than themselves, claimed that there was thunder, an omen that meant no public business could be conducted. Saturninus and his supporters, many from the countryside surrounding Rome, nonetheless continued with the assembly, intending to push the law through. Their opponents armed themselves with clubs, and they did likewise. An all-out brawl ensued. Saturninus's side won the street battle, and the laws were passed, including the provision that senators swear an oath to uphold them. Marius was never one to bind himself to another's authority, and now in his sixth consulship, he would find swearing the oath intolerable, no matter if the legislation benefitted his former soldiers and his supporters among the Italian allies. His optimate consular colleague Metellus likewise had no desire to swear the oath, a fact Saturninus had counted on. Unlike Metellus, however, Marius had to worry about opposing Saturninus and alienating his popular supporters. As the deadline approached for swearing the oath, which would be done at the Temple of Saturn before quaestors, Marius believed he had found a solution, worthy of a clever lawyer. When he stepped forward to deliver his oath, he swore that he would "obey the law insofar as it was a law." Since there had been thunder on the day of the voting, and violence was used to pass it, there were legal and religious grounds to consider the law invalid. The people would be satisfied that he took the oath, but to his thinking there would be no binding obligation to keep it. Many of the other senators followed his lead and swore as he did. Metellus, however, refused to resort to this wordplay and did not take the oath. He left the city before the inevitable official decree of exile was passed against him for disobeying the law.

Marius may have attempted a middle path between the people and the *optimates* in the senate, but he risked satisfying neither side rather than pleasing both. The Greek biographer Plutarch tells a rather comical story of the difficulties Marius faced trying to hold the middle ground between the *populares* and the *optimates*:

> Marius owed Saturninus for his support, so now he had to keep quiet as Saturninus became overly daring and extremely powerful. Although he didn't intend to, Marius created a disease without a cure, and with violence and bloodshed this disease spread, developing into tyranny and the overthrow of the republic. Because Marius was in awe of the nobles and at the same time tried to please the masses, he did something despicable and deceitful. One night, the leading men of the Senate came to his house in an attempt to turn him against Saturninus. Marius let Saturninus into his house by another door without the men from the Senate noticing. Then, pretending he had diarrhea, Marius ran back and forth through the house, now to the nobles and now to Saturninus, trying to anger them and bring them into conflict. (Plutarch, *Marius* 30)

The scene is out of a bad sitcom, but the result was that Marius no longer had enough influence over Saturninus, who had carried the day through unscrupulous means, to restrain him from actions that put further pressure on him. In trying to play both sides, Marius lost both sides. He would be expected to run for the office of censor as the culmination of his political career. However, he now felt that he did not have enough support from either faction and feared an inglorious defeat. Given his prestige and standing at Rome, choosing not to run was almost as bad as running and losing. It was certainly a loss of *dignitas*.

Saturninus, on the other hand, was reelected as a tribune of the plebs for 99, and when the election for the consuls arrived, he hoped to have his political ally and partner Glaucia elected. One optimate had already been elected, and Saturninus feared that another candidate would defeat Glaucia. To ensure Glaucia's victory, Saturninus sent a gang to the voting assembly where they clubbed the other candidate to death in full view of everyone. The voting assembly broke up, but soon other armed men returned to seek their revenge on Saturninus, Glaucia, and their followers. They fled to the Capitol to defend themselves, whereupon the senate issued the *senatus consultum ultimum*. Since his term in office not yet over, Marius would be expected to assist with eliminating this threat to the public order, while Saturninus and Glaucia would expect Marius to deal with them without violence. According to one historian, these two, now declared "enemies of the state," surrendered to Marius. He locked them and their supporters in the senate house, as if he intended to deal with them in some legal manner, rather than put them to death immediately, as he had the authority to do. Many *optimates* would expect him to carry out the executions at once. Impatient with any delay in doling out punishment, the city inhabitants who had grown to detest Saturninus and his followers climbed the roof of the Curia, ripped off the roof tiles, and threw them down onto Saturninus, Glaucia, and the rest, killing them all.

The senate promptly repealed all of Saturninus's legislation, and Metellus was recalled from exile. Marius left Rome for the eastern Mediterranean, supposedly to fulfill a religious vow he had made. Some said he could not bear the sight of Metellus returning to acclamation, while others suspected he realized that his place was on the battlefield, and without a military command to maintain his power and glory, he could not bear to fade away in the domestic politics at Rome. It might have seemed his life of service to Rome was over. It was for the moment, but he would return.

The Bull and the Wolf: The Social War

Sources for the decade of the 90s are particularly scarce, which is not to say nothing of serious importance happened. However, what didn't happen may be of more importance than what did. None of the underlying tensions and factionalism had gone away, and the economic and social issues, particularly the question of citizenship rights for the Italian allies, remained. Many of the political battles at this time were carried out through the law courts, and charges of extortion and bribery were leveled against those who tried to curb those crimes as well as those who committed them. Actual guilt or innocence was, in most cases, a secondary concern, and what was at stake was more a matter of politics than justice.

The Italian allies had continued to clamor for citizenship rights since the first attempts to provide them with citizenship during the time of the Gracchi. Among the *optimates*, there were always politicians who recognized the need for some reform, not only as a matter of what was right, but as a matter of political expediency, to maintain their positions of power and authority in the face of *populares* reformers. In 91 BC, Marcus Livius Drusus was one of the tribunes of the plebs. He was the son of the Marcus Livius Drusus who had made the unrealistic and unrealized popular proposals in 121 in order to undercut Gaius Gracchus. Like his father, the son Drusus was no popular reformer, but he proposed legislation that will sound very familiar. The laws were intended to address the long-standing problems the *populares* rallied around, as well as to break the opposition of the *equites* and the Italian allies to senatorial authority. In fact, each of his proposed laws seems aimed specifically to win the support of the different factions at Rome.

First, in regard to the equestrian order, he proposed to enroll 300 of the most prominent *equites* into the senate, doubling its size and bringing them into positions of political power. Just as important was an additional provision about juries for the criminal courts, which would now be drawn from this mixed senate rather than exclusively from the *equites*. This change would restore at least in part the position of senators as jurors, which the equestrian order had controlled since the legislation of Gaius Gracchus, without fully excluding *equites*. Second, in regard to the people, Drusus introduced a law that was straight out of the *popularis* playbook: grain distributions at a low fixed price, as well as the establishment of colonies with allotments of land. Third, and most notably, he proposed granting citizenship to the Italian allies.

On the face of it, these three proposals would seem to represent the best possible solution to the social, economic, and political turmoil that had convulsed Rome for the last three decades. Yet as a sign of how fractured politics were in Rome, all three proposals met with opposition from at least one of the groups. Instead of seeing what might be gained from these reforms, members of each group could only see what they would lose, unable or unwilling to envision politics that were not a winner-take-all competition. The senators, even though they would regain their influence in the law courts, felt that the new equestrian senators would form a faction against them. They saw the addition not as a concession to the equestrian order, an attempt to bring the most influential among them into the fold, but as handing the *equites* a powerful weapon to wield against the senatorial elite. For their part, the *equites* saw not the gain of access to the senate, but the loss of control of the juries. The establishment of the colonies, which the people supported, was worrisome to the Italian allies, who feared possible loss of their lands, which might be declared public lands and handed over to colonists. And finally, the plebs of Rome feared that the grant of citizenship to the allies would diminish their own political influence, since their votes would not count as much.

Any attempt at a solution seemed impossible, even more so when Drusus was assassinated. No one knows who did it. Even though not all the Italian allies supported the grant of citizenship, since they might not only lose some land but also local political control, the assassination of Drusus was in the eyes of many of the allies proof of the lengths those in power at Rome would go to prevent them from acquiring a political voice in Rome. Many allied communities throughout Italy thus decided to form a confederacy among themselves, in effect declaring their independence from Rome. They went about this quietly, but when the Romans heard rumors, they dispatched agents throughout Italy to gather information. One of these agents happened to see a young Roman taken as a hostage in the town of Asculum and notified a Roman praetor in the area. The praetor hurried to Asculum, and publicly accused the people, who had gathered for a festival. Fearing that their plans had been discovered, they killed the praetor as well as all the other Romans in the town. There was no turning back now, and the allies began a full-scale uprising, a bloody conflict known as "The Social War" (from the Latin word for "ally," *socius*). The Romans themselves refer to it as the "Marsic War," after the Marsi, an Italic people who inhabited territory roughly 70 miles west of Rome. They were the fiercest of Rome's opponents during the war, holding out to the end. The Samnites, Rome's bitter enemy in the wars of the late fourth century BC, also put up staunch resistance.

The confederation of Italian allies was given the name "Italia," and they even formed a senate, elected consuls, and issued their own coinage (see image at beginning of chapter). They had no shortage of soldiers, and some estimates give 100,000 as the total size of the Italian army. In fact, Rome had to use troops provided by allies overseas to match their strength. Not all of the Italian allies joined the revolt, however. Those in Latium and Campania, the areas closest to Rome, remained loyal, which in no small part helped Rome to meet this serious challenge to its existence. Marius, now close to 70, even offered his services to Rome as a commander. His offer was rebuffed, and he became a staff officer instead.

Rome was ultimately victorious in a military sense, but their victory came mostly by granting their former allies what they had wanted in the first place. In 90, a consul passed a law granting citizenship to all allies throughout Italy, provided that they did not take up arms against Rome or laid them down if they had. Two further laws extended the citizenship to free (non-slave) residents in allied communities as well as the province of Cisalpine Gaul in the north of modern-day Italy, just south of the Alps. These laws naturally weakened Italian opposition to Rome, though the Marsi continued to fight until their final defeat in 88. For these few brief years, an enemy had briefly brought the political factionalism at Rome to an end, but, of course, it was only a momentary pause. Civil war was around the corner.

Roman Engineering: Roads and Aqueducts

The Romans have a reputation for being extremely pragmatic, and roads and aqueducts are two of the best examples of their practical skills and mastery of engineering. The famous saying "all roads lead to Rome" derives from the extensive network of roads the Romans constructed throughout Italy, most of which ended (or began) in the city of Rome itself. By the end of the republic, there were 13 roads that radiated out from Roman in every direction. Most roads carried the name of the magistrate responsible for its construction, such as the Via Appia, after the censor Appius Claudius Caecus, whom we met in chapter 5. While these roads certainly were beneficial for citizens and for commerce, their primary purpose was military.

As in so many other areas, the Romans built upon what other peoples had accomplished first, and in this case it was literally true. The Etruscans had established a network of roads in their territory, and Rome's roads in those areas of Italy sensibly developed on that foundation, particularly as these were trade routes of long standing. As Rome expanded its colonization and control over the Italian peninsula, they gleaned ideas from the well-developed roads in the eastern Mediterranean. The "King's Highway" or "Royal Road" of the Persian Empire, almost 1700 miles in length, provided a model for public roadways such as the Via Appia, known as "the Queen of Roads." In fact, the famous Roman mile markers were likely an import from the Greek east. The development of the Roman road network accelerated in the years after the Second Punic War, with both increased overseas contacts in the eastern Mediterranean, and increasing

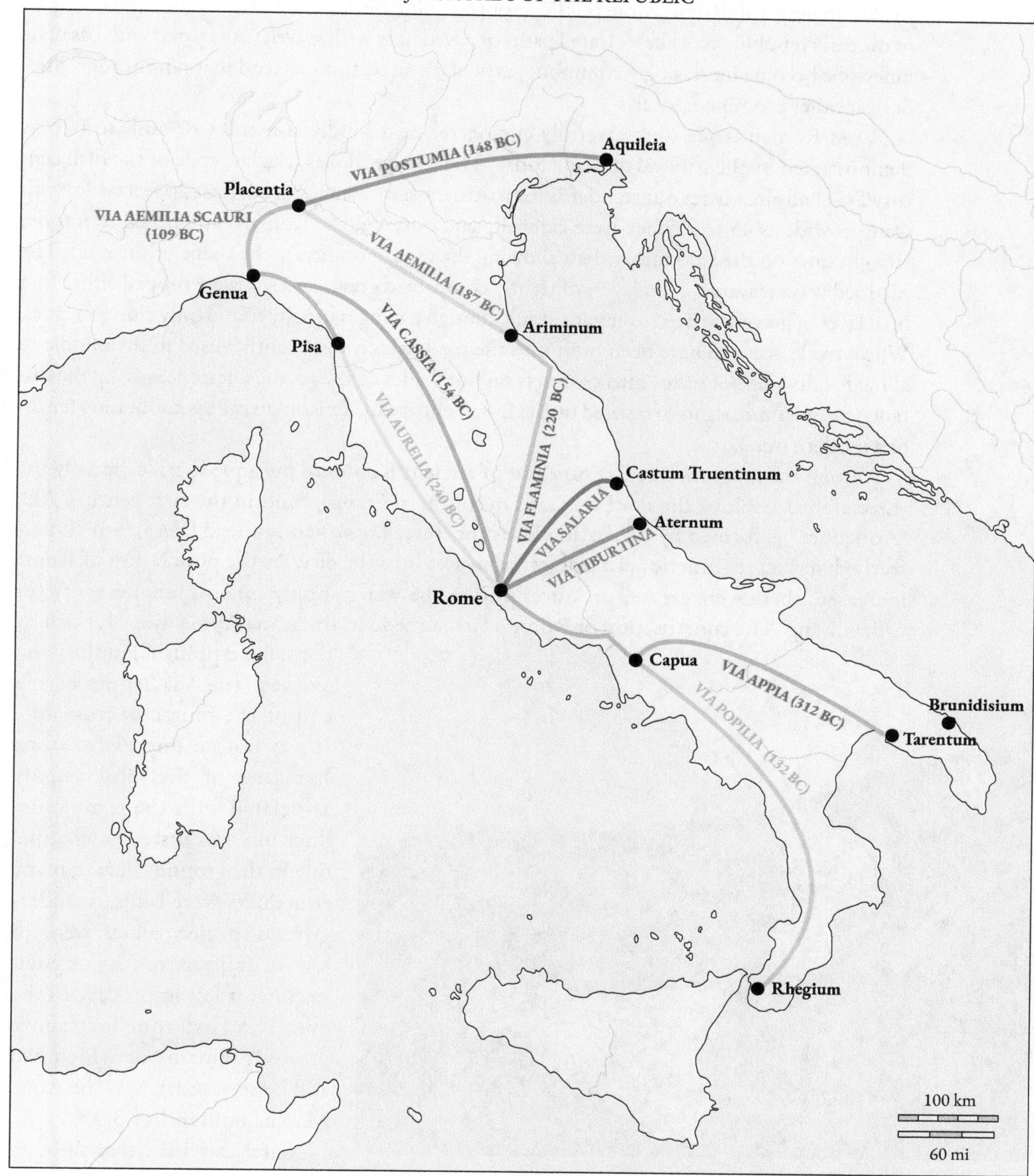

FIG. 8.6 Roman roads of the Republic.

wealth flowing into Rome. More public resources could be devoted to roads, and even the roads of the early republic were likely cleared paths or paved only with gravel; roads paved with basalt or limestone become increasingly common, particularly in sections of road that ran through cities or near other prominent locales.

Paved Roman roads were carefully engineered and solidly constructed, built to last, as demonstrated by the survival of many today. The Twelve Tables (the law code of the fifth century BC) had already set out standards for roads, most of which were at least 20 feet wide, with some as wide as 45 feet. They were carefully laid out, and the Romans attempted to impose straight lines on the land rather than allowing the terrain to dictate the shape of the road. The roadbed was excavated, then layers of tightly compacted gravel and soil were topped either by a final layer of gravel or paved over with stone, though paving is usually found only closer to cities. Wheel tracks seem to have been built into the road, which was slightly raised in the middle to allow for drainage of water into channels on both sides of the road. Milestones giving the distance from Rome began to be used by the third century BC (a Roman mile is about nine tenths of a modern mile).

Among the most spectacular survivals of ancient Rome are the aqueducts, especially the three arched levels of the Pont du Gard in southern France, built in the first century AD. "Aqueduct" is formed by the Latin words for water (*aqua*) and to lead (*duco*), which perfectly describes its function, to bring fresh water into the city. As the population of Rome increased, there were greater pressures put on the water supply, an absolute necessity for urban living. The construction of Rome's first aqueduct, the Aqua Appia, was overseen by the same Appius Claudius who oversaw the Via Appia at the end of the fourth century BC. It was not an impressive stone structure of the kind usually associated with the term aqueduct but was instead a channel dug in the ground. In fact, many aqueducts were built as underground tunnels, which were no less an impressive feat of engineering, if less impressive to the eye. The first aqueduct above ground, remains of which can still be seen today, was the Aqua Marcia, built in 144 BC.

FIG. 8.7 The remains of an aqueduct built in the 2nd c. BC, near modern-day Tivoli.

Water traveled either through a pipe or tunnel or along an open conduit, on top of an above-ground aqueduct. Stone slabs, however, were placed on top of the open channels to protect the water, and the channel itself was made waterproof with a layer of cement or plaster. One of the real challenges in constructing this type of aqueduct is maintaining a slight downward angle from the source to the end point, since the flow of the water is driven entirely by gravity. Moreover, to keep the water level as it flows, the angle of decline must be consistent for the entire length of the aqueduct. When the aqueduct encountered a hill, this presented a real challenge, and though tunneling through a hill seems more difficult and laborious, it avoided this difficulty. Several vertical shafts would be dug leading down to the tunnel, which not only released air pressure, but allowed workers to be lowered into the water channel for maintenance or repairs.

When an aqueduct reached its end point in a town or city, it usually emptied into a basin from which a number of pipes directed water to different parts of the city. Pipes in Rome were usually lead, likely because of the presence of lead mines in Spain (pipes in the eastern Mediterranean tended to be ceramic). Most water was channeled to a public fountain, the main source of drinking water for Rome and other cities, though some houses of the elite had water piped in directly. The public baths, which have left some of the grandest ruins in Rome, were a development of the first century BC and most were built after the end of the republic. The has been some debate on whether aqueducts were truly necessary, and whether they were built as monuments expressing Rome's might rather than as a public good.

Credits

CHAPTER 9

Rome Versus Rome

FIG. 9.1 A portrait of Sulla on a coin issued in 54 BC (COS = consul).

Overview

The end of the Social War might have brought greater unity to Rome and Italy, but the political divisions between the *optimates* and *populares* threatened to make any political compromise impossible. In the past, a foreign enemy compelled different political factions to work together, but now a serious threat from an enemy from the eastern Mediterranean, Mithridates VI of Pontus, became yet another arena where Rome's internal conflicts played out. These conflicts reach their natural conclusion in the civil wars between the followers of Marius and Cinna and the supporters of Sulla, the training ground for the last generation of the republic. In their aftermath, one former supporter of Marius raised a rebellion in Spain, with the possibility of creating a new Rome, while a slave revolt in southern Italy, led by the famous Spartacus, was put down with difficulty. One of the most important and flawed figures from the end of the republic, Pompey the Great, emerged at this time. The chapter ends with a brief overview of Roman law.

Timeline

88	End of the Social War
	Mithridates VI massacres Romans and Italians in Asia
87–81	Wars with Mithridates
87–84	Cinna's consulships
82	Sulla marches on Rome, becomes dictator
78	Death of Sulla
77–73	War against Sertorius
73–71	Slave revolt of Spartacus

Down the Drain

It is easy to see, as many Romans did, the history of the republic after the time of the Gracchi as a downward spiral to its final disappearance under Julius Caesar. The same problems seem to constantly reemerge as political flashpoints, and the same conflicts occur over and over again. Conflicts about the distribution of land, especially to military veterans, and the role of the Italian allies in Rome's political processes continued, while widespread debt added to the burdens of the urban and rural lower classes. All of this, combined with individual ambition, greed, and corruption, made for a volatile mixture. The republic seemed to be falling apart in slow motion, and perhaps what is most remarkable is that it managed to survive for as long as it did. Perhaps this is a testament to the idea of the republic and its traditions, both real and invented, that stretched back for more than 400 years. Even as its institutional foundations crumbled, Romans seemed to feel that words like "republic," "senate," and "liberty" were worth holding onto and worth fighting for, even against other Romans. There was still a belief that major reforms could turn back the clock, and the republic could be reestablished on its former footing.

The civil turmoil of these years may be more visible to us because we have more contemporary sources for this last generation, and many of the problems that seem to arise after the Gracchi were likely there all along, though the scale and intensity increased dramatically as the power and wealth of Rome itself did. Yet another kind of unraveling, one less tied to the material conditions of life, may have begun during these last generations: a loss of the idea of Rome. What did it mean to be a Roman during its final decades? What did the republic or its near synonym "liberty" mean anymore? Was there any meaning in which all the groups—senate, people, *equites*, and allies—could share? The political, social, and economic divisions among these groups were real enough, and certainly seemed to widen at this time, but the gaps between their understanding of the republic—what it was and what it did—seems even wider. When the realities at Rome became too far removed from the idea of the republic, could survive much longer? This is the world in which the last generation of the Roman Republic was raised, and the two leaders of the republic's final civil war—Caesar and Pompey—cut their teeth on its conflicts. This was their education, and we shall see what they learned from it, as well as what they did not.

The Social War provided, if briefly, a greater sense of unity among Rome's political factions, which had always come together when a common enemy gave them a common purpose. Its aftermath opened the possibility of a greater political cohesion throughout Italy, not only because the allies now shared in Roman citizenship, but because Italian communities, which had operated with some independence, now began to show greater uniformity in their governance. They might now claim to be a part of Rome rather than under it. But Rome was still the center, where things happened and things got done (or not). Citizenship, of course, came with benefits and protections as well as obligations, but the reality of it might be less important than its symbolic value, the sense of belonging to something greater. Allies would no longer fight for Romans, but as Romans.

Yet this opportunity was squandered by the same blindness that seemed to affect everyone. These new citizens had to be enrolled into voting tribes, and this became another source of conflict. The Plebeian and Tribal Assemblies voted in blocks of tribes, and since 241 BC there had been a fixed number of 35 tribes, even as the population increased. Each tribe cast a single vote, determined by the majority of individual votes within each tribe, and thus 18 votes constituted a majority. Four of the tribes were "urban," since originally residents of the city of Rome were assigned to one of these. These tribes eventually contained more and more people, dominated by the poorer Romans of the city, but only counted for 4 of the 35 votes. The "rural" tribes outside the city, with fewer members, would be dominated by wealthier citizens, and account for the remaining 31 votes in these assemblies. A citizen was originally assigned to a tribe according to place of residence, but later new citizens were simply assigned to a tribe. Even if many of the new Italian citizens would not cast a vote, there was still a fear among those at Rome that this influx of new voters into the tribes would drastically change the political landscape at Rome. Whether this would actually happen was less important than the fear it would.

FIG. 9.2 A copy of an original bust dating to 80–50 BC, sometimes thought to be Sulla.

There were two competing proposals on the enrollment of new citizens into tribes. One was to distribute the Italians throughout all 35 tribes, which seems reasonable and fair. However, the wealthier citizens feared their influence in the rural tribes would be diluted, which led to a proposal to restrict the new citizens to the four urban tribes, minimizing the impact of their vote. In general, the *populares* supported distribution among all tribes, while *optimates* favored limited distribution to the four urban tribes. Thus, the grant of citizenship to the Italian allies, a major source of conflict that had inflamed Rome since the time of the Gracchi until it ended with the bloodshed of the social war, became yet another source of conflict. In late republican Rome, every solution was just another problem.

The Fortunate One

One of the consuls in 88 BC was Lucius Cornelius Sulla, who much to Marius's displeasure had taken credit for capturing Jugurtha. He also served under Marius against the Germanic tribes from 103 to 101, and in the 90s had gone on campaign in the eastern Mediterranean. Sulla was the first Roman to have contact with the Parthians, a people who would prove troublesome to the Romans for generations to come, even under the emperors. He also commanded Roman troops in the Social War, overcoming the determined resistance of the Samnites. A full generation younger than Marius, he came from a patrician family that had lost its prestige. In fact, there had not been much political success among his ancestors for almost two centuries. However, he was helped to the consulship in 88 with the support of the Metelli, the family who first supported Marius but became his foe after his underhanded maneuver against his commander Metellus in the Jugurthine War. Sulla's rivalry with Marius had truly begun when he promoted the image that he had captured Jugurtha, and this rivalry was inflamed when in 91, more than a decade after the event, the senate allowed the Numidian king Bocchus, who had betrayed Jugurtha to Sulla, to place in the Roman Forum a statue memorializing this event. To a Roman walking through the Forum, Sulla, not Marius, was the victor over Jugurtha. As if often the case in Roman politics, the rivalry between Marius and Sulla was not only political—*popularis* against optimate—it was personal. Their rivalry would soon erupt into violence, thanks to a new foreign enemy.

The "Poison King": Mithridates VI of Pontus

The new threat to Rome was no minor matter of a rebellious tribe in Europe or a dynastic upstart from North Africa, but a shrewd eastern king with vast resources at his disposal. Mithridates VI was king of Pontus, a large kingdom on the south coast of the Black Sea in modern-day Turkey. (His name, derived from the eastern cult of Mithras, is sometimes spelled Mithradates.) Born in 132 BC, Mithridates came to the throne together with his mother and younger brother in 120, but within a few years eliminated them. Known as the "poison king" for his supposed habit of taking small doses of poison every day to build up an immunity, his reign would last for more than fifty years, not ending until his death in 63. He had been causing Rome trouble for some time through aggressive diplomacy and military maneuverings when in 100 he placed an ally on the throne of the neighboring kingdom of Cappadocia. Five years later Sulla was sent by the senate to reinstate the king Mithridates had driven out and to keep an eye on Mithridates himself. The Roman province of Asia, in the west of modern-day Turkey, was a major source of tax revenue for Rome, and any possible threat to their interests there would demand swift action. Mithridates was nothing if not cautious and would push the limits of Rome's tolerance without provoking a war. In 90, Mithridates invaded Cappadocia, and for good measure also invaded another neighboring kingdom, Bithynia. He replaced the kings Rome had installed with his hand-picked allies. After the two kings friendly to Rome were restored by force, a Roman delegation sent to handle the situation urged these two kings to invade Mithridates's territory, even though they were reluctant to do so. This provocation was sufficient cause for Mithridates to counterattack, and unlike the Romans, he had prepared for it. In 89, he swiftly made his way west and took possession of Rome's province of Asia. He met with little resistance, and demonstrations of loyalty to Rome were almost nonexistent. He promised cities in Asia that no harm would come to them if they handed over their Roman officers, and he won over many communities when he expelled Roman tax collectors and money lenders. As an act of public humiliation, and a display of his ability to overcome Rome, he would lead captive Roman commanders around on a donkey. After he captured a member of the Roman delegation that had persuaded the two kings to invade Mithridates's kingdom, he poured molten gold down his throat to mock the Romans' reputation for taking bribes. Such treatment was an affront to Rome, but far worse was to come.

Rome immediately declared war. Mithridates, however, was just getting started, and he made preparations to push his war farther west, threatening not only the islands along the coast of Turkey, but mainland Greece as well. From there, it would be a quick trip to Italy. Mithridates first sent

THE EASTERN MEDITERRANEAN AT THE TIME OF THE MITHRIDATIC WARS

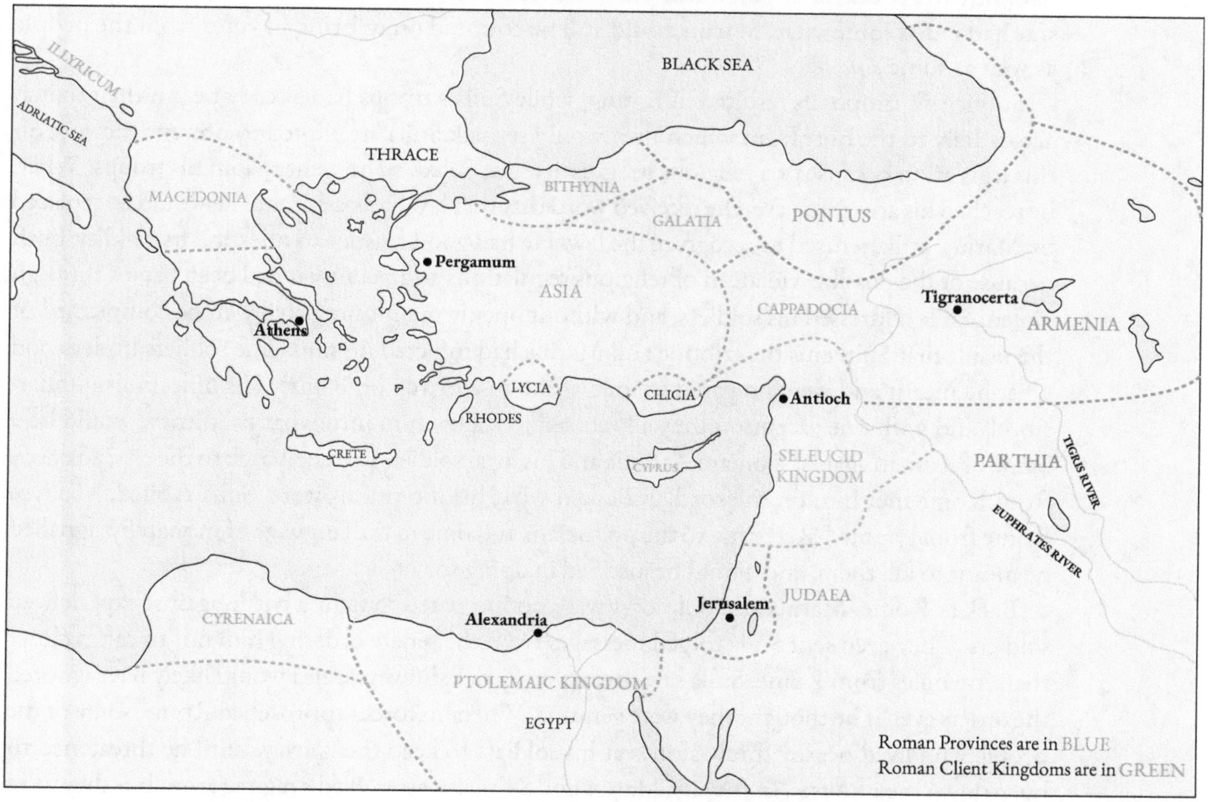

FIG. 9.3 Mithridatic Wars.

secret orders to the local rulers in the province of Asia that in thirty days, time they should kill every single Roman and Italian—man, woman, and child—and toss their bodies out into the streets. Slaves who killed their masters would gain their freedom, debtors who killed their creditors would be free of debt. The orders were carried out with brutal efficiency, and some 80,000 Romans were massacred in a single day. All property possessed by Roman citizens was seized by Mithridates.

Prelude to Civil War

This horrific act demanded an immediate and forceful response, and as consul of 88, Sulla was put in command of the war against Mithridates. One of the tribunes of the plebs that year was Publius Sulpicius Rufus, who had given up his patrician status in order to become eligible for the office. He introduced a law that would distribute the new Italian citizens among all 35 voting tribes, which would, of course, arouse intense opposition from the senatorial elite. But Sulpicius added another clause that was guaranteed to cause conflict. He proposed replacing Sulla with Marius as commander of the war against Mithridates, which held out the promise of glory and plunder. Although he was now nearing seventy and his star had faded somewhat, Marius could still be counted on to bring in votes from the people as well as some *equites*.

Sulpicius's proposals resulted in rioting, while Sulla's troops had already begun their march across Italy to the port from which they would set sail. Sulla attempted to prevent the vote on this legislation because of a religious irregularity, but failed, so he went to join his troops. When he reached his army, however, he received word that that law had passed and he would be replaced by Marius. Sulla refused to recognize the law. He had good reasons to question its validity, both because of the possible violation of religious regulations and because it had been passed through violence. He addressed his soldiers, and without openly mentioning civil war, he complained of the insult that Sulpicius the tribune and Marius had inflicted on him. The soldiers understood what he meant and were prepared to follow him in a march on Rome. His officers also understood, and with one exception they all refused to follow him into what they knew would be a battle of Roman against Roman. As Sulla and his loyal soldiers marched back to the city, an envoy from Rome met him on the road and asked what his intentions were. Sulla replied, "To free Rome from tyrants." Referring to the politicians at Rome in the language of monarchy signalled he meant to kill them, and would be justified in doing so.

Back at Rome, Marius and Sulpicius were not prepared to fight a battle against experienced soldiers. They even sent Sulla forged messages from the senate ordering him not to camp closer than five miles from Rome. Sulla saw through the trick, however, and would likely have ignored the orders even if he thought they were genuine. When his forces approached Rome, some of the people who lived nearby threw stones at his soldiers to keep them away, until he threatened to burn down their houses. In the city, Marius and Sulpicius assembled a rag-tag army, but they were no match for Sulla. They called on the people of Rome to help, and even offered slaves freedom if they came to their aid. No one came, so they quickly fled the city. Although it was not much of a battle, and the streets of Rome had seen citizens fighting and killing citizens, this was something new, as a later Greek historian wrote. It was:

> a conflict between enemies, the first in Rome that was not a battle between political factions, but exactly like a war, with legionary standards and the sounds of war-trumpets. (Appian, *Civil Wars* 7.58)

As consul, Sulla took charge. He immediately repealed the laws passed by the tribune Sulpicius, and both Sulpicius and Marius were declared "enemies of the state." Sulpicius was soon killed, and Marius fled to North Africa, barely escaping with his life. Sulla was still eager to head out for the campaign against Mithridates, especially since another army had already been sent out from Rome, led by a political opponent. He was also concerned about what might happen in Rome during his absence, so he attempted to arrange for the election of close allies as the two consuls for 87. Yet Sulla could not marshal the popular support that his opponents could, nor did he possess the standing of a Scipio that might sway the populace to support his preferred candidates. He managed to get one of his candidates elected, but the other was Lucius Cornelius Cinna, who belonged to the faction supporting Marius. Sulla made Cinna swear an oath not to do anything contrary to his wishes, but as soon as Sulla left for the campaign against Mithridates, Cinna tried to undo all of Sulla's acts of the previous year. He reintroduced legislation to distribute the new Italian citizens across all 35 voting tribes and proposed to recall Marius from his exile. When his optimate colleague attempted to stop both of these measures, rioting broke out. Italians who happened to be in the Forum were killed, and Cinna was driven out of Rome, now an enemy of the state himself. However, he found a welcome reception among the Italian allies who supported his legislation and began to assemble his own army. In addition, he summoned Marius from North Africa, who also gathered some troops, and both men led a march on Rome. They converged on the city, cut off its supplies, and captured it.

Meanwhile, Sulla had departed Italy to restore Roman control in areas that had switched their allegiance to Mithridates. He did not have far to go. One of Mithridates's generals, after overcoming Roman forces in the north of Greece, had established his headquarters in Athens, the renowned intellectual and cultural capital of Greece, famous throughout the Mediterranean. Even though its political influence had waned after the fourth century, Athens could still boast of its legendary resistance to the Persian invasion at Marathon, and it was where Socrates and Plato had taught, where the tragedies of Sophocles and the comedies of Aristophanes were performed, where Demosthenes had delivered his famed orations. Many elite Romans at this time would spend time there to complete their education and acquire an air of cultural sophistication. The people of Athens may not have all wished to side with Mithridates, but they had little choice. Sulla, however, was only interested in bringing the city under Roman control and put Athens undersiege. Given the situation back in Rome, he made every effort to take the city as soon as he could. Mithridates's general sent representatives to call for peace, but all they talked about was

Athens's past glories, expecting that would be persuasive enough for an elite Roman. Sulla would have none of it and gave a curt reply:

> Get out of here, and take your speeches with you! The Romans didn't send me to Athens to learn about its history, but to defeat its rebels. (Plutarch, *Sulla* 13.4)

He soon captured Athens and unleashed his soldiers to plunder the city's treasures and slaughter its citizens. The streets of this fabled city flowed with blood. Brutal as the violence was, there may have been a strategic purpose behind it, not just Sulla's tendency to indulge in senseless cruelty. Mithridates was still in Pergamum, near the coast of modern Turkey, and the territories between him and Sulla were under his control. Sulla's savage treatment of a city everyone in the Mediterranean respected—even the Romans—sent a clear message that no one who resisted him would be spared. Other cities in his path would be persuaded to welcome him without delay, and possibly turn against any forces Mithridates had set over them. Moreover, Sulla no longer had the support of Rome for his expenses and supplies. He needed to allow his soldiers plunder as payment to keep their loyalty, and also needed food and basic supplies from the peoples he encountered. Sulla's sack of Athens did have one cultural consequence for the future of western European culture. A library containing many of the works of Aristotle was taken from the city and sent back to Rome, providing Roman intellectuals with copies of the great philosopher's works. In addition, Greek sculptures and other artworks were shipped back to Rome to become part of the personal collections of the Roman elite.

Athens was not the only great city whose streets flowed with blood. When Cinna and Marius had occupied Rome in 87, they set about conducting a purge of all the supporters of Sulla. Cinna's optimate colleague in the consulship, Octavius, was beheaded, and his head put on display in the Forum. His was only the first of many. There are several stories from this period about members of the Roman nobility who were hunted down and killed. One of Rome's greatest orators, Marcus Antonius, fled to the countryside, where he found refuge at a farmhouse. With such a distinguished guest, the farmer decided he needed to buy better wine than he usually did. He sent a slave to a nearby tavern to purchase some, and when the tavernkeeper asked why he was buying such fine wine, the slave told him in a whisper about the distinguished guest. The tavern keeper immediately informed Marius, who sent soldiers to execute Antonius. His head joined Octavius's and others in the Forum. Another noble was saved by his slaves, who put a corpse on a funeral pyre and set it aflame. When assassins came looking for their master, they claimed the corpse on the pyre was his, since he had hanged himself that morning. All of Sulla's friends and supporters were hunted down and his house razed to the ground. His wife and children would have been killed, but they managed to escape. After the bloody elimination of their opponents, Cinna and Marius simply declared that they would be the consuls for 86. However, Marius did not get to enjoy his seventh consulship for long, dying only two weeks into the year. He was replaced by Lucius Valerius Flaccus, who was immediately sent out to relieve Sulla of his command and continue the war against Mithridates.

After his brutal conquest of Athens in 86, Sulla continued to harass Mithridates's forces in Greece. Flaccus and his army soon met up with him, but Sulla refused to hand over command of his troops. Some of Flaccus's troops even defected to Sulla. Flaccus then began to head east to the province of Asia to confront Mithridates on his own, but along the way, a member of his staff named Fimbria, who had roused the soldiers against him, killed him and took command of the army. Fimbria continued the campaign against Mithridates, who was still in Pergamum, and Sulla was making his way there as well. Mithridates might normally fear the approach of two separate Roman armies, but these two were competing rather than cooperating, a situation Mithridates would know how to exploit. Fimbria had advanced to the province of Asia and began to punish the cities that had gone over to Mithridates. He even besieged the city of Troy, site of the legendary Trojan war. When he was told by the inhabitants that they had entrusted themselves to Sulla, he demolished the city's walls, burned it to the ground, and slaughtered the inhabitants, an unheroic reenactment of the Fall of Troy a thousand years earlier. Fimbria then defeated the forces sent against him by Mithridates and headed for Pergamum. Mithridates, however, took advantage of the strife between the Roman armies, and in 85 negotiated a treaty with Sulla, who was eager to conclude the war both to prevent Fimbria from winning any glory and return to Rome as soon as possible. As a result, Mithridates, the man responsible for the slaughter of thousands of Romans, secured very favorable terms. He had to leave the province of Asia, as well as pay a heavy fine and turn over his navy, but he got to keep his kingdom of Pontus and remained, at least officially, an ally of Rome. Many of Sulla's soldiers were angry that the man responsible for the murder of tens of thousands of Romans and Italians a few years earlier got off so easy. Sulla then attacked the army of Fimbria, and after many of Fimbria's troops deserted to Sulla and many others refused to attack their fellow citizens, Fimbria committed suicide. Sulla allowed him to be buried, saying he would not treat the dead like Marius and Cinna had. To some, this seemed a noble act.

Sulla placed one of his officers in charge of Fimbria's troops and left them as a garrison in the province of Asia. He then turned back to Rome, where he knew another war awaited. Cinna, who essentially ruled Rome as consul from 86 to 84 with his handpicked colleagues, began to prepare for Sulla's return. He had hoped to meet Sulla not in Italy, but across the Adriatic Sea on Greek soil. His soldiers, however, were not eager for a battle against other Roman soldiers, especially in a war that offered no promise of plunder. When a ship carrying some of his soldiers across the Adriatic sank, their attitude did not improve, so Cinna assembled his troops, intending to berate them into following his orders. As they gathered in a tense atmosphere, one of Cinna's lictors struck a soldier for refusing to get out of the way, and the situation spiraled out of control into a riot. Cinna himself was killed in a storm of stones and daggers. His colleague as consul, Gnaeus Papirius Carbo, then took up the fight against the supporters of Sulla, as did the two subsequent consuls of 83. In this year, Sulla arrived at Brundisium, a city on

FIG. 9.4 A bust of Mithridates. He wears a lion skin, associating him with Hercules.

FIG. 9.5 A bust of Pompey, perhaps as he looked in 55 BC.

the southeast "heel" of Italy that was the usual departure and arrival point for sea voyages to Greece and the eastern Mediterranean. He was, technically, a declared enemy of the state and his actions constituted a rebellion, but such distinctions meant very little in these circumstances. Many of the *optimates* who had escaped the carnage at Rome came to meet him, and many brought funds and troops.

Enter Pompey

One remarkable young man who came to join him was Gnaeus Pompeius Magnus, better known now as Pompey or Pompey the Great (*magnus* means "great" in Latin and harkens back to Alexander the Great). Born in 106 BC, Pompey had served in the Social War under his father, who commanded Roman troops against the Samnites. At the time of Sulla's arrival back to Italy, Pompey was 23, and even though he had no official position as a military commander, he raised on his own an army of three legions from cities in northwest Italy, around his hometown of Picenum. Everywhere he went, he drove out supporters of the consul Carbo and all those who had supported Cinna during his reign of terror. He was confronted by forces sent out from Rome but defeated them all. He then drew up his soldiers into formation and marched to Brundisium to meet up with Sulla, hoping to make a good first impression. When Sulla saw Pompey's troops arrive, he got down from his horse, and the young Pompey saluted him as *imperator*, a title given by soldiers to their victorious commander. Much to everyone's surprise, Sulla returned the favor, and hailed Pompey as *imperator*—it may well have been something of a joke, but it certainly would have pleased this young upstart.

Sulla's New Republic

Sulla began his march on Rome with plenty of support, and the consular armies sent against him from Rome did not offer much resistance. In one case, the opposing soldiers simply defected to Sulla, much as they had done when he had met rival Roman commanders in the east. In 82 BC, Carbo was once again consul, this time together with Marius's son, also named Gaius Marius and only in his 20s. The young Marius was defeated in battle by Sulla outside of Rome, so he instructed his colleague to evacuate the city and kill anyone suspected of supporting Sulla. The victims included his own father-in-law, the pontifex maximus. Sulla and his forces finally reached Rome near the end of 82, and the last battle of the civil war, if not the last bloodshed, took place at the Colline Gate, at the northern side of the city walls supposedly built by king Servius five hundred years earlier. Although the Roman forces arrayed against Sulla were not well organized, they had been reinforced by Samnite and Lucanian troops, and the fighting lasted into the night. Eventually, Sulla's armies overwhelmed their opponents and, after 50,000 or so had died, Sulla entered Rome as a victor. After his defeat by Sulla, young Marius had retreated to a town 20 miles east of Rome, where Sulla's forces put him under siege. Samnite troops failed to rescue him, and when he attempted to flee the city, he was caught. His arms and legs were broken, his ears sliced off, and his eyes gouged out. Then, following a new tradition, his head was cut off and displayed in the Forum.

The government of the republic had essentially ceased to function, so an *interrex* was appointed from among the patricians to conduct elections. This office, as the title suggests, went back to the days of the kings and was used when a king, or later the consuls, died or were otherwise incapacitated. Each *interrex* held office for five days until a new king was chosen, or under the republic until new elections were held. In this case, a crisis that went beyond the deaths of the consuls, the *interrex* appointed Sulla as dictator. This was an old republican office used at times of crisis, but a dictator had not been appointed for well over one hundred years. Although a dictator had supreme legal authority for the six-month term of his office, Sulla took measures to make sure that everything he did during this time would not face legal challenges afterward. He later even passed a law that made all his prior actions as dictator legal. Technically, he had been an exile during his war against Mithridates, and thus the treaty he made with this long-standing enemy of Rome, it could be argued, was not legally binding. Moreover, his refusal to hand over command of the army to a consul, who was the legally appointed commander, could be considered a treasonous act. As dictator, he had the authority to execute citizens without a trial, but such actions would undoubtedly cause him serious trouble should the political tide later turn against him.

Sulla first set about purging the republic of enemies and opponents, settling old scores at the same time. The supporters of Marius, Cinna, and the others who opposed him were hunted down and killed. In one story, when a few thousand Romans sent a representative to beg for mercy on their behalf, Sulla promised to pardon them should they prove themselves by attacking his other enemies. He arranged to have these 3000 Romans seeking clemency gather together with 6000 others who had been on the wrong side or at least suspected of such. As Sulla was speaking at a meeting of the senate at a nearby temple, the one group began to prove their loyalty to the new regime by butchering the larger group. The cries and shrieks of the slaughter disturbed the senators, but Sulla told them not to worry—it was just some criminals being punished. The story sounds unbelievable, but even the possibility of it hints at how much carnage filled the streets of Rome at the time.

Sulla also introduced "proscription," a procedure by which his political enemies and their supporters could be legally killed. If a person's name was put on an official list ("proscribed"), then that person became an official enemy of the state and could be legally killed by anyone else. The killer would receive a portion of the person's property. It was basically the same as putting a bounty on someone's head. Of course, this process was open to abuse, and wealthy individuals might find their names on the list of the proscribed simply because someone with influence in Sulla's regime had their eyes on their property. It is not clear how many people were actually proscribed under Sulla, but estimates range from 1500 to 5000, including 40–90 senators and over 1000 members of the equestrian order. The property of the proscribed was put up for auction, and so much went up for sale at this time that the real estate market collapsed. Some

Romans became very rich at this time by buying up wealthy estates at bargain-basement prices. The proscriptions also affected the sons and grandsons of the proscribed, since they were barred from holding political office. They might very well wish to seek legal or political revenge, but this exclusion kept them out of power and made it far more difficult to do so.

But Sulla put the powers of the dictatorship to real use in recreating the constitution of the Roman Republic. In fact, his official title alludes to this as his real purpose: *dictator legibus scribundis et rei publicae constituendae*, "dictator for writing laws and establishing the republic." With this title, he embarked on a major program of legislative and political reform. His constitution, or re-constitution, of the republic is often simply known as "the Sullan constitution." The basic idea underlying all his reforms was restoring the primacy of the senate and the patricians in the governance of the republic, in line with optimate ideals. He not only strengthened the senate's position, he also weakened the political forces opposed to it, especially the office of tribune of the plebs.

First, he doubled the size of the senate and also restored the position of senators as jurors in criminal courts. However, it was difficult to find individuals who could meet the high wealth qualification for the senate after the loss of dozens of senators in the civil war and through proscriptions. Sulla thus found it necessary to turn to the equestrian in order to fill the senate to its new capacity of 600 members. (Though it began with a different purpose, his reform ended up looking very much like the proposal the tribune Drusus put forward in 91, before he was assassinated.) Sulla also increased the number of quaestors from 12 to 20, and since holding this office meant automatic entry to the senate, he ensured there would be an extra 8 new senators every year. He also suspended the office of censor, which could be used to expel individuals from the senate for misconduct, and had been abused for political purposes.

To weaken the office of tribune of the plebs, he first made those who held the office ineligible for any other political office. Thus an ambitious Roman who hoped to become consul would likely not choose the route of tribune and would be compelled to work through the other offices that were aligned much more closely with the senate. Moreover, tribunes could no longer initiate legislation on their own and take it straight to the assembly. They had to consult the senate first, which was a return to the customary practice from earlier in the republic. The Tribal Assembly was itself weakened, at least from the perspective of the *populares*, by reorganizing it so that the wealthiest members had even more influence, and the Centuriate Assembly, already dominated by the wealthy, would now ratify all laws. In addition, priesthoods would no longer be elected, but would be chosen by "co-optation," meaning the priests themselves would choose a new member when they needed to fill a vacancy. He revived an older law from almost 100 years earlier that set minimum ages for offices (29 for quaestors, 39 for praetors, and 42 for consul), and put other restrictions on office holding, including a 10-year period between consulships. Reelection to other offices was also restricted, and the *cursus honorum* became more rigidly fixed. Even provincial governors were put under new restrictions and were now forbidden from leaving their provinces or taking an army over its borders without permission from the senate.

All of this severely weakened the political influence of the people of Rome and those who wished to represent them, or at least pretend to. Now there was no question that the senate came first in SPQR. Following proper legal procedure, Sulla stepped down from his dictatorship after his six-month term was up, but he was elected consul for 80. He was thus was able to enjoy the benefits of his new constitution but could also ensure that it would function properly in its first year. After this uneventful transition, in which there were no legal challenges to his reform of the Republican constitution or criminal charges against himself, he retired from politics and from Rome to enjoy a secluded retirement as a private citizen. He supposedly spent his last days in the company of low-born individuals such as actors and musicians, the kind of people an aristocratic Roman should be ashamed to associate with. He died shortly after in 78 and did not live to see the immediate outbreak of new civil turmoil. His epitaph, which he supposedly composed himself, proudly declared that no one ever did more good as a friend, or caused more harm as an enemy.

Sulla's changes had lasting effects, though not necessarily the ones he intended. And it may be that the way he gained power and exercised influence as a commander and politician had more of a political impact on Rome than any of the concrete reforms he instituted. The republic's political ills could no longer be cured by political reforms or constitutional tinkering and required a change in the character of the individuals who would lead it. But with Rome in such a condition, what it took to acquire power, and to exercise it, was the opposite of it was needed to make it right, and this was thus likely beyond Sulla's or anyone else's capability. It was almost as if the Roman Republic could no longer survive in Rome, and what was needed was a new start, maybe in a new place. Two Romans in the years after Sulla tried just that.

The First Cracks

Some later Romans thought that Sulla's greatest mistake was stepping away from his position of power, and the events that soon followed his retirement and death suggests this may be right. In fact, Sulla was still alive when the first cracks in his newly restored republic began to show.

Lepidus: Rebel or Freedom Fighter?

In 79 BC, immediately after Sulla's retirement, one of his political enemies, Marcus Aemilius Lepidus, was elected consul for 78. Lepidus had profited from the proscriptions and had been charged with extortion for his governorship of the province of Sicily in 80. Though he held office under Sulla, Sulla did not trust him. Pompey, however, the young man Sulla might have seen as his political heir, had supported Lepidus in his bid for the consulship. When Sulla saw Pompey during the election, he warned Pompey that he was giving his own enemy power over himself. Lepidus's colleague, on the other hand, was an unabashed optimate who had Sulla's approval, setting up another clash between consuls.

Lepidus did not even wait until Sulla was dead before he began to call for the repeal of much of Sulla's legislation, and in particular the return of lands that had been seized during the civil war. The historian Sallust, writing only a generation after Sulla, gave Lepidus a speech accusing Sulla of being a tyrant and urging Romans to stand up for their liberty. Lepidus presents a stark choice. There is, in this view, no middle road, no compromise:

> You must act, citizens, and you must resist! If you don't, the Sullans will take everything you've won. There can be no delay, and prayers to the gods will be of no help. Do you really think that Sulla is so bored with his tyranny, or so ashamed of it, that at great danger to himself he will give up everything he has criminally stolen? For him now the only thing that is glorious is what he has secured, and the only thing honorable is what helps him hold on to power. Honest men once aimed for a calm and peaceful liberty rather than the toil of political offices, but this no longer exists. Now you must be either a slave or a commander; you must either feel fear, citizens, or makes others fear you. What other choice is there? (Sallust, *Histories* 1.49)

The civil war had given Sulla the opportunity to confiscate land throughout Italy from the communities that fought against him, especially in Samnite territory. He used this land to reward his veterans, settling them in new colonies in Italy as well as in communities that did not always welcome them, and resented the loss of their lands. The veterans also seemed to have special privileges, which created even more tensions with the Italians among whom they lived. An opponent of Sulla and his reforms could use this discontent to his advantage, and Lepidus did just that. Lepidus's supporters believed he was standing up for the rights of those who had lost their lands, and in some cases their citizenship, because of Sulla. His opponents claimed that he was bringing back the tyranny and turmoil of Cinna.

In 78, veterans of Sulla who had been settled in Etruria, just north of Rome, were attacked by the local inhabitants, and many were killed. Lepidus was sent at the head of an army to put down this uprising against Sulla's veterans, but instead seized the opportunity to turn it into a revolt against Rome. He even sent troop commanded by one his officers to take control of Cisalpine Gaul, the province north of Etruria, where Lepidus was supposed to go to take up his governorship. The senate ordered Lepidus to return to Rome, supposedly to oversee the elections for 77, but it was clear he would be stripped of his command and disciplined. His actions made it clear that he had no intention of relinquishing his troops, and he marched on Rome to demand a second consulship and the repeal of Sulla's reforms. Because no elections could be held, an *interrex* was appointed, and the senate issued the *senatus consultum ultimum*. Lepidus's former colleague in the consulship was charged with the task of putting Lepidus's revolt down. To confront the forces Lepidus had sent to Cisalpine Gaul, the senate appointed Pompey to a special command. Lepidus and his troops managed to reach the Milvian Bridge, which crosses the Tiber just north of Rome. (The Milvian Bridge is more famous for the victory of the emperor Constantine the Great four hundred years later, associated with his conversion to Christianity.) Lepidus was defeated and fled to Sardinia, where he died shortly afterward.

Sertorius: Traitor or Tragic Hero?

Lepidus's brief revolt was only the prelude to a more serious rebellion, undertaken by a supporter of Cinna and Marius who had fought against Sulla. Quintus Sertorius is one of the more fascinating and polarizing figures of this period. To some he was a traitor to Rome, to others he was its possible savior. These opposing views began with the first Roman historians who wrote about him, including his contemporaries. In some ways, the different historical views about Sertorius represent the same conflict that was so prevalent in Rome between *populares* and *optimates*.

Sertorius came from an equestrian background, but most of what we know about his early life is his military career. He served in the wars against the Cimbri and Teutones under Marius, winning recognition for daring feats such as swimming across the Rhone in full armor after the disastrous battle at Arausio in 105 BC. A few years later, Sertorius was a soldier in Spain, where among other deeds, he saved the Romans from a treacherous surprise attack. Upon his return to Rome, the people greeted him as a hero, cheering him when he entered the theater. In 89 or 88, he entered the election for tribune of the plebs, but the Sullan faction made sure he was defeated. During the tumult of Rome in 87, he sided with Cinna, but in some sources is credited with keeping his distance from any faction, refraining from the bloodshed carried out by the other Marians. In one instance, he even fought against a troop of slaves that Marius had assembled to carry out killings in Rome. During Cinna's reign as consul, Sertorius was elected to the praetorship, but when Sulla returned to Rome, he openly criticized the way the followers of Cinna behaved. It seems he attempted to follow the course that Lepidus had deemed impossible: "In the midst of civil wars, he sought a reputation for justice and virtue." (Sallust, *Histories* 1.90)

After Sulla's victory at the Colline Gate in 82, Sertorius was in a dangerous position. Sulla would not care how moderate and independent he had been. Sertorius, however, seemed to despair more for Rome's future than for his own. He left the city and went to Spain, where he had been a soldier twenty years earlier. While there, he raised a rebellion of his own against the Roman provincial governors, though it does not appear he intended to march on Rome and seize power. Instead, he assembled together other Roman exiles in Spain, including soldiers from Lepidus's short-lived uprising, and won over the local population with his fair treatment of them. He even organized an "anti-senate" in Spain and had boys from the local elite educated in Latin. To all appearances, Sertorius was trying to refound Rome in Spain, though there is some suggestion he planned to use Spain as a base to conquer Italy, entering into an alliance with Mithridates. During the 70s, Rome sent legions against him under various commanders, including Pompey, yet Sertorius continually fought them off with guerilla tactics. Although Pompey fared somewhat better than the others, not even he could defeat Sertorius, and in one battle just barely escaped with his life. Although successful in war, Sertorius's attempt to found his own version of Rome ends with his death, not in battle, but in an act of treachery, when he is assassinated in 73 at the hands of his own officers.

Pompey the Great

As you may have noticed, one name that connects all of the events described above is Pompey, who was introduced when he first brought his own personal army to Sulla at the beginning of his march on Rome. A brilliant military strategist and outrageously ambitious, Pompey was one of the greatest Romans of the late republic, and might have been remembered as *the* greatest if not for Julius Caesar, who would defeat him in the civil war that brought the republic to an end. Although Pompey at times seemed he could be the savior of the *optimates*'s republic, especially when Caesar relied on the power and influence of the people and the *populares* for his rise to power, he did not fit the mold of a traditional aristocrat. Pompey's first appearance on the pages of Roman history is in command of three legions he raised himself, despite holding no office or having any official authority, which certainly did not conform to any traditional aristocratic ideal. In fact, Pompey was never one to follow tradition or accepted procedure if it did not suit his goals.

From a young age, Pompey had received special commands from the senate, including putting down Lepidus and defeating Sertorius. Some years later, when the senate debated giving Pompey an even more extraordinary command, the famous orator Cicero bent over backward to support the proposal in favor of Pompey by acknowledging that almost nothing Pompey did was in accordance with Rome's traditions, beginning with his first appearance before Sulla:

> What could be a bigger break with tradition than such a young man, without a political office, raising an army during a crisis in the republic? Yet Pompey raised one. ... What could be more opposed to our traditions than giving a military command to someone too young to be a senator, and giving him the responsibility of leading a military campaign to Sicily and Africa? ... Could there be anything stranger to our eyes than an *eques* holding a triumph? ... Or anything as unprecedented as sending an *eques* to a dangerous war with a consul's authority? Yet Pompey was sent. (Cicero, *On the Manilian Law* 60-2)

Cicero continues from there, listing all the ways in which Pompey had upended Rome's traditional practices, all to support the argument Pompey should be allowed to do so again. But in breaking with tradition, Pompey was nevertheless doing so within the traditional framework of the republic. It was the senate, after all, that granted him special exemptions from the laws. However, at the same time it was arguing for its primacy in the republic, the senate undermined its own authority by granting extraordinary individuals special powers and privileges. If Pompey, or someone like him, should ever regard the senate as subservient to him, the senate gave him plenty of reason to think it so.

The *optimates* who placed their faith in him were often disappointed, but it may be that Pompey saw what they could not: Traditional ways no longer mattered, and the times now called for daring individuals, ready to set aside the political ideals that had long dominated Rome. In many ways, Pompey was not only the heir of Sulla, but of the Gracchi, and it is no wonder that the final conflict of the Roman Republic would involve two singular men, both of whom acquired their own personal prestige and influence by using soldiers more loyal to them than the "senate and people of Rome." In fact, senate and people were both now means to their individual ends, to be used as the circumstances dictated. The senate and people might serve them, but they were not going to serve the senate or the people.

FIG. 9.6 A bust of Pompey, copied from of an original dating to 70-60 BC.

Pompey saw his first military action in the Social War at the age of 18, serving under his father, the consul of 89. His father had reached the consulship largely because of his success as a military commander, and, during the civil wars of the 80s, was summoned by Sulla to defend Rome. However, the elder Pompey was also willing to listen to offers from Cinna, especially if they involved another consulship for himself. He died in 87, probably of an illness, when Pompey was not yet 20 years old, and before he reached any agreement with either side in the civil wars. His corpse was dragged by an angry mob through the streets of Rome.

Not long after his father's death, Pompey joined forces with Sulla, who was impressed enough by the young man that he persuaded him to get a divorce so he could marry his step-daughter. Sulla also entrusted Pompey with other important military commands, and after taking Rome in 82, Sulla sent Pompey to Sicily, where he captured and executed the anti-Sullan consul Carbo. He did so in a rather cruel way, by placing the three-time consul in chains and forcing him to kneel at his feet. After insulting Carbo, Pompey had his head cut off and sent to Sulla. In 81, he sailed from Sicily to Africa with four legions in order to finish off some other anti-Sullan resistance by Marius's veterans. He made quick work of the other Roman soldiers there, and also restored Roman authority in North Africa. Sulla then ordered him to send all his legions except one back to Italy, while he stayed in Africa with the single legion left to him. Sulla himself may have begun to have concerns about Pompey's ambitions, and these were certainly justified. Pompey, in fact, refused the order and instead demanded a triumph, a particularly audacious request for a 24-year-old with no political office to his name. Sulla refused, citing historical precedents such as Scipio Africanus, as well as the fact that only a praetor or consul was permitted to hold a triumph. Pompey was not even a senator. Moreover, having this young upstart ride in a triumphal chariot through the streets of Rome would look bad for Sulla's newly restored republic, and would likely make Pompey unpopular among the senatorial elite. Pompey, however, would not listen and instead retorted to the aged Sulla that "more people worship the rising sun than the setting sun." Sulla gave in. Not satisfied with simply holding a triumph, Pompey attempted to make it all the more remarkable by having his chariot drawn by four elephants rather than the usual horses. Apparently, the four elephants could not fit through the city gate, and he had to abandon the idea.

Yet whatever ill-will Pompey may have earned from his unprecedented triumph in 79, it did not harm his political career. His successes and his cruelties continued, and he made it clear he was a force to be reckoned with. When he was chosen to subdue the forces Lepidus had sent to Gaul during his revolt, Pompey had to be given a special command as a "propraetor," since he still had not held any office. After accepting the surrender of the Roman commander there, he then sent someone to kill him. Pompey's cruelty would lead one Roman to label him a "teenage butcher" (*adulescentulus carnifex*). In search of further military glory, he then wished to be sent to fight Sertorius in Spain where previous commanders had failed. Instead, the senate ordered him to disband his troops, but Pompey refused and remained camped outside Rome, keeping the senate waiting with excuses. Fortunately for him, the war against Sertorius was not going well, and once again, in recognition of his military prowess, he was sent to Spain. He did not defeat Sertorius militarily but did keep him in check until Sertorius was undone by treachery. While there, he wrote a letter to the senate begging for funds to continue the war, and threatening to bring the war to Italy if his demands were not met. Once Sertorius had been assassinated, he could count his Spanish campaign as a success. His attention then turned back to Italy, where another military threat seemed to require his services.

Quest for Freedom?: The Slave Revolt of Spartacus

Spartacus was a gladiator from Thrace, a rugged area corresponding to modern-day Bulgaria, and had also served in the Roman army in one of the allied auxiliary units. In 73 BC, he led an escape from a gladiator school from the town of Capua, about 15 miles north of Naples. What began as a breakout of about 80 individuals grew within a short time into an army of as many 120,000 slaves, gladiators, and even freeborn poor Italians. The escaped gladiators first grabbed cleavers and meat spits from the kitchen of the school to use as weapons, but then coming across some wagons carrying gladiator weapons, seized these to arm themselves. Soldiers from Capua attempted to stop them, but the band led by Spartacus defeated them and took their weapons. After defeating another small force, Spartacus seems to have realized that in the long run defeating Rome was unlikely, and he decided to take his growing band north over the Alps. From there those who had followed him could return home. However, his "army" refused to heed his plan and instead continued to wreak havoc in Italy. Two consular armies were sent against him, and he defeated them as well. Spartacus then headed back south, perhaps intending to cross the small strait from the toe of Italy into Sicily, and to reignite the slave wars that had occurred there in the past. He made a deal with some pirates in the area to ferry his men to Sicily, but the pirates tricked him and took his money.

The first armies sent against Spartacus were not full legions, which suggests Rome did not initially recognize the magnitude of the problem. But after two defeats, the senate decided to send legions under Marcus Licinius Crassus, an officer who had served under Sulla and had grown extraordinarily wealthy thanks to the proscriptions. Crassus trapped Spartacus and his army in the south of Italy and finally destroyed them. A few thousand stragglers managed to escape, and Pompey came down from Spain to finish them off. Pompey developed something of a reputation for swooping at the end of a difficult battle or war and taking credit for the victory even if he really only mopped up at the end. Some 6000 followers of Spartacus were captured and crucified along the Via Appia between Rome and Capua.

Spartacus was clearly an exceptional leader, and some ancient historians praise him for his kindness and intelligence. Some sources say that he attempted to keep the men following him under control, and to prevent excessive violence. It is said he even banned gold and silver from his camp. Yet as his army swelled, his ability to control it diminished. It is remarkable he managed to hold this rag-tag band together for so long. Spartacus's revolt did not bring about any lasting changes, but he has lived on in the popular imagination, helped by the 1960 film *Spartacus* and more recently by the raunchy television series *Spartacus: Blood and Sand*. Before these cinematic portrayals, he served as inspiration to the oppressed who fought against entrenched political powers. Early communists adopted him as a hero of class warfare, an embodiment of the proletariat's struggle against the forces of capitalism and imperialism. During World War I, a "Spartacus League" was founded in Germany, one of whose original members was the prominent thinker and activist Rosa Luxemburg. This league eventually was folded into the German communist party, but not before they attempted to start a revolution in 1918, producing a pamphlet entitled *Spartakusbriefen* ("Spartacus Letters").

FIG. 9.7 A poster for the Spartacus League, a Marxist organization founded in Germany in opposition to World War I.

Two's Company: Pompey and Crassus

Pompey finally returned to Rome in 71 BC with his eyes set on a second triumph for his victories in Spain in the war against Sertorius, and also with hopes of a consulship. Both would be extraordinary accomplishments for a man in his thirties, and a consulship for someone who was not only too young for the office, but also had held no previous elected office, would be a violation of Sulla's constitution. However, as long as Pompey appeared to support the senatorial elite, they would allow him to continue with his extraordinary and unprecedented career. Any suspicion that he might turn to the *populares*, however, would meet with immediate resistance. Some senators did in fact have this concern, for even though Pompey had proved himself a loyal Sullan during the civil wars, his popularity among the soldiers would be worrisome. He had already shown he was willing to use the army for political leverage. He eased those fears by disbanding his army, but only after he was granted his triumph. Yet the worry remained that he would still seek the support of the people, going as far as to restore the powers of the tribune of the plebs that Sulla had removed. In a dangerous dance, the senate would feed Pompey's ambitions as long as he appeared to respect its authority, but he would respect their authority only as long as they allowed him to pursue his individual ambitions.

Crassus was understandably annoyed that Pompey would take credit for the defeat of Spartacus, especially since Crassus, no matter what credit he deserved, could not celebrate a triumph, since a victory over runaway slaves and gladiators was not usually considered worthy of a triumph. In fact, Pompey wrote a letter to the senate to remind them that while Crassus had defeated the slaves, he had ended the war. Crassus did, however, celebrate an *ovatio* ("ovation"), far less of an honor than a triumph and lacking much of the spectacle. Nonetheless, some people still criticized him for celebrating a victory over slaves.

The end of the war against Spartacus was the beginning of a political rivalry between Pompey and Crassus, which only grew with the suspicions that Pompey was turning *popularis*. Crassus, like Pompey, had been a loyal Sullan, though his use of the proscriptions to enrich himself did not endear himself to the dictator. He purchased burned-out houses and other properties at bargain-basement prices during the civil wars between the Sullans and Marians. He would then hire out his workers to build large apartment buildings on the properties so he could collect rent off the apartments for years to come. It was also said he would show up when a building was on fire and offer to buy it, as well the buildings next to it, while the flames were still burning, offering a lower and lower price as the building was slowly destroyed. This might not be true, but he certainly did reap enormous financial gains from the civil wars, and he became legendary as Rome's richest man. In one famous saying attributed to him, he said that no man could be considered rich unless he could support a Roman legion out his own pocket. Crassus is best known for his wealth, but he was a shrewd politician. While Pompey used his military success and the support of his soldiers for political influence, Crassus used his money for the same purpose, especially in giving out loans.

Pompey, on the other hand, rose to power through his exploits on the battlefield, and was able to turn his success and the personal loyalty of his soldiers into political influence. In this regard, he was much like Marius, even though he was a political opponent of Marius and all those who succeeded him. Also like Marius, he was most at home on the battlefield, which makes sense given that he had essentially lived on one since his teen years. Even when Pompey finally entered the political arena after the defeat of Spartacus, he seemed always to be looking for ways to find his way back to military command. As the political difficulties that were soon to face him showed, he was right to do so.

Despite the tensions and rivalry between Pompey and Crassus, they could work together as long it was to their mutual benefit. In fact, they did so to become colleagues in the consulship of 70. While Crassus had experience in the senate, Pompey had yet to hold any other office, and a scholarly friend of his wrote a handbook for him on how the senate worked. Once in office, their political differences prevented them from undertaking any notable actions, but at least they managed to avoid creating any serious conflicts or hostilities. In the decade following, the two men would take different paths, but would soon join together again thanks to the efforts of a third, Julius Caesar.

Law and Order at Rome

Law is one the most important and most lasting legacies that Rome passed on to the contemporary world and Roman law deeply influenced European traditions of legal theory and practice. While in many ways the Roman legal system might look somewhat familiar, there were also significant differences from the way modern legal systems function, especially in the operation of law courts. Over the course of the republic, the administration of law changed drastically, and also became another arena of conflict in late Republican political conflicts.

Much like today, in the Roman Republic there were two different types of law, civil and criminal, which were handled by separate courts. However, the division between the two at Rome does not perfectly match the modern distinction between civil and criminal law. Basically, civil law at Rome concerned actions carried out against another individual, so that theft, today considered a crime, was originally a civil matter between two individuals. (Later in the republic, however, it was considered a crime.) Criminal law covered acts considered to involve the state, such as corruption by a Roman magistrate.

For civil law, there were two courts run by praetors, one that handled cases between Roman citizens and another cases involving noncitizens. A plaintiff would summon the defendant to appear before the praetor, who then determined if the case had merit to proceed. If the praetor determined it did not, that was the end of the matter. Another magistrate, such as a tribune of the plebs or consul, could also halt the proceedings at this point. The case could also come to an end if the defendant admitted guilt, or either party swore an oath of guilt or innocence. The plaintiff could also take his complaint to another praetor, or simply wait for the following year when new praetors would be elected and try again. If there was no admission of guilt or no oath sworn, the praetor then came up with what was known as a *formula*, which was a simple expression of the case. The *formula* would serve to guide whomever served as judge at the next stage of the trial. Developing a *formula* was tricky business, as the specific wording shaped the trial, and both sides could request that clauses be added to it. An example of a praetor's *formula* is preserved in a later collection:

> Marcus Silanus shall be judge. If it appears that Aulus Agerius deposited a silver table with Numerius Negidius, and, through the fraud of the said Numerius Negidius, the said table has not been restored to the said Aulus Agerius, you, judge, will condemn Numerius Negidius to pay Aulus Agerius a sum of money equal to the value of the property, and if the case is not proved let him be released. (Gaius, *Institutes* 4.47)

In the first sentence, the praetor assigns a judge to the case. The judge chosen could be most anyone, and in some cases consisted of a small group of three to five individuals. There were also some larger juries, but in most instances, a single judge decided these cases. Once the verdict was given, both parties were expected to adhere to whatever penalties had been specified in the *formula*, but there was no police force or government authority that would help them to enforce it.

If, for example, a defendant failed to pay restitution after a judgment, the plaintiff would have to bring another action against him. (The closest Rome came to police force were the aediles and three magistrates known as the *tresviri capitales,* who were the officials in charge of maintaining public order, including fighting fires.) Losing a civil trial, however, could involve more than legal penalties. A Roman citizen would be branded with "infamy" (*infamia*), which brought social disapproval among his peers, and for a member of the senatorial elite, could result in expulsion from the senate.

In criminal law, trials were at first conducted before an assembly, which meant that the juries consisted of hundreds of men. The first permanent courts were established in 149 BC, and at first these were only for trials of Roman magistrates charged with extortion. By the time of Sulla, several other permanent courts had been set up, each one for a particular crime, such as treason or election bribery. After Sulla, it was rare that a trial was held before an assembly. Instead, at the beginning of the year, a list of jurors was drawn up. The pool of jurors, depending on the period in question, would be either senators or *equites* or a mixture of both. The jury for a particular trial would be selected by lot from this list. The size of the jury varied, depending on the particular court, but seemed to range from 32 to 75. The courts met in the Forum, with the jurors seated on benches. The prosecutor would be a private citizen, while the defendant would usually have advocates represent him. The defendant would also bring friends and supporters along with him to the trial, the more the better. Lawyers in the modern sense did not exist, though there were Romans who were considered experts in the law and could be consulted on technical points of law. These individuals were not professionals, in the sense that they were paid. It was, in fact, illegal to receive fees for speaking for someone. But an individual who needed to defend himself in court, or wished to prosecute someone else, would often rely on a trained speaker, though in truth almost all upper-class Romans, and especially senators, had some rhetorical education. Some Romans were better speakers than others, but often more important than the speaker's rhetorical gifts was his political standing. Simply having a prominent Roman speak on your behalf, no matter what he said, could often make the difference between conviction or acquittal.

For a trial, the defendant often put on mourning clothes, usually a dark-colored robe, and made sure to look his worst not only at the trial but everywhere he went for the duration of the trial. He would make sure to appear in public in this sad state and might even drag his wife and children into court, all to make the jurors feel pity for him. Once all the paperwork was taken care of, with the names of the prosecutor and defendants listed as well as the specific charges, the prosecutor had ten days to prepare evidence, during which time the defendant would either be held in jail or given some kind of bail. For example, the accused might stay with a friend who would guarantee his appearance at the trial. Each side made an opening speech, then followed the presentation of evidence, and finally there was questioning, much like a modern trial. When both sides had finished presenting their case, the jurors deliberated. Each juror had a wooden tablet covered with wax on both sides. On one side was the letter A for *absolvo* ("I acquit, find not guilty") and C on the other, for *condemno* ("I condemn, find guilty").

The juror would rub out one of the letters and leave visible the letter representing his verdict. He would then drop his tablet into a large urn, and then all the votes were counted and the final verdict given. If a juror could not come to a verdict, he could erase both the A and C and write N L, for *non liquet* (literally "it is not clear"). The Roman magistrate in charge of the trial would pronounce the verdict and determine the punishment. Aside from capital cases where execution was the punishment, the most severe penalty was exile from Italy, to which the Romans gave the name *interdictio aquae et ignis* ("prohibition of fire and water"), since fire and water symbolized the essentials of life.

Credits

CHAPTER 10

The Rise of Pompey

FIG. 10.1 *Cicero Denouncing Catiline*, by Cesare Maccari (1889). One of five paintings of his in the Italian Senato della Repubblica, each of which depicts a notable moment in the history of the Roman Republican Senate.

Overview

During the decade of the 60s, Pompey the Great received from the senate two extraordinary military commands, one to stamp out piracy and the other to defeat Mithridates. During his absence from Rome, a political and military rival was rapidly ascending, and by the end of the decade, Julius Caesar had established himself as the most powerful leader of Rome, setting the stage for a collision with Pompey that would lead to civil war and the end of the republic. The decade also saw the rise to prominence of another leading figure of the last generation of the republic, Marcus Tullius Cicero, who more than any other Roman would have a lasting intellectual influence on the Middle Ages and Renaissance. Consul in 63, he successfully put down a conspiracy against the republic by a corrupted patrician known as Catiline. Thanks in large part to Cicero's own self-promotion, it remains one of the most famous episodes of the period. The chapter concludes with a brief section on money.

Timeline

70	Consulship of Pompey and Crassus
70	Cicero's prosecution of Verres
67	Pompey given command against pirates (*lex Gabinia*)
66	Pompey given command of war against Mithridates (*lex Manilia*)
63	Cicero's consulship and the conspiracy of Catiline
62	Pompey returns to Rome
59	First consulship of Julius Caesar

Pompey's Special Commands

Sulla's constitutional reforms were an attempt to place the republic back on its traditional footing. For Sulla and his supporters, "traditional" meant a government dominated by the conservative senatorial elite with the influence of the plebs and the *populares* diminished. When Pompey held the consulship together with Crassus in 70 BC, he had done so in violation of the rules for officeholding established by Sulla just over a decade earlier. At the time of his election, Pompey was technically six years too young to be consul, and he had not yet held any of the lower offices required before holding the consulship as part of the *cursus honorum*. He had not yet even qualified to be a senator. In fact, when Pompey was elected consul, he had not yet set foot in the senate house. His colleague Crassus, however, was more of a traditional aristocratic politician, and from one perspective, the two men might look like a standard opposition between a *popularis* politician, who relied on the support of the plebs and the soldiers, and an old-school optimate, who was supported by the other members of the senatorial aristocracy. However, neither Pompey nor Crassus were cookie-cutter representatives of political factions, and each went his own way.

In a telling concession, the senate granted Pompey a special exemption and allowed him to hold the consulship. To some degree, the senate was forced to acknowledge Pompey's popularity, and some senators felt it necessary to give him special treatment in order to avoid any outbreak of violence on the part of the people or the soldiers. Some in the senate also felt that Pompey could be won over to their side. By giving him what he wanted, they thought they could maintain some control over him or make use of his popularity. While the senate's treatment of Pompey was prudent and perhaps necessary to avoid the kind of conflicts that led to the civil bloodshed of the 80s, the relationship between the two showed how broken the system was even when it seemed to work. In fact, the special commands granted to Pompey were not a sign of health, but further proof that the constitution was broken beyond repair. Unable to accommodate an ambitious young man without making exceptions of this sort, the cracks in the republic's foundations began to widen.

The Sullan constitution, in fact, was already in the process of being undermined when Pompey and Crassus became consuls. The power of the tribunes of the plebs, which Sulla had limited, was slowly being restored, censors were chosen for the first time since Sulla, and laws authorizing distributions of grain in Rome, one of the hallmarks of *popularis* policy, were passed. The Italians who had been granted citizenship at the end of the Social War were officially enrolled in the register of citizens, across all 35 tribes, just as the *popularis* politicians wanted. Jurors as well were no longer chosen exclusively from senators. In some ways, the legislation of this period was the ultimate victory of the Gracchan reforms.

Pompey had risen to power through his military victories, which had begun with the offer of his service and his troops to Sulla as he began his march on Rome. This rather than his family connections or political maneuvering had brought him to the consulship. And despite his attachment to Sulla as a young man, he did not seem all that attached to Sulla's principles or his ideas about the republic. Now that Pompey possessed his own prestige and influence, he supported positions quite at odds with the Sullan reforms. Pompey, however, was never one to adhere to principles, and in this he was not so different from most Roman politicians, for whom personal standing and glory were more important than the ultimate victory of some political ideal.

Once Pompey's year in the consulship was over, there was little else to accomplish in the political arena, and he was only 36 years old. A censorship, while a feather in the cap for many consuls, would not add much to his accomplishments when there was more of the world to conquer. Moreover, domestic politics was not the arena where he felt most comfortable. His place was on the battlefield, but it would take a few more years before he could return to a conflict worthy of his standing.

The Republic's Spokesperson

The year 70 also saw the rise to greater prominence of Marcus Tullius Cicero, another figure who would go down in history as one of the greatest members of the republic's last generation. An ambitious young man from the town of Arpinum (Marius's hometown), Cicero was born in 106 BC, the same year as Pompey. He was from a wealthy Italian family of the equestrian order, but not from an elite senatorial family with a tradition of political prominence. However, he received an elite education, including two years in Athens where he learned rhetoric from the finest Greek teachers and attended lectures on philosophy. Over the course of his long political career, he would use his speech-making abilities to acquire political influence, by defending or prosecuting cases as political favors, or by swaying the senate or the people through political speeches. His talents made him a formidable presence at Rome, even if he never seemed to possess the standing of a Pompey or Caesar. In due time, he reached the consulship, at the minimum age required by law, in 63. Yet his attainment of the consulship was in a way more exceptional than Pompey's, since Cicero was a *novus homo*, meaning he was the first in his family to reach that office, and did not even have in his family a history of political service. He was not only first in his family to be consul, but also the first to reach the senate, putting him in the company of Cato the Elder and Marius (a distant relative).

Cicero was not only one of the most important Romans of his generation, he is also one of the most important sources for the history of this period. In fact, this last generation of the republic is one of the most studied and most well known because of him. Thanks to Cicero we have much more information than for any other period of Roman history. In particular, we have over 800 letters written by Cicero to his friends and relations, the vast majority to his close friend and confidant Atticus. His letters, covering the period from 69 until shortly before his death in 43, were collected and edited for publication by Cicero's trusted slave and confidant, Tiro, after his master's brutal murder in the aftermath of Caesar's assassination. These letters give us a rare behind-the-scenes look at Republican politics. There are gaps in the correspondence, and we do not have many of the letters written to Cicero, which can make interpretation difficult. Nonetheless, we do not have anything like it for any other period of Roman history. In addition to providing us with a glimpse into history that we do not often have, these letters allow us to get to know Cicero as a private man as well as a political figure, something we do not have for people like Pompey, Crassus, and Caesar. Cicero does not always come off looking very well because of this, and he often receives more criticism for personal failings than other figures, simply because we have a better view of his weaknesses and flaws. He was, as with many notable historical figures, a complex person, at times showing courageous resolve, and at other times wallowing in doubt and lacking all conviction.

We also have numerous speeches by Cicero, like his letters edited for publication, and not all of which were actually delivered. However, they all provide a close view of particular moments at the end of the republic. As with the letters, we do not have the speeches by those on the other side from Cicero. Like all lawyers, Cicero used misdirection and clever wording to present his case in the best possible light, which often meant presenting his opponent in the worst, so interpretation can be tricky. He is considered the greatest orator Rome ever produced, and for centuries to come his speeches would be studied as ideal examples of eloquence and argumentation. Cicero also wrote numerous other works on philosophy, religion, and political theory, weaving together his deep study of Greek and Latin literature, history, and philosophy. These works would survive to become some of the most important texts of the European Middle Ages and the Renaissance. He also dabbled in poetry, but very little survives (which likely benefited Cicero's literary reputation). To some of the Renaissance humanists of the fifteenth and sixteenth century, Cicero was the ideal statesman, who used his broad learning in service of the republic, at least when he could. In the view of some historians, the discovery of a lost manuscript of Cicero's letters to Atticus by the fourteenth-century Italian poet and scholar Petrarch, sometimes called the "father of humanism," gave birth to the Renaissance. This is an overstatement, but Cicero's writings remained the bedrock on which much of the Renaissance was built.

FIG. 10.2 A bust of Cicero from the 1st c. AD, in the Musei Capitolini in Rome.

Cicero had become politically active in the aftermath of the civil wars under Sulla, and one of his first speeches, in the year 80, was on behalf of a young man named Roscius. (The speech is known as *Pro Roscio*, which is the standard form of a defense speech, since *pro* means "on behalf of." A prosecution speech has a title with *in*, meaning "against," followed by the defendant's name, as *In Catilinam*.) Roscius's father had been murdered, and some relatives of Roscius subsequently made a pact with a powerful and influential associate of Sulla, a Greek freedman named Chrysogonus, to profit off the murder. The dead man's property would normally be inherited by the son. However, Chrysogonus placed the murdered father's name in the list of the proscribed, meaning the son would be disinherited and his father's property would be auctioned off to the highest bidder. Chrysogonus won the auction, since no one would dare to outbid a powerful ally of Sulla during such a dangerous time, and Roscius's relatives were set to take possession of the property and pay off Chrysogonus. In order to make sure that young Roscius would not try to claim his father's property for himself, these relatives accused him of murdering his father. It was on this charge that Cicero defended Roscius, and though he managed to have the young man acquitted of murder, it is unlikely Roscius managed to recover his father's property. Even attempting to recover it might endanger his life.

This was Cicero's first public case, and he claims he undertook it when no one else would, since everyone was afraid to stand up to Chrysogonus (which meant standing up to Sulla). It did take courage, even if Cicero exaggerated the danger to enhance his own reputation. He was very careful to make it clear he was not accusing Sulla of any wrongdoing. In fact, he even drew a flattering comparison between Sulla and Jupiter, ruler of the universe, in order to explain why Sulla would have no knowledge of what Chrysogonus was up to:

> Many people did a lot of things without Sulla's approval or knowledge, because everyone knew that Sulla was busy with so many things at this time. ... Even Jupiter Optimus Maximus, who governs the universe with the nod of his head, has sometimes harmed mortals, destroyed cities, and ruined crops with strong winds, violent storms, excessive heat, or frigid cold. According to our beliefs, these things don't happen because it was the god's intention to cause harm, but simply came about because of the great power inherent in the universe. On the other hand, we see that all the benefits we take advantage of, the light we enjoy and the air we breathe, have been granted us by Jupiter. Is it so strange, members of the jury, that Sulla, who alone rules the Republic, governs the world, and strengthens with laws the great empire he took by arms, might have failed to notice a few things? (Cicero, *In Defense of Roscius Amerinus* 131)

There is no telling if Sulla felt flattered, but if Cicero demonstrated courage in defending Roscius, his fawning treatment of Sulla seems cowardly and pathetic. Yet walking a political tightrope was a skill Cicero made use of throughout much of his career, not always successfully or admirably. Nonetheless, the political delicacy and argumentative skill he showed in this speech succeeded, though he still thought it prudent to leave Rome immediately afterward for a couple of years and continue his education in Greece.

He served as a quaestor in Sicily in 75, his first political office, and by all accounts he carried out his duties with honesty and integrity, or at least without the greed and corruption that had become more prevalent among Roman provincial administrators. As a result of his fair treatment of the Sicilians, and his growing reputation for legal and rhetorical prowess, in 70, during the consulship of Pompey and Crassus, some Sicilians approached Cicero to prosecute Gaius Verres, the extremely corrupt and greedy governor of Sicily from 74 to 71. There was little question that Verres had abused his office, essentially treating the province as a personal piggybank and even stealing valuable artworks from temples. However, the jury would consist of his fellow senators, and Verres had enlisted for his defense the leading orator of the day, the distinguished aristocrat Quintus Hortensius. Unfortunately for Verres, the praetor who would serve as judge had a reputation for honesty and could not be easily corrupted. Verres and Hortensius tried to delay the trial until the following year when they could expect a judge who was more kindly disposed to them or more receptive to their bribes, but failed, thanks in part to Cicero's energetic preparations.

In his prosecution, Cicero attacked Verres's character and produced evidence of his crimes, as would be expected. He also used to his advantage the political question about the make-up of the juries, which had long been an issue between the equestrian order and the senatorial order. Sulla had returned the juries to their original form, which consisted exclusively of senators and excluded members of the equestrian order. However, with Pompey and other *popularis* politicians on the rise, there was pressure once again to include members of the equestrian order on the juries. Cicero thus hinted to the senators of his jury that they were on trial as much as Verres, warning that if they did not convict one of their own in a case of obvious guilt, they would lose all credibility. Their reputation would be so damaged that they might lose control of the juries altogether. On the other hand, if they were willing to sacrifice one of their own by finding Verres guilty, they might save their valued position as jurors. Essentially, Cicero was daring them to acquit Verres, and he opens up his prosecution with this issue, rather than anything about Verres or his crimes. In fact, he tells the senators they are lucky to have the opportunity to convict a fellow senator:

> This is something, members of the jury, you should want more than anything else, the one thing that will help to get rid of your order's unpopularity and the bad reputation of your verdicts. It's as if, at this critical moment for the Republic, the gods, and not any human planning, have given you this opportunity. There is a belief out there— everyone talks about it here in Rome and even overseas—a belief harmful to the Republic and a danger to you, that no one who is wealthy, no matter how guilty he is, will be found guilty by a jury such as this. (*Against Verres* 1.1)

Given his own political ambitions and optimate leanings, Cicero had to tread lightly if he did not want to make too many enemies too soon. As well as flattering the jury of senators, he also took pains to make sure that Pompey, who had his own connections to Sicily, was not tainted by any association with Verres's crimes. Conviction would not be easy, but Cicero did such a masterful job in his first speech that Verres fled into exile to Massillia, modern-day Marseilles on the south coast of France. (Cicero published a second speech against Verres, a self-advertisement of sorts, but it was never delivered.) More important than the exposure of Verres's guilt was Cicero's arrival on the political stage of Rome. In 69, the following year, he was elected as aedile, a major step on his way to his consulship in 63. In the years between holding these offices, he played a major role in Pompey's continued rise, even defending a supporter of Pompey against an optimate attack because he wanted Pompey's influence to help him to the consulship in 63. These were the kinds of political bargains he would have occasion to regret.

Pompey and the Pirates

One of the constant problems that had plagued Rome once its power and influence had spread across the entire Mediterranean was piracy. Pirates traveled over the sea regularly, capturing vessels and cargo and selling into slavery any passengers, including freeborn Roman citizens. At one major slave market on the island of Delos, thousands of slaves were bought, sold, and traded every day. The pirates themselves were based for the most part in Cilicia, a region on the southern coast of Turkey, and on the island of Crete. Even though their bases were in the eastern Mediterranean, the pirates had begun to threaten the coast of Italy directly. In addition to the capture of Roman citizens, the pirates also disrupted trade, in particular the all-important shipments of grain used to feed the urban plebs. Despite military action against the pirates taken by Rome in the previous decades, piracy had continued to be a problem. By the beginning of the 60s, they controlled the waters around Sicily, one of the major sources of grain. In 68, they reached the Roman port of Ostia, at the mouth of the Tiber just down the river from Rome, and set fire to the granaries. They even kidnapped two Roman senators.

Because piracy had become a serious crisis, there was a clamor in Rome for immediate action, and given the scope of the piracy, a six-month appointment of a dictator seemed insufficient. Moreover, the horrors of Sulla's dictatorship made Romans wary of using the office. In 67, a tribune by the name of Gabinius, who had already been active in promoting legislation that undermined many of the Sullan reforms, proposed a law to create a special command to defeat the pirates. And this was not just a means of investing someone with consular authority to take command of some forces. The appointed commander would be given an authority that would supersede all other commanders, even those of consular rank, and the command would stretch not only over the entire Mediterranean Sea, but would cover all territory up to 40 miles from the coast. While such an extension of the area of command makes sense, given that pirates might flee inland up a river, this special command would supersede the territorial command of numerous provincial governors. The commander appointed under Gabinius's law would also have the authority to raise a fleet of 500 ships and an army of up to 125,000 men, as well as have access to extraordinary sums from the public treasury. He could also select 24 legates to serve under his direct command, and the period of this command would last for three years. Gabinius's proposed law did not mention anyone by name as a candidate for appointment to this special command, but there was no need to. Everyone knew the law was written for Pompey.

Needless to say, there was strong opposition to the proposal, and not only because of political opposition to Pompey himself. Placing so much power in the hands of any single man struck many senators as extremely dangerous, almost asking for an ambitious Roman to seize control of Rome and the entire Mediterranean, like a powerful king. Fifteen years prior, Rome had witnessed a military commander march on the city after returning from the east at the head of troops loyal to him, and many senators had lived through the bloodshed that followed in the civil wars between Sulla, Cinna, and Marius. A consul attempted to block the bill and Pompey's appointment along with it, causing the people to riot. Then one of the other tribunes of the plebs stepped forward to veto the proposed law, clearly at the request of some of the optimate senators. In the face of further popular violence, the tribune withdrew his veto. The law passed, and Pompey took command.

When Pompey's appointment was announced, confidence in his abilities was so high that the price of grain immediately dropped. The confidence of the people and the markets was not misplaced, and Pompey took care of the pirates with astonishing speed. Although he was given a three-year appointment, he finished the job in three months. Pompey's real strength was his ability to organize large-scale operations and carry them out with brutal efficiency. So rapidly did he conclude his campaign against the pirates that some at Rome accused him of paying them off. There were grounds for the charge, at least from one perspective, since Pompey did not simply defeat the pirates in battle or chase them away. Instead, he addressed the root cause of piracy and settled many of the pirates on land given to them in newly founded cities some distance from the sea. To a critic, it might appear that Pompey rewarded the pirates for their criminal behavior, and in a sense he did. But from a practical point of view, he gave the pirates a means of living that would be less dangerous to themselves, and also a future benefit for Rome. These former pirates, now turned into settled farmers, would produce future citizens and taxpayers—and future soldiers of the Roman army. Moreover, Pompey could rely on their support for him if needed, since they would look on him as their patron—these new cities were part of his own personal power base in the eastern Mediterranean.

Pompey and the "Poison King"

While the successful conclusion of Pompey's war against the pirates brought him added prestige, the command he really sought was in the war against Rome's nemesis Mithridates. After Sulla's settlement with Mithridates, criticized as being far too favorable, the "poison king" had begun to rebuild his military forces, more to control rebellious territories in his kingdom than to seek revenge on Rome. He had made some overtures to the rebellious Sertorius in the mid-70s, likely to form a coalition against Rome, but there is no evidence Sertorius had any interest in a partnership. However, there was little question he would confront Rome again. In 75, the king of Bithynia died and in his will left his kingdom to Rome. Bithynia was a kingdom on the southwest coast of the Black Sea and a neighbor to Mithridates's kingdom of Pontus. Mithridates declared the will invalid, and in 73 invaded Bithynia. Rome sent out both naval forces and infantry to confront Mithridates and his allies, and so began what is commonly known as the Third Mithridatic War. Lucius Licinius Lucullus, an optimate senator from a distinguished family and consul of 74, was put in command of the land forces in 73. At first, he met with success in many battles and conducted successful sieges, and by 69, Lucullus had driven Mithridates into his son-in-law's kingdom of Armenia. He had not delivered a knock-out blow, however, and the campaign had not gone as smoothly and rapidly as some would have liked, providing an opening for supporters of Pompey to promote him as a replacement for Lucullus. Their cause was helped when Lucullus's troops mutinied, complaining that their long service had not brought the expected rewards, especially since Lucullus preferred to come to terms with cities rather than let his soldiers plunder them. Some blamed the soldiers for their greed and lack of discipline, claiming their long exposure to the wealth and immorality of the east had corrupted them. Moreover, Lucullus had eased the burden of debt under which many of the cities in Asia suffered, thanks to the taxes they owed. While a sensible policy, this angered many of those back at Rome who had financial interests in the east, and they also worked against Lucullus. Most damaging of all, Lucullus's brother-in-law, Publius Clodius Pulcher, a troublemaker we will meet again, stirred up Lucullus's soldiers against him by an unfavorable comparison to Pompey's soldiers in Spain. The soldiers serving under Lucullus, Clodius told them, wear out their lives in battle after battle in these distant lands without the reward due to them. Instead, they are forced to drag along Lucullus's carts filled with golden cups covered in gemstones, while Pompey's soldiers are already enjoying life with their wives and children on the farmlands they had received or in prosperous cities founded for them. He concluded:

> If our battles will never end, why don't we save the rest of our strength
> and of our life for a commander who believes his greatest honor is
> to make his soldiers wealthy? (Plutarch, *Lucullus* 34.4)

With all of these forces working against Lucullus and in support of Pompey, it seemed only a matter of time before a change of command came about. In 66, only a year after the law granting Pompey special command against the pirates, another tribune of the plebs, named Manilius, put forward a law that would give Pompey supreme command over the forces in Asia Minor. This law, the *lex Manilia*, was opposed, naturally enough, by many of the optimate senators who had opposed the *lex Gabinia*, including the patricians Quintus Catulus and Hortensius (the orator who defended Verres). But given Pompey's successful completion of the campaign against the pirates, their opposition to that law made their opposition to this one much weaker. Catulus said his opposition was not to Pompey, but to the danger of placing so much power in any man's hands—Pompey could be trusted with such power, but what would happen, he said, if some accident happened to Pompey? Whom could they trust with so much power? The crowd had an answer: "You, Catulus!" Cicero also gave a speech in favor of the law (but made sure to praise

Lucullus to appease his supporters). He also tried to make that case that there was a precedent for giving Pompey unprecedented commands, arguing that breaking tradition when necessary was in fact a Roman tradition:

> But they say there should be nothing unprecedented, nothing contrary to the examples our ancestors established. I won't discuss here how our ancestors always followed our usual practices in times of peace, but in war were always guided by what was practical, and always made new plans to meet the new crises of the moment. Nor will I mention that one commander brought an end to two of our greatest wars, the Punic war and the Spanish war, or that the same Scipio destroyed Carthage and Numantia, two powerful cities that were the most serious threats to our empire. I won't remind you that very recently you and your ancestors decided to place all the hopes of our empire on Gaius Marius, and same man led the wars against Jugurtha, against the Cimbri, and against the Teutones. (Cicero, *On the Manilian Law* 60)

Cicero brings up two historical precedents, neither all that far in the past, for Pompey's second extraordinary command, using the common rhetorical device known as *praeteritio* ("passing over," which means mentioning something by claiming you will not mention it). Although there were differences between the situations of Scipio and Marius, the comparison is politically effective since Marius was a hero to the *populares*, Scipio to the *optimates.*

Not only were the people and soldiers in support of Pompey, but now also the equestrian order would support a change to Pompey, since he could be expected to protect their financial interests. Needless to say, the law passed, and Pompey would take over from Lucullus the war against Mithridates, almost certainly leading to a glorious triumph and even greater wealth and prestige for Pompey. Lucullus suffered the fate that Crassus had before him, when Pompey swooped in at the end of a campaign and appeared to receive the credit for the work others had done. Since Lucullus had severely weakened Rome's enemies in the east, some senators said what Pompey was taking away from Lucullus was not a military command, but a triumph—Lucullus would be handing over not his army, but his victory. Lucullus's troubles with Pompey and his supporters did not end when he returned to Rome. He applied to the senate for a triumph, but a tribune of the plebs, with Pompey's blessing, blocked it, and it would take many months of political maneuvering before he was granted one in 63.

The real triumph, of course, would belong to Pompey, and he would make sure that Rome and the world knew it. He quickly transitioned from his campaign against the pirates to war against Mithridates. Pompey soon defeated the "poison king," who then fled to Crimea. Even Mithridates's own family members were now either on friendly terms with Rome or weary of his stubborn struggle against it. His own son led a rebellion against him, and eventually Mithridates, recognizing that it was all over, tried to commit suicide by drinking poison. Unfortunately, his lifelong practice of building up a resistance to poison had worked, so he had to ask a bodyguard to kill him with a sword. One of Rome's greatest enemies, he died in 63.

Eastern Settlements: Rome and Jerusalem

Pompey did much more than defeat a foreign enemy on the battlefield. He engaged in diplomacy throughout the eastern Mediterranean, making political arrangements with various rulers as well as founding new cities (including Pompeiopolis, "Pompey City"). He also annexed some territories as new Roman provinces, including Syria. In one notable example, Pompey intervened in a political dispute in Jerusalem, leading to a siege and the occupation of the city. According to one source, Pompey even entered the inner sanctuary of the Temple Mount, known as the "Holy of Holies" and believed to contain the Ark of the Covenant, in which the original stone tablets of the Ten Commandments were kept. Only the high priest was permitted to enter the Holy of Holies, and thus Pompey's entry was an act of desecration. But by all accounts, he did not touch anything, and on the following day had the temple cleansed and purified in accordance with Jewish custom. Yet his brazen walk into the temple's inner sanctum revealed something of Rome's arrogant attitude toward the peoples and cultures that fell under its dominion. Pompey's entry into Jerusalem itself marked the beginning of Rome's close involvement with Jewish politics and the loss of Jewish independence. Judea became a client kingdom of Rome, and subsequently a province. Much later, in 70 AD, a Roman army under the emperor Titus would sack Jerusalem and destroy the Second Temple.

Pompey had established Roman dominion over the world of the eastern Mediterranean as far inland as the Euphrates river, but he had also established his own personal authority over the same areas. A later historian has preserved a copy of an inscription in stone that Pompey set up in Asia. It is in the style that the people of Asia would recognize as typical of one of their rulers, but might make a Roman of the republic uneasy:

> Pompey the Great, son of Gnaeus, *imperator*, freed the world's coastlines and every island in the world from war with the pirates. He liberated the kingdom of Ariobarzanes, Galatia and the territories beyond it, and Bithynia. He defended Paphlagonia, Pontus, Armenia, Achaea, Iberia, Colchis, Mesopotamia, Sophene, and Gordyene. He conquered Darius, king of the Persians; Artoles, king of the Iberians; Aristobolus, king of the Jews, and Aretas, king of the Nabatean Arabs, as well as Ciclician Syria, Judaea, Arabia, Cyrenaica, the Achaeans, the Iozygi, the Soani, the Heniochi, and all the other peoples that live between Colchis and Lake Maeotis together with their kings, nine in total, and all the peoples who live between the Sea of Pontus and the Red Sea. Pompey extended the empire's borders to the edges of the world, maintaining or increasing the revenues of the Romans. He carried away the statues and images of the gods and other enemy treasure, and dedicated to Minerva 12,060 pieces of gold and 307 talents of silver. (Diodorus Siculus, *The Library of History* 40.4)

In some cases, it might not be clear if these overseas communities were dealing with Pompey as a representative of the senate and people of Rome, or simply Pompey himself. His political and economic arrangements with cities and rulers of the eastern Mediterranean would need to be approved by the senate, but Pompey had already either established new provinces or arranged for indirect control through alliances. On the whole, there would be no need for a large Roman military presence to ensure Roman control over this vast area. More importantly, the peoples in the east would view Pompey as their personal benefactor and their patron. To many inhabitants, Pompey would be very much like another of the Hellenistic monarchs who had ruled kingdoms in the eastern Mediterranean following the death of Alexander the Great in 323, and to treat him as such was simply the customary way of doing things in this area. The question at Rome would be to what degree Pompey would welcome this royal treatment and attempt to bring it back to Rome, and this was precisely the fear of those who had opposed his special commands.

Rotting at the Core: The Conspiracy of Catiline

Before Pompey returned to Rome, there was a domestic political crisis at Rome, one of the more famous incidents from the republic's final decades. It owes its fame to Cicero, who was its hero and whose speeches against the villain have been read by students of Latin for centuries. How serious this conspiracy truly was has been a matter of some debate, and it may have achieved greater prominence than it warrants thanks to the survival of a short account of the events by the Roman historian Sallust, who did not participate directly but was alive at the time. As well, many of the most important figures of the last generation of the republic—Cicero, Cato, and Caesar—played prominent roles in it.

Lucius Sergius Catilina (usually known in English as Catiline) was born into an old patrician family that had fallen into political decline. Catiline seemed to maintain the haughtiness and pride of an aristocrat, while behaving in ways traditional-minded Romans found scandalous. In fact, he seemed to have the potential to be an outstanding Roman, equal to the military and political heroes of earlier generations, but he turned all of his gifts and talents to wrongdoing. Sallust introduces him as follows:

> Lucius Catiline was from a noble family, mentally and physically strong, but his character was evil and depraved. Beginning in his early years, he found pleasure in civil wars, bloodshed, looting, and political conflict, and as a young man he spent his time on these. Physically, he could endure hunger, cold, and lack of sleep to an unbelievable extent. Mentally, he was reckless, cunning, and wily; he could think up any kind of lie or trick. He was greedy for what others had, and wasted what he had. His passions were intense, and while he could speak well, he did so carelessly. His mind, never satisfied, always craved what was excessive, incredible, and impossible. (Sallust, *Catiline's Conspiracy* 5)

Much of our information about him comes from hostile sources and cannot be fully trusted. It was rumored that he killed his first wife out of love for another woman, a consul's daughter with a bad reputation. When this new lover could not stand having his son by his first wife around, Catiline killed him too. His character was likely of a sort that would generate lurid stories to indicate his depraved and violent character, especially in light of his later actions. And though he may not have murdered his step-son, he did kill his brother-in-law. This, however, was not some wanton act, but was carried out during Sulla's proscriptions as a favor to the patrician Quintus Lutatius Catulus, who became one of the leaders of the *optimates*. In 73, Catiline was charged with committing adultery with a Vestal Virgin, though he was acquitted thanks to his close association with Catulus. After reaching the praetorship in 68, he governed the province of Africa for two years. A natural next step would be the consulship, and he declared his candidacy for 65. However, he was charged with corruption for his actions while governor of Africa, and though he was acquitted (likely through bribery), he was barred from running for office that year. Undeterred, he put himself up for election in the following year, hoping to be consul in 63. Despite his political connections, including the support of Crassus and Julius Caesar, there were concerns about Catiline, less for his corruption than for his talk of abolishing debts, which would frighten off many members of both the equestrian order and the senate. Because of his birth, he felt he belonged with the patricians and *optimates*, but since he felt his political ambitions had been thwarted by them, he had turned into a *popularis* politician. In order to ensure his defeat, many of the *optimates* threw their support behind Cicero, for even though he was a "new man," he was a reliable supporter of tradition and order. He would certainly never entertain the idea of canceling debts and would work to oppose any movement in that direction. Cicero won, and had as his colleague Gaius Antonius Hybrida, who had earlier partnered with Catiline. Hybrida agreed to support Cicero as long as Cicero allowed him to have the lucrative province of Macedonia, which Cicero had been lucky enough to draw as his province to govern after the consulship.

Twice thwarted in his attempt to reach the consulship, Catiline decided to resort to violent overthrow of the government. He could appeal to some of the most desperate citizens of Rome, especially young aristocrats who had squandered family fortunes and had nothing to lose. Catiline would either succeed in instituting debt reforms that would save his supporters from a debtor's prison or exile, or he would bring the whole system down. Although it may be an exaggeration, Catiline was rumored to be planning to set fire to the city of Rome and to murder a number of senators. He sent an associate, a former centurion who had fought under Sulla, to gather an army in Etruria north of Rome in preparation for an attack.

In November 63, Cicero was told of Catiline's plans by the lover of one Catiline's confederates, and Crassus also supplied him with some damning letters from the conspirators. Cicero learned there was a plan to assassinate him at the beginning of the plot, but forewarned, he managed to take precautions, including wearing an armored breastplate (perhaps more for the dramatic effect). On the next day, he convened the senate at the Temple of Jupiter Stator and delivered a scathing denunciation against Catiline, who to the surprise of many was in attendance. This speech of Cicero's, known as the *First Catilinarian* (there were four in total), became famous for its opening lines, which sound better in Latin rather than English:

> *Quo usque tandem abutere, Catilina, patientia nostra? Quam diu etiam furor iste tuus nos eludet? Quem ad finem sese effrenata iactabit audacia?*
>
> To what extreme, Catiline, will your abuse of our patience go? How much longer will your madness mock us? Where will your unrestrained recklessness end? (Cicero, *Against Catiline* 1.1)

Cicero's speech had the effect of driving Catiline out of the city, though not until Catiline had sneered at Cicero's status as a "new man" and pointed to his own illustrious family history. Catiline went not to hide in shame, but to join the army his co-conspirator had been gathering in Etruria.

The senate did not yet seem to be convinced of the danger that Catiline presented and suspected Cicero of exaggerating. He wanted the senate to issue the *senatus consultum ultimum*, but he needed definitive proof that Catiline and his associates were an immediate threat to the republic. Fortunately, help came to him from an unexpected source. Representatives from a Gallic tribe, the Allobroges, had been approached by the conspirators to join them in the attack on Rome, but the Allobroges had instead contacted Cicero. He told the Allobroges to reply that they agreed to join in the conspiracy, and to include a request for something in writing to take back to their leaders in Gaul. Cicero then set up an ambush so when the conspirators met the Allobroges to hand over the incriminating documents, they were captured. There could now be little doubt about their guilt and the danger of the conspiracy.

At this point the senate was convinced, and finally issued the "ultimate decree," or SCU. Cicero thus had the authority to execute the conspirators without a trial if he so chose. The senate met to debate whether to execute them, since despite their treasonous actions they were still legally Roman citizens. In the historian Sallust's account, there are two speeches in this debate, the first by Caesar, and the second by Cato. (He did not include Cicero's speech.) These speeches were crafted for the purposes of his history, but as Sallust was writing it 20 years after the event, when there were still living witnesses to the trial, they would have accurately represented the arguments both speakers made, if not their exact words. Caesar, who had been elected as praetor and was soon to take up his office, gave a speech arguing against execution. Instead, he proposed keeping the conspirators in a kind of house arrest outside of Rome and confiscating all of their property. Part of his argument was that death would be a relief to the guilty, but he had a more serious argument. Executing these conspirators would be a drastic departure from tradition and would set a dangerous new precedent:

> As far as I'm concerned, we have nothing to fear from Cicero or this crisis, but in a large population there are many different kinds of people. It's possible that something untrue now will be true later, when someone else is consul

> and has an army under his control. When that consul, using Cicero as a precedent, kills someone in accordance with the decree of the Senate, who will stop him, who will restrain him? (Sallust, *Catiline's Conspiracy* 52.35)

This argument echoes earlier speeches made by senators who opposed Pompey's special commands against the pirates and Mithridates. They claimed to have no concerns about Pompey himself—he was an honorable man, of course—but feared what would happen if someone less trustworthy than Pompey obtained such a position of power, perhaps even using Pompey's special commands as a precedent for their own. Here, Caesar claims he is not worried Cicero will act in any tyrannical way, but that some future consul will use the SCU for his own nefarious purposes with no check on his power—a consul could thus act like a king. This future wicked consul could execute innocent Roman citizens without a trial because they were deemed a threat to Rome by the SCU, just as the honorable Cicero will have executed the wicked Catilinarian conspirators. In fact, as Sallust well knew when he wrote this speech for Caesar, Cicero would be later charged with illegally executing Roman citizens.

Caesar's speech swayed many of the senators, the majority of whom initially seemed inclined to vote for execution. The optimate leader Catulus accused Caesar of being involved in the conspiracy, and his plea for leniency heightened those suspicions. There is, however, no firm evidence that he was, though given Caesar's extraordinary shrewdness, one might guess he was either informed of it, or hoped by this speech to make use of the conspirators for his own purpose at some future date. But after Caesar appeared to weaken the senate's resolve to hand out the harshest punishment possible, the stern Cato rose to speak in opposition. This Cato, great-grandson of Cato the censor, was in his early 30s, a bit younger than Caesar, Cicero, and the others, but already had a reputation for his upright morality and unyielding adherence to principles. One of his main points was that these were men who wished to destroy Rome and kill many of the very men debating their execution. Saving them from execution would not be "compassionate," Cato argued, but extremely foolish. What punishment short of death would prevent individuals determined to murder senators and burn down Rome from trying again later? And what kind of precedent would such "compassion" set? In fact, Cato suggested there was a more serious problem, which echoed Gaius Gracchus's argument about the definition of a "tribune." The republic was on the brink of ruin, Cato said, because the meaning of words such as compassion, courage, and generosity had been lost:

> The issue now is not whether our morals are good or bad, not how great and glorious the empire of the Roman people is, but whether everything around us including control of our very own lives, however it appears now, will belong to us or to the enemy. At this moment of crisis, is someone really talking about clemency and compassion? Well, I suppose we lost the true names for things long ago, and this is the very reason the Republic is close to ruin: Wasting other people's wealth is called generosity and reckless criminal behavior is called courage. So, my colleagues, by all means, spend

> freely at the expense of our allies, show mercy to robbers of the treasury, since that's the way things are done now. But don't waste the blood we've spent, and don't bring ruin upon all good men by sparing a few scoundrels. (Sallust, *Catiline's Conspiracy* 53.13)

Cato's proposal carried the day, and the conspirators, including the patrician Publius Cornelius Lentulus Sura, were immediately taken to the Tullianum, a chamber in the nearby prison in the Forum, where executioners strangled them with a rope. Catiline himself, however, was in Etruria at the head of a sizeable army, amounting to two legions, but once news of the executions reached his followers, many began to desert his cause. Then, surrounded by troops sent out from Rome, he made a desperate last stand and died fighting with what some would call courage.

Pompey: Power and Weakness

Shortly after the conspiracy of Catiline was over, Pompey returned from his lightning-quick suppression of the pirates and his victorious march against Mithridates. In addition to bringing untold wealth back to Rome, he also brought with him a great fear. He had received exceptional treatment from the senate on the basis of his standing in Rome, and now his successful campaigns would elevate him even higher. Would he demand even more special treatment? Would he expect to rule over Rome like a king from the east? What limits to his ambitions would he accept? Pompey was in fact becoming something like a Hellenistic monarch in his relation to Rome, not in the sense of a tyrant, but as a personal benefactor, a wealthy and powerful individual who showered the people of Rome with gifts for both their glory and his own. Indeed, he looked not to earlier Roman consuls as a model, but to Alexander the Great, the young Greek monarch who conquered much of the known world. Associating himself with Alexander would be a politically useful form of propaganda in the eastern Mediterranean, but how would it be received in the Roman Republic?

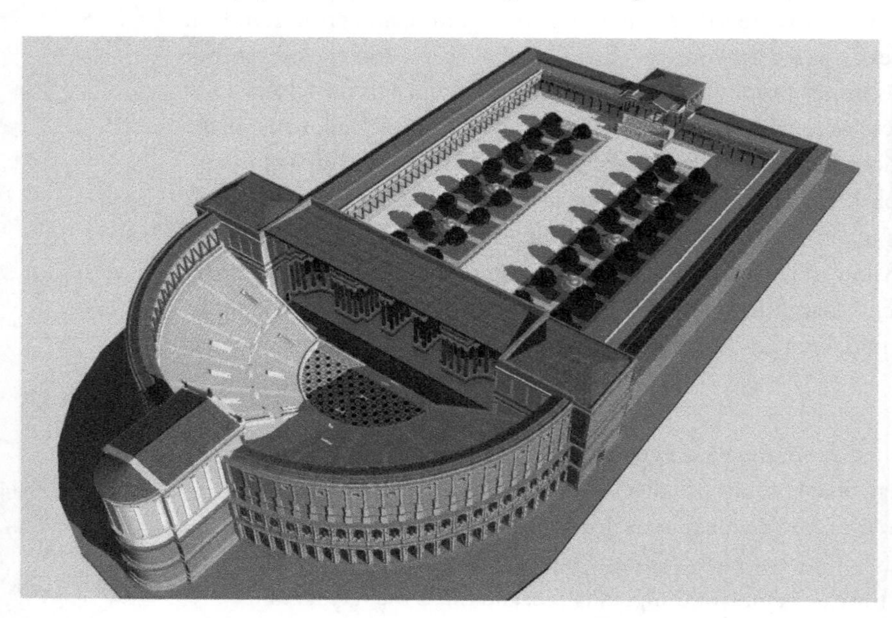

FIG. 10.3 A digital reconstruction of the Theater of Pompey.

The wealth he brought back from the east basically tripled the size of the public treasury at Rome, and even with his contributions to the public good, Pompey himself became enormously wealthy from his eastern conquests, as had the legates whom he had personally appointed to serve under him. Much of his generosity was made possible by wealthy eastern rulers, who rewarded Roman commanders as well as troops with gifts of money. While Pompey recognized that plunder from war was in part to be paid into the public treasury, or to be vowed for the purpose of adorning the city of Rome with new buildings and extravagant games, this public service would redound more to his personal prestige. One example is the Theater of Pompey, completed in 55 BC after six years of construction. It was the first permanent theater in Rome, built of stone rather than wood, as temporary stages and seating had usually been built. Parts of it are still visible today.

Despite the fear of what he might do shortly after his return to Italy, Pompey disbanded his army. To the relief of many, he did not attempt to impose himself as a ruler over the senate and people of Rome. He did, however, treat Rome to one of the most spectacular triumphs ever seen in September of 61, on his 45th birthday. This was, in fact, Pompey's third triumph, and it was treated not just as a celebration of the defeat of Mithridates, but as the culmination of his conquests, a triumph over the world. As the Greek biographer Plutarch noted, even though he was not the first Roman to celebrate three triumphs, he was the first who could claim triumphs over the entire world, as represented by three different regions: Africa, for his conquest of Numidia while fighting for Sulla; Europe, for fighting in Spain against Sertorius, and lastly Asia, for his defeat of Mithridates. One might question how deserved the first two triumphs were, but other Roman commanders had sought them for far less. No one would question Pompey's achievements now. According to our sources, the triumph lasted for two full days, and even that was not long enough to display all his victories and their treasures. Pompey rode on a chariot covered with gemstones and wore a cloak that once belonged to Alexander the Great. Placards carried in the triumph displayed the names of the territories and peoples he conquered. In addition to the pirates he subdued, there were the peoples of Iberia, Albania, Pontus, Armenia, Cappadocia, Paphlagonia, Media, Colchis, Syria, Cilicia, Mesopotamia, Phoenicia Palestine, Judaea, and Arabia. He boasted of conquering over 900 cities, while founding another 39 new ones.

At the time of his triumph, Pompey could claim to be the most prominent individual not only in Rome, but in the entire world known to the Romans. Yet even though he had numerous supporters who protected his interests while he was abroad fighting the pirates and Mithridates, his opponents in Rome had not remained idle, and he was not the only Roman who sought to be at the top of the heap. Crassus, his colleague in the consulship of 70, was using his own vast financial resources to work against Pompey's interests, and there were powerful senators who used the political arena and the courts to go after those who supported Pompey. For example, Pompey wanted a law passed to provide land for his former soldiers, but this effort was blocked in the senate. Moreover, the efforts to have his political arrangements with the rulers in the eastern Mediterranean ratified by the senate were stalled, with some senators claiming they needed to examine each one on its own terms rather than approve them all in one vote, basically an extreme version of a bureaucratic slow-walk. There were also extraordinary honors proposed for Pompey, and again these come to nothing, despite the presence of his supporters in the consulship for 62 and 61. The machinations of the domestic political scene frustrated the great military conqueror, justifying his preference for command in the field. At a time when Pompey seemed to be at the height of his power and influence, his political weakness was being exposed, and within a few years he would find himself playing second fiddle to his great rival and eventual foe, Julius Caesar.

A Necessary End: The Rise of Caesar

Julius Caesar, six years younger than Pompey, was born in 100 BC. Despite being one of the best-known historical figures in the history of Rome, and indeed of the world, we have very little information about his early years. Caesar's father died when he was 16, but it was his family connections on his mother's side that were of greater importance to his early career. These connections did not completely determine his character and politics, but they certainly shaped how others viewed him—and nearly cost him his life. His mother's brother was Marius, making him the nephew of the great and flawed *popularis* general. He also married the daughter of Cinna, the ruthless ally of Marius who essentially ruled Rome during the bloody civil wars against Sulla, only to be killed by his own soldiers in 84. When Sulla emerged victorious and began a murderous purge of his opponents, young Caesar's life would have been in serious danger. According to the sources on Caesar's life, Sulla tried to force him to divorce Cinna's daughter Cornelia, but Caesar refused to do so. This marriage would last until Cornelia's death in 69, producing his only legitimate child, his daughter Julia, despite two later marriages lasting over twenty years combined. (He later fathered a son outside of marriage to Cleopatra, and there were rumors of other children born from his affairs—Caesar had a reputation as an adulterer.)

For a young man so closely associated with Sulla's greatest enemies, this opposition to Sulla's wishes certainly took a great deal of courage and put his life in even greater danger. He is said to have gone into hiding during Sulla's reign of terror, forced to sleep in a different place every night. At one point he had to pay off the agents Sulla sent to kill him. It was only through the intervention of prominent relatives that Caesar's life was spared. Sulla is said to have first resisted their pleas, but they persisted until he threw up his hands and said,

> You win, you can have him! But I'm telling you this man whose life you're so desperate to save will one day be the death of the *optimates* we've tried to protect. There's more than one Marius in Caesar! (Suetonius, *Julius Caesar* 1)

Sulla's exasperated outburst is suspiciously prophetic, and many of the stories about Julius Caesar have been amplified in hindsight to add to his later luster, or have been exaggerated to emphasize his future ruthlessness.

One of the best-known dramatic episodes of his early life is his capture by pirates. Sources place it at different moments, either when he fled Rome to avoid Sulla, or later when he was sailing to the island of Rhodes off the southwest coast of modern Turkey in order to study rhetoric with a Greek teacher. In either case, the incident would have occurred when he was still in his early 20s, though it has clearly been embellished. Aside from highlighting the dangers piracy posed for those sailing the Mediterranean, the story is meant to demonstrate Caesar's daring and fortitude. The Greek biographer Plutarch provides a colorful version:

> The pirates demanded twenty talents for Caesar's ransom, but he just laughed at them for not knowing who they had captured. He promised to pay them fifty talents on his own, and to raise the money he sent some of the men with him around to different cities. This left him with only one companion and two attendants in the middle of these bloodthirsty Cilician pirates, but so little did he think of them that whenever he went to bed he ordered them to stop talking. He was their prisoner for 38 days, and the whole time he exercised and played sports with them without worry. It was as if he was not a hostage of these pirates, but the pirates were his bodyguards! He read them poems and speeches he wrote, and if any of the pirates did not express admiration for them, he called them illiterate barbarians to their face, and with a smile threatened he would hang them all. All this amused the pirates, who assumed Caesar spoke so boldly because he was young and foolish. When the ransom finally arrived from Miletus, Caesar was released. He immediately assembled ships and men, set sail from Miletus in pursuit of the pirates, and came upon them while their ships were still at anchor near the island. He captured most of them, seized all of their money, and threw them in prison at Pergamum. It was the responsibility of the praetor who was the governor of Asia to punish the pirates, so Caesar first approached him. But since he had his eyes on the large sum of money, the greedy praetor said only that he would look into the matter when he had the time. Caesar departed, went to Pergamum, took the pirates out of prison, and crucified them all. He had warned them more than once that one day he would crucify them, but they thought he was joking. (Suetonius, *The Deified Julius Caesar* 2.1-7)

Caesar was likely captured by pirates and ransomed, but this entertaining episode is meant to inform readers about Caesar's character—to tell us what kind of man Caesar was—rather than provide us a history of what he did. The details that make it such a lively read portray Caesar with the same qualities he would demonstrate when he seized political supremacy at Rome with steely-eyed determination. Indeed, Caesar usually seemed to have the last laugh, particularly when others failed to take him seriously.

In 80 BC, Caesar served on the staff of the governor of Asia and was awarded a military decoration for saving the life of a fellow citizen during a battle at Miletus, the city from which he launched his pursuit of the pirates in the story presented. He also took part in operations directed against piracy, but after the death of Sulla, he returned to Rome and won a reputation for speaking in the law courts. In 69, he took the first step on the *cursus honorum* when he was elected quaestor. In the senate, he supported the legislation authorizing Pompey's extraordinary commands, which helped him in his election as aedile for 65. One of the aedile's duties was to oversee the public games, and the more lavish and spectacular these were, the better an aedile's chances for election to higher office. While there were public funds available, an aedile would use his own wealth—or at least money he would borrow—in order to put on truly memorable games, and Caesar was no exception. The successful animal hunts and gladiator combats he supervised were necessary for his political ascent but placed him in serious debt. Debt would be a constant issue for Caesar as he continued his rise, and in one sense the large sums he borrowed early in his career suggested he was prepared to gamble everything on himself. Caesar may have been a gambler, but he was no fool. He always seemed to know the true odds better than anyone, and his throws of the dice seemed always to pay off—at least for himself.

Roman Money

Throughout this book are images of Roman coins, which are an important source of historical information (the study of coins is known as "numismatics.") Coins were the principal source of money and were minted on a regular basis; paper money did not exist, and would not until centuries later in China. The first coins in the ancient Mediterranean seem to have originated in Caria, corresponding to the modern area of central Turkey, in the seventh century BC. The first kind of money in Rome dates from the period of the kings (753–509 BC) and the beginnings of the republic. It was a lump of bronze, weighing one Roman pound (*libra*, thus the abbreviation "lb." for the modern pound) and divided into 12 Roman ounces (*uncia*). The first bronze coins did not appear until the fourth century, likely thanks to contacts with Greek communities in southern Italy. Roman coins were not regularly minted until the beginning of the third century BC. The basic unit of this bronze currency was the *as*, and it was the unit used for the census classes in the so-called "Servian Reforms" for the Centuriate Assembly (the first class, for example, was those with property worth 100,000 *asses* or more).

FIG. 10.4 Bronze *as* from the 3rd c. BC. On the obverse is a portrait of Janus, the two-faced god. On the reverse is an image of a ship's prow (*rostrum*) with the ram for use in naval warfare. Above it is the Roman numeral I to indicate the value of one *as*.

During the Second Punic War, the older system of currency was replaced by a new one, and the main coin became the silver *denarius*, which was initially worth 10 *asses* but later was adjusted to a value of 16 *asses*. When the *denarius* was established, another silver coin of lower value, the *sestertius*, replaced the bronze *as* as the basic unit for counting money. A *sestertius* was originally worth one fourth of a *denarius*, or 2-and-one-half *asses*, just as the American quarter is a quarter, or one fourth, of a dollar. *Sestertius* means 2 and one half in Latin, literally "half third." With the adjustment of the *denarius* to 16 *asses*, the value of the *sestertius* became 4 *asses*, still one fourth of a *denarius*. A gold coin, known as an *aureus* from the Lain word for gold (*aurum*), became more common as a means to pay soldiers beginning with Sulla, and was worth 25 *denarii*.

Coins were struck by hand with a hammer and anvil. An image in reverse would be carved on a hard metal, one for each side of the coin; these were known as the "dies" (as in die-cast). A flat piece of metal, known as a blank, would be placed between the two dies and hammered, producing a coin with the images.

FIG. 10.5 The obverse of a silver denarius. The Roman numeral XVI indicates it was worth 16 asses, and thus minted after the revaluation.

FIG. 10.6 The obverse of a sestertius with the head of Roma. To the left is the abbreviation for sestertius, IIS (the Roman numeral II and S = *semi*, or one half).

Coins were also a useful instrument for self-advertisement, and the use of portraits becomes common in the second century BC. The officials in charge of minting money, the *tresviri monetales*, would use the coins to promote an ancestor or a patron, and thus promote himself. The front of a coin, known as the obverse, usually carried the portrait, who by tradition would have to be deceased, while the other side, known as the reverse, often had a deity or an object of symbolic value. Later, Caesar would place his own portrait on coins, and to mint a coin with a portrait of a living person was something Hellenistic kings had done (Brutus, Caesar's assassin, also issued coins with his own portrait). Other magistrates could produce coins with the senate's approval, and so could military commanders if there was a need. The mint at Rome, at least according to a late source, was next to the temple of Juno Moneta on the Capitol, though this may be a guess based on the name's resemblance to the word for money.

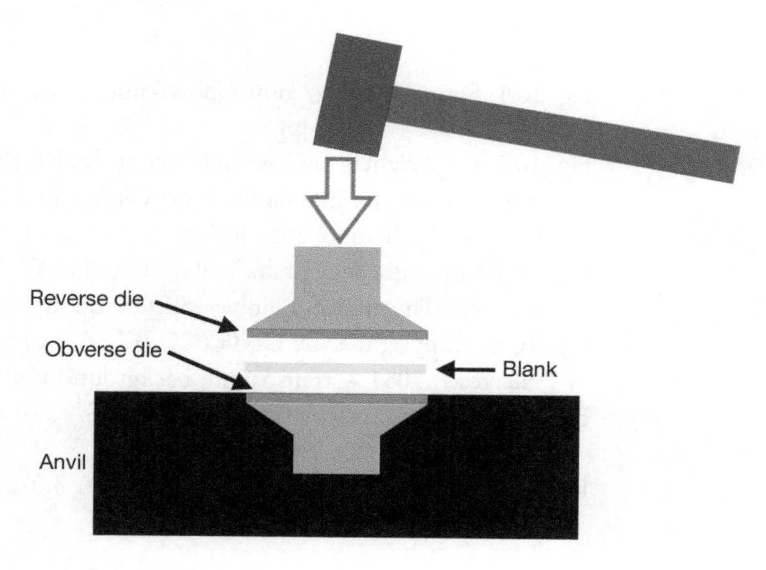

FIG. 10.7 The minting of coins.

Banks as we think of them today did not exist, and many Romans would keep their money at home or in a temple, protected by religious sanctity. By the end of the fourth century BC, however, there were individuals who acted something like modern bankers. *Argentarii*, whose name derives from the Latin word for silver (*argentum*), received deposits of money from individuals, and in some cases would use the deposited money for their own and pay interest on the deposits. Sometimes they simply kept the money, and a depositor could have the *argentarius* make payments on his behalf from his account. An *argentarius* would also change money, especially exchanging foreign currency for Roman coins, for a slight fee. Finally, an *argentarius* would inspect coins to make sure they had not been debased with less valuable metals or counterfeit (testing coins is known as "assaying"). Counterfeit coinage does not seem to have become an issue until the first century BC, after the tribune Livius Drusus had suggested that Rome mix copper into its silver coinage to alleviate a financial crisis.

Although some of these bankers and money-changers became wealthy, they did not seem to be of high status, and some were freed slaves. Senators and members of the equestrian orders, who were the wealthiest men in Rome, did not use these services, but would themselves make loans from their own funds and often among themselves. Crassus, for example, would loan money to individuals such as Caesar and Cicero, which was a useful way to win friends and influence others. Senators were legally forbidden to engage in trade, though obviously many found ways around this prohibition, or simply ignored it.

Credits

Fig. 10.1: Source: https://commons.wikimedia.org/wiki/File:Cicerón_denuncia_a_Catilina,_por_Cesare_Maccari.jpg.

Fig. 10.2: Copyright © by José Luiz Bernardes Ribeiro (CC BY-SA 4.0) at https://commons.wikimedia.org/wiki/File:Bust_of_Cicero_(1st-cent._BC)_-_Palazzo_Nuovo_-_Musei_Capitolini_-_Rome_2016.jpg.

Fig. 10.3: Copyright © by Lasha Tshkondia (CC BY-SA 3.0) at https://commons.wikimedia.org/wiki/File:Theatre_of_Pompey_Sketch_up_model.png.

Fig. 10.4: Copyright © by CNG (CC BY-SA 3.0) at https://commons.wikimedia.org/wiki/File:Vecchi_051_-_transparent_background.PNG.

Fig. 10.5: Copyright © by Curtius (CC BY-SA 3.0) at https://commons.wikimedia.org/wiki/File:Crawford_224-1-Obverse.jpg.

Fig. 10.6: Copyright © by CNG (CC BY-SA 3.0) at https://commons.wikimedia.org/wiki/File:ArSestertiusDioscuri.jpg.

CHAPTER 11

Caesar in Charge

FIG. 11.1 A bust of Julius Caesar, produced shortly after his death.

Overview

Only two years after Pompey's spectacular triumph of 61, Julius Caesar was elected as consul and formed an alliance with both Pompey and Crassus. These three men essentially controlled the republic, dividing up the provinces among themselves and controlling access to political offices. Caesar took Gaul and spent much of the next decade conquering it, killing hundreds of thousands and enriching himself. The political situation at Rome devolved into further corruption and violence, and by the end of the decade regular elections could not be held. With the death of Crassus, the alliance of the three men was over, setting Pompey and Caesar on a collision course and leading Rome to the brink of civil war.

Timeline

59	Caesar's first consulship and the "First Triumvirate"
59–52	Caesar's conquest of Gaul
58	Exile of Cicero
56	Return of Cicero
54	Death of Julia, Caesar's daughter and Pompey's wife
53	Death of Crassus
52	Pompey's "sole consulship"

Caesar's Path to the Consulship

Though Caesar had lost the debate about the execution of Catiline's fellow conspirators, and even came under suspicion of involvement with them, his argument about the dangerous precedent Cicero set by executing them without trial would prove to be right—in part because he himself made it so. By the end of the 60s, when Pompey seemed to be at the height of his prestige and power, it was, in fact, Caesar who was becoming stronger while Pompey's political weakness was being exposed. If anything, Caesar revealed how much more skilled he was in political maneuvering than the "great" commander, and he would soon show he was more than his equal on the battlefield. Caesar had supported efforts to summon Pompey back from his military campaign against Mithridates in Asia to put an end to the conspiracy of Catiline. And as praetor in 62, he had attempted to give the honor of restoring the Temple of Capitoline Jupiter to Pompey instead of the patrician optimate Catulus. (The temple had burned in 83 BC.) At the time, Caesar might have appeared to be one of Pompey's biggest supporters, but he always took a longer view in his political ambitions. In hindsight, Caesar seemed from the beginning to be laying the groundwork for his own rise to power. Of course, since many of our sources for Caesar were written after his death, hindsight will make his life seem more planned than perhaps it was. Yet there was no question there was something special about Caesar.

In addition to climbing the *cursus honorum* during the 60s, Caesar had also become pontifex maximus, the chief priest of Rome and a powerful position held for life. In 63, the current holder of the office died, leaving an opening that would normally be filled by one of Rome's distinguished elder statesmen, not a younger man who had not yet achieved the office of praetor. In fact, Catulus was a candidate, yet Caesar made a daring political move and put himself forward. The votes appeared to be evenly split between the Catulus and Caesar, and both were expending large sums of money, mostly in bribes, to win. Catulus, to avoid the embarrassment of losing to an upstart, offered Caesar a substantial sum of money if he would withdraw. He knew that Caesar, who did not have Catulus's resources, was running up huge debts in his attempt to win the office, in addition to the debts he already had from his aedileship. Caesar refused the offer and said he would borrow even more if he had to. In one story, as Caesar was saying goodbye to his mother on the morning of the election, he told her that he would return home as pontifex maximus or he would not return at all. But Caesar won, becoming the chief religious official at Rome.

Following his praetorship in 62, Caesar governed the province of Farther Spain (*Hispania Ulterior*, in western Spain and Portugal), a welcome opportunity to accumulate funds to repay his creditors. However, his creditors were not keen to let him leave Rome. Since he was immune from prosecution while in office, he could only be hauled into court during the short time between the end of his term as praetor and the beginning of his governorship in Spain as a propraetor, when he would legally be a private citizen. However, the wealthy Marcus Crassus stepped in to serve as guarantor of Caesar's loans, which was a wise political investment. Nevertheless, to be on the safe side, Caesar left for his province before his term of office was up. The senatorial elite had grown concerned about his political success and his growing popularity, and for good reason. Some had even wanted Cicero, when the *senatus consultum ultimum* (SCU) was in effect during the conspiracy of Catiline, to have Caesar killed on the grounds of his suspected involvement—a convenient pretext to eliminate a political threat. After Caesar's election as pontifex maximus, they blamed Cicero for his failure to strike when he had the opportunity. Now it was too late.

Scandalous Clodius

We met Publius Clodius Pulcher in the previous chapter, when he stirred up Lucullus's troops against him with an unfavorable comparison to Pompey. His troublemaking in Roman politics, for which he had a talent, had just begun, and he would be a major force in Roman politics for several years. A useful attack dog for his allies and a dangerous and cunning snake to his enemies, he seemed to be beyond anyone's control. Much of the political turbulence that roiled the streets of Rome in the 50s can be traced back to him.

Clodius also had a reputation as something of a playboy and was even rumored to have a sexual relationship with his alluring sister, Clodia. Some believe she is the subject of a number of witty, charming, and occasionally obscene poems written by the poet Catullus in the 50s BC. (Don't confuse the poet Catullus with the patrician Catulus!) Many of Catullus's poems depict a tumultuous and maddening love affair with an aristocratic married woman who is given the pseudonym Lesbia. The name Lesbia refers to a woman from the Greek island of Lesbos (from which the modern term "lesbian" derives). Women from Lesbos had a reputation for learning and beauty, and this is the sense in which it was applied to the Lesbia of Catullus's poems. One of the more famous examples of the love poems is as follows:

> Let's live, Lesbia, and let's love—
> all the gossip of old grouches
> won't count for anything to us.
> When the sun sets, it will rise again,
> but when our life's brief light goes out,

we sleep through a night that never ends.
So kiss me a thousand times, then a hundred,
then another thousand and another hundred,
and keep kissing by the thousands and hundreds.
Once we've accrued thousands on thousands,
we'll scramble the accounting until noone knows
the total, so they can't give us the evil eye. (Catullus 5)

Another couplet captures the torment of the love affair, beginning in Latin *odi et amo* ("I hate and I love"):

I hate and I love. "Why?" you ask.
I don't know, but I feel it and am tortured. (Catullus 85)

As tender as some of the love poems, when Catullus feels betrayed by his beloved Lesbia, he can descend into bitter insult:

Hey Caelius, my Lesbia, that Lesbia,
the one Catullus loved more than himself,
more than all the rest? She's now
on streetcorners and in alleys
sucking off great Remus's offspring. (Catullus 58)

Whether or not this Lesbia is Clodius's sister, Clodius belongs to the world of the poems, filled with young and dissolute elite Romans who enjoy a good party and are happy to mock traditional morality. Wealthy, good-looking, and aristocratic, this younger generation lacked the seriousness and respect for the past that previous generations possessed, at least in the eyes of the "old grouches," and behaved in a disgraceful manner that undermined the moral foundations of Rome.

In 62 BC, Clodius found himself in serious trouble as a result of what appeared to be a rather humorous prank, exactly the kind of thing a dissolute and brazen young aristocrat would do. Every year, rites to a goddess known simply as *Bona Dea*, the "Good Goddess," were held at the house of the wife of the consul or praetor. These secret rituals, lasting overnight under the supervision of the Vestal Virgins, were for women alone, and men were absolutely forbidden from being in the house for the duration of the ritual. In 62, Caesar was both praetor and also pontifex maximus, so the rites were hosted at his house by his current wife, Pompeia (a granddaughter of Sulla) and his mother Aurelia. There were rumors that Pompeia

Translated from Catullus, "Catallus 5."
Translated from Catullus, "Catallus 85."
Translated from Catullus, "Catallus 58."

and Clodius were having an affair, or at least trying to have one, but Caesar's mother kept a close eye on her daughter-in-law. On the night of the *Bona Dea* rites, Clodius, whether to find his way to Pompeia or simply for the thrill of it, dressed up as a female musician and snuck into the house with the help of a female slave. After the slave girl went to find Pompeia for him, Clodius became impatient and began to wander through the large house. One of Aurelia's slaves saw him and invited him to play some music, but when Clodius tried to speak, his voice gave him away as a man. The slave ran screaming to tell the women that a man was present. The rituals were brought to a halt and the house searched. Clodius was found hiding in the room of the slave who helped him enter the house. He was driven out, and the matter was reported to all the husbands, including the pontifex maximus Caesar. As funny as the story sounds, there was a political dimension to it. The scandal took place on the one-year anniversary of the execution of the Catilinarian conspirators, and that year the rites had been held at Cicero's house. Cicero even seems to have appealed to the "Good Goddess" in his decision to carry out the executions. Clodius's offense was in truth not all that serious, but he had very powerful enemies among the senatorial elite. They saw this as an opportunity to destroy him, and as a result he was charged with committing a serious act of religious desecration, *incestum*. A Vestal Virgin who violated her vow of chastity would be charged with the same crime. The punishment was death.

FIG. 11.2 A statuette of *Bona Dea*, the "Good Goddess," dating from the 2nd c. AD (the head belongs to the 3rd c.). The inscription says that Callistus, a slave of Rufina, dedicated it because he was ordered by the goddess in a dream.

Clodius's trial was something of a sensation at Rome given the popularity and prestige of the individuals involved, the scandalous story, and the seriousness of the charge. The optimate senators used the opportunity to attack Clodius, though he was protected not only by his overwhelming popularity with the urban plebs, but by some powerful allies, including Crassus. Caesar had immediately divorced his wife after the scandal came to light and was called to testify at the trial. However, when questioned, he claimed to have no knowledge of what happened that night, hinting that Clodius might be innocent after all. When the prosecutor then asked him why he had divorced his wife if he thought Clodius might be innocent, he replied, "Caesar's wife must be above suspicion." Whatever Caesar's personal embarrassment or feelings about his wife, he knew that Clodius was a valuable political ally. Clodius actually proclaimed his innocence, claiming he was not at Rome at the time. Cicero, however, proved at the trial that his alibi was a lie. It was in vain, since to ensure Clodius's acquittal, Crassus had used his immense wealth to bribe the jury. Cicero's embarrassment of Clodius would soon come back to haunt him.

The Catilinarian Conspiracy and the *Bona Dea* scandal were both moments of political uproar, with the courts used as the political field of battle. For Cicero in particular, the outcomes of each could not have been more different, and within a few years he went from heroic consul to pathetic exile. Given the honorific title *Pater Patriae* ("Father of the Fatherland") for putting down the conspiracy, he reveled in the glory he won for being the savior of his country, often serving as his own best promoter. His vanity even led him to snub Pompey on his return to Italy from the east, only one of the many ways in which the *optimates* humiliated Pompey. As the popularity of Caesar grew, senators like Cicero believed Pompey could be their best defense against him. At times the *optimates* tried to play the two rivals off one another, but they never fully trusted Pompey. Moreover, since they believed the leaders of the senate should be the leaders of the republic, elevating either of the two to a position of power over the other was unacceptable. At the end of the 60s, however, Pompey might have seemed the lesser of two evils, but optimate refusal to support Pompey to the degree he felt he deserved ended up bringing Pompey and Caesar together. When the *optimates* realized their mistake, it was too late.

Principles Over Politics: Cato the Younger

Marcus Porcius Cato, who had won the debate over the execution of the Catilinarian conspirators, became one of the leading voices of *optimate* opposition to Pompey. Born in 95 BC, Cato was a bit younger than Pompey, Caesar, and Cicero, though he often seems much older, almost like one of Catullus's "grouchy old men" and principled to a fault. The great-grandson of Cato the Censor, many Romans would have seen a family resemblance in their outlook and severe moral standards. Both his parents died when he was young, so he was raised in the household of his uncle Livius Drusus, whose sister had once been married to Cato's father. Drusus, you may recall, was the tribune of the plebs in 91 who proposed granting citizenship to the Italian allies, and whose murder helped to bring about the Social War. One story from Cato's childhood, meant to exemplify his unyielding character and his hard-line optimate stance as an adult, involves the controversy over citizenship for the Italians. A group of Italian allies were staying at the house of Livius Drusus, seeking political support for citizenship. One of them was Quintus Poppaedius Silo, leader of the Marsi, who would serve as their general in the coming war against Rome. In the telling of the Greek biographer Plutarch, as a child Cato already displayed both his virtues and his flaws:

> Poppaedius Silo became friendly with the young children, and once asked them, "Why don't you ask your uncle to help us in our fight for citizenship?" Caepio agreed with a smile, but Cato said nothing and kept his eyes fixed on the Italian visitors with a fierce stare. Poppaedius turned to Cato and said, "What do you have to say, young man? Won't you help out your visitors, just like your brother?" Cato again did not reply, but the look on his face was a silent refusal to help. Poppaedius picked up Cato and held him out a window, in harsh tones commanding him to agree

> to help or else he would toss him out. He even shook Cato as he held him out the window. Cato showed no signs of being frightened at this, though he put up with it for some time. Poppaedius put him back down, then turned to the other Italians and quietly said, "Italy is lucky he's still a little boy! If he were a grown man, I don't think a single person would give us their vote." (Plutarch, *Cato the Younger* 2.1-4)

Cato would have been four years old when this incident occurred, if it actually did. The other child mentioned, Caepio, was Cato's older half-brother. His father would become an enemy of Livius Drusus, with some suspecting him of being involved in Drusus's assassination. He fought against the Marsi in the Social War, and in one tradition was killed in battle by Poppaedius Silo. The presence in this anecdote of representatives of the major factions involved in the politics of the Social War might seem suspicious, but the family relations portrayed are historically accurate. It is a good reminder of how deeply intertwined personal and political ties were in the late republic. The four-year-old Cato's political views might not have been so firmly fixed at the time, but much as with the story of Caesar and the pirates, his later character is on full display: fearless, unyielding, and exasperating.

By the time he was twenty, Cato held one of the minor priesthoods, and then began his military service, volunteering to serve in the campaign against Spartacus. His successful speech in favor of executing the Catilinarian conspirators caused a stir, helping him to become tribune of the plebs the next year, in 62. As tribune, he was a thorn in the side to both Pompey and Caesar, an opposition that would continue to the bitter end. While Cato's stands on political issues were often based on an admirable adherence to his principles, his unwillingness to compromise or yield an inch to the political realities of the day contributed to the dissolution of the republic as much as anything else. It was Cato who led the opposition in the senate to granting formal approval of Pompey's political arrangements in the east, and when the tax collectors (*publicani*) sought to revise downward their bid on the contracts for collecting taxes in Asia, since they were at risk of incurring heavy losses, Cato blocked that as well. In principle, Cicero agreed with Cato's opposition to the bill—the tax collectors had agreed to a contract, and should adhere to it; otherwise, they would always seek to revise contracts. But to maintain political harmony between the senate and the equestrian order (to which many tax collectors belonged), Cicero supported the bill. It was pragmatic if not principled. Cicero once quipped in a letter that Cato seemed to act as if he were living in the utopian republic of the Greek philosopher Plato rather than in the cesspool of Rome.

Cato also allowed his strict scruples to alienate Caesar when there was little need to. On his return from Spain in 60, Caesar wished to hold a triumph and to declare his candidacy for the consulship. According to the letter of the law, Caesar could not do both, since the law required him to make his declaration as a candidate in person in the city of Rome, but if he crossed the city boundary (*pomerium*) to do so, he would have to set aside his command and thus lose the opportunity to celebrate a triumph. The senate would often make exceptions, especially for exceptional individuals, and had already done so on more than one occasion for Pompey. This would seem to be the case where it would be wise to let Caesar have his cake and eat it too, but Cato would not budge. Faced with a choice, Caesar gave up the triumph and instead declared himself a candidate for the consulship of 59. His triumphs would come later, and one of them would be over Cato.

Prelude to Power

The thought of Caesar reaching the consulship frightened many of the *optimates*, and they mobilized in an attempt to stop the unstoppable. Recognizing that Caesar's election, supported by Pompey and Crassus, was all but inevitable, the *optimates* decided that the best they could hope for was to elect one of their own as Caesar's colleague. Even Cato, in one of his rare departures from principle, claimed that in a situation such as this bribery was good for the republic. They coordinated their bribery to elect Marcus Bibulus as the second consul in place of Caesar's preferred colleague. Yet they once again underestimated Caesar, for when Bibulus attempted at every turn to veto Caesar's actions, Caesar simply ignored him—he was pontifex maximus after all. Bibulus eventually gave up resisting Caesar and spent most of the consular year at home. For his last attempt at resistance he resorted to religion. Since every meeting had to begin by taking auspices, Bibulus would claim he was watching the skies for any omens, which would technically mean anything that was done in the senate was invalid. Even if Caesar pressed on, a future magistrate could challenge the legality of everything Caesar had done. Yet Caesar pressed on, and Bibulus was irrelevant. Usually, the year at Rome was designated by the names of the two consuls, and thus the year 70 would be known as "the consulship of Pompey and Crassus." The year 59 BC should have been "the consulship of Caesar and Bibulus," but people joked that it was really "the consulship of Julius and Caesar."

Although Pompey and Crassus had become political enemies since their consulship together, Caesar had managed to reconcile them. The three together formed an alliance that is often called the "First Triumvirate," though there was nothing official about their decision to work together (in contrast to the "Second Triumvirate," a legally recognized group that governed the republic in the aftermath of Caesar's assassination). However, these three men for all practical purposes controlled Roman politics, and largely determined who would hold which offices for the next several years. To solidify the pact, Pompey married Caesar's daughter Julia. Even though she was thirty years younger, by all accounts they were in love (Pompey's friends even made fun of him for being so smitten with her). Some might be surprised that Pompey, not much more than a year after his spectacular triumph in 61, would play second fiddle to Caesar, and for the moment, he might not have seen it that way. Moreover, Caesar could help him to accomplish what he and all his other supporters had failed to do after his glorious return to Rome: ratification of all his political arrangements with cities and kingdoms in the eastern Mediterranean, and distribution of plots of land in Italy for his veterans. From Crassus's perspective, by joining together with Caesar and Pompey, he could further his political and financial influence with the wealthy equestrian class, especially in regard to the lucrative contracts for collecting taxes in the province of Asia. What would Caesar get? First and foremost, he would receive the territory of Gaul as his province to govern for a period of five years. This would allow him to accumulate vast wealth, comparable to what Pompey had collected in the east, especially if, unlike Pompey, he kept most of it for himself instead of turning it over to the public treasury. He would also, like Pompey, win the loyalty of soldiers in the legions he commanded.

Though he tried at first to work with the *optimates* in the senate, Caesar found their constant delays and attempts at obstruction intolerable. At one point he had Cato arrested, but not wishing to make a martyr of him, had him released. Caesar thus decided to take his legislation directly to the Tribal Assembly, and one of his early acts as consul was to put forward a massive land bill for Pompey's veterans, the constant bane of *optimates*. Bibulus announced there had been thunder, an omen that should have brought a halt to the proceedings, but Caesar ignored it. When tribunes of the plebs tried to veto the legislation, Caesar appeared before the people, with Pompey on one side and Crassus on the other. He asked both of them in the presence of all if they supported his land bill, and they both declared they did. Caesar exhorted them to defend his laws with swords if necessary. To the dismay of the *optimates*, Pompey added he would bring his shield as well as his sword. Bibulus tried once more to halt the voting, but Caesar's supporters violently drove him out of the Forum after dumping a basket of dung on his head. Some might have seemed this coalition of the most powerful men at Rome as a three-headed monster, but there was no question as to who was in charge: Caesar. The initial appearance in the Forum when he had Pompey and Crassus by his side would have made that clear enough.

After his consular year, Caesar would head to Gaul, and while he had the support of Pompey and Crassus, he needed to take further precautions to ensure that no *optimates* would attempt to meddle with his legislation or attempt to undermine him politically. The consuls for 58 were Caesar's father-in-law and Gabinius, who had proposed the law for Pompey's command against the pirates in 67. However, there was still fear that Cicero would put his eloquence to use and oppose him in his absence. Caesar first offered him a position on the commission he established to oversee his land reform bill, and then offered him a position on his staff in Gaul. Cicero refused these positions, naively believing his previous glory and support of Pompey would protect him. He was mistaken.

For additional insurance, Caesar could rely on Clodius who became tribune of the plebs in 58, a few years after his acquittal in the Bona Dea scandal. Clodius was a member of the patrician Claudian line, but in 59 he underwent a ritual adoption in which he renounced his patrician status and became a plebeian, changing the spelling of his name from the traditional patrician form "Claudius" to the plebeian "Clodius." The purpose of the adoption was to make Clodius eligible to be a tribune of the plebs, which would make him a useful political ally and allow him to cause all sorts of political trouble. In fact, Caesar, as pontifex maximus, had supervised the adoption, and Pompey served as an augur at the ceremony. (Clodius's adoptive father was actually younger than he was!) The year of the adoption—Caesar's consulship—is not coincidental. Clodius would be their attack dog against the *optimates*, and he had personal reasons for attacking Cicero.

Clodius Against the *Optimates*

One of the most noteworthy victims of the coalition between Caesar, Pompey, and Crassus was Cicero, who found himself politically isolated and vulnerable. His execution of the conspirators in 63 BC, which he considered his greatest glory, made him vulnerable. As Caesar's speech in Sallust made clear, executing Roman citizens without a trial, even under the authority of the *senatus consultum ultimum*, was a politically risky move, even if at the time a necessary and prudent one for the republic. Caesar himself had helped to set the legal precedent for Cicero's downfall. In 100, the tribune Saturninus had been killed during political violence that arose following his introduction of *popularis* legislation. He was one of those Marius had taken from the Capitol and placed in the senate house, only to have people climb on the roof, rip up the roof tiles, and hurl them down at Saturninus and others, killing them. The deaths occurred after the senate had passed the SCU.

In 63, a tribune of the plebs charged Gaius Rabirius, now an old man, with the murder of Saturninus 37 years earlier. The charge was made with the backing of Pompey and Caesar in an effort to nullify the senate's use of the SCU as a means to legitimize violence against *populares*. Instead of a regular charge of homicide, Rabirius was brought to trial on a charge of *perduellio*, which required an ancient form of legal procedure used for religious crimes. In this process, there was no trial before a jury, and no arguments for the defense. Two judges would render the verdict, and the penalty was death by hanging or being thrown from the Tarpeian rock on the Capitoline hill. Caesar was one of the two judges, and the other was his brother, so Rabirius was found guilty without much trouble. However, Rabirius made use of the right of a Roman citizen to appeal a death penalty before the Plebeian Assembly, and Cicero, as consul, defended him. Cicero's strategy was to admit that Rabirius killed Saturninus, but argue that if Rabirius was guilty, so were many prominent Romans, many of whom, like Gaius Marius, were dead. Thus, Cicero implies, a guilty verdict against Rabirius is tantamount to passing judgment on great Roman heroes of the past:

> But why speak of everyone who obeyed the authority of the consuls? What will happen to the reputation of the consuls themselves? ... Will Gaius Marius' name be branded with the infamy of that killing? We could rightly call Gaius Marius the father of his country, the parent of your liberty and our state—now that he is dead, will we convict him of a horrific murder? (Cicero, *Pro Rabirio* 27)

Despite Cicero's efforts, curtailed by the tribune, it appeared that the death penalty against Rabirius would be upheld. To stave off a guilty verdict, an augur lowered a flag on the Janiculum, an ancient method of indicating an enemy was approaching. This clever use of an old ritual brought a halt to Rabirius's appeal, allowing him to go into exile rather than face execution. The matter was then dropped, especially as the real object of the prosecution had been accomplished.

With this trial in the background, Clodius introduced in 58 legislation directly aimed at Cicero. It declared that anyone who had put to death a Roman citizen without a trial or an appeal to the people would be sent into exile. Cicero's rejection of Caesar's overtures and offers of a post left him vulnerable, especially since he could not be assured of Pompey's protection. In truth, this was a no-win situation for Cicero, as it would be for many *optimates* or supporters of the senate's traditional authority. It was, however, a situation as much of their own making as Caesar's. Cicero still had friends and supporters, including the consuls of 58, Piso and Gabinius, but they knew which way the wind was blowing. Most hurtful to Cicero was feeling abandoned by Pompey, whom he thought would protect him. Pompey, however, avoided him, and, according to one source, when Cicero showed up at his house to beg him for help, he snuck out the back door.

Cicero was forced to flee Rome. To add insult to injury, Clodius passed another law that prevented Cicero from approaching within 500 Roman miles of Italy (approximately 400 modern miles). Some of his former friends wished him well but would not receive him in their homes, not even in Sicily, where he had developed close connections thanks to his prosecution of Verres. Cicero traveled to Thessalonica in Greece, and though he was welcome and honored by Greek cities as a famous orator and politician, he could not but feel rejected and humbled, only a few years after he was hailed as savior of his country. Plutarch describes his sad state:

> Many people visited him out of goodwill, and Greek cities competed with one another to send him official visitors. Nonetheless, he spent most of his time dejected and in great sorrow. He would stare into the distance towards Italy like an abandoned lover, and his misfortune made him petty and mean-spirited. He was brought low, more than one would expect in a man who had enjoyed such a lofty education. (*Cicero* 32.5)

Cicero himself reveals his state of mind in a series of letters he wrote to his friend Atticus from his exile in Thessalonica. While we do not have Atticus's letters to Cicero, we can tell he frequently encourages Cicero to take heart and criticizes him for his despondency. In one letter, Cicero complains bitterly of his own stupidity for trusting in the patrician Hortensius:

> I've been struck by a disaster that is beyond belief and like no other, but my disordered thoughts, which you can see from my letters, is not caused by my unhappiness. No, the cause is the memory that this is all my fault. You now know who the villain is who spurred me on and betrayed me. I wish you had seen it sooner, and not given up your soul entirely to sorrow, as I did! So when you hear that I have sunk to the lowest depths of misery, consider that the punishment for my foolishness is a heavier burden to me than what happened, since I trusted a man I didn't think was wicked. (*Letters to Atticus.* 3.8)

To add even further insult, shortly after Cicero fled into exile, supporters of Clodius tore down his house in the Forum, and on its site Clodius had a shrine to Liberty built. Cicero's luxurious villas outside of Rome, in Tusculum and Formiae, were also torn down, and his property put up for auction, though no one wanted to buy it out of respect for the great orator.

Cicero was not the only optimate opponent who was removed from Rome. Cato's principles could at times be a political liability, but his reputation for strict adherence to the law won him great respect, even among the plebs who might otherwise be politically opposed to him. And even when Cato lost a political argument, his opponents would often have to expose their own corruption to defeat him. Pompey, Caesar, and Crassus would prefer if he were not around to constantly block their political plans.

In 58, Rome had become embroiled in political unrest in Egypt. Thirty years earlier, the pharaoh of Egypt had died and left his kingdom to Rome in his will, and in 65, Crassus had proposed making Egypt a Roman province. There was even talk of distributing land to veterans in Egypt. These efforts did not come to fruition, but the ruler of Egypt, Ptolemy XII, cultivated close ties with Rome and supported Pompey with funds while he was in the East. A descendant of Alexander the Great's general Ptolemy, who had established a ruling dynasty in Egypt after Alexander's death in 323 BC, Ptolemy XII did not quite live up to his forebears. He was nicknamed "Auletes," which means "flute player," since he acquired a reputation for playing the flute at religious celebrations of Dionysus. The people of Alexandria, the city founded by Alexander the Great, had already rioted in 63 to protest high taxes, and Ptolemy's pro-Roman stance did not endear him to his subjects. In 59, he was made an official ally of Rome, thanks to an enormous bribe paid to Pompey and Caesar, by some estimates a sum equal to a year's revenue for all Egypt.

Rome then decided to annex the island of Cyprus, seizing control of it from Ptolemy XII's brother and making it a Roman province. Someone needed to be sent on a special commission to carry out this policy, which promised to be a lucrative one, ripe with possibilities of receiving bribes. Many Roman politicians wanted it, but Clodius had a plan. He approached Cato, declaring that he was the perfect man to undertake the annexation of Cyprus. After all, he was the most upright of all the Romans, and now he could prove his purity on Cyprus, where there would be an abundance of temptations for corruption. Cato alone was worthy of the task, and thus Clodius offered him the honor of this special commission. Cato, of course, knew it was no honor, but a trap, and told Clodius as much. Clodius cheekily replied, "If you don't think of it as an honor, consider it a punishment!" He went before the Plebeian Assembly and had them pass a law that appointed Cato as the official in charge of annexing Cyprus. Cato went, in obedience to the law. Before he left, he had warned Cicero against taking any steps that would lead to civil strife and bloodshed, declaring Cicero could once again be the savior of Rome. Shortly afterward, however, Cicero was made an exile of it.

The Wars in Gaul

Caesar was already in Gaul when Clodius began his attack on Cicero. Thanks to his consulship and coalition with Pompey and Crassus, he had special legislation passed that gave him proconsular authority over two provinces, Cisalpine Gaul and Illyricum. When the governor of Transalpine Gaul died, Pompey pushed forward legislation transferring command of that

CAESAR'S CAMPAIGNS IN GAUL 58-51 BC

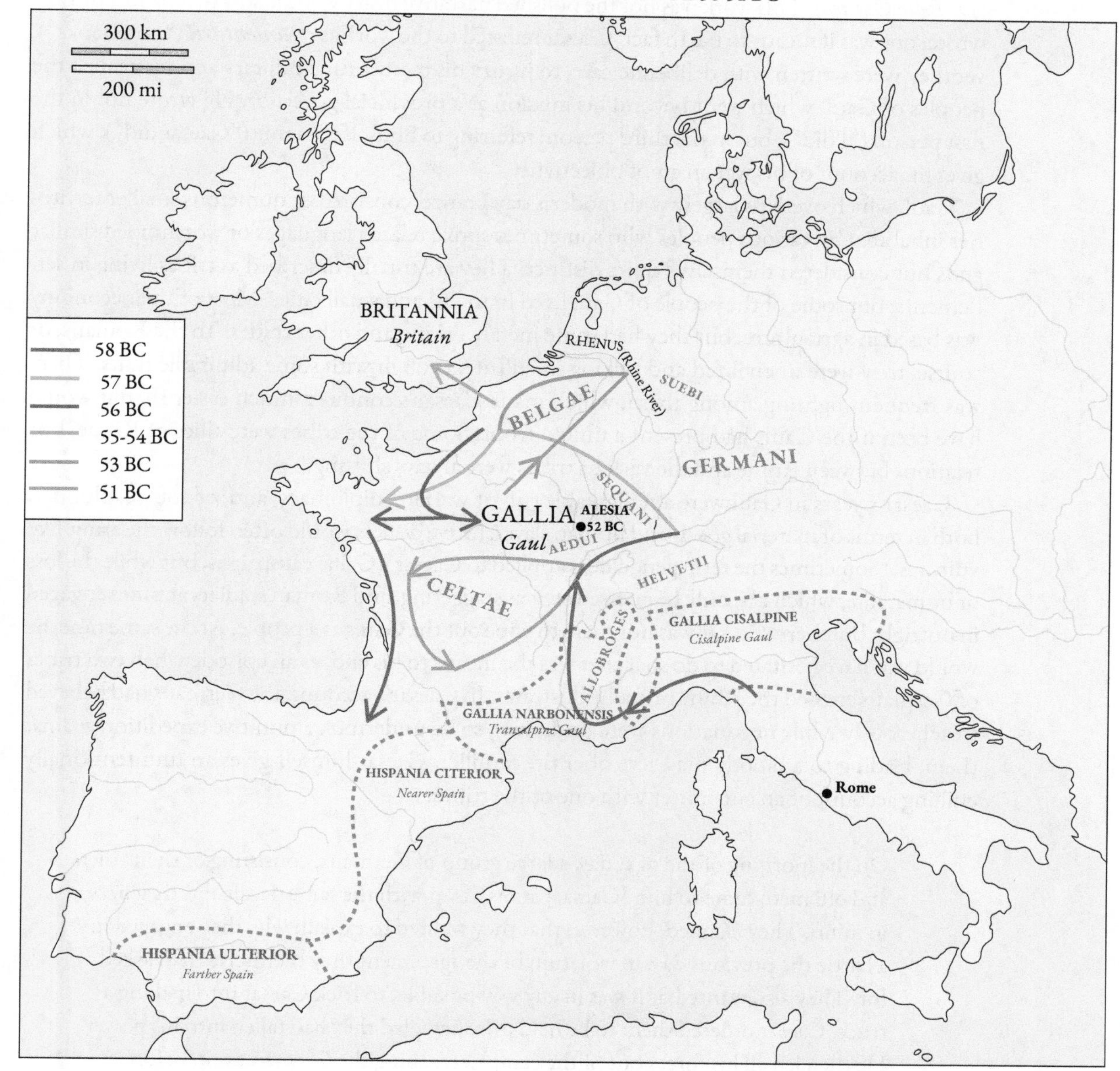

FIG. 11.3 **Gaul.**

province to Caesar as well. Caesar would have command of four legions and had the authority to levy new troops. He would spend the next six years campaigning throughout Gaul, amassing wealth and glory for himself more than for the republic. Much of our information about Caesar's Gallic campaign comes from his own hand, in a book he wrote known as *The Gallic War*

(*De Bello Gallico*). This work was not the polished narrative history of the sort that Sallust or Livy wrote, nor was it meant to be. In fact, Caesar referred to the work as *commentarii* ("notebooks"), yet they were written with deliberate care, to justify his many brutal military actions against the peoples of Gaul, which went beyond his mission as a provincial governor. He wrote not in the first person ("I did"), but in the third person, referring to himself by name ("Caesar did"), which gives his account of his war an air of objectivity.

Gaul, which overlaps largely with modern-day France, consisted of numerous smaller territories inhabited by various peoples who sometimes spoke related languages or worshipped similar gods but considered themselves quite distinct. They are usually described as tribes living in settlements, but some of the people of Gaul lived in towns and small cities. Most of their economy was based in agriculture, but they had some metalworking and other trades. To the Romans, of course, they were uncivilized and lacking in culture, though with some admirable traits. There was frequent fighting among them, which made Caesar's conquest much easier than it would have been if the Gauls had present a united front. Some of the tribes were allies of Rome, but relations between Rome and the various tribes were always shifting.

Caesar's years in Gaul were a remarkable run of warfare, diplomacy, and, of course, plunder, both in terms of material goods and human slaves. (Slave dealers would often follow the army, like vultures.) Sometimes the term genocide is applied to Caesar's Gallic campaigns, but while the loss of human life, which can only be guessed at, was staggering, and Roman soldiers at times engaged in outright butchery, Caesar was not there to wipe out the Gauls as a people. At the same time, he would not have hesitated to do so if that was the means to his end, as an episode when two tribes of Germans crossed the Rhine brutally illustrates. In Caesar's account, the Germans had behaved treacherously while negotiations were underway, so he undertook a punitive expedition against them, leading to a bloody massacre of entire families. Caesar himself gives an unintentionally chilling account of an encounter with one of the tribes:

> On the morning of the next day, a large group of Germans, consisting of their rulers and old men, came to him [Caesar] at his camp with the same deceit and treachery in mind. They claimed, however, that they wanted to explain why they engaged in a battle the previous day, in violation of the agreement they themselves had asked for. They also wanted, if it was in any way possible, to trick Caesar into making a truce. Caesar ordered them to be held prisoner, glad they had fallen into his power. He then led all his forces out of the camp ... reaching the German camp before they realized what was happening. Alarmed by our sudden arrival when their own commanders were away, they had no time to get organized or grab their weapons ... our soldiers, angered by their treachery the day before, rushed into the camp. Some Germans who did grab their weapons held out against our soldiers for a short time ... but the rest of the people, boys and women, ran away, scattering in every direction. Caesar sent the cavalry in pursuit. When the Germans saw that their families were being killed, they threw down their weapons, abandoned their military standards,

Translated from Julius Caesar, *The Gallic Wars*, 2008.

> and fled from their camp. When they reached the place where the Meuse and the Rhine rivers flowed together, the surviving Germans, with no hope of escape and so many of them killed, threw themselves into the river. There they died, overcome by fear, exhaustion, and the strong current. (Caesar, *The Gallic War* 4.13-14)

Caesar emphasizes the "treachery" and "deceit" of these people as a justification for slaughtering them, including unarmed women and children. As well, he often writes as if he is defending Gauls from other invading tribes. Some of Caesar's actions were simply to demonstrate Roman might. For example, he built a massive bridge over the Rhine river, and when he crossed spent only 18 days in German territory. He also later invaded Britain, the first Roman commander to do so. The invasion did not lead to any real practical benefit, but it made for excellent propaganda. (Britain would not be conquered until over one hundred years later, when it was made a province under the emperor Claudius). Not all Romans were convinced by Caesar's justifications for his actions or believed the glory and wealth he acquired in the name of Rome balanced out the means he used to get it. Cato even proposed that Caesar be handed over to the Germans as a war criminal.

The climax of Caesar's Gallic campaign was the Battle of Alesia in 52 BC, waged against one of the most remarkable Gallic leaders. Vercingetorix, as this leader was named (pronounced vur-sin-GE-tor-icks), attempted a coordinated rebellion of several tribes against the Romans, coming close to unifying the peoples of Gaul against the Romans as their common foe. When confronted by the overwhelming power of the Roman legions, he turned to guerilla warfare with some success. After one particular defeat at the hands of Caesar, he encouraged his people to keep their spirits up and promised that no one would be able to stand up to them once the other Gauls joined together. Caesar himself gives a report of this speech:

> On the following day, when the council had been called together, Vercingetorix consoled them and encouraged them. They should not feel at all dejected, he said, nor be worried at the defeat. The Romans had not been victorious in courage or in combat, but only won through their skill in deceit and trickery, which the Gauls themselves had no experience in. They were mistaken if they expected everyone to always be successful in war. It was not his decision to defend Aviacus, as they themselves could bear witness. It was the carelessness of the Biturgi and the slavish obedience of the other Gauls that caused this setback. He would soon remedy this to their advantage. He would work hard to reunify the tribes that were not in harmony with the rest of the Gauls, and make one policy for all Gaul. Once Gaul was united, not even the whole world could resist. And he had already nearly brought this about. In the meantime, he thought it fair that for the sake of their common safety they agree to begin fortifying their camps in order to more easily hold out against sudden attacks by the enemy. (Caesar, *The Gallic War* 7.29)

Caesar eventually surrounded Vercingetorix in the town of Alesia, building a wall around the town to put it under siege. At the same time, he had to build a wall to his rear, to protect his forces from attacks by Vercingetorix's allies. The Romans besieging Alesia were themselves under siege, and Caesar's troops were within a double wall, much like a donut. The Romans first defeated the Gallic troops surrounding them. The enemy, still within the walls of Alesia, including Vercingetorix, were unaware of the Roman victory until they saw Romans carrying bloody Gallic armor into their camp. Vercingetorix eventually surrendered, riding out on his best horse and wearing his most beautiful armor. He rode in a circle around Caesar, who remained seated, then leapt down from his horse, removed his armor, and sat motionless at Caesar's feet until he was taken into custody. He would remain a prisoner at Rome for six years, until he could be displayed in Caesar's triumph of 46 BC.

FIG. 11.4 A statue of Vercingetorix at Alise-Saine-Reine in east-central France, where the battle of Alesia may have taken place. The statue was erected in 1865, under Napoleon III, as a monument to French nationalism. The French inscription, an inflated version of a line from Vercingetorix's speech in Caesar's *Gallic War*, reads, "Gaul united, forming one nation, inspired by the same spirit, can defy the world."

Things Fall Apart—Again

While Caesar remained in Gaul, the political situation in Rome began to deteriorate. There were public demonstrations against the three-man alliance, and someone claimed to have information that some *optimates* were planning to assassinate Pompey. This informer, however, was himself murdered under mysterious circumstances. Then there were rumblings in the senate about whether Caesar's laws during his consulship were legal, and a tribune of the plebs even suggested putting him on trial, which is what Caesar feared. As long as he held an official position, however, he was safe from prosecution. Moreover, Clodius was immensely popular, thanks in part to a law he had passed that provided free grain for the people of Rome, the first time grain was made free instead of sold at a low price. With Crassus's backing, Clodius continued to create problems for the *optimates*, organizing armed bands of supporters who made political street violence a part of everyday life at Rome. Clodius also started to attack Pompey, and Pompey and Crassus fell back into their mutual hostility. At one point, Pompey was forced to hide in his house from Clodius's gangs.

Now Pompey began to work for Cicero's recall from exile, in which he succeeded by receiving guarantees that Cicero would not work against the interests of the three-man coalition. Caesar also gave his blessings to his return. Cicero made a grand entrance into Rome in 57, receiving praise and admiration from numerous supporters, and soon after managed to prosecute Clodius for the destruction of his house. Clodius's free grain distributions had won him the support of the plebs in the city but contributed to food shortages, leading to a riot in Rome. In order to meet this crisis, Pompey was given yet another extraordinary command, this time for five years in charge of the grain supply throughout the Roman empire. The *optimates* opposed this command, just as some had opposed Pompey's commands in the previous decade. Clodius was also in the opposition, claiming the food shortage was a ploy to give Pompey more power, but Cicero, repaying Pompey for supporting his return, spoke in favor of it. However, as he had in his earlier commands, Pompey, with fifteen legates under his command, used his organizational abilities to quickly end the crisis. He collected so much grain there was enough left over for people outside of Italy.

Rome's annexation of Cyprus, undertaken by Cato with his usual scrupulous behavior, also had an impact on domestic politics. In 57, Ptolemy XII had been driven out of Alexandria, in part for allowing the Romans to take Cyprus, and fled to Rome where he and his money might find a welcome reception. Ptolemy sought Pompey's help, while his opponents in Egypt, fearing Ptolemy would convince the Romans to restore him to Egypt, sent an embassy of 100 men to represent their side and ensure Ptolemy would not be let off the hook. Following in the footsteps of Jugurtha, Ptolemy resorted to extensive bribery of Roman senators and assassinations of the Egyptian ambassadors opposed to him. Ptolemy wanted the senate to appoint Pompey to a special command to restore him to the throne of Egypt, but for the optimate senators this special command for Pompey was unacceptable in the current political situation. They found a useful oracle in the Sibylline Books, which the Romans had consulted for centuries at moments of crisis, and blocked the appointment on religious grounds. Ptolemy XII was forced to flee Rome in 56, but if he was done with Rome, he was not done yet with Roman assistance.

The Roman governor of Syria in 55 was Aulus Gabinius, who as tribune of the plebs in the previous decade had sponsored the law that gave Pompey his command against the pirates. Backed by Pompey, Caesar, and Crassus, he had been consul in 58, receiving Syria as his province to govern after his consulship. Stymied by the senate in Rome, Ptolemy XII sought Gabinius's assistance, for which he had Pompey's blessing. For the massive sum of 10,000 talents, Gabinius used the troops at his disposal as provincial governor to restore Ptolemy XII to the throne in Egypt, and even left a garrison of troops there for support. (A "talent" is a measure of money, roughly 60 pounds of gold or silver. In buying power, 1 gold talent was roughly the equivalent of the pay received for ten years of skilled labor.) Gabinius undertook this mission in complete defiance of the law, which prohibited a governor from leading an army outside of his province. In fact, this was considered an act of treason. There was also the matter of bribery. But Gabinius's real crime, at least in the eyes of the *publicani*, was taking the profits of tax collection in his province for himself. Although Gabinius had broken some serious laws, it was when he lost political support back in Rome that he became vulnerable to criminal prosecution. Gabinius was acquitted on the charge of treason (*maiestas*), but was found guilty of corruption for his bribery, even though Cicero unhappily defended him at Pompey's insistence. He went into exile and would not return until recalled by Caesar in 49. What is most telling in the actions of Gabinius is his willingness to act as a mercenary to a foreign ruler, in total disregard to the policy of the senate or the law. In a way, he represents the type of behavior that was becoming more the norm and makes the future actions of Pompey and Caesar less exceptional.

Since relations between Caesar, Pompey, and Crassus had become strained, in 56 they decided to meet in person at the town of Luca in northern Italy, a midway point between Rome and Gaul (modern-day Lucca, just outside Pisa). At this meeting, they renewed their alliance and made sure each got what they wanted. Pompey and Crassus would once again be colleagues as consuls for the following year of 55. (Some of Caesar's soldiers on leave in Rome conveniently drove away the supporters of their opponents during the election.) Caesar's proconsular authority in Gaul would be renewed for another five-year term. Pompey and Crassus would also receive five-year proconsular commands after their consulship, Pompey in Spain and Crassus in Syria. Pompey, however, took the unusual and unprecedented step of governing his province *in absentia*—meaning he remained in Rome while governor of Spain. His reasons for doing so are not entirely clear, but it did allow one of the three men to keep an eye on events in Rome, and Pompey still could recruit an army in Spain. Crassus, however, was eager to head to his province and wage war against the Parthians, a people who inhabited modern-day Iran and Turkey, and would prove to be a thorn in Rome's side for generations to come.

Despite this renewed agreement, the coalition of Caesar, Pompey, and Crassus began to fall apart. First, in 54, Julia, Pompey's wife and Caesar's daughter, died in childbirth along with her infant. Pompey seemed to have developed a deep emotional attachment to Julia and was by all accounts deeply saddened by her death. For political purposes, their union, especially if it produced a child, might have drawn Caesar and Pompey closer together, or at least prevented them from open conflict. Caesar proposed a new marriage alliance, with Caesar marrying Pompey's daughter and Pompey marrying Caesar's grandniece (both women already had husbands and would be compelled to divorce them). Pompey rejected the offer, less because of his grief over Julia than his suspicion of Caesar's power. The following year, in 53, Crassus suffered a catastrophic defeat in his campaign against the Parthians at the Battle of Carrhae, on the border of modern-day Turkey and Syria. Crassus was killed together with his son, and Crassus's severed head was used as a stage prop in a Greek tragedy put on at the Parthian court. This was a horrific enough outcome, but to many even more horrific was the loss of the legionary standards to the Parthians (their recovery thirty years later through diplomatic means was a celebrated event). Pompey ended up marrying the widow of Crassus's son, which further distanced him from Caesar and his political supporters.

With Crassus dead, Caesar and Pompey began to behave as rivals rather than partners. The situation at Rome deteriorated even further. Clodius's supporters continued to create havoc but were now opposed by other street gangs. One of these was headed by Titus Pomponius Milo, a former wrestler and tribune of the plebs who supported the optimate cause. Clodius had attempted to prosecute Milo in 56 for committing acts of violence when Milo was defending his own house against Clodius's gang, and somewhat ironically charged him with maintaining an armed band. Even more ironically, the trial ended without any resolution because of the violence that erupted around it. Elections also became violent affairs, rife with bribery, leading to battles in the courts and in the streets. In 54, there were four candidates for consul, and three were charged with bribery. As a result, at the start of 53 there were no consuls or any other magistrates except tribunes of the plebs. There was talk of appointing a dictator, but instead Pompey was given the authority to hold elections. Though he managed to do so, the consuls who were elected that year once again could not manage to hold elections, and once again there would be no magistrates except tribunes for 52. Needless to say, the street violence intensified, and at the beginning of 52, just outside Rome on the Appian Way Clodius and Milo, who had both run for office, came to blows with their gangs. Clodius was beaten to death. His outraged supporters took his corpse to the Forum and rioted, burning down the senate house.

Given the disorder, there were renewed calls for a dictator to restore stability, and Pompey was the natural choice. Many of the optimate senators, however, found this idea unacceptable, as it would signal to them the end point to which the formation of the "First Triumvirate" was headed—the return to a kind of monarchy. Cato in particular was opposed to naming a dictator, but even he recognized the need for a strong hand to bring order back to the streets of Rome. As a compromise, Pompey was made "sole consul" for 52, another kind of innovation within republican tradition. One of his first acts was to prosecute those responsible for the violence, and he did not make an exception for his supporter Milo. Even though the great Cicero was defending him, in this case the golden tongue of Rome's most famous orator failed him. Pompey's armed soldiers surrounded the court to maintain order and to demonstrate who was in charge. Cicero was so frightened by their presence that he lost his nerve and forgot his speech. Milo was convicted and went into exile.

Pompey's Grip on Rome

Pompey eased concerns about his sole consulship by holding elections later in the year, and his father-in-law was elected as his colleague for the last months of 52. But while Pompey managed to quiet the streets of Rome, he also passed legislation that strengthened his position in relation to Caesar. One was a law against bribery that was retroactive to 70, meaning it could be used against Caesar for actions he took during his climb to power in the 60s. Another law set a mandatory five-year waiting period between holding a political office and governing a province. This too was retroactive and could be applied to Caesar's command in Gaul, meaning he could be removed at once. As soon as Caesar became a private citizen, he could be prosecuted on any number of charges, a fact of which he was well aware. Pompey's own governorship of Spain could also be subject to this law, but Pompey made sure a special law was passed to extend his command in Spain for another five years. Finally, a law was passed that made it even more difficult to run for office without being present in Rome. Even though a law similar to this had earlier forced Caesar to choose between a triumph and consulship, the new law would compel Caesar to put down his command before he held another office, since as soon as he crossed the border of his province he would no longer hold *imperium*. In this period when he would be a private citizen, he would be liable to legal prosecution. Pompey gave Caesar a special exception to this law, but he made clear that Caesar's fate was in his hands.

Caesar was certainly nobody's fool and would not be outmaneuvered by Pompey. He had ten legions at his command in Gaul, not a long march from Rome. And in addition to thousands of loyal soldiers, he had plenty of loyal officers and supporters who would begin to hold office in Rome and counter Pompey's efforts, as well as the efforts of *optimates* who feared Caesar more than they supported Pompey. It was clear by now that the two rivals were locked in a battle for supremacy at Rome, and it was only if their conflict could not be settled in the Forum, it would be settled on the battlefield.

The Latin Language

Of Rome's many legacies to modern Europe and the Western world, perhaps the most profound and lasting is its language. Of course, Latin is essentially a dead language, though it is spoken at the Vatican and by a growing number of proponents of teaching Latin as a living language. However, it was a living language for over 2,500 years, and even in the early modern period, scientists, philosophers, mathematicians, and other scholars wrote their works in Latin in order to make them accessible to speakers of other languages. Even though many people in Europe and beyond were multilingual, one could not assume that intellectuals in other countries knew English, German, French, Italian, Spanish, or Russian, but every educated person would be assumed to have a knowledge of Latin. For example, Isaac Newton wrote his groundbreaking *Principia Mathematica*, published in 1687, in Latin. Latin was, to use a Latin term, the *lingua franca* of intellectuals in Europe and around the globe. (The term *lingua franca*, "Frankish tongue," means a mish-mash of multiple languages that can be used by a diverse group in which there is no one single language spoken by everyone, such as sailors from around the Mediterranean.)

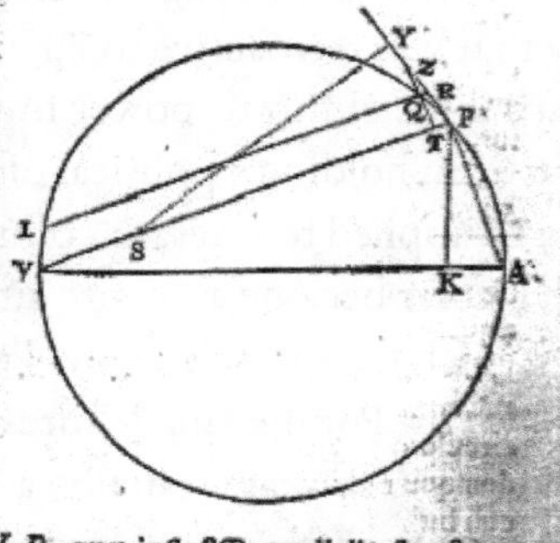

PROPOSITIO VII. PROBLEMA II.

Gyretur corpus in circumferentia circuli, requiritur lex vis centripetæ tendentis ad punctum quodcunque datum.

Eſto circuli circumferentia *VQPA*; punctum datum, ad quod vis ceu ad centrum ſuum tendit, *S*; corpus in circumferentia latum *P*; locus proximus, in quem movebitur *Q*; & circuli tangens ad locum priorem *PRZ*. Per punctum *S* ducatur chorda *PV*; & acta circuli diametro *VA*, jungatur *AP*; & ad *SP* demittatur perpendiculum *QT*, quod productum occurrat tangenti *PR* in *Z*; ac denique per punctum *Q* agatur *LR*, quæ ipſi *SP* parallella ſit, & occurrat tum circulo in *L*, tum tangenti *PZ* in *R*. Et ob ſimilia triangula *ZQR*, *ZTP*, *VPA*; erit *RP quad.* hoc eſt *QRL* ad *QT quad.*

8

FIG. 11.5 A page from a 1726 edition of Newton's *Philosophiae Naturalis Principia Mathematica* (*Mathematical Foundations of Natural Philosophy*), on centripetal force.

After the slow fragmentation of the Roman empire and the emergence of new kingdoms and peoples in Europe and around the Mediterranean, Latin was still very much a living language, and remained so throughout the Middle Ages. However, the everyday form of Latin had long diverged from the "proper" Latin that was learned in schools rather than on the streets. The Latin spoken by everyday people is known as "vulgar Latin." We do not have a great deal of evidence for vulgar Latin today, in part because those who spoke it would not write it, even if they were literate. "Vulgar" today usually means rude, crude, or obscene, but the root of the word is the Latin *vulgus*, which simply means "the people" (though there is some obscene literary Latin). The Latin Bible translated by Saint Jerome at the end of the fourth century AD, which was the standard bible of the Middle Ages, is known as the Vulgate, since it was produced for people who could not read the original Hebrew and Greek.

Although it is a complex history, the "Romance" languages of Europe developed out of vulgar Latin. The Romance languages are French, Italian, Spanish, and Portuguese, and take their name not directly from Rome or Roman, but from the term for literature written in the everyday speech of the people (such as early forms of French, Spanish, or Italian). These works of fiction, often involving tales of knights and courtly love, were known as "romances." Thus, the German word for a novel, once considered a low form of literature, is *Roman*, and in French it is the same, *roman*. The "vulgar" language of this low-brow literature came to be known as romance, and the term also lives on in the very popular and formulaic paperback books known as romance novels. One of the early literary masterpieces in a "vulgar" language was Dante's *Divine Comedy*, best known for the first of its three parts, *Inferno*, which describes the poet's journey through the circles of hell with the Latin poet Vergil as his guide. Dante's use of Italian to write a major epic, rather than a "romance," would have been shocking to some intellectuals. Dante, in fact, had started to write a Latin treatise, *De vulgari eloquentia*, about the relationship of everyday Italian to Latin.

Latin also influenced other languages, either directly or indirectly through the Romance languages. English is not a Romance language, but roughly one third of English words have Latin roots, in part because of the French influence following the Norman conquest in 1066. A knowledge of Latin can be a tremendous help in building vocabulary and recognizing unfamiliar words. Many English words are formed from Latin prefixes and suffixes; *pre, de, ante, sub, post, in, ex, ob*, are some of the most common. An ability to recognize Latin suffixes in English words can also be helpful. For example, *-ance* and *-ence* are from the Latin *-ntia*, a suffix attached to a verbal root to form abstract nouns, representing an idea or concept, as in "difference" (when things differ, *differo*) or "intelligence" (understanding, the abstract notion from the verb to understand, *intelligo*). The common word ending *-ous* comes from a Latin suffix *-osus*, which means "filled with," such as gaseous, dangerous, or nebulous (from *nebula*, Latin for cloud). In addition to everyday words, Latin is particularly helpful with scientific and technical terms in chemistry, physics, biology, anatomy, pharmacology, botany and many others (most also have ancient Greek mixed in). For example, many symbols from the periodic table of elements might appear confusing, if not downright absurd, but some are from the Latin names of the metals. For example, *aurum* is Latin for gold, so the symbol for gold on the period table is Au.

Other examples:

Silver	Ar	*argentum* (cf. French *argent*, money)

Lead	Pb	*plumbum* (cf. plumber, from lead pipes).
Iron	Fe	*ferrum* (cf. Italian *ferrovia*, railroad, lit. "iron road")
Copper	Cu	*cuprum*
Tin	Sn	*stannum*

Moreover, the structure of a Latin sentence, and the styles in which various Latin authors wrote, had a deep impact on the way that later writers in English and other languages wrote. Clear and logical, except when it does not wish to be, Latin demands a close attention to detail that modern languages often do without. Software coders and math majors often have an easier time with Latin grammar than speakers of modern Romance languages, who are sometimes fooled into believing they know what a Latin sentence says.

Latin's influence runs deeper than this, however, since with the vocabulary comes ways of thinking about the world. A Latin word is not just a word, but an idea, and if we wish to know why many people think the way they do (or did), knowing something of the Latin language and its history is crucial (crucial, from Latin *crux*, "cross, cross-shaped," as in the point where two roads cross). Many Latin philosophical terms, which themselves were attempts to translate Greek philosophical terms, are now common terms in English. For example, "essence" (*essentia*, from the verb to be, *esse*) and "substance" (*substantia*, formed from the prefix *sub-* under, and the verb *stare*, "to stand" or simply "to exist").

Latin is also found in common abbreviations:

cf.	*confer*	compare
etc.	*et cetera*	and the rest
et al.	*et alii* (or *alia*)	and others
e.g.	*exempli gratia*	for the sake of example
ibid.	*ibidem*	in the same place
i.e.	*id est*	that is
op. cit.	*opus citatum*	work cited
sc.	*scilicet* (*scire licet*)	namely, that is ("it is permitted to know")
viz.	*videlicet* (*videre licet*)	namely, that is ("it is permitted to see")
vs.	*versus*	against
CV	*curriculum vitae*	"course of life"; a document listing someone's credentials and qualifications, often submitted as part of a job application

Common Latin words and phrases, some of which are from the world of law:

ad hoc	"for this"	Usually in reference to a temporary measure, as an ad hoc committee, which is formed not as a permanent or standing committee but as one formed to address a single issue in a determined time.
agenda	"things to be done"	A Latin verbal form that simply means "what has to be done," and now refers to a list of items to be covered in a meeting, or something that someone wants to be done (as in a "hidden agenda").
alibi	"elsewhere"	A Latin word that now refers to the claim of a person to have been somewhere else when a crime was committed, thus demonstrating their innocence.
bona fide	"in good faith"	On its own, it means that something is genuine or real. Often refers to someone's credentials, or the information listed on a CV, meaning it was made without any attempt to deceive.
cui bono?	"for whom is it good?" or "who benefits"?	A terse phrase that is often used in legal contexts, suggesting that the guilty party is the one that benefits from the crime.
ego	"I"	The Latin first-person pronoun, now taken to mean one's sense of personal identity, and in particular one's self-esteem or self-worth, often with reference to an overly inflated pride. This word was used to translate Sigmund Freud's *Das Ich* (the "I"), and so ego is often associated with Freud's psychoanalytic theories, along with superego and id. *id* is just the Latin pronoun "it," a translation of Freud's original *Das Es* (the "it").
ergo	"therefore"	Used in English to represent the logical conclusion to an argument. One famous example if from the sixteenth-century French philosopher Descartes, who famously wrote *cogito, ergo sum* ("I think, therefore I am.").
habeas corpus	"you may have the body"	This is a fundamental principle of American law. A "writ of habeas corpus" is a document that requires that a person under arrest be brought into court to secure their release unless grounds can be shown for continued detention. *Habeas corpus* allows for someone charged with a crime to be released on bail.
memorandum	"something to be remembered"	Usually found in the shortened form "memo," referring to a document that contains important information. A form similar to *agenda*, and from a root where we get the English word "memory."
prima facie	"on first appearance"	The Latin word *facies* is related to the English word "face," and this phrase means "on first impression" or "on the surface."
pro bono	"for the good"	A shortened form of *pro bono publico* ("for the public good"), referring to work done free of charge. Most often used in reference to legal work undertaken for those who cannot afford or a lawyer or on behalf of a charity.
quid pro quo	"something for something"	This phrase means there has been an exchange of favors, and often has a negative sense in reference to corruption or a criminal act.
re		Found in email headings, a form of the Latin noun *res*, the same word that forms republic, *res publica. Res* means a "thing, matter, business," so *re* simply means "in the matter of, in regard to." Court cases often use the fuller phrase *in re* ("in the matter of ...").
vice versa	"with a change in turn"	In reference to reversing the order of items in a statement. Examples: "Mike finds Xi attractive, but not vice versa." (That is, Xi does not find Mike attractive.) "A triangle is made of lines, but not vice versa. (A line is not made of triangles.)

Credits

Fig. 11.1: Source: https://commons.wikimedia.org/wiki/File:Gaius_Iulius_Caesar_(Vatican_Museum).jpg.

Fig. 11.2: Copyright © by Andrea Pancotti (CC BY-SA 4.0) at https://commons.wikimedia.org/wiki/File:Bona_Dea_Marble_Statue_with_Epigraph.jpg.

Fig. 11.3: Adapted from d-maps.com.

Fig. 11.4: Copyright © by Myrabella (CC BY-SA 4.0) at https://commons.wikimedia.org/wiki/File:Alise-Sainte-Reine_statue_Vercingetorix_par_Millet_2.jpg.

Fig. 11.5: Source: https://commons.wikimedia.org/wiki/File:Principia_Page_1726.jpg.

CHAPTER 12

The Republic Is Dead. Long Live the Republic!

FIG. 12.1 A coin issued by Brutus to commemorate the assassination of Julius Caesar. The obverse has Brutus's portrait, with BRUT IMP (Brutus Imperator; the B and T are missing) and the name of the moneyer L. PLAET. CEST (Lucius Plaetius Cestius). On the reverse are daggers and a cap worn by slaves when they are freed, with the inscription EID MART (Ides of March).

Overview

The rift between Pompey and Caesar intensified following the deaths of Crassus and Julia, exacerbated by the stubbornness of their supporters. The optimate senators, in particular, refused to yield any ground to Caesar, though Caesar's offers of political compromise with Pompey may have only been a political ploy to provide a justification for following through on his ambitions. Civil war had longed seemed inevitable, and it became a reality when Caesar crossed the border of his province into Italy at the head of an army. Within a few years, he had defeated Pompey and eliminated other resistance, becoming supreme ruler of Rome with unprecedented powers couched in traditional forms. His time in power was short-lived, and his assassination by a group of senators often marks the end of the republic in history books. Caesar, however, had perhaps already recognized that the republic was dead. Yet in another sense, the Roman Republic continues to live on as an inspiration, an ideal, and a warning.

Timeline

49	Caesar crosses the Rubicon
48	Defeat of Pompey at Pharsalus
46	Defeat at Thapsus, suicide of Cato
44	Assassination of Julius Caesar on the Ides of March

March to War

After the political turmoil and irregular elections of the late 50s, Pompey held onto his position of preeminence in the city of Rome, in large part because the *optimates* saw him as their last best hope against Caesar. Caesar's provincial command would end on March 1, 50, and he planned on his election to the consulship of 49, which would begin on January 1. In the nine months between those two dates, he would be subject to criminal prosecution, and his opponents were eagerly looking forward to the opportunity to bring charges. Caesar's official position was under attack, and already in 51 BC, a consul had attempted to remove Caesar from his command in Gaul. Loss of his command would mean loss of his legions, at least legally, though many of his soldiers would be loyal to him, not to the senate. Caesar had already lost two legions when the senate requested that Pompey and Caesar each supply a legion, purportedly for a war to defend the province of Syria against the Parthians. Since Pompey had loaned Caesar one of his legions, he forced Caesar to return that one as his contribution. These two legions were not sent to the east, but were kept near Rome. However, before Caesar released these legions, he presented each soldier with a substantial gift of money, ensuring that they would remain well disposed to him should it come down to a question of following him or Pompey. Moreover, Caesar spent some of the vast funds now at his disposal to create a favorable outcome in the upcoming elections, which were particularly important since the censor, Appius Claudius Pulcher, could use the powers of that office to remove supporters of Caesar from the senate. Caesar purchased the loyalty of one of the consuls of 50, who needed the money to complete the reconstruction of the Basilica Aemilia in the Forum, and also of a tribune of the plebs, Gaius Scribonius Curio. Curio's father had fiercely opposed Caesar, and Curio himself had optimate leanings, but he was in serious debt and welcomed the opportunity to be well compensated for political services to Caesar.

At the beginning of 50 BC, the senate began to debate what should be done about this looming crisis, and while some hoped to avoid another civil war, others almost seemed willing to risk a military conflict between Caesar and Pompey rather than compromise in any way. On March 1, the consul who was not paid off by Caesar proposed that Caesar resign from his command immediately. Curio, proving he was a wise investment, vetoed the bill as tribune of the plebs. However, Curio offered to withdraw his veto on the condition that Pompey give up his five-year command of Spain, which had not yet expired. Pompey rejected this suggestion, so the senate offered as a compromise to extend Caesar's command until November of 50, but at Caesar's request Curio vetoed this proposal as well.

Since neither Caesar nor Pompey wished to be at a disadvantage in relation to the other, both of them would need to give up their provincial commands at the same time. Curio proposed just such a measure, and the senators voted for it in a landslide, 370–22. While this seems like it should have put an end to the matter, and it appeared a peaceful solution was in sight, neither Caesar nor Pompey wished to give up their commands, nor did either one of them trust the other to do so. Curio was praised for this proposal, but it is likely that he knew it would never be put into effect. In fact, it broke down over mutual suspicions and haggling over who would lay down his command first. The proposals and compromises put forward to end the tension between Pompey and Caesar were as much about propaganda as practical policy. Each side wanted to portray the other as unwilling to make reasonable compromises, and Caesar needed to present himself as the reasonable peacemaker before he invaded Italy at the head of an army.

A poet writing a century later under the emperor Nero neatly summed up the rivalry between Pompey and Caesar, suggesting why no real compromise was possible: "Caesar could not bear to have a superior, and Pompey could not tolerate an equal." (Lucan, *Pharsalia* 1.120-125) We do not have writings by Pompey, and thus he is at a disadvantage in the history of this time, since we do not get to hear his own voice. Caesar won this battle over its history since in addition to his history of the Gallic War, Caesar also wrote his own account of the Civil War. Though he could reasonably be blamed for beginning the war, Caesar portrays his actions as necessary, and he paints an unflattering portrait of his opponents, which are not necessarily inaccurate. Writing about himself in the third person, he had an explanation for Pompey's behavior in a debate about what the two men should do with their troops:

> Pompey was spurred on by Caesar's enemies, and since he did not want anyone to be his equal, he had rejected any friendly relations with Caesar and became friends with the enemies they once had in common. Pompey had forced most of these on Caesar when he was married to Julia. Also, Pompey was upset at the harsh criticism he received for diverting the two legions on their way to Asia and Syria to his own quest for political supremacy, and so he was eager for a fight. (Caesar, *Civil War* 1.4)

Caesar highlights that Pompey held onto control of two legions in Rome for his own purposes, even though they were supposed to be deployed in the eastern Mediterranean—an act that certainly looks bad, especially if Pompey claims to be defending the authority of the senate. The source of the "harsh criticism" Pompey received is left unnamed, but as written does not come from Caesar himself. The real message behind Caesar's portrait of Pompey is that Pompey is no leader, but is rather being led—it is Caesar's enemies who spur him on, and the criticism from others makes him eager for a fight. Caesar subtly suggests Pompey is not making his own rational decisions, but his emotions are being manipulated.

Caesar likely had a good idea of the optimate reaction to Curio's proposal. On the day after it was made, the optimate consul hostile to Caesar called a special meeting in the hopes the senate would issue the *senatus ultimum consultum* for use against Caesar. Once again, the motion met with the Curio's veto, at which point the consul simply urged Pompey to lead his troops against Caesar, though there was no senate authorization to do so. In a sense, the consul was urging Pompey to act in the way he feared Caesar would act—a version of fighting fire with fire. Caesar then offered yet another compromise: He would release eight of the ten legions under his command, keeping only two until he was elected consul. At the same time, Marcus Antonius (or Antony), one of the tribunes of the plebs, attempted to pass a motion that the troops intended for Syria, which Pompey had detained in Rome, must now be sent there. In addition, it would not be permitted to levy troops in Italy. There was no concealing that this was an attempt to weaken Pompey, effectively stripping him of his command without formally doing so. He would be a commander with no soldiers to command. The time for compromise was nearing an end, especially since the consuls elected for 49 were enemies of Caesar and would do what they could to destroy him.

On January 1, 49, a letter from Caesar was read aloud to the senate. It was really an ultimatum disguised as an offer to make accommodations. He declared that the senate should not try to take away from him a provincial command that the people, represented by the assembly, had given him, suggesting the senate was usurping the authority of the people of Rome. However, if the senate would not allow him to keep his command, then they should force Pompey to resign his command at the same time. If neither of these options was satisfactory, then the senate should expect war. Of course, Caesar felt confident that even if both of them disbanded their troops, he could gather his veterans to his side much more quickly and easily than Pompey could find new recruits to follow him, so he would still have an advantage. Instead, the senate passed a motion that Caesar must relinquish his command at once, well knowing this would never happen. When this motion was yet again vetoed by a tribune of the plebs, the senate bypassed the veto by issuing the *senatus consultum ultimum*. Caesar was declared an enemy of the state. The tribunes who were Caesar's supporters, including Antony, attempted to veto the passage of the SCU but were threatened with their lives. They fled Rome and headed to Caesar, stationed at Ravenna in northeastern Italy, the border of his province of Cisalpine Gaul. He was there, he claimed, awaiting the response to his "very mild demands" in the hope that "out of a sense of human fairness" matters could be brought to a peaceful conclusion.

However, when he realized his "mild demands" were not to be granted, and he sensed events were moving to war rather than peace, he addressed the soldiers of the 13th legion who were with him (he would soon be joined by two legions summoned from Gaul):

> Caesar recalled the constant insults he had suffered at the hands of his enemies. These men, he complained, who out of jealousy belittled his own glory, had now seduced Pompey into error, though he had always been a supporter of Pompey, and aided his political career. He also complained that when armed

> force was used to override a tribune's veto, treating it as a criminal act, a dangerous precedent was introduced into the republic. (Caesar, *Civil War* 1.7)

Caesar seems to go out of his way to excuse Pompey from any direct blame, claiming that he was being led astray by others. Of course, the fact that Pompey could be led astray fits with his portrayal in the passage quoted above. Caesar again suggests he was too much under the influence of others and lacked a will of his own—not a quality one expects in one of Rome's greatest commanders. No one would lead Caesar astray! Caesar also emphasizes that the senate's disregard of the veto by the tribune of the plebs was contrary to the traditions of the republic, unprecedented and intolerable. True, but somewhat ironic coming from Caesar. Nonetheless, he can portray himself as the upholder of the republic's traditions, especially in defending the rights of the tribunes of the plebs, champions of the people of Rome, if not the senate.

The border between Italy and Cisalpine Gaul, and the line between Caesar as legitimate military commander and armed rebel, was a small river known as the Rubicon. In this case, crossing over it at the head of an army was not simply a violation of the law prohibiting governors from leading an army outside their province without permission from the senate. That was a serious enough crime, one committed a few years earlier by Gabinius when he restored Ptolemy XII to Egypt for a tidy sum of money. But when Caesar crossed his provincial boundary, he would enter not just another province, but Italy itself, on a march toward Rome. This was more than *maiestas*, it was tantamount to armed insurrection and an invasion of the republic. When the tribunes arrived from Rome, Caesar may well have believed that a line had already been crossed by the optimate senators who seemed hell-bent on destroying him. If there was to be no compromise at all, no recognition for his extraordinary deeds, no special treatment as had often been granted to others, then there was only one choice to make: destroy or be destroyed. Even so, to cross the Rubicon into Italy was not a simple decision. To save the republic, should he sacrifice himself, relinquish his hard-won prestige and power? But this battle was now bigger than Rome, and bigger than the republic—the entire Mediterranean world was at stake, and so was his place in it. The biographer Suetonius paints the scene of Caesar's momentous step:

> After sunset, he quietly set out with a few others, taking mules from a nearby bakery and harnessing them to a wagon. His torches went out and he lost his way, but at dawn he found a guide and used narrow paths to walk back to the main road. He caught up with his troops at the river Rubicon, which was the boundary of his province. He paused for a while, then realizing the momentous step he was taking turned to those around him and said: "We can still turn back, but once we cross that small bridge everything will be settled by the sword." He was standing there in doubt, when he suddenly received a sign—an amazingly large and beautiful figure appeared, sitting nearby and playing a reed pipe. Shepherds gathered to listen to him, and many of the soldiers left their posts, among whom were some trumpeters. The figure snatched one of their trumpets, ran to the river, and while loudly playing

> the call to war, walked to the other side of the river. At that point Caesar cried out: "We'll take the course the signs of the gods and the false dealing of our enemies show to us. The dice have been thrown!" (Suetonius, *The Deified Julius Caesar* 31-32)

The divine signs again attest to the moment's historical importance. "Crossing the Rubicon" is a phrase that has come to mean passing the point of no return, and this indeed it was. Whether actually spoken by him or not, Caesar's final words before taking this momentous step, "The dice have been thrown!" nicely sums up Caesar's approach. (In Latin, it is *alea iacta est!* Literally, "the die is cast," as it is often translated.) Always cool and calculating, when the time came, he was willing to throw the dice and take his chances. But it was not all luck, and Caesar knew that if he acted with speed, he would have the upper hand over any forces that Pompey and the senate could muster. His immediate objective after crossing was to seize Ariminum (modern Rimini), the first sizeable city south of the Rubicon, and this he did at the beginning of January 49, taking it and those who opposed him by surprise.

The senate's treatment of the tribunes supporting Caesar had provided an excellent pretext for his invasion of Italy, since he could portray himself as standing up for the people of Rome against the tyrannical actions of the senate. When Caesar describes his motives, the treatment of tribunes is one of the reasons he gives for his launching a civil war, but not the only one:

> It was with no evil intent that I left my province, but to defend myself from the insults of my enemies, to restore to their rightful standing [*dignitas*] the tribunes of the plebs who were driven from the state, and to assert my freedom [*libertas*] and the freedom of the Roman people, oppressed by a small faction. (*Civil War* 1.22)

Restoring the tribunes to their rightful place in the Republic takes second place to the personal insults he received from his political opponents. This might seem egotistical and even petty, but to the Romans it would not seem out of place at the head of the list, especially not during the last decades of the Republic. *Dignitas*, a Latin term for one's personal standing and prestige, was a serious matter, and personal attacks would demand revenge. Caesar also deploys the slogan of "liberty," both his own and that of the Roman people. It is, in his presentation, a "small faction" that is acting like a tyrannical oppressor, and he thus places himself in the long tradition of anti-monarchical Republicans. It just happens that in this case, the "small faction" is a large part of the Senate. He is a defender of the *populus Romanus* against the *Senatus*—the Republic, as SPQR, was at war with itself, each side represented by a single individual who achieved power and prestige by leveraging his military prowess.

Running Resistance

Caesar's swift action had the element of surprise. Pompey and others would have expected Caesar to wait for the two legions from Gaul to arrive before he went on the offensive, especially since it was the middle of January. As a result of this calculated throw of the dice, he created a panic in Rome. Senators fled the city, essentially abandoning it to Caesar's supporters, and Pompey himself prudently fled to Brundisium, at the "heel" of Italy and the launch point for Greece and points east. If he was to match Caesar militarily, he needed to gather his forces and his funds, and both of these would be available to him in greater numbers outside of Italy. Thanks to his campaigns in the 60s, he had his connections in the eastern Mediterranean, and because of his governorship of Spain, he could call on troops there. In addition, Pompey would have control of the sea, and there was the potential to blockade Rome, preventing shipments of grain from reaching the city. Pompey's departure from Italy was not running away from a challenge, but a strategic move, even if he had to make it earlier than expected. Many senators, but not all, joined Pompey on the eastern seaboard of Greece, which became the de facto headquarters of the Republican resistance to Caesar. Caesar had marched to Brundisium to prevent Pompey from setting sail for Greece, setting siege to the Pompeian forces there, but when this failed, he knew that an immediate and direct confrontation with Pompey in Greece would be foolhardy. Moreover, Caesar was now in complete control of Italy.

Caesar entered Rome at the end of March 49. This was the first time he had set foot in the city since he departed for Gaul almost a decade earlier. One of his first tasks was to reestablish a government at Rome, and to do so he needed men of standing and prestige. He had already approached Cicero, who unlike many others had wavered about which course of action to take. He would have been a valuable ally for Caesar, who could make use of his optimate credentials to demonstrate his own willingness to let bygones be bygones. Cicero, however, ultimately rejected Caesar's overtures and fled to Pompey. Some leading Romans who had opposed Caesar were now more than happy to accept his offer of mercy and become a part of his new government. Caesar's willingness to forgive past offenses against him, even though he had made much of the insults and injuries he received in the lead-up to the civil war, was a virtue he liked to promote. On his earlier march to Brundisium, he defeated Roman troops, but instead of killing the commanders or taking any retribution, he released them as well as the money they carried. Such mild and surprising treatment was effective propaganda and won him popularity in Italy. The Latin term for this forgiveness is *clementia* (the origin of the English word "clemency"), and it would become a virtue emperors would later claim for themselves. For Caesar, offering foes *clementia* had the advantage of removing any fear of reprisals and would thus encourage more and more people to join him. Individuals who accepted Caesar's *clementia* would also be under an obligation to him, though, as we shall, see, some felt this obligation to Caesar less than their obligation to the republic, or their idea of it.

FIG. 12.2 A denarius with a temple and CLEM CAESARIS ("Caesar's clemecy"). The coin may celebrate the temple decreed by the senate to honor Caesar's mercy on his enemies (especially the senators!) when he took Rome.

Of course, Caesar's *clementia* had its limits, and those who continued to oppose him would feel his wrath.

Just as he had mercilessly butchered German tribes who he felt mistreated him, this same impulse, if not on the same scale, governed his relations with those who resisted him now that he was master of Rome. One anecdote is telling in this regard. The funds in Rome's public treasury, at the base of the Capitoline hill, had been left behind in the panicked flight from Rome at Caesar's approach. A tribune attempting to fulfill his duty to protect the treasury encountered Caesar, who was in need of funds. As Plutarch relates in his life of Caesar,

> Metellus, a tribune of the plebs, tried citing laws in order to stop Caesar from taking money from the Republic's reserve funds, to which Caesar responded that there was a time for laws, and a time for weapons. He then said: "If you believe what I'm doing is wrong, stay out of the way for now. Free speech has no place in war. You can make speeches against me in front of a crowd after I reach an agreement with my enemies and the fighting stops. In giving you this advice, I'm not making use of the authority I now have by right, since you and everyone opposed are now in my power." Caesar then walked up to the treasury door, but the keys were nowhere to be found. He ordered some blacksmiths to break down the door, when Metellus again tried to stop him. Some found this praiseworthy, but Caesar, raising his voice, threatened to kill him if he didn't stop interfering. "I want you to understand, young man," he said, "that threatening to kill you is more trouble than actually killing you." Metellus left in terror. After this, everything Caesar needed for the war was provided to him quickly and without difficulty. (Plutarch, *Caesar* 35.4-11)

This small episode perfectly sums up Caesar's seizure of control at Rome, and Metellus is a suitable stand-in for many of the ruling class who remained in the city.

Caesar quickly put the affairs of the city in order, then headed for Spain to tackle the Pompeian forces there. He left the praetor Lepidus, son of the "rebel" of chapter 9, in charge of Rome, while Antony watched over Italy, then sent other loyal followers and former tribunes to secure Sicily and North Africa, crucial for the grain supply of Rome. Others were dispatched to Illyria, across the Adriatic Sea, to prevent an invasion of Italy from the north. After first overcoming some stubborn resistance at the port of Massillia on the southern coast of modern-day France (modern-day Marseille), Caesar subdued the Pompeian forces left in Spain, in some cases offering opposing commanders and soldiers his *clementia*. This first major success was crucial, raising expectations among his followers of ultimate success against Pompey. At the end of 49, he returned to Rome, where he was appointed dictator for the first time. The alleged reason was to oversee elections, since at the time there were no consuls in Rome. Of course, Caesar was elected as one of the consuls for 48, and immediately began to pass legislation that helped to alleviate the financial problems that afflicted many who were in debt and crushed by heavy interest payments. He also recalled those who had been sent into exile under Pompey, gaining more supporters and goodwill.

FROM THE RUBICON TO PHARSALUS: CAESAR'S MARCH ON ROME
& DEFEAT OF POMPEY 49-48 BC

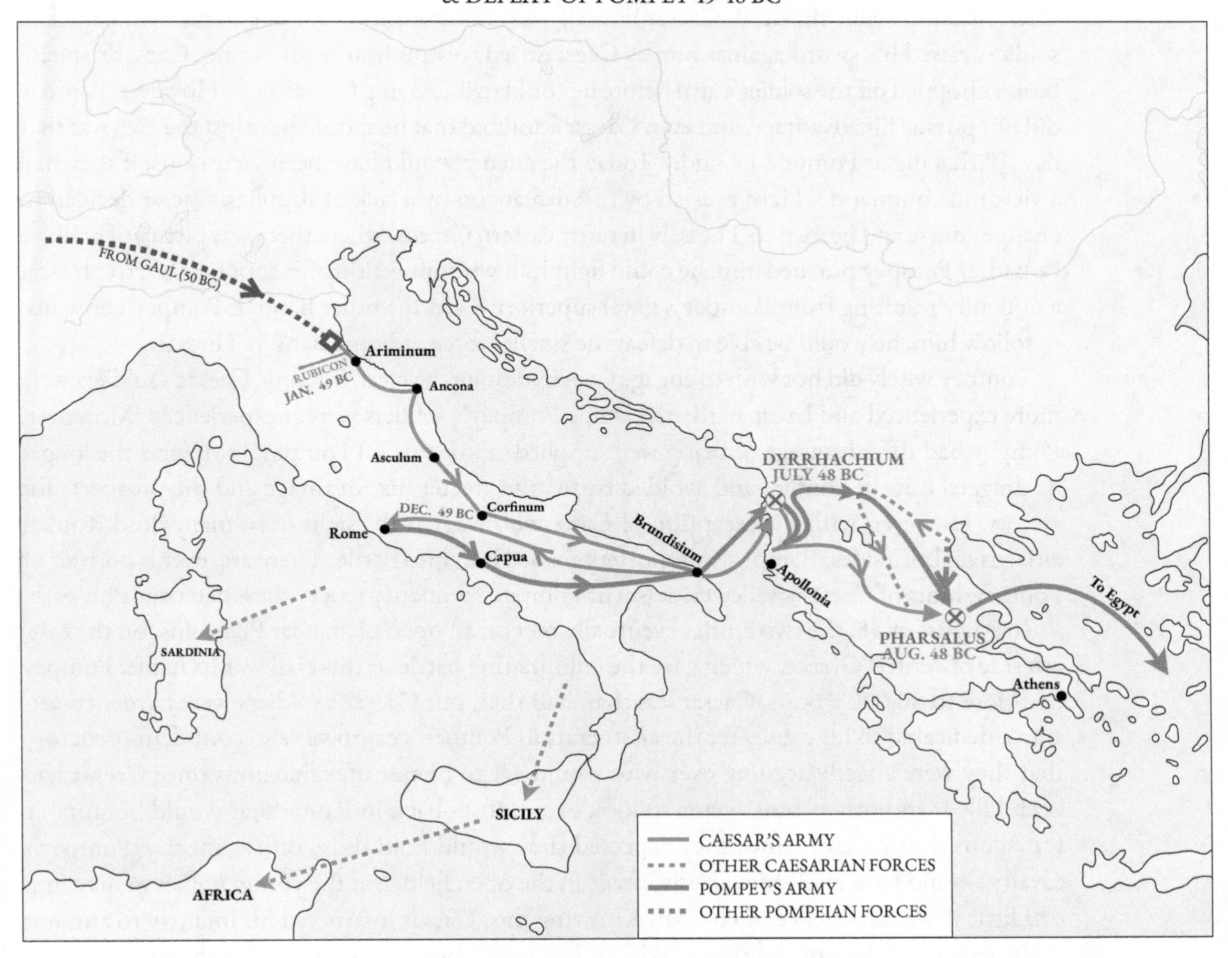

FIG. 12.3 The Civil War.

On a Beach in Egypt: The End of Pompey

Pompey had established his camp at Apollonia, on the eastern coast of Greece, and had stationed part of his fleet nearby. He had access to fresh water and food supplies and held an advantageous position. Caesar, emboldened by his early success, decided to sail to meet Pompey, and in another daring January move, crossed over the Adriatic with five legions and awaited more troops to sail from Brundisium to meet him. Caesar's veteran soldiers, many of whom had been with him for the better part of a decade, began to complain as they made their way to the port for their voyage to Greece, but when they found out he had already sailed, they instead become all the more eager to join their beloved general. Antony eventually sailed with the reinforcements to join Caesar near Pompey's camp.

In an early battle of 48 BC, Pompey's forces overran Caesar's troops, filling the moat of Caesar's camps with the dead. Caesar himself was almost killed when one of his own panicked soldiers raised his sword against him as Caesar tried to stop him from fleeing. Caesar's shield-bearer chopped off the soldier's arm before he could strike, saving Caesar's life. However, Pompey did not pursue his advantage, and even Caesar admitted that he should have lost the civil war that day. With a dig at Pompey, he said: "Today the enemy would have been victorious, if they had a victor in command." Hard pressed by this defeat and by a lack of supplies, Caesar decided to change course and headed to Thessaly in northeastern Greece, where there was plenty of grain to be had. If Pompey pursued him, he could fight him without waiting for supplies to arrive by sea, a difficulty resulting from Pompey's naval superiority. On the other hand, if Pompey chose not to follow him, he would be able to defeat the smaller force of Pompeians in Thessaly.

Pompey wisely did not wish to engage Caesar, despite the recent victory. Caesar's soldiers were more experienced and battle hardened, while Pompey's soldiers were inexperienced. Moreover, Pompey had the advantage of being well supplied. Time was on Pompey's side, and the longer he dragged out the conflict and avoided battle, the greater his advantage and the prospects for victory. However, with the exception of Cato, who wept at the sight of so many dead Roman citizens on both sides, Pompey's supporters goaded him into battle. There are, in this portrait of Pompey, hints of Caesar's veiled criticism of Pompey's tendency to let others determine his path.

In August of 48, the two armies eventually met on an open plain near Pharsalus, on the eastern side of central Greece, which gave the culminating battle of this civil war its name. Pompey had close to 50,000 troops, Caesar less than half that, but Caesar's soldiers were hardened veterans, dedicated to his cause. Yet the aristocrats in Pompey's camp were so confident of victory that they were already arguing over who would get to be pontifex maximus once Caesar had been killed, and others sent agents to look over houses back in Rome that would be suitable for a consul or praetor, since they expected they would hold those offices shortly. Pompey's cavalry should have given him an advantage in the open field, but the young nobles in his camp had little if any experience of combat. Knowing this, Caesar instructed his infantry to aim not at the legs and thighs of the riders, as would be usual, but to aim upward at their faces. These handsome and inexperienced youth would be especially fearful of receiving a wound to the face. The tactic was a shrewd one, and when the battle began, Pompey's cavalry soon turned from the spearpoints in fear, eliminating his advantage. Caesar's experienced infantry carried the day. When defeat was inevitable, Pompey changed out of his general's cloak, disguised himself as a fugitive, and escaped.

Caesar's reaction to his victory was recorded by a contemporary historian, whose works have unfortunately not survived, but quotations are found in later authors. According to his account, when Caesar saw his fellow Romans dead and dying on the battlefield of Pharsalus, he lamented:

> This is what they wanted. They're the ones who made it so that if I, Gaius Caesar, had dismissed my troops after such great victories, I would have been condemned in their courts. (Plutarch, *Caesar* 46.1)

In essence, he blames the *optimates* who opposed him and now followed Pompey for the civil war and the deaths of so many Roman citizens—he had no choice but to do what he did. It might strike some as odd that he presents condemnation in court as a drastic alternative to civil war, but such an outcome would have meant the end of Caesar. He simply could not conceive of a world in which he was not at the top.

When Pompey fled the battlefield, he was accompanied by only a few followers. No one pursued him, which might have been a relief, but it was also a sign of how far he had fallen. A short while before he had been master of the world, and now no one bothered to hunt him down. He told his slaves to go back to Caesar, reassuring them that they had nothing to fear. Pompey made his way east to the sea, spending the night in a fisherman's hut. On the coast he found a merchant ship, owned by a man who recognized Pompey, and sailed to the Greek island of Mytilene. There he brought his wife and son on board. Eventually, he fled with them to Egypt, where he expected to receive a welcome from the current king, the 13-year-old son of Ptolemy XII. Pompey had a relationship with his father, supporting his restoration to the throne of Egypt (for which Ptolemy had rewarded Pompey handsomely). Pompey might expect to find a safe haven, and perhaps a base from which to rebuild, with access to funds and soldiers. Unfortunately for Pompey, the young king was now controlled by a group of older advisers and was also engaged in a civil war over the throne with his older sister, Cleopatra, one of the most remarkable individuals in world history. The advisers debated what to do about Pompey, since his arrival in a single ship accompanied only by his wife and child was a clear signal of Caesar's victory.

When Pompey was anchored in the harbor of Alexandria, he was quite disappointed to see a small rowboat approach with only a few figures, instead of a royal reception befitting his former status. One of the passengers in the rowboat was a former soldier of his, Septimius, lessening Pompey's suspicions. He boarded the boat and began to read a speech he had prepared for the young king Ptolemy XIII, but as they approached the shore, his former soldier Septimius stabbed him. The others finished him off. It was nothing personal, only political calculation. They reasoned that this was the safest course, since Caesar would not be too upset at the death of his vanquished enemy, and they would have nothing to fear from Pompey. "Dead men don't bite," as one of them said. On the day after his 59th birthday, Pompey's head was cut off and preserved by pickling so it could later be shown to Caesar. The headless corpse was abandoned on the Egyptian shore, where one of his former slaves washed it, wrapped it some of his clothes, and built a small funeral pyre from the planks of a rotting boat.

Caesar and Cleopatra

The advisers to Ptolemy XIII had, like many others, misread Caesar and miscalculated his reaction. When he arrived in Egypt at the beginning of October, now as a Roman consul with full legal authority, the young king's advisers presented him with Pompey's head. Caesar is said to have turned away in disgust and wept. He then executed all those involved in the assassination and gave the head a proper burial. Caesar remained in Alexandria and informed Ptolemy XIII that he wished to collect the enormous sum of money promised him earlier by his father Ptolemy XII. The young king's advisers suggested that Caesar attend to his other affairs, and they would send him the money later. Caesar did not receive a warm welcome from either the court of the people of Alexandria and soon found himself under siege in the city. The 13-year-old Ptolemy XIII had inherited his father's throne together with his older sister, Cleopatra VII, now 21 years old. However, she had been driven into exile but was trying to reclaim her place on the throne at the head of an army. Caesar had offered to settle this sibling dispute between monarchs but could not make any headway while Ptolemy XIII was in charge of Alexandria. Cleopatra might make a good ally, if he could find a way to meet her.

According to most ancient sources, Cleopatra was not physically beautiful but had a powerful personality, alluring charm, and a keen intelligence that men found irresistible. She spoke several languages and was the first of the Ptolemaic dynasty, which had ruled Egypt for nearly three centuries, to learn the language spoken by the native Egyptians (the rulers spoke Greek). Since her brother's advisers were keeping a close eye on her as well as on Caesar, she had herself smuggled into his room in a rolled-up rug. Caesar was impressed by her cunning and daring and was captivated enough by her that their meeting produced a son, named Caesarion, which means "Little Caesar" in Greek. (He formally became Ptolemy XV, but in 30 BC was hunted down and killed by Caesar's heir Octavian, the future Augustus.) Concerned with the more immediate political situation, Caesar reconciled Cleopatra with her brother Ptolemy XIII, but his royal advisers continued to cause trouble. They called in an army to put Caesar under siege, but with the help of forces that arrived from Pergamum, raised by a son of the "poison king" Mithridates, Caesar defeated the Egyptian forces. The young king Ptolemy died when he drowned in the Nile, and Caesar then placed Cleopatra on the throne as queen alongside Ptolemy XIV, another brother and, following Egyptian tradition, now husband. (Cleopatra had him killed after Caesar's assassination.) He then headed to Pontus, the kingdom in north central

FIGS. 12.4 & 12.5 Two representations of Cleopatra. On the left, a marble bust dating to the time she visited Rome, discovered at a villa along the Via Appia. Note she wears a royal diadem. On the right, Cleopatra and her son Caesarion at the Temple of Dendera on the Nile in central Egypt.

Turkey, where a king had rebelled against Roman authority. In a lightning campaign, Caesar quickly took care of this king, described in his famous jingle *veni, vidi, vici* ("I came, I saw, I conquered").

End of the Resistance

Caesar now headed for Italy after spending nearly a year in Egypt. He arrived back in Rome in October of 47 after an absence of nearly two years. He had, however, been appointed dictator for that year, the second time he held the office. Antony, left in charge of Italy as "Master of the Horse" (*magister equitum*) had a reputation for drunkenness and partying and had not maintained order in the way Caesar would have liked. Some of his veterans had even mutinied, but Caesar brought them back into order by addressing them not as "soldiers" but with the humiliating "citizens." Caesar was elected consul for 46, his third consulship, but at the end of the year, only two months after his return, he was needed elsewhere. While Caesar had been with Cleopatra in Egypt, Cato had assembled an army in North Africa, joining forces with King Juba of Mauretania, who had earlier defeated Caesarian forces at the onset of the civil war. Unfortunately, Cato's adherence to protocol and the rule of law did not serve him well in this case, since he turned over his command to Metellus Scipio, a scion of an illustrious patrician family whose daughter had married Pompey. He had commanded the center of Pompey's battle line at Pharsalus, and as a former consul, outranked Cato. He was not the man for the job, but Cato followed the rules.

Near the town of Thapsus, on the north coast of Africa in modern-day Tunisia, Caesar met these holdouts of the republic in April of 46 BC. With Scipio in command, the fight was hardly fair, and Caesar's forces wiped out the Republican armies. Cato, the uncompromising enemy of tyranny and defender of liberty, chose to end his life rather than live to see Caesar's victory and to receive his *clementia*. He had retreated to the city of Utica, whose inhabitants were considering handing over the Roman senators to Caesar when he arrived. With nowhere left to run, Cato advised the remaining senators to appeal to Caesar's mercy. At the approach of Caesar's troops, Cato's thoughts turned to death. He enjoyed a bath, then a dinner with friends, where the wine and philosophical arguments flowed. He then headed off to bed with a copy of Plato's *Phaedo*, a dialogue on the immortality of the soul that ends with the famous scene of Socrates's death, drinking a cup of poison hemlock in an Athenian prison. Plutarch describes the vivid scene of Cato's last hours, a suicide Cato performed with less panache than Socrates:

> The birds were already beginning to sing when he fell asleep again for a little while. Butas [a slave] came and told him that there was no activity in the harbor, so Cato ordered him to close the door. He then lay down in his bed as if he intended to rest there for the rest of the night. But after Butas left the room, Cato drew his sword from its sheath and stabbed himself below the heart. His thrust, however, was rather weak because his hand was injured [Cato had earlier punched a slave in the mouth when

> he didn't bring him his sword], and so he did not manage to kill himself immediately. In his death struggle he fell from the bed, making a loud noise by knocking over an abacus. His slaves heard the noise and cried out, and his son rushed in together with his friends. They saw Cato covered in blood and his guts hanging out, but his eyes were still open. To their amazement, he was still alive. The doctor came and tried to pack his guts back in, since they were still intact, and to sew up the wound. When Cato recovered and realized what was happening, he pushed the doctor away, tore out his guts with his hands, opened up the wound even more, and died. (Plutarch, *Cato* 70.4)

Cato's suicide, at the age of 48, became immortalized in art and literature, and he remained a symbol of resistance to tyranny for centuries. His death, which seemed the last possible way to oppose Caesar, was elevated into a heroic martyrdom. Cicero even wrote a pamphlet in praise of him, simply entitled *Cato,* and Caesar, always aware of the power of written histories, felt compelled to respond with his own treatise, the *Anti-Cato.* Neither work survives, but it was the beginning of a long debate about Cato's legacy. If anyone among the republicans could claim to have conquered Caesar in death, it was Cato. Caesar, in fact, bemoaned Cato's suicide, complaining that it had robbed him of the chance to display his *clementia*. Metellus Scipio managed to flee from the Utica but was pursued by the Caesarians. When he realized there was no escape, no more battles to be fought, he too committed suicide. When his pursuers asked where he was, they were told "All is well with the commander." Though he had not quite managed to live up to the traditions of his family in life, these final words allowed him a dignified death, which was the best he or any other opponent of Caesar could hope for.

Return of the Conqueror

After the defeat of Scipio and Cato, Caesar was the unquestioned master of Rome and its empire. He was also master of the Roman Senate, which granted him extraordinary honors and powers, unprecedented but cloaked in traditional republican forms. He had been consul in 48, the year he defeated Pompey, and after his victory at Pharsalus was appointed dictator for one year. This same year, the senate granted him "tribunician power," meaning he had all the authority and privileges of a tribune of the plebs without actually being one. (This was to set a precedent for future emperors, who would date their reigns by the number of years they held tribunician power.) He was also consul in 46, 45, and 44. In 46, he was granted the dictatorship for ten years, with the possibility for renewal, and took on a new title, *praefectus morum* ("Supervisor of Morals"), for a period of three years. The powers of this office were much like those of a censor and allowed him to decide who would be in the senate. In February of 44, shortly before his assassination, the pretense was given up and the senate simply made him "dictator for life." He was also granted the privilege of speaking first in any discussion in the senate, a permanent *princeps senatus*. This position had been an honor given to a distinguished senator, a former consul or censor, who could set the tone of any debate and discussion. Under Caesar, the senate would want him to speak first, so they would know what they were supposed to think.

The senate also decreed that when Caesar went out in public he would be preceded by 72 lictors. A consul traditionally received 12, and a dictator 24. Upon Caesar's return to Rome, a *supplicatio* lasting for 40 days was also decreed. A *supplicatio*, often translated as "thanksgiving," was a holiday from all public business, and Romans went to shrines and temples to offer the gods thanks for whatever the senate had decreed, usually a major military victory. It normally lasted two or three days, though they had grown longer as the republic declined. Pompey had earned a *supplicatio* of 12 days on his return from the east in 62, while Caesar's defeat of Vercingetorix in Gaul was celebrated for 15 days. In 45 BC, the year after his 40-day *supplicatio*, Caesar would be honored with one lasting 50 days. Caesar returned the favor to Rome by celebrating a triumph that outdid Pompey's triple triumph of 61. His was a quadruple triumph, for victories over the Gauls, over Egypt, over Pharnaces II in Pontus, and over Juba in North Africa. (It was the first time a giraffe was seen at Rome.) There was no mention of the defeat of Pompey or the Republican forces at Thapsus, with whom Juba was allied. Cleopatra also arrived in Rome, with the son she claimed was Caesar's. A statue of her, appearing as the Egyptian goddess Isis, was set up in the Temple of Venus, the goddess from whom Caesar claimed descent. In a generation, Cleopatra's name would become unspeakable at Rome, after she allied with Antony in a civil war against Caesar's grandnephew, the future emperor Augustus.

Despite the celebrations, there was one final battle to be fought. In 45, Pompey's two sons and one of Caesar's former loyal commanders raised a revolt in the town of Munda in Spain. It was a last dying gasp of the republic, and 30,000 soldiers fighting on the side of the Pompeians lost their life. Caesar even said that he had often fought for victory, but at Munda he had to fight for his life. One of Pompey's sons, Sextus, survived the battle, and would live on to cause trouble in the civil wars that followed Caesar's assassination. Perhaps what is most notable about the battle of Munda is that Caesar celebrated another triumph in late 45 for this victory, and this time the fact that it was over Roman citizens was not concealed. This angered many Romans, which Caesar would have foreseen. His triumph over fellow Romans, including the sons of Pompey, was perhaps a sign that Caesar would no longer tolerate any resistance. It would be met with force, no matter who resisted, and its defeat would be celebrated, not covered up. To his opponents, however, it was a sign of a further step away from the traditions of the Roman Republic and toward new forms of tyranny.

The Republic Transformed

While the Romans never shied away from innovation, they nevertheless held dear the idea of tradition and precedent, and thus everything new was made to look old. Almost every argument, whether in a legal trial or in a senate debate, was based as much on appeals to famous incidents or figures from the Roman past as on logic and reason. For example, when Cicero defended Milo against the charge of murdering Clodius in 52 BC, he could appeal to the example of Quintus Horatius, a legendary figure from the regal period, almost seven hundred years earlier.

> Some people claim that someone who kills another and admits it has no right to live. In what city do people make this foolish claim? The very city that witnessed the trial of the heroic Marcus Horatius, the first case involving the death penalty. But Horatius was freed by the assembly of the Roman people, even though he confessed that he had killed his sister with his own hand, and this happened even before the Republic had been founded. (Cicero, *In Defense of Milo* 7)

Quintus Horatius comes from one of the better-known stories of early Roman history, set in the regal period. The Horatii and Curiatii were two sets of triplets, one from Rome and the other from nearby from Alba Longa. The two cities were at war, and it was decided that combat between the two sets of triplets would determine the outcome of the war. Two of the Horatii were killed before any of the Curiatii, but Quintus Horatius managed on his own to slay all three Curiatii, giving Rome the victory. Upon his glorious return home, carrying the spoils from his defeated enemy, his sister broke down into tears. She was to marry one of the Curiatii, and the bloody cloak her brother carried home was the one she had made for her future husband. Enraged by her reaction, Quintus stabbed her with his sword. He was then sentenced to be executed on the charge of murder, until his father made an appeal for his life. He argued that even though his son had committed a heinous crime, one that normally deserved the death penalty, his extraordinary deeds in killing the Curiatii and saving Rome demanded that an exception be made in his case. Essentially a fairy tale, it could still be used as part of a serious legal argument in a murder trial. In his defense of Milo for the murder of Clodius, Cicero acknowledges Milo has admitted to the crime, but uses this historical legend to suggest Milo should not be found guilty because of the benefits he has brought to Rome.

But the use of this history required some shared understanding of what it meant. During the final years of the republic, it became increasingly difficult to maintain shared traditions. Caesar's honors, powers, and offices in one way seemed to defy all traditions—no one had been a dictator for ten years, for example. But in another way it was still within the bounds of the traditions of the republic, if barely. The dictatorship, after all, was an established office to be used in extraordinary times, and more importantly it was the senate and people of Rome that had authorized it and his other honors. But if the senate and people of Rome authorized something, no matter what it was, would that fact alone make it "republican"? Or could the very institutions that defined the republic, the SPQR, act contrary to the republic? To some at Rome, Caesar had crossed another Rubicon and had begun to make a mockery of traditional titles and practices. A special *supplicatio*? Yes, but for fifty days? A quadruple triumph? Okay, but to celebrate the defeat of Roman citizens? A dictator? Of course, but for life? Caesar did not do away with the institutions of the republic, but these too he transformed beyond recognition. There would still be consuls, praetors, and elections, even if these would be predetermined by Caesar. And the senate and assemblies would still perform their role, even if it was to carry out Caesar's will. Yet all of this change cannot be attributed to Caesar alone—his special commands and extraordinary privileges were in some way simply the logical extension of the way Pompey and others had been treated before him.

One of the hallmarks of an authoritarian ruler is the construction of monuments and other buildings that transform a city into his image, providing employment for the people as well. Caesar was no different and began a building program that would dramatically alter the landscape of Rome. With the plunder from the Gallic War, he built a new forum, the Forum Julium, which housed a Temple of Venus Genetrix (*genetrix* means "mother," and refers to Venus as Caesar's ancestor). There was a new hall for the law courts, the Basilica Julia, and a new Rostra (speaker's platform). He had even more construction plans, including a new library, a new senate house, and a new theater, which would remain unbuilt, at least in his lifetime.

He also planned for large-scale projects throughout Italy, including a new harbor and a road that crossed the Apennine mountains. For his veterans, he established new colonies throughout Europe, including on the sites of the modern-day Geneva, Seville, and Lyons, as well as in North Africa and Greece. He granted citizenship to provincials, and some even made it into his senate, which he had expanded with an additional 300 members to a total of 900. Caesar not only transformed Roman space, he transformed Roman time as well, reforming the Roman calendar to a more precise form. The Julian calendar, as it is called, remained in use until the late sixteenth century, when it was replaced by the Gregorian calendar (named after Pope Gregory, and in truth only a minor adjustment to the Julian calendar). In honor of Caesar, the fifth month, Quintilis, was renamed Julius, from which we get the modern July (July was originally the fifth month because the Roman year originally began on March 1).

But of all the plans he had, realized and unrealized, his campaign against the Parthians is one of the most tantalizing. He had an immediate strategic reason to march against the Parthians. In Syria, there had been a flicker of a revolt against Rome, but the commander sent to deal with it was beaten back by a Parthian army. Caesar, however, had larger ambitions than another triumph. There was, of course, the matter of avenging the ignominious defeat suffered by Crassus in 53, and the recovery of the lost legionary standards. (That task, however, would be left to his adopted son, later known as Augustus.) Caesar was thinking in terms of history and his place in it. In one story, Caesar laments that while Alexander the Great had conquered the world by the time he died at age 33, he could not point to any truly glorious achievements of his own at the same age. From his perspective, for all that he had done, there was still lacking a grand, epic campaign against a worthy opponent. The Parthians would certainly provide such an opportunity for him to march in the footsteps of Alexander the Great, and perhaps go beyond them. Pompey had attempted to imitate Alexander but failed; Caesar was going to surpass him. Had he lived, he might have succeeded.

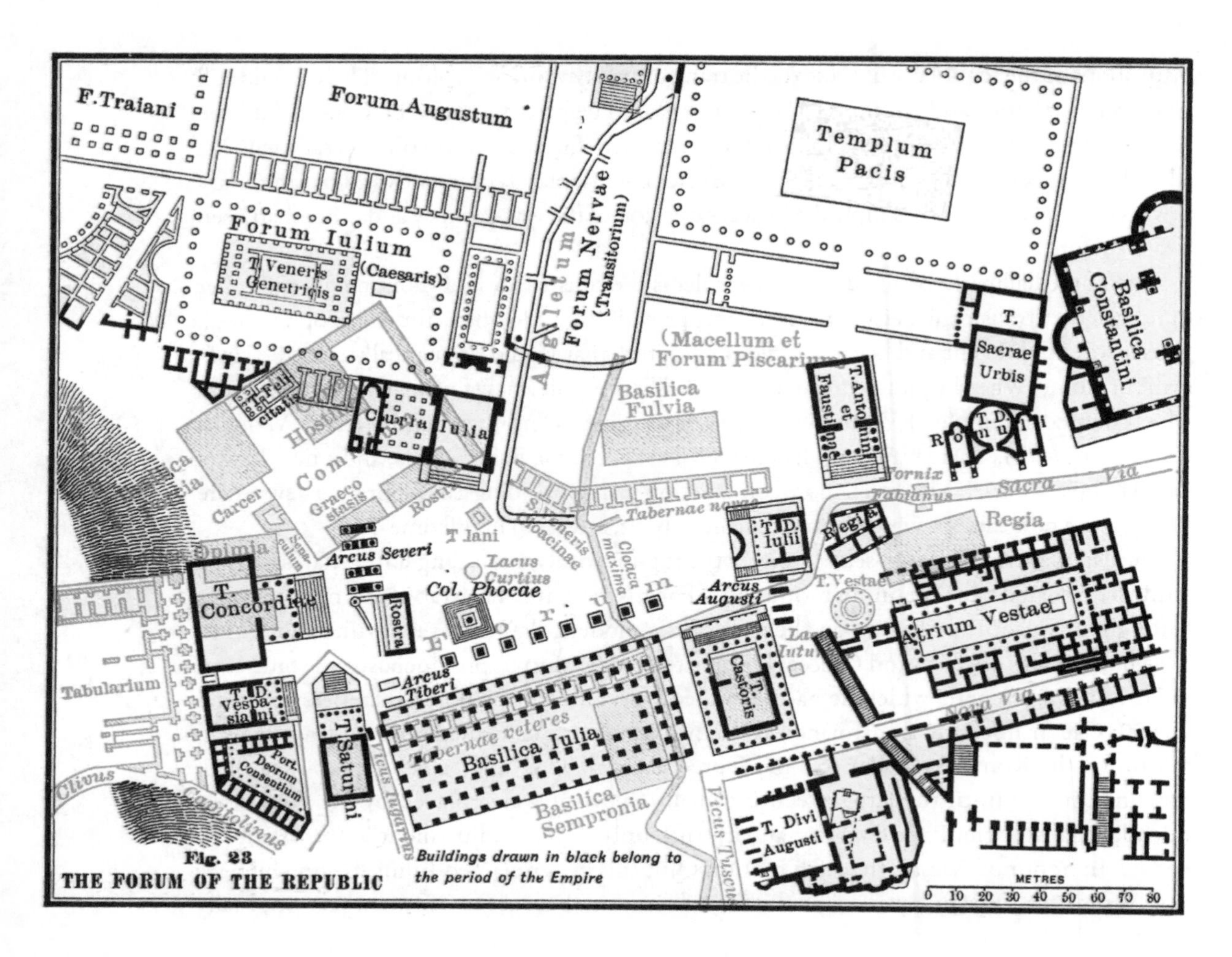

FIG. 12.6 An older plan of the Roman Forum, showing how it was built in layers. Caesar's Basilica Julia is bottom center, and the Forum Julium, with its Temple of Venus Genetrix, is in the upper left. Note how the later fora (plural of forum) built by emperors Augustus, Trajan, and Nerva are attached to Caesar's.

The Ides of March

Despite all the honors and powers bestowed on him, it could be said Caesar used them for the greater good of Rome. And even if one found him overly authoritarian in his methods, it is difficult to find fault with much of what he managed to accomplish, given the disorder into which the republic had fallen. Yet despite his defeat of the Republican resistance, the republican ideal of "liberty" still lived on in the hearts and minds of some Romans. One of the most prominent of these was Marcus Junius Brutus, who shared a name with the Brutus who 450 years earlier had stood over the corpse of Lucretia and sworn that no king would ever rule Rome again. As Caesar continued to consolidate power and inch toward monarchy in all but name, some Romans began to remind Brutus of his ancestry. Notes were left on statues of the earlier Brutus urging him to follow in the footsteps of his famous forebear: "If only Brutus were alive!", "Are you asleep, Brutus?", and "You're no Brutus!"

Born in 85 BC, Brutus belonged to a younger generation than Pompey, Caesar, and Cicero. Cato was his uncle and oversaw his education when he was a young boy. His mother Servilia, a remarkable individual about whom we know too little, was one of Caesar's favorite mistresses, and there were rumors Brutus was really Caesar's son. In his late 20s, Brutus went with Cato on his mission to Cyprus, returning to Rome in 53. Later, he would take Cato's daughter Porcia for his second wife. He was initially opposed to Pompey since his father had been killed in 78, apparently on Pompey's orders. However, he fought on the side of the Pompeians at Pharsalus, and after the defeat received Caesar's *clementia*. Although he is now best known as one of Caesar's killers, in the years before the assassination, he was associated with supporters of Caesar. Caesar himself placed him in various offices and had even designated him to be consul in 41. His decision to take part in the conspiracy against Caesar was a momentous one. The final straw, perhaps, was Caesar's acceptance of the title of *dictator perpetuus*, "dictator for life."

The past was a powerful force at Rome, and as the notes on the statues suggest, the history of his family and the republic must have weighed on Brutus as Caesar continued to accumulate power. And when the conspiracy, consisting of as many as sixty senators, finally began to come together, they looked to young Brutus as their leader not only because of his history, but because he had a widespread reputation for nobility of character. He was like Cato in this regard, but without the hard edge. If Brutus would kill Caesar, then it must be honorable. His close personal ties to Caesar, as well as his mother's, would help him to avoid suspicion. Even when rumors were reported to Caesar about Brutus and an assassination, he is said to have brushed them off, with the remark Brutus need only wait for him to die. Like many others, he had faith in Brutus's character.

The other leading conspirator was Cassius, known for being hot-headed, in stark contrast to Brutus, and the two of them had a falling out over the praetorship, when Caesar had passed over Cassius for the office and gave it to Brutus. Indeed, it was said that while Brutus was opposed to Caesar's rule, but not Caesar the man, Cassius was the opposite. He personally hated Caesar, and the politics were secondary. The leaders of the conspiracy debated whether to include Cicero in their plans, and in the end decided to leave him out. As one of the leaders of the older generation, his participation would have helped them in the aftermath, and they certainly could have used his rhetorical skills. He was still popular and respected, and there was real danger of a popular uprising if the killing of Caesar could not be quickly justified to the people of Rome. Above all, the assassination needed to be a group effort, not the work of a single individual, in order to demonstrate that it was the senate as a whole that regarded Caesar as a king to be killed.

The conspirators decided a meeting of the senate would be the best occasion to carry out the assassination, since there would be nothing suspicious about all of them being together there. A meeting was called for the Ides of March (the 15th), at a meeting hall attached to the Theater of Pompey. It was rumored that Caesar would be proclaimed king at the meeting, and three days later he was scheduled to leave for his campaign against the Parthians. (Some thought if he went he would never make it back.) There are several accounts of Caesar's assassination, and

Shakespeare's play *Julius Caesar,* based on historical sources, is one of the most memorable. The sources Shakespeare used provide a dramatic account of the time leading up to the assassination, which was filled with foreboding omens, signs and dreams, as would be expected before an event of such significance. Caesar's wife Calpurnia had a dream in which an ornament on the roof of their house, an honor bestowed by the senate, came crashing down, and a "king bird" was said to have carried a sprig of laurel into the Theater of Pompey, where other birds pecked it to death. Caesar himself is said to have dreamt he was flying among the clouds when Jupiter took him by the hand. Somewhat more realistically, Caesar considered not attending the meeting because he was not feeling well, and his delay in arriving worried the conspirators, who thought he might have discovered their plot. One of the conspirators went to Caesar's house and persuaded him he should not disappoint all those who were waiting for him. On the way, someone who had learned of the conspiracy passed Caesar a note warning him, which Caesar stuck in the middle of the other documents he carried. The man shouted to him to read it first, but Caesar did not hear. Of course, there is the famous story that a seer had warned him "Beware the Ides of March!" Caesar saw him as he was about to enter the meeting, and reminded the seer of his prophecy, claiming that nothing bad had happened. The seer reminded Caesar that the Ides of March had come, but they had not passed. All of these anecdotes sound very much like details added for dramatic purposes, things Shakespeare himself would dream up. At times, it seems the authors of these incidents are still desperately trying to warn Caesar, or by drawing out the numerous signs trying to keep him alive longer by delaying the inevitable final scene.

As Caesar finally entered the meeting of the senate in the recently completed Theater of Pompey, one of the conspirators approached him with a petition to recall his brother from exile. When Caesar tried to dismiss him, he grabbed Caesar's toga and pulled it down from his neck, the signal for the others to step forward. The first blow struck him on the neck but did not cut deeply. The rest of the conspirators soon surrounded Caesar with their daggers while he tried to pull his toga over his head, to maintain in this undignified death some semblance of the *dignitas* he earned in life. He fell dead before a statue of Pompey, stabbed 23 times. Brutus had hesitated, until he too stepped and delivered what Shakespeare called, with a double superlative, "the most unkindest cut of all." According to tradition, Caesar uttered *et tu, Brute?* ("Even you, Brutus?), which is how Shakespeare has it. But according to the biographer Suetonius, most sources report Caesar said nothing, but if he did say anything it was the Greek *kai su, teknon*? This is close to *et tu, Brute?* but with one important difference: *Teknon* means "child," and so the Greek phrase means "Even you, my child?" While *teknon* could be a term of endearment, or even belittlement, for the much younger Brutus, rumored to be his child, it would have been a striking word to hear, whether or not he knew the truth of the matter. There is also evidence that *kai su* was in fact a Greek curse, and thus Caesar really said something like "Go to hell, son!"

While the conspirators successfully carried off their plan to kill Caesar, they seemed to have planned little for the aftermath, assuming that their prestige and authority would carry the day. They seemed to have believed they would shout "Liberty!" at Caesar's fall, and that this would mean to everyone else what it meant to them. Antony had been purposely detained outside of the senate meeting during the assassination. Some of the conspirators argued that he needed to be killed as well, but Brutus persuaded them that only Caesar would be assassinated. Brutus attempted to speak to the senators not involved in the plot, but they scattered before he could say anything. Antony fled in the immediate aftermath but quickly returned to conduct negotiations with the conspirators about a path forward. The conspirators had headed for the Capitol, proclaiming that the people of Rome were now free, but no one seemed to listen. Marcus Aemilius Lepidus, who had replaced Antony as Caesar's *magister equitum*, led soldiers into the Forum and urged the people to take revenge on Caesar's murderers. One unfortunate individual, a poet who had the same name as a prominent conspirator, was torn apart by an angry mob.

Two days after Caesar's death, an agreement was reached between Antony and the conspirators. Caesar's acts and laws while he was dictator would remain valid, and Caesar's killers would be given amnesty. It was an uneasy truce at best, and when Antony spoke at Caesar's funeral, he roused the people to anger, especially when he read part of Caesar's will. Caesar had not only donated many of his properties as parks and gardens to the people, he gave every citizen a gift of money. Worse yet, some of the conspirators themselves were benefactors of Caesar's will. The people rioted and piled up benches and any other wooden object they could to make an impromptu pyre. While given legal amnesty, many conspirators thought it prudent to flee Rome, and some were given official positions overseas for that purpose.

The Noblest Roman of Them All?

In Shakespeare's dramatic telling, it is Brutus who first goes into the Forum to address the people. He provides a succinct explanation of his reasons for killing Caesar, by claiming while he did love, honor, and admire Caesar, he loved the republic more.

> If there be any in this assembly, any dear friend of Caesar's, to him I say, that Brutus' love to Caesar was no less than his. If then that friend demand why Brutus rose against Caesar, this is my answer: –Not that I loved Caesar less, but that I loved Rome more. Had you rather Caesar were living and die all slaves, than that Caesar were dead, to live all free men? As Caesar loved me, I weep for him; as he was fortunate, I rejoice at it; as he was valiant, I honour him: but, as he was ambitious, I slew him. There is tears for his love; joy for his fortune; honour for his valour; and death for his ambition. (*Julius Caesar* III.2.19-30)

Although Brutus did not in fact give a speech, Shakespeare has captured one of the fundamental problems that Caesar presented to those who still believed in the republic. To Brutus and others who held to principles, the assassination of Caesar was not something they wanted to do, but had to do. And it was not about Caesar, but about the republic. In this fictional speech, Brutus recognizes all the good qualities Caesar possessed, but it was his "ambition," his desire for personal supremacy, which had forced the conspirators to kill him, even those that loved him.

In Shakespeare's version of Antony's funeral speech, one of the most famous orations in the history of literature, Antony takes Caesar's bloody cloak in his hand as a prop and uses Brutus's own words against him to rouse the crowd to a fury.

> Friends, Romans, countrymen, lend me your ears;
> I come to bury Caesar, not to praise him.
> The evil that men do lives after them;
> The good is oft interred with their bones;
> So let it be with Caesar. The noble Brutus
> Hath told you Caesar was ambitious:
> If it were so, it was a grievous fault,
> And grievously hath Caesar answer'd it.
> Here, under leave of Brutus and the rest—
> For Brutus is an honourable man;
> So are they all, all honourable men—
> Come I to speak in Caesar's funeral.
> He was my friend, faithful and just to me:
> But Brutus says he was ambitious;
> And Brutus is an honourable man.
> He hath brought many captives home to Rome
> Whose ransoms did the general coffers fill:
> Did this in Caesar seem ambitious?
> When that the poor have cried, Caesar hath wept:
> Ambition should be made of sterner stuff:
> Yet Brutus says he was ambitious;
> And Brutus is an honourable man.
> You all did see that on the Lupercal
> I thrice presented him a kingly crown,
> Which he did thrice refuse: was this ambition?
> Yet Brutus says he was ambitious;
> And, sure, he is an honourable man.
> I speak not to disprove what Brutus spoke,
> But here I am to speak what I do know.
> You all did love him once, not without cause:
> What cause withholds you then, to mourn for him? (*Julius Caesar* III.2.82-113)

William Shakespeare, *Julius Caesar*, 1599.

The opening lines are some of the most famous, but more notable is Antony's constant refrain that "Brutus was an honorable man," each instance dripping with more and more sarcasm. While the speech is not historical, it does capture Brutus's tragic adherence to a notion of honor that no longer had meaning at Rome. Antony also questions if Caesar really had the "ambition" Brutus ascribed to him, using his refusal of the diadem at the Lupercalia as evidence.

This opposition between Brutus and Antony would play out in real history two years later after Caesar's assassination. On another battlefield in Greece, Brutus would commit suicide after fighting in vain for the Republican cause, much like Cato before him. The victors in this battle were Antony and Caesar's grandnephew, Gaius Octavius, who as Caesar's primary heir was the greatest benefactor of the will. He is often called Octavian in histories at this point, but in 20 years he would be known as Augustus, the first emperor of Rome, though he would not call himself that. At the time of Caesar's death, Octavian was a young man of 18 years, engaged in military training exercises in Illyricum, across the Adriatic Sea from Italy. Caesar had not only named Octavian his first heir, meaning he would inherit immense wealth (two thirds of his estate), he had also adopted him in his will, making him his son. At Caesar's death, Gaius Octavius became Gaius Julius Caesar Octavianus, heir not only to Caesar's fortune, but to something far more valuable, his name. Caesar's soldiers would accord him some of the same reverence they had for the man who was now his father.

Octavian did not have to accept the inheritance, in which case he could avoid being immediately thrust into political prominence and mortal danger and could instead live out his life comfortably and in peace. Octavian's family advised him to take this safer course. After all, Caesar's closest friends had killed him, and for all they knew the entire senate was in on the conspiracy. The killers of Caesar might well want to kill his heir and namesake as well. Antony, who had long served Caesar as his right-hand man, might wish to have the boy removed as well, since he would be a rival to his own claim to power and prestige. The situation was unstable and far too dangerous for the 18-year-old. Others advised him to flee east to Macedonia, where there were troops loyal to Caesar, whose officers would protect him. Yet in a bold and daring move, a sign of things to come, Octavian immediately sailed across the Adriatic to Italy. At first, he planned to maintain a low profile to ascertain the situation, but upon his landing on shore, an army came to meet him. At this good sign, he accepted Caesar's inheritance, and using his new wealth and new name, he marched on Rome. Crowds flocked to him, and Caesar's veterans followed him.

Vengeance against Caesar's assassins was on his mind, as well as his uneasy relationship with Antony. He would soon have his vengeance, and there would be another triumvirate, another defeat of forces claiming to defend the republic and liberty, another immortalized suicide (Brutus instead of Cato), and finally, another civil war, this time against Antony and Cleopatra. Octavian, like his adoptive father, would become master of Rome and the world, but unlike him, he would remain so for another generation and die a natural death in his bed.

Res Publica Aeterna

Not long after the assassination, Octavian sponsored a religious festival in honor of Venus Genetrix, the goddess from whom Caesar claimed descent and whose temple he had built in his new Forum. On the first day of the games there appeared in the sky a blazing star, which remained for seven days. This was a comet, now often called Caesar's Comet, and its appearance on the first day of the games put on by Caesar's heir was a miraculous coincidence. Many believed the comet was a sign that Caesar's soul had joined the immortal gods, and soon, in 42 BC, Caesar would have his own temple in Rome, the Temple of Divus Julius ("the divine Julius"). Caesar was immortal not only in a historical sense—he had become a god.

At the beginning of the fourteenth century AD, one of the great poets of world literature, Dante, wrote an epic poem that told the story of his journey through hell, into purgatory, and finally to a vision of paradise. Each of these regions has its own book—*Inferno*, *Purgatorio*, and *Paradiso*—which together make up the *Divine Comedy*. Not only is this poem one of the most important and influential in the history of literature, it also paved the way for the writing of serious literature in the "vulgar" tongue of Italian rather than in Latin. The best-known and most widely read of the three sections is *Inferno*, not only because it is the first, but also because it is filled with fascinating characters who suffer imaginative punishments. The work opens with Dante himself, who has lost his way in life, but finds in the Roman epic poet Vergil a guide who will lead him on this first part of his journey. Vergil has a special status among the dead souls, but since he died before the arrival of Christianity, he cannot leave hell. The *Inferno* is famous for its circles of hell, each corresponding to a particular sin, which get worse as one descends, until, in the ninth and final circle, Satan himself can be found, spreading an icy chill among the lower depths. (As it turns out, hell is frozen over.)

When Dante, as the narrator of his poem, finally gazes upon the figure of Satan in the final lines of *Inferno*, this is what he sees:

> With six eyes he wept, down three chins
>
> dropped tears and bloodsoaked drool.
> In each mouth his teeth tore up a sinner
> like a thresher, bringing the three of them pain.
>
> For the one in front, the biting was nothing
> compared to the clawing, which sometimes
> left his back stripped of all its skin.
>
> "That soul there in the greatest pain,"
> said my master, "is Judas Iscariot,
> his head within, his legs thrashing without.

> Of those other two, with their heads down,
> the one hanging from the black jaws is Brutus—
> Look how he writhes without making a sound!
>
> The other is Cassius, who seems so muscular." (Dante, *Inferno* 34.53-67)

The vivid portrait of the weeping three-headed Satan, chewing on the world's three worst sinners in each of his three mouths, is hard to forget. The image is a reversal of the crucifixion scene, in which Jesus is set between two criminals, by tradition known as the good thief and the impenitent thief. In the worldview of Dante's poem, the worst sinner of all is, of course, Judas, who betrayed Jesus to the Roman authorities for thirty pieces of silver. The two other sinners, the worst in history after Judas, are Brutus and Cassius, the assassins of Julius Caesar. Their betrayal of Caesar places them next to the man who betrayed, in this perspective, the savior of all humankind, and thus elevates Caesar to a position as lofty as any pagan could hope for. After all, Caesar had, in this view, ushered in the Roman Empire, and thus made it possible for Christianity to spread throughout the world. A nineteenth-century author of a life of Caesar, who was the Regius Professor of Modern History at Oxford University and a failed clergyman, also drew a close parallel between Jesus and Caesar at the conclusion of his book:

> Strange and startling resemblance between the fate of the founder of the kingdom of this world and of the Founder of the Kingdom not of this world, for which the first was a preparation. Each was denounced for making himself a king. Each was maligned as the friend of publicans and sinners; each was betrayed by those whom he had loved and cared for; each was put to death; and Caesar also was believed to have risen again and ascended into heaven and become a divine being. (James Anthony Froude, *Caesar: A Sketch* (1879))

The comparison is remarkable, and the correspondence might be difficult to take seriously, yet, it is worth remembering that many people over the centuries have. Indeed, Caesar has had many afterlives and has over the centuries become many things to many people. That there have always been such complicated and contrasting views of him is perhaps the greatest proof his achievements were beyond that of most mortals.

Adopted into the Christian tradition, which was heir to the Roman empire, Caesar became in the Middle Ages one of the "Nine Worthies," the models of chivalry and ideals of medieval courtly behavior drawn from history. Three of the nine were pagan, which meant they belonged to the world of ancient Greece and Rome, whose gods were from the Christian perspective only poetic fictions. Alongside Hector, the Trojan hero of the *Iliad* killed by Achilles, and Alexander the Great, stood Caesar. Even he might have been surprised to find himself revered as an example for aspiring knights. In the sixteenth century, Charles V of Spain was ruler of the Holy Roman Empire (which, according to a well-known quip by the eighteenth-century French thinker

Voltaire, was neither Holy, nor Roman, nor an empire). As emperor, he saw himself as heir to the line of Rome's emperors, but he chose as his particular model Caesar, and would be greeted with cries of "Cesare, Cesare, Carlo, Carlo, Imperio, Imperio!" When he marched into battle against Sultan Suleiman I, ruler of the Ottoman Empire, many saw the conflict as a war not just between two earthly empires, but between Christianity and Islam. Charles and Suleiman, however, also saw it as a battle over who was the true heir of Caesar, for Suleiman also admired him.

Not all, however, would place Caesar, whose name lives on in the German *Kaiser* and the Russian *tzar,* in such lofty company, and think of him as a martyr or a just and honorable ruler of a world empire. Others have seen him less as a good king and more a brutal tyrant, whose assassination served as the model for future revolutions in the name of freedom and liberty. It is no accident that in the build-up to the American revolution, King George of England would be equated with Caesar, and the American revolutionaries looked to figures such as Brutus and Cato as their heroes. George Washington's favorite play, which he had performed for his troops at Valley Forge, was *Cato* by Joseph Addison (1713), which glorifies his suicide at Utica. At the conclusion of the play, Cato advises his daughter to marry King Juba. He explains that it is unusual for a Roman senator to marry his daughter to a king, but Caesar has upended all Roman traditions:

> A senator of Rome, while Rome survived,
> Would not have match'd his daughter with a king,
> But Caesar's arms have thrown down all distinction;
> Whoe'er is brave and virtuous, is a Roman. (V.4.87-90)

The positive side of Cato's suicide is that Rome will survive as long as there are people who will courageously sacrifice their life for the good and right, like Cato. And in this view, it may be Caesar's Rome that survives in the halls of power, in the creation of empires, in the domination and subjection of other peoples, but it is Cato's Rome that survives in the hearts of the brave and the free. Both of these could be considered gross simplifications of complex characters, but this is often the case when historical figures have powerful meanings attached to them.

In the debate about the ratification of the Constitution, the writers of the Federalist Papers—Alexander Hamilton, John Jay, and James Madison—used the pseudonym "Publius" to argue for a stronger and more centralized federal authority. Those who opposed them, the Anti-Federalists who feared the abuses of power and corruption that would inevitably result from strong centralized national government, used the pseudonyms Brutus and Cato. In doing so, they implicitly associated the federalists with the political ambitions of a domineering Caesar rather than the republicanism of a Publicola. Their constitutional arguments were the real threat to the liberty provided by a republic. The French Revolution, shortly following the American, also turned to the Roman Republic for inspiration. Brutus became one of their most potent symbols for the violent overthrow of the monarchy, and in their revolutionary people's assembly, there was a bust of Brutus on which speakers would swear an oath.

But Caesar and Brutus could be put to other uses, and any person who considered themselves a freedom-fighter might portray their enemy as a tyrannical Caesar. John Wilkes Booth, when he fired the shot that killed Abraham Lincoln, shouted *Sic semper tyrannis!* ("Thus always to tyrants!" meaning tyrants should always be killed). The phrase has long been associated with the assassins of Caesar, and Booth drew the same analogy in the diary entry he wrote after killing Lincoln:

FIG. 12.7 The 1875 version of the seal of Virginia, with the motto *sic semper tyrannis*! Note that the goddess, representing the state, stands victorious over the tyrant king, whose crown has fallen from his head. In his right hand is a flail used to whip slaves, and the chains of slavery are in his left.

> After being hunted like a dog through swamps, woods, and last night being chased by gunboats till I was forced to return wet, cold, and starving, with every man's hand against me, I am here in despair. And why? For doing what Brutus was honored for. ... And yet I, for striking down a greater tyrant than they ever knew, am looked upon as a common cutthroat.

At the same time, African American units of the Union Army used the same motto in their banner, the tyrants now the slave owners of the Confederacy. And the phrase had already in 1851 become part of the seal of the State of Virginia, the tyrant in their case being King George III of England.

This phrase, in which any self-proclaimed Brutus or Cato can make most anyone a "tyrant" Caesar, shows that not only Caesar, but also the Roman Republic itself can be used and abused. Each generation must decide anew what meaning to give to its history, and even what its history was. What does Rome have to do with Virginia? It is an odd question that can be easily dismissed, but a more thoughtful approach might examine how a single historical thread can be woven into the fabric of the present. The history of the Roman Republic, like all history, is a question, not an answer. The way we read history, and even what we read as history, are ways of shaping who we are, of forming an identity—defining what we want to be, and what we don't. That is, in the end, every history's question, and every generation will fashion its own Caesar and its own Brutus, finding them in other traditions, in other translations, and in other parts of the world.

Credits

Fig. 12.1: Source: https://commons.wikimedia.org/wiki/File:Brutus_Eid_Mar.jpg.

Fig. 12.2: Source: http://www.wildwinds.com/coins/imp/julius_caesar/RSC_0044.2.jpg.

Fig. 12.3: Adapted from d-maps.com.

Fig. 12.4: Source: https://commons.wikimedia.org/wiki/File:Kleopatra-VII.-Altes-Museum-Berlin1.jpg.

Fig. 12.5: Source: https://commons.wikimedia.org/wiki/File:Dendera_Cesarion.jpg.

Fig. 12.6: Source: https://commons.wikimedia.org/wiki/File:Platner-forum-republic-96_reconstructed_color.jpg.

Fig. 12.7: Source: https://commons.wikimedia.org/wiki/File:Seal_of_Virginia_(1875).png.

Glossary of Latin Terms

Definitions of political and social terms can be found in chapter 1, and religious terms at the end of chapter 3.

comitium the name of an area in the Forum near the senate where the Romans gathered to vote. In the plural form, *comitia*, it refers specifically to the voting assemblies, such as the Centuriate Assembly, *Comitia Centuriata*.

Curia a term used to designate a building where the senate met, but most often used in reference to the *Curia Hostilia* in the Forum, next to the Comitium. Its construction was attributed to Tullus Hostilius, the third king of Rome. There were others, such as the *Curia Julia*, begun by Julius Caesar just before his assassination, and the *Curia Pompeii*, built by Pompey but closed after Caesar was assassinated there.

diadema a word borrowed from Greek, it is a headband worn as a marker of royalty among Greek kings in the eastern Mediterranean. Originally made of cloth, they were later made of gold and other precious metals.

dignitas a term related to the English word "dignity," but with specific reference to one's actual political and social standing, as recognized by others. The term can also be used specifically of political offices.

evocatio a religious process in which the Romans would "call out" the god or gods of a city under attack, inviting them to desert their current city and become gods of Rome.

fasces the bundle of wooden rods around an axe, bound together with red straps, carried by lictors (see *lictor*). The bundle was the symbol of a Roman magistrate's ability to punish (rods) and execute (axe); the axe was usually removed when the *fasces* were carried in Rome in recognition of the right of *provocatio*. Consuls had 12 *fasces*, praetors 6, and dictators 24.

feriae a plural noun referring to a religious festival or holiday.

foedus a treaty, root of "federation."

haruspex an Etruscan religious official interpreted the will of the gods by inspecting the organs and innards of a sacrificed animal.

imperium from the Latin verb "to command" (*impero*), and the origin of the English word empire, *imperium* in its basic sense is the authority a magistrate possesses to command soldiers and order civilians to be punished, including executions. From this sense, the word took on the meaning of an area over which someone had this authority, and thus an "empire."

lex Latin for law; most laws are followed by a feminine adjective form of the name of the magistrate who proposed it. For example, the *lex Gabinia* was proposed by a tribune of the plebs Aulus Gabinius. On occasion, the name of the law will be followed by a description of it, though these titles are not always ancient: *lex Aufidia de ambitu*, "the law of Aufidius on election corruption."

libertus, liberta the terms for a freed (or "emancipated") slave, often called a freedman or freedwoman. The plurals are *liberti* and *libertae*. Freed slaves in Rome usually became citizens, though they also remained partly dependent on their former masters and were required to perform some services for them.

lictor an attendant of a Roman magistrate who possessed *imperium* (usually a praetor, consul, or dictator), who carried the *fasces* when they walked before the magistrate in the city. The number of lictors corresponds to the number of *fasces* a magistrate had: 12 for consuls, 6 for praetors, and 24 for dictators.

ludi athletic contests and entertainments, such as chariot races, gladiator combats, staged animal hunts, and theatrical performances, usually held over a period of days, much like a public holiday.

lupa a she-wolf, often used with particular reference to the she-wolf who nurtured Romulus and Remus. The term is also used to refer to a prostitute.

magister equitum usually translated "Master of the Horse," though "Horse" in this translation really means cavalry (the Latin word is from *eques*). A dictator, upon appointment, chose a *magister equitatum* as his second-in-command.

mos maiorum "the way of the ancestors," used by Romans to designate traditional practices and beliefs imbued with the authority of the past.

nexum the institution of debt bondage, according to which a debtor unable to pay back creditors could be legally bound to perform services for the creditor, and in some cases could be put in chains by his creditor.

novus homo "new man," the Latin term for an individual who did not have any consuls in his family history, though in same cases it may refer to someone without even a senator among their ancestors. Such individuals had to overcome extraordinary obstacles to reach high office. Well-known examples are Cato the Elder, Marius, and Cicero.

paterfamilias "father of a household," a designation for a male head of a household, all members of which were under his legal authority, known as *patria potestas*, "fatherly power," which included the power of life and death. Children, even as adults, were considered to be under the authority of the father. Upon the death of a *paterfamilias*, adult males would take on the role of *paterfamilias*, while women would be subject to the authority of their husband or a male relative.

patres a plural noun meaning "fathers," it was a regular term for senators.

plebiscitum, plural plebiscita a decree passed by the Plebeian Assembly, in contrast to a decree of the senate (*senatus consultum*). These eventually acquired the force of law.

pomerium the sacred city limit of the city of Rome.

princeps the root of the English "prince," the word originally referred to someone or something that was first in order. In the phrase *princeps senatus*, it is a formal designation of the leader of the senate, an honorary title held for life that gave the bearer the right to speak first in a debate.

provocatio the right of a Roman citizen to appeal any action taken by a magistrate.

res novae "new things," the Roman expression for political revolution or rebellion.

rex the Latin word for king, which during the republic had a negative sense, a tyrant; *regina* is the word for queen, and *regnum* is a kingdom or monarchy.

rostra a plural noun from the singular *rostrum*, meaning "beak" or "prow of a ship." In the plural it most often refers to the speakers platform in the Forum in front of the senate house from which public speeches were delivered, named after the captured prows of enemy ships that formed its base.

sella curulis the "curule chair," an ivory folding stool used by high-ranking Roman officials as a mark of their privileged status.

senatus consultum ultimum "the final decree of the senate," often abbreviated SCU, was a declaration by the senate of an extreme crisis, usually empowering a consul to take any measures necessary to restore order and protect the republic. A normal decree of the senate would simply be a *senatus consultum*.

SPQR the abbreviation for *Senatus Populusque Romanus*, "the Senate and the People of Rome," the usual designation of the republic on inscriptions, which continued to be used even under the emperors.

A Note on Translations

All translations from the Latin and Greek sources are my own, and I have in some cases added or deleted phrases for the sake of clarity and ease of understanding, without, I hope, taking too many liberties with the original. Since for almost all students of Roman history the original sources must be read in translation, it is recommended that, when possible, more than one translation be consulted. Different translations may offer quite different readings without being wrong in any one case.

Because the texts we use as sources have been read and studied for centuries, there are many translations freely available on the web. In many cases, however, these translations are quite old and filled with stilted and archaic English, such as "thou" and "dost." Fortunately, there are many modern translations readily available, particularly in the Oxford World Classics series as well as Penguin Classics.

For translations available online:

- Perseus Digital Library (perseus.tufts.edu)

  This site has been around for some time, and while it is a bit clunky, it is an invaluable resource. In addition to translations, there are the original Greek and Latin texts along with commentaries, dictionaries, and other study aids.

- Loeb Classical Library (loebclassics.com)

  This series, published by Harvard University Press, has been ongoing for over one hundred years. There are translations of Latin or Greek classical texts, with the original on the facing page. They originally produced small hardback copies—green for Greek, red for Latin—designed to fit in a young gentleman's coat pocket. They have since gone digital, with the full library online. Older translations are regularly replaced with newer, updated versions. Full access requires a subscription, but shorter passages can be consulted for free.

Following are affordable modern translations for the texts quoted in each chapter, as well as specific references to the Loeb translations, which will also have the original Greek or Latin.

Chapter 1

Cicero. *Philippics*. Edited and translated by D.R. Shackleton-Bailey. Chapel Hill, NC: University of North Carolina Press, 1986.

Cicero. *Political Speeches.* Translated by D.H. Berry. New York, NY: Oxford University Press, 2009.

Cicero, *Philippics*, Edited and translated by D.R. Shackleton-Bailey, revised by John T. Ramsey and Gesine Manuwald. Cambridge, MA: Loeb Classical Library, 2010. DOI: 10.4159/DLCL.marcus_tullius_cicero-philippic_2.2010

Plutarch. *Roman Lives: A Selection of Eight Roman Lives.* Translated by Robin Waterfield. New York, NY: Oxford University Press, 1999.

Plutarch. *Fall of the Roman Republic.* Translated by Rex Warner. Revised and expanded edition. New York, NY: Penguin Classics, 2005.

Plutarch. *Lives, Volume VII: Demosthenes and Cicero. Alexander and Caesar.* Translated by Bernadotte Perrin. Cambridge, MA: Loeb Classical Library, 1919. DOI: 10.4159/DLCL.plutarch-lives_caesar.1919

Sallust. *Catiline's Conspiracy, The Jugurthine War, Histories.* Translated by W.W. Batstone. New York, NY: Oxford University Press, 2010.

Sallust. *Catiline's War, The Jurgurthine War, Histories.* Translated by A.J. Woodman. New York, NY: Penguin Classics, 2008.

Sallust. *The War with Catiline. The War with Jugurtha.* Edited by John T. Ramsey. Translated by J. C. Rolfe. Cambridge, MA: Harvard University Press, 2013. DOI: 10.4159/DLCL.sallust-war_catiline.2013

Tacitus. *The Annals: The Reigns of Tiberius, Claudius, and Nero.* Translated by A.J. Yardley. New York, NY: Oxford University Press, 2008.

Tacitus. *The Annals of Imperial Rome.* Translated by Michael Grant. Revised edition. New York, NY: Penguin Classics, 1996.

Tacitus. *Histories: Books 4-5. Annals: Books 1-3.* Translated by Clifford H. Moore, John Jackson. Cambridge, MA: Harvard University Press, 1931. DOI: 10.4159/DLCL.tacitus-annals.1931

Chapter 2

Livy. *The Rise of Rome: Books 1–5.* Translated by T.J. Luce. New York, NY: Oxford University Press, 2009.

Livy. *The Early History of Rome: Books 1–5.* Translated by Aubrey de Selincourt. Revised edition. New York, NY: Penguin Classics, 2002.

Livy. *History of Rome, Volume I: Books 1–2.* Translated by B. O. Foster. Cambridge, MA: Harvard University Press, 1919. DOI: 10.4159/DLCL.livy-history_rome_1.1919

Chapter 3

Livy. *The Rise of Rome: Books 1–5.* Translated by T.J. Luce. New York, NY: Oxford University Press, 2009.

Livy. *The Early History of Rome: Books 1–5.* Translated by Aubrey de Selincourt. Revised edition. New York, NY: Penguin Classics, 2002.

Livy. *History of Rome, Volume I: Books 1–2.* Translated by B. O. Foster. Cambridge, MA: Harvard University Press, 1919. DOI: 10.4159/DLCL.livy-history_rome_1.1919

Chapter 4

Livy. *Rome's Italian Wars: Books 6–10.* Translated by J.C. Yardley. New York, NY: Oxford University Press, 2013.

Livy. *Rome and Italy: Books 6–10.* Translated by Betty Radice. Revised edition. New York, NY: Penguin Classics, 1982.

Livy. *History of Rome, Volume III: Books 5–7.* Translated by B. O. Foster. Cambridge, MA: Harvard University Press, 1924. DOI: 10.4159/DLCL.livy-history_rome_5.1924

Plutarch. *The Rise of Rome.* Translated by Ian Scott-Kilvert. New York, NY: Penguin Classics, 2013.

Plutarch. *Lives, Volume II: Themistocles and Camillus. Aristides and Cato Major. Cimon and Lucullus.* Translated by Bernadotte Perrin. Cambridge, MA: Harvard University Press, 1914. DOI: 10.4159/DLCL.plutarch-lives_marcus_cato.1914

Chapter 5

Livy. *Hannibal's War: Books 21–30.* Translated by J.C. Yardley. New York, NY: Oxford University Press, 2009.

Livy. *The War with Hannibal: Books 21–30.* Translated by Aubrey de Selincourt. New York, NY: Penguin Classics, 1965.

Livy. *History of Rome, Volume V: Books 21–22.* Edited and translated by J. C. Yardley. Cambridge, MA: Harvard University Press, 2019. DOI: 10.4159/DLCL.livy-history_rome_21.2019

Plutarch. *The Rise of Rome.* Translated by Ian Scott-Kilvert. New York, NY: Penguin Classics, 2013.

Plutarch. *Lives, Volume III: Pericles and Fabius Maximus. Nicias and Crassus.* Translated by Bernadotte Perrin. Cambridge, MA: Harvard University Press, 1916. DOI: 10.4159/DLCL.plutarch-lives_fabius_maximus.1916

Chapter 6

Cato, Varro. *On Agriculture*. Translated by W. D. Hooper, Harrison Boyd Ash. Cambridge, MA: Harvard University Press, 1934. DOI: 10.4159/DLCL.cato-agriculture.1934

Livy. *The Dawn of the Roman Empire: Books 31–40*. Translated by J.C. Yardley. New York, NY: Oxford University Press, 2009.

Livy. *Rome and the Mediterranean: Books 31–45.* Translated by Henry Bettenson. New York, NY: Penguin Classics, 1976.

Livy. *History of Rome, Volume XI: Books 38–40*. Edited and translated by J. C. Yardley. Cambridge, MA: Harvard University Press, 2018. DOI: 10.4159/DLCL.livy-history_rome_38.2018

Polybius. *The Histories.* Translated by Robin Waterfield. New York, NY: Oxford University Press, 2010.

Polybius. *The Rise of the Roman Empire.* Translated by Ian Scott-Kilvert. New York, NY: Penguin Classics, 1980.

Polybius. *The Histories, Volume VI: Books 28–39. Fragments.* Edited and translated by S. Douglas Olson. Translated by W. R. Paton. Revised by F. W. Walbank, Christian Habicht. Cambridge, MA: Harvard University Press, 2012. DOI: 10.4159/DLCL.polybius-histories.2010

Suetonius. *Lives of the Caesars*. Translated by Catherine Edwards. New York, NY: Oxford University Press, 2009.

Suetonius. *The Twelve Caesars.* Translated by Robert Graves. Revised by James Rives. New York, NY: Penguin Classics, 2007.

Suetonius. *Lives of the Caesars, Volume I: Julius. Augustus. Tiberius. Gaius. Caligula.* Translated by J. C. Rolfe. Cambridge, MA: Harvard University Press, 1914. DOI: 10.4159/DLCL.suetonius-lives_caesars_book_i_deified_julius.1914

Chapter 7

Apicius. *Cookery and Dining in Ancient Rome*. Translated by J.D. Vehling. Chicago, IL: Walter M. Hill, 1936. https://www.gutenberg.org/files/29728/29728-h/29728-h.htm

Appian. *The Civil Wars.* Translated by John Carter. New York, NY: Penguin Classics, 1996.

Appian. *Roman History, Volume I.* Edited and translated by Brian McGing. Cambridge, MA: Harvard University Press, 2019. DOI: 10.4159/DLCL.appian-roman_history_civil_wars.2020

Appian. *Roman History, Volume III.* Edited and translated by Brian McGing. Loeb Classical Library 4. Cambridge, MA: Harvard University Press, 2019. DOI: 10.4159/DLCL.appian-roman_history_book_vi_wars_spain_fragments.2019

Cornelius Nepos. *On Great Generals. On Historians.* Translated by J. C. Rolfe. Cambridge, MA: Harvard University Press, 1929. DOI: 10.4159/DLCL.cornelius_nepos-fragments.1929

Livy. *Rome's Mediterranean Empire: Books 41–45 and the Periochae*. Translated by Jane D. Champlin. New York, NY: Oxford University Press, 2010.

Livy, Julius Obsequens. *History of Rome, Volume XIV: Summaries. Fragments.* Julius Obsequens. *General Index.* Translated by Alfred C. Schlesinger. Index by Russel M. Geer. Cambridge, MA: Harvard University Press, 1959. DOI: 10.4159/DLCL.livy-history_rome_summaries.1959

Plutarch. *The Makers of Rome.* Translated by Ian Scott-Kilvert. New York, NY: Penguin Classics, 1965.

Plutarch. *Roman Lives: A Selection of Eight Roman Lives.* Translated by Robin Waterfield. New York, NY: Oxford University Press, 1999.

Plutarch. *Lives, Volume X: Agis and Cleomenes. Tiberius and Gaius Gracchus. Philopoemen and Flamininus.* Translated by Bernadotte Perrin. Cambridge, MA: Harvard University Press, 1921. DOI: 10.4159/DLCL.plutarch-lives_tiberius_gaius_gracchus.1921

Chapter 8

Plutarch. *Fall of the Roman Republic.* Translated by Rex Warner. Revised and expanded edition. New York, NY: Penguin Classics, 2005.

Plutarch. *Roman Lives: A Selection of Eight Roman Lives.* Translated by Robin Waterfield. New York, NY: Oxford University Press, 1999.

Plutarch. *Lives, Volume IX: Demetrius and Antony. Pyrrhus and Gaius Marius.* Translated by Bernadotte Perrin. Cambridge, MA: Harvard University Press, 1920. DOI: 10.4159/DLCL.plutarch-lives_caius_marius.1920

Sallust. *Catiline's Conspiracy, The Jugurthine War, Histories.* Translated by W.W. Batstone. New York, NY: Oxford University Press, 2010.

Sallust. *Catiline's War, The Jurgurthine War, Histories.* Translated by A.J. Woodman. New York, NY: Penguin Classics, 2008.

Sallust. *The War with Catiline. The War with Jugurtha.* Edited by John T. Ramsey. Translated by J. C. Rolfe. Cambridge, MA: Harvard University Press, 2013. DOI: 10.4159/DLCL.sallust-war_jugurtha.2013

Chapter 9

Appian. *The Civil Wars.* Translated by John Carter. New York, NY: Penguin Classics, 1996.

Appian. *Roman History, Volume III.* Edited and translated by Brian McGing. Loeb Classical Library 4. Cambridge, MA: Harvard University Press, 2019. DOI: 10.4159/DLCL.appian-roman_history_book_vi_wars_spain_fragments.2019

Cicero. *Ten Speeches*. Translated J.E.G. Zetzel. Indianapolis, IN: Hackett, 2009.

Cicero. *Political Speeches.* Translated by D.H. Berry. New York, NY: Oxford University Press, 2009.

Cicero. *Pro Lege Manilia. Pro Caecina. Pro Cluentio. Pro Rabirio Perduellionis Reo.* Translated by H. Grose Hodge. Cambridge, MA: Harvard University Press, 1927. DOI: 10.4159/DLCL.marcus_tullius_cicero-pro_lege_manilia.1927

Plutarch. *Roman Lives: A Selection of Eight Roman Lives*. Translated by Robin Waterfield. New York, NY: Oxford University Press, 1999.

Plutarch. *Fall of the Roman Republic.* Translated by Rex Warner. Revised and expanded edition. New York, NY: Penguin Classics, 2005.

Plutarch. *Lives, Volume IV: Alcibiades and Coriolanus. Lysander and Sulla*. Translated by Bernadotte Perrin. Cambridge, MA: Harvard University Press, 1916. DOI: 10.4159/DLCL.plutarch-lives_sulla.1916

Sallust. *Catiline's Conspiracy, The Jugurthine War, Histories.* Translated by W.W. Batstone. New York, NY: Oxford University Press, 2010.

Sallust. *Catiline's War, The Jurgurthine War, Histories.* Translated by A.J. Woodman. New York, NY: Penguin Classics, 2008.

Sallust. *The War with Catiline. The War with Jugurtha.* Edited by John T. Ramsey. Translated by J. C. Rolfe. Cambridge, MA: Harvard University Press, 2013. DOI: 10.4159/DLCL.sallust-war_jugurtha.2013

Sallust. *Fragments of the Histories. Letters to Caesar.* Edited and translated by John T. Ramsey. Loeb Cambridge, MA: Harvard University Press, 2015. DOI: 10.4159/DLCL.sallust-histories.2015

Roman Civil Law: Including The Twelve Tables, The Institutes of Gaius, The Rules of Ulpian & The Opinions of Paulus. Translated by S.P. Scott. Cincinnati, OH: The Central Trust Company, 1932.

Chapter 10

Cicero. *Ten Speeches*. Translated J.E.G. Zetzel. Indianapolis, IN: Hackett, 2009.

Cicero. *Political Speeches.* Translated by D.H. Berry. New York, NY: Oxford University Press, 2009.

Cicero. *In Catilinam 1–4. Pro Murena. Pro Sulla. Pro Flacco.* Translated by C. Macdonald. Cambridge, MA: Harvard University Press, 1976. DOI: 10.4159/DLCL.marcus_tullius_cicero-in_catilinam_i_iv.1976

Cicero. *Pro Quinctio. Pro Roscio Amerino. Pro Roscio Comoedo. On the Agrarian Law*. Translated by J. H. Freese. Cambridge, MA: Harvard University Press, 1930. DOI: 10.4159/DLCL.marcus_tullius_cicero-de_lege_agraria.1930

Plutarch. *Roman Lives: A Selection of Eight Roman Lives.* Translated by Robin Waterfield. New York, NY: Oxford University Press, 1999.

Plutarch. *Fall of the Roman Republic.* Translated by Rex Warner. Revised and expanded edition. New York, NY: Penguin Classics, 2005.

Plutarch. *The Rise of Rome.* Translated by Ian Scott-Kilvert. New York, NY: Penguin Classics, 2013.

Plutarch. *Lives, Volume II: Themistocles and Camillus. Aristides and Cato Major. Cimon and Lucullus.* Translated by Bernadotte Perrin. Cambridge, MA: Harvard University Press, 1914. DOI: 10.4159/DLCL.plutarch-lives_marcus_cato.1914

Plutarch. *Lives, Volume VII: Demosthenes and Cicero. Alexander and Caesar.* Translated by Bernadotte Perrin. Cambridge, MA: Loeb Classical Library, 1919. DOI: 10.4159/DLCL.plutarch-lives_caesar.1919

Sallust. *Catiline's Conspiracy, The Jugurthine War, Histories.* Translated by W.W. Batstone. New York, NY: Oxford University Press, 2010.

Sallust. *Catiline's War, The Jurgurthine War, Histories.* Translated by A.J. Woodman. New York, NY: Penguin Classics, 2008.

Sallust. *The War with Catiline. The War with Jugurtha.* Edited by John T. Ramsey. Translated by J. C. Rolfe. Cambridge, MA: Harvard University Press, 2013. DOI: 10.4159/DLCL.sallust-war_jugurtha.2013

Suetonius. *Lives of the Caesars.* Translated by Catherine Edwards. New York, NY: Oxford University Press, 2009.

Suetonius. *The Twelve Caesars.* Translated by Robert Graves. Revised by James Rives. New York, NY: Penguin Classics, 2007.

Suetonius. *Lives of the Caesars, Volume I: Julius. Augustus. Tiberius. Gaius. Caligula.* Translated by J. C. Rolfe. Cambridge, MA: Harvard University Press, 1914. DOI: 10.4159/DLCL.suetonius-lives_caesars_book_i_deified_julius.1914

Chapter 11

Caesar. *The Gallic War.* Translated by Carolyn Hammond. New York, NY: Oxford University Press, 2008.

Caesar. *The Conquest of Gaul.* Translated by S.A. Handford. New York, NY: Penguin Classics, 1983.

Caesar. *The Gallic War.* Translated by H. J. Edwards. Cambridge, MA: Harvard University Press, 1917. DOI: 10.4159/DLCL.caesar-gallic_wars.1917Caesar. *The Civil War.* Translated by John Carter. New York, NY: Oxford University Press, 2008.

Caesar. *The Civil War.* Translated by Jane P. Gardner. New York, NY: Penguin Classics, 1976.

Caesar. *Civil War.* Edited and translated by Cynthia Damon. Cambridge, MA: Harvard University Press, 2016. DOI: 10.4159/DLCL.caesar-civil_war.2016

Catullus. *Catullus. Tibullus. Pervigilium Veneris.* Translated by F. W. Cornish, J. P. Postgate, J. W. Mackail. Revised by G. P. Goold. Cambridge, MA: Harvard University Press, 1913. https://www.loebclassics.com/view/LCL006/1913/volume.xml

Catullus. *The Complete Poems.* Translated by Guy Lee. New York, NY: Oxford University Press, 2008.

Catullus. *The Poems of Catullus.* Translated by Peter Green. Berkeley, CA: University of California Press, 2007.

Cicero. *Pro Lege Manilia. Pro Caecina. Pro Cluentio. Pro Rabirio Perduellionis Reo.* Translated by H. Grose Hodge. Cambridge, MA: Harvard University Press, 1927. DOI: 10.4159/DLCL.marcus_tullius_cicero-pro_lege_manilia.1927

Cicero. *Selected Letters*. Translated by P.G. Walsh. New York, NY: Oxford University Press, 2009.

Cicero. *Letters to Atticus, Volume I.* Edited and translated by D. R. Shackleton Bailey. Cambridge, MA: Harvard University Press, 1999. DOI: 10.4159/DLCL.marcus_tullius_cicero-letters_atticus.1999

Plutarch. *Rome in Crisis.* Translated by Ian Scott-Kilvert. New York, NY: Penguin Classics, 2010.

Plutarch. *Fall of the Roman Republic.* Translated by Rex Warner. Revised and expanded edition. New York, NY: Penguin Classics, 2005.

Plutarch. *Lives, Volume VII: Demosthenes and Cicero. Alexander and Caesar.* Translated by Bernadotte Perrin. Cambridge, MA: Loeb Classical Library, 1919. DOI: 10.4159/DLCL.plutarch-lives_caesar.1919

Plutarch. *Lives, Volume VIII: Sertorius and Eumenes. Phocion and Cato the Younger.* Translated by Bernadotte Perrin. Cambridge, MA: Harvard University Press, 1919. DOI: 10.4159/DLCL.plutarch-lives_cato_younger.1919

Chapter 12

Caesar. *The Civil War*. Translated by John Carter. New York, NY: Oxford University Press, 2008.

Caesar. *The Civil War*. Translated by Jane P. Gardner. New York, NY: Penguin Classics, 1976.

Caesar. *Civil War.* Edited and translated by Cynthia Damon. Cambridge, MA: Harvard University Press, 2016. DOI: 10.4159/DLCL.caesar-civil_war.2016

Cicero. *Pro Milone. In Pisonem. Pro Scauro. Pro Fonteio. Pro Rabirio Postumo. Pro Marcello. Pro Ligario. Pro Rege Deiotaro.* Translated by N. H. Watts. Cambridge, MA: Harvard University Press, 1931. DOI: 10.4159/DLCL.marcus_tullius_cicero-pro_milone.1931

Plutarch. *Rome in Crisis.* Translated by Ian Scott-Kilvert. New York, NY: Penguin Classics, 2010.

Plutarch. *Fall of the Roman Republic.* Translated by Rex Warner. Revised and expanded edition. New York, NY: Penguin Classics, 2005.

Plutarch. *Lives, Volume VII: Demosthenes and Cicero. Alexander and Caesar.* Translated by Bernadotte Perrin. Cambridge, MA: Loeb Classical Library, 1919. DOI: 10.4159/DLCL.plutarch-lives_caesar.1919

Plutarch. *Lives, Volume VIII: Sertorius and Eumenes. Phocion and Cato the Younger.* Translated by Bernadotte Perrin. Cambridge, MA: Harvard University Press, 1919. DOI: 10.4159/DLCL.plutarch-lives_cato_younger.1919

Shakespeare, William. *Julius Caesar.* shakespeare.mit.edu

Suetonius. *Lives of the Caesars*. Translated by Catherine Edwards. New York, NY: Oxford University Press, 2009.

Suetonius. *The Twelve Caesars.* Translated by Robert Graves. Revised by James Rives. New York, NY: Penguin Classics, 2007.

Suetonius. *Lives of the Caesars, Volume I: Julius. Augustus. Tiberius. Gaius. Caligula.* Translated by J. C. Rolfe. Cambridge, MA: Harvard University Press, 1914. DOI: 10.4159/DLCL.suetonius-lives_caesars_book_i_deified_julius.1914

Index

D

E

F

G

H

I

J

L

Q

R

S

T

U

V

W

Z

Printed in the USA
CPSIA information can be obtained
at www.ICGtesting.com
LVHW060013301124
797814LV00008B/26

* 9 7 8 1 5 1 6 5 4 3 8 1 6 *